THE BOOK OF THE
COCKER SPANIEL

Acknowledgments

Much time and many people are involved before a book is finally published. All those who have contributed so generously to help make this book a lasting tribute to a magnificent breed have my sincerest thanks for giving so generously of their knowledge, memorabilia, and photographs. Irene Gaddy Zimmerman was of great help in providing old photos and information, for which I am grateful. Special thanks are due Aaron Norman for his glorious color photograph for the cover as well as other photos within the book; Michael Allen for information, old publications, photographs and reproductions of her marvelous art work; Margaret Saari, D.V.M. for her statistics, some of which have not been published anywhere before; Robert R. Shomer, V.M.D. for his expert counsel on this book as well as all those that preceded this one; and to my parents, Stephen and Lillian McDonald, who have helped care for and enjoyed my dogs with me all through the years.

Most of all I owe a very special thanks and appreciation to Bill Gorodner, a friend of many years standing, a devoted dog person, and a source of constant encouragement and information during the many months this book was in preparation. It was Bill who convinced me that I should write it and who constantly offered his kind assistance when it was asked for, and it is my sincerest hope that he is pleased with the final result.

Joan Brearley

Endpapers: Two exquisite chocolate and white brothers, BeGay's Abbott O. Hershey (left) and Ch. BeGay's Shot P. Hershey (right), bred by Gay Ernst of East Hampton, New York. William Gilbert photo.

Title Page:
Ch. Phoebe Fireworks ("Paget"), owned by Bill Gorodner and Lloyd Alton of the Ging Kennels, Leesburg, Virginia. Photo by Aaron Norman.

ISBN 0-87666-737-X

© 1982 by TFH Publications, Inc. Ltd.

Distributed in the U.S. by T.F.H. Publications, Inc., 211 West Sylvania Avenue, PO Box 427, Neptune, NJ 07753; in England by T.F.H. (Gt. Britain) Ltd., 13 Nutley Lane, Reigate, Surrey; in Canada to the pet trade by Rolf C. Hagen Ltd., 3225 Sartelon Street, Montreal 382, Quebec; in Canada to the book trade by H & L Pet Supplies, Inc., 27 Kingston Crescent, Kitchener, Ontario N28 2T6; in Southeast Asia by Y.W. Ong, 9 Lorong 36 Geylang, Singapore 14; in Australia and the South Pacific by Pet Imports Pty. Ltd., P.O. Box 149, Brookvale 2100, N.S.W. Australia; in South Africa by Valid Agencies, P.O. Box 51901, Randburg 2125 South Africa. Published by T.F.H. Publications, Inc., Ltd., the British Crown Colony of Hong Kong. Printed in Hong Kong

THE BOOK OF THE
COCKER SPANIEL

Joan McDonald Brearley

Contents

Acknowledgments......................4
About the Author 9

Chapter One
The History of the Breed...............11
Breed Development — Sensory
Perception — How the Spaniel Got Its
Name — Early Written Records — England

Chapter Two
The Cocker Spaniel in England........17
James Farrow and Obo — Show Dogs and
Dog Shows in England — The First Field
Trials — The Cocker Spaniel Club in
England — England's Kennel Club — The
1940's — The 1950's — The 1960's — The
1970's

Chapter Three
The Cocker Spaniel Arrives in America..23
Chloe II — Obo II — It Paid to
Advertise — The Breed's First Best in
Show Winner — The 1930's — The
1940's — Petts — The 1950's — The
1960's — The End of the Old Timers
Group — The 1970's — Knebworth
Marches On — The 1980's

Chapter Four
The American Spaniel Club...........81
Field Trials — The A.S.C. Versus the
A.K.C. — The First Specialty — Revision
of the Standard — Color Jurisdictions —
A.S.C. Year Books — The Centennial
Books — The A.S.C. Centennial
Celebration — The Futurity — Junior
Showmanship — Trophies — Catalogs —
Breeder of the Century — The Second
Hundred Years

Chapter Five
The Cocker Spaniel as a Breed..........91
The American Kennel Club — What Are
Breed Standards? — Standard for the Cocker
Spaniel — Cocker Spaniel Colors — A Breed
Survey — Your Zoological Chart — Cocker
Spaniel Publications — Earliest Records

Chapter Six
Cocker Spaniel People and Places......101
Top Ten Breeders in the History of the
Breed — Owners and Handlers — Cocker
Spaniel Tales — Newsworthy Cocker
Spaniels — Self Service — The Cocker
Spaniel in Art — The Cocker Spaniel in
Literature — Cocker Spaniels in Politics —
Cocker Spaniels in Foreign Lands

Chapter Seven
**Buying Your First Cocker
Spaniel Puppy**.....................129
What to Look for in a Cocker Spaniel
Puppy — Male or Female? — The Planned
Parenthood Behind Your Puppy — Puppies
and Worms — Veterinary Inspection — The
Conditions of Sale — Buying a Show
Puppy — The Purchase Price — The Cost of
Buying Adult Stock

Chapter Eight
Grooming Your Cocker Spaniel........143
Grooming Equipment — Bathing Your
Cocker Spaniel — Clipping and Trimming
Your Dog — Grooming the Head — The
Combing — Grooming Shops

Chapter Nine
The Dog Show World..................151
Match Shows — Point Shows — Point Show
Classes — Obedience Trials — Junior
Showmanship — Dog Show
Photographers — Two Types of Dog
Shows — Benched or Unbenched Dog
Shows — If Your Dog Wins a Class — The
Prize Ribbons and What They Stand
For — Qualifying for Championship —
Professional Handlers — Do You Really
Need a Handler? — The Cost of
Campaigning a Dog with a Handler

Chapter Ten
Showing and Judging the Cocker........177
Entering the Ring — Move Them Out —
Judging the Head — Individual Gaiting —
The Games People Play — Children in the
Show Ring — Baiting — Double-handling —
Applause, Applause! — Sins When Showing
Dogs

Chapter Eleven
Statistics and the Phillips System........185
What is the Phillips System? — How the
System Works — 1956 and Ch. Gail's Ebony
Don D — In 1957 It's Ch. Gail's Ebony
Don D Again — In 1958 Ch. Artru Hot Rod
Makes It to the Top — 1959 and Ch.
Clarkdale Capital Stock — 1960 and the
"Dog of the Year" is Ch. Pinetop's Fancy
Parade — 1961 and the Newcomers —
1962 — 1963 — Moving Up in 1964 —
1965 — 1966 — 1967 — 1968 — 1969 —
The Decade of the 1970's — 1971 — 1972
is the Year of Toccoa — 1975 — Further
Ratings — Top Sires and Dams — "Les
Girls" — Top Producing Sires and Dams

for 1962 — 1965 — Top Producing Dams for 1965 — Other Top Producer Statistics — Great Show Dogs of America — Our Westminster Winners — Westminster Group Winners — Margaret Saari and her Statistics for the American Spaniel Club — The Decade of the 1980's

Chapter Twelve
Cocker Spaniel in Obedience.........**201**
The Obedience Rating Systems — 1975 Obedience Winners — 1976 Winners — 1977 — 1978 — 1979 — 1980 — The Dog Obedience Classics — The Gaines' Dog Obedience "Fido" — Milru-1930's — San-D-Glyn — Obedience and the Movies — Other Obedience Activities — Latest Obedience Rules and Regulations — How to Understand and Enjoy an Obedience Trial — Training Your Dog — Early Training at Home — When to Start Formal Training — The Reward Method — What You Need to Start Training — Formal School Training — Obedience Degrees — Obedience Trial Championship Titles — Check Points for Obedience Competitors

Chapter Thirteen
Cockers in the Field.................**229**
In the Beginning — "Breaking" for the Field — Actual Training — Field Trials at the Turn of the Century — Field Trials in America — Field Trials Today — Working Titles — Finding the Facts — Choosing a Field Dog — Buying the Older Field Dog — Joining a Field Trial Club — Kinds of Field Trials — Ribbons and Prizes — Judges — Entering a Field Trial — Eligibility for Entry — Special Awards — The Various Kinds of Stakes — National Championship Stakes — What is Required of a Field Champion — The Guns — Judging the Game — Weather Conditions — Some of the Finer Points — The "Old" Versus the "New" — Parting Shot — Don Ploke

Chapter Fourteen
Breeding Your Cocker Spaniel........**239**
The Power in Pedigrees — The Health of the Breeding Stock — When to Breed a Grown Bitch — The Day of the Mating — How Much Does the Stud Fee Cost? — The Actual Mating — Artificial

Insemination — The Gestation Period — Probing for Puppies — Alerting Your Veterinarian — Do You Need a Veterinarian in Attendance? — Labor — The Arrival of the Puppies — Feeding the Bitch Between Births — Breech Births — Dry Births — The Twenty-four Hour Checkup — False Pregnancy — Caesarean Section — Episiotomy — Socializing Your Puppy — Rearing the Family — Evaluating the Litter — Spaying and Castrating — Sterilizing for Health

Chapter Fifteen
Feeding and Nutrition.................**251**
Feeding Puppies — Weaning the Puppies — Feeding the Adult Dog — The All-meat Diet Controversy — Obesity — Orphaned Puppies — How to Feed the Newborn Puppies — Gastric Torsion

Chapter Sixteen
The Blight of Parasites................**273**
Internal Parasites — How to Test for Worms

Chapter Seventeen
Your Dog, Your Veterinarian and You..**277**
Aspirin: A Danger — What the Thermometer Can Tell You — Coprophagy — Masturbation — Rabies — Vaccinations — Snakebite — Emergencies — Burns — Drowning — Fits and Convulsions — Frostbite — Heart Attack — Shock — Suffocation — Sun Stroke — Wounds — The First Aid Kit — How Not to Poison Your Dog — Symptoms of Poisoning — The Curse of Allergy — Allergies in Dogs — Do All Dogs Chew? — Some Reasons for Chewing — Hip Dysplasia — Elbow Dysplasia — Patellar Dysplasia — The United States Registry — HD Program in Great Britain — Geriatrics — Dog Insurance — The High Cost of Burial — In the Event of Your Death — Keeping Records

Chapter Eighteen
Pursuing a Career in Dogs.............**291**
Part-time Kennel Work — Professional Handling — Dog Training — Grooming Parlors — The Pet Shop — Dog Judging

Chapter Nineteen
A Glossary of Cocker Spaniel Terms....**297**

Cocker Spaniel Statistics.................**307**
Cocker Spaniel Conformation **323**
Index **328**

DEDICATION

for

ROBERTA McDONALD POOLE

A WONDERFUL COUSIN, WONDERFUL
FRIEND AND A GREAT LADY

and for

BLACK CREST CHARCOAL CHAMPION

my first Cocker—which endeared the
breed to me forever

The author with her first Cocker Spaniel, photographed in 1946.

About The Author

Joan Brearley is the first to admit that animals in general—and dogs in particular—are a most important part of her life. Since childhood there has been a steady stream of dogs, cats, birds, fish, rabbits, snakes, alligators, etc., for her own personal menagerie. Over the years she has owned over thirty breeds of purebred dogs as well as countless mixtures, since the door was never closed to a needy or homeless animal.

A graduate of the American Academy of Dramatic Arts where she studied acting and directing, Joan started her career as a writer for movie magazines, actress, and dancer. She studied ballet at the Agnes DeMille Studios in Carnegie Hall and appeared with an Oriental dance company which performed at the Carnegie Recital Hall. She studied journalism at Columbia University and has written for radio, television, and magazines, and she was a copywriter for some of the major New York City advertising agencies working on material for Metro-Goldwyn-Mayer Studios, Burlington Mills, *Cosmopolitan* magazine, White Owl Cigars, and "World-Telegram and Sun," to name just a few.

While a television producer-director for a major network, she worked on Nick Carter, Master Detective; Did Justice Triumph; and news and special feature programs. Joan has written, cast, directed, produced and, on occasion, starred in television commercials. She has written special material for such personalities as Dick Van Dyke, Amy Vanderbilt, William B. Williams, Gene Rayburn, Bill Stern, Herman Hickman, and many other people prominent in the entertainment world. She has appeared as a guest on several of the nation's most popular talk shows, including Mike Douglas, Joe Franklin, Cleveland Amory, David Susskind and the *Today Show*. Joan was selected for inclusion in the Directory of the Foremost Women in Communications in 1969, and the book *Two Thousand Women of Achievement in 1971*.

Her accomplishments in the dog fancy include breeding and exhibiting top show dogs, being a writer and columnist for various magazines, and being author of over 30 books on dogs and cats. For five years she was Executive Vice President of the Popular Dogs Publishing Company and editor of *Popular Dogs* magazine, the national prestige publication for the fancy at that time. Her editorials on the status and welfare of animals have been reproduced as educational pamphlets by dog clubs and organizations in many countries of the world.

Joan is as active in the cat fancy and in almost as many capacities. The same year her Afghan Hound Ch. Sahadi Shikari won the Ken-L Ration Award as Top Hound of the Year, one of her Siamese cats won the comparable honor in the cat fancy.

In addition to breeding and showing dogs since 1955, Joan has been active as a member and on the Board of Directors of the Kennel Club of Northern New Jersey, the Afghan Hound Club of America, the Stewards Club of America, The Dog Writers Association of America, and the Dog Fanciers Club. She has been an American Kennel Club judge of several breeds since 1961. As a guest speaker at many dog and cat clubs and humane organizations, she has crusaded for humane legislation for animals and won several awards and citations for her work in this field. She is one of the best known and one of the most knowledgeable people in the animal world. Joan is proud of the fact that her Ch. Sahadi Shikari was top-winning Afghan Hound in the history of the breed for several years and still remains in the #2 position today. No other breeder can claim to have bred a Westminster Group winner in their first home-bred litter, an honor also won by Shikari.

Joan looks forward to the near future when she will once again breed dogs at her Sahadi Kennels and Cattery to continue her line of dogs which excel in the breed rings, obedience trials, in the field and on the race tracks. Meantime, Joan continues to write dog books (a novel about the dog fancy is also in the works), does free lance publicity and public relations work, exhibits her needlepoint (for which she has also won awards), is an active member of the Daughters of the American Revolution, the New York Genealogical and Biographical Society, and the New Jersey Film Advisory Board. Whatever time is left finds her at the art and auction galleries or maintaining her reputation as a movie buff.

This impressive list does not include all of her accomplishments or interests, since Joan Brearley has never been content to have just one interest at a time but has always managed to dovetail several occupations at the same time to make for a fascinating career.

Ch. Bondale's Willie Thompson, shown by handler Ray McGinnis for owner Marjorie E. Bond, Bondale Kennels, Eugene, Oregon.

CHAPTER ONE

The History of
the Breed

Helen Rice's Ch. Corwin Chances Are symbolizes our reflection back to the early history of the Cocker Spaniel.

Many millions of years ago dinosaurs and other strange-looking creatures roamed the earth. As "recently" as sixty million years ago a mammal existed which resembled a civet cat and is believed to have been the common ancestor of dogs, cats, wolves, and coyotes. This animal was the long extinct Miacis (pronounced *My-a-Kiss*).

The Miacis were long-bodied, long-tailed, short-legged beasts that stalked and chased their prey, grasped it in their long, powerful, fanged jaws and gnashed their food with their teeth. Just 15 million years ago the Tomcartus evolved from the earlier Miacis and provided an even truer genetic basis for the more highly intelligent prototype of the domesticated dog.

It is only fifteen to twenty thousand years since the first attempts were made to domesticate these ferocious, tree-climbing animals. Archaeologists have uncovered the skeletal remains of dogs that date back to the age of the cave man, and co-existed with them as members of their families in several ancient civilizations.

There are several schools of thought among the scholars and scientists on the exact location of the very first creatures to live with man. Some contend that the continent of Africa was the original locale. Ancient remains unearthed near Lake Baikal date back to 9,000 years B.C. Recent diggings in nearby Iraq that are said to date back 12,000 years have produced evidences of what is called the Palegawra dog. Siberian remains are said to date back 20,000 years. The Jaguar Cave Dogs of North America have been dated circa 8,400 B.C. Others say Asia and claim the Chinese wolf to be the ancestor of the dog.

Advocates of the theory of the Chinese wolf point out that the language barrier was responsible for the Chinese wolf not being known or acknowledged in earlier comparisons. When scientists could not translate Chinese writing, they could not study or authenticate the early Oriental findings. Their theory is also based on the presence of the overhanging bone found in the jawbone of both the Chinese wolf and the dog. This is believed to be significant in the change from their being strictly carnivorous creatures to creatures that eventually became omnivorous carnivores.

The general consensus of opinion among scientists dealing with prehistoric and archaelogical studies seems to settle on the likelihood that dogs were being domesticated in many parts of the world at approximately the same period in time. Since dogs were to become so essential to man's very existence, they were naturally absorbed into family life wherever and whenever they were found.

Climate, geography, and other environmental conditions all played a part in the evolution of the dog, and much later, the individual types and sizes and breeds of dogs.

The three most primitive types originated in three parts of the globe. While all bore certain very exact characteristics, the wolf-type seemed to evolve in southern Asia and Australia, the Pariahs in Asia Minor and Japan, and the Basenjis in Africa.

The Dingo found its way north to Russia and Alaska, across what is now the Bering Strait, into North America. The Pariahs moved far north and learned to pull sleds and developed into the various northern breeds in the arctic regions. The Basenjis and Greyhounds coursed the desert sands and hunted in the jungles of Africa when they weren't guarding royal palaces in Egypt. As dogs found their way across Europe, they served as guard dogs in the castles, rescue dogs in the Alps, barge dogs on the canals, and hunting dogs in the forests. The smaller dogs were bred down even smaller and became companions and pets for the aristocracy. Kings and queens of the world have always maintained their own personal kennels for their favorite breeds.

Ch. Pett's Trick or Treat, one of the Roland Pett's early top-winning show dogs. Photograph by Gunderson.

Ch. Chess King's Board Boss, bred and owned by Chuck and Billie Ballantine of Phoenix, Arizona. The sire was Ch. Lurola's Royal Lancer ex Ch. Rinky Dink's Serendipity. Photo by Bill Kohler.

BREED DEVELOPMENT

While the cave man used the dog primarily as a hunter to help provide meat and to provide meat themselves, he also made use of the fur as clothing and used the warmth from the dogs' bodies when sleeping. Dogs were to become even more functional as time went by, according to the dictates of the climates and geographical regions. Definite physical changes were taking place which eventually would distinguish one dog from another even within the same area. Ears ranged in size from little flaps that we see on terriers to the large upright ears on the Ibizan Hounds. Noses either flattened greatly as they did with Pekingese, or they grew to amazing lengths as we see in the Borzoi. Tails grew to be long and plumey such as those we see on the Siberian Husky or doubled up into a curl such as those we see on the Pug. Legs grew long and thin for coursing Greyhounds or were short and bent for the digging breeds such as the Dachshunds and the Bassetts. Sizes went from one extreme to the other, ranging from the tiniest Chihuahua all the way up to the biggest of all breeds, the Irish Wolfhound. Coat lengths became longer or shorter. There were thick, woolly coats for the northern breeds and smooth, short coats for the dogs that worked in the warm climates.

SENSORY PERCEPTION

As the dogs changed in physical appearance, their instincts and sensory perceptions also developed. Their sense of smell is said to be thirty million times keener than their human counterparts, allowing them to pick up and follow the scents of other animals miles in the distance. Their eyes developed to such a sharpness that they could spot moving prey on the horizon far across desert sands. Their hearing became so acute that they were able to pick up the sounds of the smallest creatures rustling in the leaves across an open field or in a dense forest.

All things considered, it becomes easy to comprehend why man and dog became such successful partners in survival and why their attraction and affection for each other is such a wondrous thing.

Ch. Baliwick Bricklayer, a black and white, sired by Ch. Baliwick Barrymore ex Ch. Bizzmar Bon Bon. Bred by Michael Allen and co-owned by Lindy Hay of Bakersfield, California, and Michael Allen.

HOW THE SPANIEL GOT ITS NAME

In ancient times when the Carthaginians invaded Spain—spelled *Spayne* in those days—they were immediately aware of the great profusion of rabbits that overran the countryside. It is little wonder then that their small dogs that flushed and pursued the rabbits in the fields with such success and enthusiasm came to be known as Spaniels, since the Carthaginian word for rabbit was *Span*. The word "Span-iel" came to mean "rabbit dog," a claim to fame they still enjoy today.

To quote from *All About the Cocker Spaniel* by John F. Gordon (Pelham Books, London): Virginia Woolf in her noted biography *Flush*, 1933 offers an interesting explanation to show how Spaniels could well have hailed from Spain. She refers to the historians who say that when the Carthaginians landed in that country (c. 238 B.C.) rabbits were to be found everywhere. The soldiery shouted 'Span! Span!', at the sight of them, this being their word for rabbits. The land became known and was eventually named *Hispania* or Rabbit-land and the dogs used by the natives to catch the rabbits called *Spaniels!* A colorful and attractive story no doubt which some might like to accept. Miss Woolf reports also that the Basques referred to the land as Espana, a word in their language signifying an edge or boundary. The dog coming from this region became known as a Spaniel; another likely explanation. We find too that in Old French, the word *espaigneul* is used in manuscripts which describe the Spanish Dog or Spaniel. In fact, there seems small doubt that the dog we know today originated in Spain. Were we able to travel back through time and inspect one of the originals we would probably have no difficulty in associating this early dog with one of the modern Spaniels, so strongly would the former's likeness have been transmitted through the many centuries of evolution. This, in spite of the manner in which the main rootstock has branched out to nine or more varieties of Spaniels which comprise the breed's family today.

As rabbits and other small rodents multiplied and became indigenous to all of Europe and the British Isles, so did all breeds of hunting dogs, including our Spaniels.

Remains of some of the earliest dogs unearthed in Ireland during the Harvard Archaeological Expedition in the 1930's, in the crannog of Lagore near Dunshaughlin, produced three of the oldest types: *Canis intermedius, Canis palustris,* and *Canis leineri,* all of which date back to the 7th and 8th centuries A.D. The largest of these "species" belonged to a large wolfdog-type. Other remains bore bent forelegs and were more diminutive in size; they had obviously belonged to the toy and terrier breeds. A third type carried the distinctly domed skull and clearly defined stop which indicated the first evidences of the Water Spaniel common to Britain, and the staunchest local contender for the Spaniel breeds which had migrated from Spain by way of France.

At this point it would be rather difficult to try to define precisely the various breeds of dogs (resulting from the early Irish diggings) which were crossbred with the Spaniels from Spain and other dogs brought to Ireland by the Celts from the south of England. Also, when Henry II of England invaded Ireland in 1154 there had already been a canine, as well as a human, integration since the people of Ireland, Scotland, and England had begun moving from country to country in sailing ships. In the 16th century a Sir Robert Cecil was importing "setting dogs" which were derived from the Spaniels in Ireland and which he presented to visiting diplomats with great ceremony.

Down there had been dogs of various breeds brought into Ireland from Belgium and the Netherlands by returning warriors through the centuries. After the Treaty of Utrecht in 1713 there was obviously mixing of the breeds from there and as far away as Germany and the Orient. There has been speculation that it might well have been one of the German imports that actually triggered the breeding of self-colored dogs, inasmuch as the German Vorstehund was certainly self-colored, while the Spaniels from Spain were said to be red and white in color.

Whatever the importations and mixtures were —either intentional or unintentional—it became more and more obvious that the Spaniels were beginning to become divided into more than one breed. A gradual but distinct evolution took place which produced both land and water dogs and certain changes from the original Spaniel into the beginnings of Field, Cocking, Clumber, Irish Water, Sussex, and Norfolk breeds.

Heather and Bonnie—double the pleasure, double the fun. These two 12-week-old buff bitches were bred by Julie Loustalot and C. Nelson. The sire was Ch. Pleasant Valley Swinger ex a Skyjack daughter. Heather is owned by Lindy Hay of Bakersfield, California.

EARLY WRITTEN RECORDS

The marvelous temperament and hunting talents of the Spaniels soon earned them a place as companions to commoners and kings alike. This is confirmed in written records dating back many centuries. One of the earliest is in the ancient tome called the Laws of Howel, written by Howel Dda in 948 A.D. He declared in this work that "the Spaniel of the King is a pound in value." Considering all that money could buy in olden times the value of our little dogs is duly noted. However, Henry VIII decreed that no dogs be kept in his court except "some small Spanyells for ladies."

Other early mentions of Spaniels in "olde Englyshe" history books are equally praiseworthy. In 1386 they were mentioned as participating in netting. (We must not forget that animals were captured in nets before the invention of firearms, so hunters were actually netting in the fields.) Later, hunting and hawking became popular when the dogs were "springing game to the gun." In the 14th century, however, Chaucer writes of the Spaniel in *The Wyf of Bathes Prologue*. Dr. Cains, in his history of Englishe Dogges, gives further insight into our breed with his comment, that the "Spaniell whose skynnes are white, and if marcked with any spottes they are commonly red . . ."

Stonehenge in the 1880's and Freeman Lloyd, an early 20th century dog man, heaped praises on the abilities of our talented little Cocking Spaniels. Further evidence of their excellence is recorded in the *Booke of Faulconorie*, by George Tumerville and published in 1575. His statement "Howe necessary a thing a spanell is to Falconrie," is written proof of their worth as sporting dogs. Stonehenge also wrote of their being "nearly mute, but whimper slightly on the scent, and when well-broken they distinguish each kind of game by the note they give out."

In 1940 in a book entitled *The Story of Pedigreed Dogs*, Arthur Roland, dog man and dog columnist for the "New York Sun," wrote an amusing piece on Stonehenge's statement. He wrote in part: "Just think of the potentialities in this! A Cocker scenting grouse could signal the fact back to his master in minor thirds or augmented fifths. A partridge ought to justify an arpeggio. The Cocker could give notice of quail in a tenor aria, and if he flushed a covey he could announce it by going into a fugue. Dissonant chords would be reserved for canards like

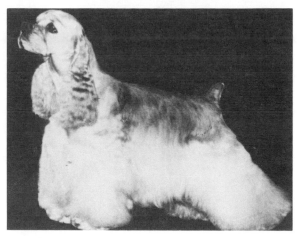

Am., Can. Ch. Bobwin's Boy Eagle owned by breeder Winnie Vick, Bobwin Kennels, Suisun, California. Sire was Ch. Pett's Golden Eagle ex Ch. Bobwin's Thumbelina.

rushing the decoy or tripping over one bird while sniffing out another."

Perhaps it is for the best that our present day requirements for the Cocker Spaniel in the field have changed to prevent just such symphonies.

ENGLAND

In England, as in America, the Cocker Spaniel has always been the smallest breed in its Group. During the years between the two World Wars there was for a short time an effort to establish a "pocket size" cocker breed with an eye toward eventually having it recognized. However, one of England's greatest proponents of the breed, the late H.S. Lloyd, member of The Kennel Club, managed to effectively eliminate the efforts to do so in what they considered to be a "retrograde step."

After World War II there was another kind of threat to the breed. Postwar breeders took readily to the Cocker Spaniel which began to suffer the adverse effects of over-popularity. They became the most popular breed in the country. A report in "The Field" stated that in retrospect they were so commercially and haphazardly bred that they suffered from loss of character, and sportsmen had difficulty in filling the field trial stakes for the breed. By the 1960's, however, the popularity of the Poodles surged up in the fancy and the Cocker Spaniel was relegated to a spot further down on the list.

Mrs. Yvonne Knapper of Dorset, England owner of the Sundust American Cocker Spaniel Kennels can take credit for founding the breed in England and she is still active and interested in the welfare of Cockers in that country today.

The 1980 Crufts winner, British and American Ch. Windy Hill Dur Bet Tis Patti of Sundust, is a top-winning American Cocker Spaniel in England. Patti has 16 challenge certificates to her credit. Owned by Mrs. Yvonne Knapper of Dorset, England, founder of the American Cocker Spaniel breed in England.

CHAPTER TWO

The Cocker Spaniel in England

Ch. Sundust Glamour Boots, a black and tan owned by Yvonne Knapper of Dorset, England, was sired by Am. Ch. Dur Bets Knight to Remember ex Sundust Ranita's Ebony Mystery.

In 1790, Bewick, the English writer, made the first written reference to the differences between the Springing Spaniels and the Cocking Spaniels. It was made clear that the Cocking Spaniels were the smallest of the Spaniels in size, weighing approximately eleven to sixteen pounds. At times they were used in packs to flush game but were reported to be too noisy and too small to be of much other use. Early in the 19th century they were used along with Greyhounds to spring the hare or rabbits after which the Greyhounds would take up the chase.

Recognition of the more "modern" Cocker Spaniel dates from about 1870, though the first Cocker Spaniel was registered with The Kennel Club in 1893. James Farrow of Ipswich founded his Obo strain in 1879, and the breed was finally recognized by The Kennel Club in 1892. By this time the Cocker had its weight limited to twenty-five pounds and the increase in weight and size helped it to gain popularity as a gun dog.

At the time of their new-found popularity, and upon a resolution made by Colonel Cane and seconded by Mr. Farrow, dogs under 25 pounds were considered Cocker Spaniels while the dogs over 25 pounds were called Springers.

JAMES FARROW AND OBO

When referring to the "modern" Cocker Spaniel in England, it cannot be denied that the Farrow Dog, Obo, had the strongest claim to fame in setting the "Standard" for the future of the breed. Obo is registered with The Kennel Club in England as being "by Fred and out of Betty." According to an article in Dalziell's *British Dogs*, Obo is described as weighing 22 pounds, 10" in height, 7¼" in length from nose to occiput, 2¼" in length from nose to eyes and 29" in length from nose to set on of tail. There are those that claim this is rather a description of one of his progeny, rather than of Obo himself, but to the best of our knowledge the argument has not been settled to anyone's satisfaction to date.

At James Farrow's suggestion Obo was bred to a bitch named Chloe II before she was shipped to Mr. F.F. Pitcher in New Hampshire. Her litter, whelped in the United States on August 7, 1882, produced Obo II, American Kennel Club registration #4911. Obo II was later sold to Mr. J. P. Willey who exhibited the dog and created a sensation in the breed in this country.

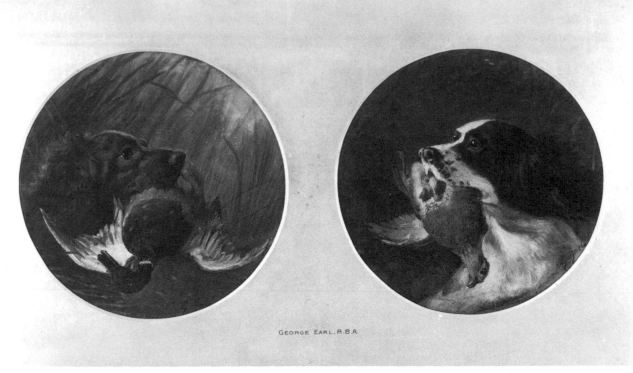

Famous dog painter George Earl painted these two ovals in oil on board many years ago. The paintings, each 8 inches in diameter, are of two famous Cocker Spaniels of yesteryear. On the left is the liver Spaniel "Beb," owned by T. Burgess, Esquire, and on the right the liver and white bitch "Nellie," owned by R. T. L. Price. The original of these drawings was offered for sale at $400 and appeared in *Portraits of Champion Dogs of England Painted by George Earl.*

While Ch. Obo can be said to be behind the first American strains, he was by no means the first or most highly prized Cocker Spaniel in England. English Ch. Brush, another black dog, which was highly thought of by fanciers on both sides of the Atlantic, was on the scene before Obo.

Rawdon B. Lee, the British dog writer, in his book, *Modern Dogs*, put aside his apparent lack of faith in the Cocker Spaniel's field abilities and praised the quality of the Farrow strain of blacks. He wrote, ". . . one or two of which are of the Cocker type of which I approve. Some of them are miniature specimens of the black field spaniels, and from which they are bred, but his Frank Obo, Ted Obo and Lily Obo are quite of the correct old-fashioned type."

It was almost as if Mr. Lee's writings were to preface things to come in the breed. New attention was given to the conformation of the Cocker Spaniel. Quite a few dogs were being sent to America and on both sides of the Atlantic new emphasis was being put on structural features which would enhance the Cocker's efficiency in the field. Great length of ear leather was said to be extremely desirable and there were reports of dogs which could boast ear spreads of up to two feet.

It was almost inevitable that the large gap between the shortlegged, long-bodied early Cockers used almost exclusively in the fields and the longer-necked, soft-eyed sloping-backed specimens that were desired in America would result in a separation between the American Spaniels and the English Cocker Spaniels, and differences between the dogs being shown in conformation classes for championship titles and those being trained for the field.

SHOW DOGS AND DOG SHOWS IN ENGLAND

Newcastle-on-Tyne was the site of the first dog show held in England. Various breeds competed at this English event, with Ireland holding their first show in 1864. Scotland was next with a dog show in 1871.

By the turn of the century breeding and showing dogs had become a popular pastime or sport. The challenge of trying to breed "the perfect dog" brought many dedicated and wealthy fanciers into the sport and several famous bloodlines gained recognition in the show rings. Huge kennels with full-time employees and trainers brought the sport of dogs into prominence.

Unfortunately, World War I and World War II made the importing or exporting of dogs almost an impossibility. During the wars many kennels completely disappeared. Feeding large breeds or maintaining large kennels became too expensive and too risky with food shortages and lack of kennel help. It was only following World War II that the most dedicated dog owners and exhibitors once again established their kennels and tried to pick up the bloodlines to carry on. Dogs once again became popular and the sport of dogs was once more a sportsman's delight.

THE FIRST FIELD TRIALS

The first field trials for Spaniels in England were run on January 3 and 4, 1899 at Sutton, Scarsdale, and were sponsored by the Sporting Spaniel Club. A 25 pound dog named Stylish Pride won both stakes that were held at that first event and were owned by Mr. Isaac Sharpe. The first field trial champion was Walhampton Judy, owned by Colonel Heseltone and bred by Mr.

A.E. Halsey in 1905. The first working certificate was won in 1909 by Mr. Phillips' bitch, Rivington's Robena, who also had her three Challenge Certificates making her a champion.

THE COCKER SPANIEL CLUB IN ENGLAND

In 1902 a Cocker Spaniel Club was established. It was largely responsible for the enormous surge in registrations after the conclusion of World War I and which lasted until the late 1940's and World War II. Just before the war Cocker Spaniel registrations in England had exceeded 27,000. In spite of the ravages of war, Cockers continued to survive but in considerably smaller numbers.

ENGLAND'S KENNEL CLUB

The Kennel Club in England was founded in 1873 and held its first dog show that first year at the Crystal Palace. Shortly thereafter came the publication of a stud book and the "Kennel Gazette," used to announce registrations and to publicize all other matters concerning pedigreed dogs.

Challenge certificate winners in England. American and English Ch. Sundust Bleuaire Repercussion. Sire was American Ch. Dreamridge Delegate, owned by Tom O'Neal, Woodstock, Illinois.

Ch. Moonmist Perchance is a winning black Cocker Spaniel owned by Mrs. W.J. and Miss P.A. Iremonger, Ferndown, Dorset, England. Sire was Sundust Johan Frisco ex Sundust Perseverance.

Am. Ch. Bobwins Bangaway of Memoir, handled by Yvonne Knapper in England.

The enormity of the sport of dogs in Britain continues to impress us when we avidly follow the results of Crufts competition. Crufts is not only the largest dog show in England, but in the world. Many of the English dog shows surpass entries of eight thousand, and Crufts with many, many more.

THE 1940's

Some of the well-known Cocker Spaniel kennels showing and breeding champion show dogs after World War II were Broomleaf, Sandover, Ide, Lochranza, Oxshott, Ware, Durban, Joywyns, Colinwood, Ulwood, Sixshot, Kenavon, Courtdale, Traquair, and Bramlyn, all producing and showing notable champions in the ring. It was due largely to their perseverance that the breed picked up once again when the war finally ended.

THE 1950's

The decade of the fifties saw the appearance of many of the same kennel names in the show catalogues. Inevitably new names appeared. Names such as Springbank, Weirdene, Dennydene, Nostrebor, Glendorgal, Goldenfields, Merryworth, Misbourne, Bartonblount, Gatehampton, Dorswick, Lucklena, Tideway, Eastlands, and Astrawin to name some of them.

THE 1960's

The sixties produced winners from kennels named Glencora, Moyhill, Quettadene, Ronfil, Eldwythe, Topbrands and with many of the names representing the past two decades clearly evident in the pedigrees just a few generations back.

THE 1970's

The same important names appeared during the decade of the 1970's and will undoubtedly do so in the 1980's, for the Cocker Spaniel remains in a place of high position among British dog fanciers. In 1980 it ranked fourth among the Top Ten dogs in England, surpassed only by Yorkshire Terriers, German Shepherds and Labrador Retrievers. As we enter the decade of the '80's, we can see no indication that our beloved little all-purpose dogs will not maintain their position. Cocker Spaniels have come a long way, just about a century after the famous Obo first endeared the breed to so many dog lovers on both sides of the Atlantic.

English and American Ch. Sundust Bleuaire's Repercussion, owned by Mrs. Yvonne Knapper of Dorset, England. Mrs. Knapper is also the owner of the Sundust American Cocker Spaniel Kennels in England and was instrumental in establishing the breed in that country. This magnificent black was photographed for the owner by Anne Cumbers.

Ch. Pett's Pamper is a magnificent buff Cocker Spaniel, owned and bred by Dorothy and Roland Pett, Dennis Port, Massachusetts.

CHAPTER THREE

The Cocker Spaniel Arrives in America

Head study of the author's black female Cocker Spaniel, Black Crest Charcoal Champion. This photograph was taken in 1951 by Edmond Vianney.

It has been said that one of the Pilgrims brought a Cocker Spaniel to America in 1620. How much it resembled our Cocker Spaniel of today is a matter of conjecture, but apparently the resemblance was such that it was recorded as being a Spaniel and of that we can be proud.

More than a century after the arrival of the Pilgrims, importations of Spaniels into this country were few and far between. When they did come over, they arrived almost simultaneously in America and Canada. At the time, when sportsmen interested in this wonderful little hunting dog first began importing them, there was not even a registry or governing body to keep a stud book. It wasn't until 1879 that the National Kennel Club—later to become the American Kennel Club—published the first stud book in St. Louis.

It was Mr. M.P. McCoon who decided to register his liver-and-white dog, Captain, and a Cocker was entered in the American Kennel Club Stud Book and was given the number 1354. It started the ball rolling and another 55 Cockers were registered in the stud book that first year. The formation of the American Spaniel Club in 1881 prompted a further increase in breeding, and registration numbers reached a total of 117 for that year. These registration figures represent both Cockers and Field Spaniels, since they were both registered in the same stud book as the same breed in those early days—the only difference being weight differential. Field Spaniels weighed in at over 28 pounds, while anything under that weight was a Cocker Spaniel.

CHLOE II

Mr. F. F. Pitcher, dog fancier of New Hampshire, was known to have imported Cockers to this country. While he did not exhibit them extensively, he did enjoy the breed and kept a few of them at his kennel. It was on the suggestion of James Farrow that he bought Farrow's black bitch, Chloe II, in whelp to his famous English Ch. Obo. It was a decision that was to lead to the establishment of the breed in this country.

On August 1, 1882 Chloe II gave birth to five puppies; 3 bitches, 2 dogs. This was the litter that included the renowned Ch. Obo II, later sold to Mr. J. P. Willey. The other dog in the litter went to Mr. J. Otis Fellows. This dog's name was Ch. Hornell Silk, and both Silk and Obo II were destined to become part of Cocker Spaniel history in this country. Both were black dogs and both produced get in a wide range of colors. And by their quality and marvelous temperament stamped the mark of the English great, Ch. Obo, on American Cocker Spaniels for all time.

This quality found in the Obo Chloe II puppies started a run on Obo importations. Obo Junior, Brock, Bob Obo, Obo III, Miss Obo II, and Snow II were brought to this country by breeders who desired to lay the foundation of their kennels on the famous English Obo line. Cocker Spaniels were off and running in America!

OBO II

While the pedigree of Obo II has been open to discussion because of questioned entries on the original registration in the English Stud Book, Volume I, published in 1874, on his sire, the influence of Obo II cannot be denied. He stands well on his own individual record, as well as upholding that of his sire and dam.

Obo II made his championship in September, 1883 at the Lowell, Massachusetts show just three months after entering a show ring to compete. Obo II was a celebrated sire and a sensation in the show ring.

Not that he didn't have his detractors. Mr. Mason, author of *Our Prize Dogs* gave a critique of Obo II that wasn't all flattering. He wrote: "Skull showing slight coarseness. Muzzle should be deeper, with a cleaner-cut appearance in every direction; it is wider than we like and the lower incisors project slightly." He also mentioned with Obo II that his neck was somewhat too heavy. But he also had good things to say about the dog. He finished his assessment by saying, "Ears correct in size, shape, position, quality, and carriage. Eyes good in color, size, and expression. Chest deep, with ribs beautifully sprung. Shoulders strong and free. Back firm. Loin compact and strong. Forelegs showing great strength and set into good feet. Stern well set. Carriage gay. Coat showing slight curliness, especially on neck and hindquarters. Feather profuse. Hindquarters of exquisite formation." The "crown of glory" finished with, "A thickset and sturdy little dog that looks exactly what he is—the prince of stud dogs—his worth to the Cocker interest of this country cannot be overestimated."

Spaniel man James Watson also heaped praise on Obo II claiming him to be ". . . a long way in front of any of his sex in this country so far, either as a show dog or sire."

Obo II was used widely at stud with many of the Canadian bitches as well as those in this country. Names such as Miss Obo, King of Obo,

Betty Obo, Ted Obo, Frank Obo, Minnie Obo, Tim Obo, Lily Obo, Ann Obo, and Miss Obo II were popping up on pedigrees and proving to be important foundation stock. Other top dogs sired by either Obo II himself, or in close lineage with him, also were contributing to the quality of the breed. Dunrobin, La Tosca, Goldstream Friar Tuck, Midkiff Demonstrator, Shina, Jersey, Doc and Red Dock, a dog called I Say, Middy, Darkie, Juno W, Beatrice W, and Helen were declared to be good potential for quality litters. It was also the time of the much talked about Braeside breeding and Baby Ruth who was whelped in 1892.

But records are made to be broken, and during the 1890's the name on everyone's list of sires was an Obo II son, called Black Duke. Following in the footsteps of his famous father, Black Duke became the greatest sire of his generation. James Luckwell was the owner/breeder, and Black Duke was out of Luckwell's Woodland Queen.

This was also the era of the Idahurst Kennels owned by the O.B. Gilmans. Idahurst Belle and Idahurst Roderic were two of their most famous Cockers, and they also used Black Duke in their breeding program.

An Irish Setter and a Cocker Spaniel circa 1840. This lithograph is part of the collection of the author.

Mr. Hildreth K. Bloodgood was the owner of the Mepal Kennels, and owner of the aforementioned Baby Ruth who was bred by W. Barclay. She was said to have the most classical headpiece up to that time. Other important kennels were the Warners' Belle Isle Kennels, Brookside, and Mount Vernon. On the West coast Governor James Rolph of California founded the Mission Kennels with his blue roan bitch Beechrove Topsy. Also prominent in the fancy were the names of Lydia Hopkins, Mrs. William Ralston, Denniston, Golden Gate, Bellmore, Louise Hering, and Richard and Helen Shute's Knebworth Kennels.

IT PAID TO ADVERTISE

As early as 1897 Cocker Kennels were beginning to breed extensively and kennel advertisements were a regular feature in trade publications offering puppies for sale and lauding their important English pedigree backgrounds. James L. Little had his Newcastle Kennels in Brookline, Massachusetts and his ads in *The American Stock-Keeper* contained phrases such as "from the best English and American bloodlines, such as Ch. Obo, Ch. Middy, Dude Paro, Jersey Nebo, Jersey Obo, Ch. Black Dufferin, and King Raven." This fascinating line-up in his front page ad in the April 3, 1897 edition read like a "Who's Who" in the breed around the turn of the century.

George Douglas owned the Havoc Kennels in Woodstock, Ontario, Canada and advertised stud fees at $25 for Ch. Black Duke, AKC #SB8494 and boasted, "Absolute winner of the American Spaniel Club Trophy and the Whitehead Cup for the best stud dog and two of his get." He included in the ad that he had puppies, grown dogs, and bitches in whelp for sale and would send photographs of same for 25 cents.

The Belle Isle Kennels in Detroit specialized in blacks and offered puppies for sale and stud service on Omo, AKC #SB42750, only son of Ch. Black Duke ex Ch. Baby Ruth. The fee, according to this ad, was $15. The advertisement also mentioned that Dude, CKC #SB1405 was also at stud. He was sired by Newton Abbott Beau ex Dinah Bennet. His stud fee was $10.

F. H. Topham of Boston, Massachusetts also advertised puppies for sale and stud service. Some of the brood bitches were listed as being for sale and sired by Black Duke, Ch. Cherry Boy, Dude, Commodore, Jersey Nebo and Rex T. One of Topham's top dogs was Home Rule, by Ch. Pickpanie out of Elsie. His Josephus was winner of the first prize at Mineola and Brooklyn shows in 1896, and was sired by Snowball ex Brunette. His stud fee was $10.

C.C. Moulton in Dorchester, Massachusetts was offering at stud his imported Cocker Spaniel, Obo III, which had been given the AKC #SB20874, and bred in England by James Farrow. Obo III also had a Canadian Kennel Club #SB414. Obo III, as the name implies, was sired by Mr. Farrow's famous Ch. Obo, #E10452 ex Gipping's Floss, #E20653. (The "E" of course represents England's Kennel Club registration numbers.) Mr. Moulton revealed in his advertisements the distinct advantages carried by Obo III. The ad read: "He is a son of grand old Ch. Obo, is solid black in color, and has immense feather, is a very active, cobby dog, standing 11 inches at shoulder, and weighs 26 pounds, has a perfectly flat coat, dark eyes and stands on straight legs. He is a great stock getter and produces excellent pups. Stud fee ten dollars. Pups for sale and orders received for six litters now due."

J. Riggs was known for his Rosamaude Cocker Kennels in 1897, and Mrs. Hester's dog Butcher Hester and J. Kennedy's Hamilton Jack were making headlines in the dog publications. In Ohio Mr. A. W. Pancoast was importing English stock. Little Prince was one of them.

In 1898 Mr. W. T. Payne sold his parti-color Cocker Mirge for $75 on the strength of his first place win at the Boston show that year. And in H.W. Lacy's "Kennel Notes" column in the March 5th issue of *The American Stock-Keeper*, it was revealed that he had sold Joe Rice, also first place winner at Boston in 1898, but the notice read, "price private."

In 1898 Mrs. H. E. Smyth's Swiss Mountain Kennels in Germantown, Pennsylvania was listed as "importers of Cockers and Skyes," and further advertised in *The American Stock-Keeper*, "Our 1897 catalog, illustrated, with half-tone pictures of individual dogs, kennels, etc., 20 cents." It was Mrs. Smythe who imported the black bitch, Trumpington Daisy.

Such was the growing interest in the Cocker breed at the turn of the century when one of the greatest Cocker breeders of all time was even more famous and revered. The name was Herman E. Mellenthin.

In addition to all the wonderful things people had to say about Herman Mellenthin as a person, the influence he was to have as an ambassador for the breed over so many decades could not have been imagined at the time. Add his well-deserved popularity to his good fortune in having a superior dog, a dog far ahead of his time in excellence and quality, and you come up with an unbeatable combination.

The dog was Red Brucie, and while he never became a champion, his contribution to the breed by way of his potency as a stud is now legend. He was the sire of 31 champions by 1931. Physical descriptions of Red Brucie make close comparisons to those of the earlier Ch. Obo II. His sire was Robinhurst Foreglow and his dam was Rees Dolly. He sired 34 champions, with many others pointed or not exhibited in spite of their worth, out of seven bitches.

As the 1920's wore on, more and more kennels, which had managed to renew themselves after the adjustments of World War I and the curtailments on importing, began to operate once again on a broad scale. In the East, especially where importing was certainly feasible, kennels such as Dorothy L'Homedieus Sand Spring, Mepal, Midkiff, Lucknow, Mrs. Ella B. Moffit's Rowcliffe, Brookside, Hornell, Overcross, Rees, Cassilis, Robinhurst, and others were breeding for both field and show. The Scioto Kennels of Dr. Phillips was dominating the midwest, and many of the top specimens were racking up impressive lists of wins. And the name of Arline Swalwell, who "championed" Cockers of all colors was well-known. She is the lady who was to go on to celebrate more than 60 years of successful breeding. At 80 years of age (in 1981) she held the honor of being active in the breed longer than any other living breeder.

A great old picture of some of the old-time greats in Cocker Spaniels! Circa 1915 banquet for Cocker people shows Ch. Knebworth Florizel sitting in the lady's lap on the extreme left in the photo; the man with glasses next to her is noted judge Dr. Knox; Helen Shute stands behind him; Richard Shute stands behind Charles Gilbert, another prominent judge at the time; and Ch. Knebworth Rowdy is the dog in the center of this illustrious group. His owner, Mary Lester Conner, sits in front of him. Judge Dr. Krandell is third from right.

The exhibit at the 1932 Olympics shows Ch. Sinaloa Moonshine among a display of trophies. He was one of the most outstanding black and white Cockers during this decade and was co-owned by Helen Shute and Helen Rice. His sire was Ch. Jack of Dara ex Bellmore Brazen. The walls behind the trophy display are lined with show ribbons for this prestigious event.

Type and general outline of the Cocker Spaniel became a popular topic of conversation in the 1920's, when the American Kennel Club divided the Cockers into two varieties. The trend seemed to go from the longer field type of dog to the square, cobby type seen in the show rings. The rule became "From tip of nose to root of tail should be about twice the height at shoulder, rather more than less." The key word being "about."

As the concept of the "ideal" Cocker began to come into reality, we began to see the straight top line start to slope and shorten, skulls became even more rounded and the reach of neck became longer to better aid the dog in scenting the ground.

It was not until April, 1924 that competition was held for Groups and Best in Show. Even then it was not a mandatory award and was not given except at some of the larger shows. Prior to that time, a Best in Show was classified as an "unclassified special" and was not reported in the *American Kennel Gazette*.

One of the Group-winning bitches at that time was Ch. Knebworth Gloriana, whelped February 27, 1923. Gloriana started her show career at just over a year old and finished with two five-point majors and three Best of Breed, including a Group first.

During this same 1924-1925 season she also took time out to whelp a litter sired by Ch. Knebworth Cyclone, a Best in Show winner. In that litter was Ch. Knebworth Buddie, another top dog at the time.

During Gloriana's career, the Best of Winners award was not given. When a Best of Breed award was made, the Winners Dog and Winners Bitch solid color and the Winners Dog and Winners Bitch parti-color—which included black/tan—went into the ring together to compete for the Best of Breed ribbon.

THE BREED'S FIRST BEST IN SHOW WINNER

But the highlight of the decade of the 1920's was obviously the winning of the coveted Best in Show award at the prestigious Westminster Kennel Club show held at Madison Square Garden. Ch. Midkiff Seductive, owned by William T. Payne, captured this tremendous honor in 1921. Payne, one of the early and most devoted dog men in the U.S., considered it a triumph for the breed as well as the individual dog. It gave a boost to the breed following the general slow-down in breeding immediately after the declaration of war and the slow process of starting over again once peace had been declared.

It was also a win that would not be repeated at this show by a Cocker Spaniel until Ch. My Own Brucie flashed across the horizon in 1940 and 1941 by winning the show two years in succession. It was not to be won again until 1954 when Mrs. Carl E. Morgan's Ch. Carmor's Rise and Shine took the top honor, though we must say Mrs. Byron Covey and Mai Wilson's beautiful Kaptain Kool came close in 1981.

THE 1930's

It was during the decade of the 1930's that the Treetops Kennels bred an excellent dog named Treetops Tristan. This dog later became Ch. Treetops Tristan of Giralda and was owned and shown by the Giralda Farms. Tristan was by Bazel Otto ex Treetops Truelove and did some nice winning for Mrs. Geraldine Dodge. A dog named Blackmoor Barnabus of Giralda was another of the Cockers at this famous kennel.

Mrs. Dodge, one of the most respected ladies of all times, owned many breeds and it was she who was largely responsible for getting the English Cocker Spaniel recognized as a separate breed in this country.

The Torohill Kennels were doing their share of winning in the 30's with their Ch. Torohill Trader. This home-bred was sired by Torohill Trouper ex Torohill Tidy.

By 1935 the Rocky Point Kennels in Oklahoma City had produced four generations of "Rocky Point reds" they could be proud of. The Rees Kennel's dog Rees The Guard produced the lovely Ch. Sugartown Pie out of Orthodox Gendye of Irolita. The Sugartown Kennels were located in Paoli, Pennsylvania. Ch. Lady Patricia of Sugar-

town was another winner out of My Own Kennel's breeding, namely My Own Pet ex My Own Lady Huntington.

By the middle of the thirties the Stockdale Kennels were well-known, not only on the West Coast where their kennels were based in Van Nuys, but the Stockdale dogs were winning all over the country. Ch. Stockdale Town Talk and Stockdale Startler were carrying the banner while Ch. Stockdale Trade-Mark was making his "mark" by the end of the decade.

The first half of the 1930's heralded the arrival of Ch. Found on the show scene. He was owned by Mrs. Leonard J. Buck and sired by My Own Ladysman out of My Own Lady Brucie. The author is pleased to note that her first black Cocker bitch, purchased early in 1940 from Marie Peterson's Black Crest Kennels, was a Found daughter named Black Crest Charcoal Champion. She was out of Black Crest Ebony Lady. Her sire was the Ch. Nonquitt Nola's Candidate. Ch. Found sired Ch. Don Juan of Dorick when bred to Mardormere Molly Bawn.

Poetry in motion—handler Ted Young puts Ch. Kamp's Kaptain Kool through his paces on the way to another Best in Show win.

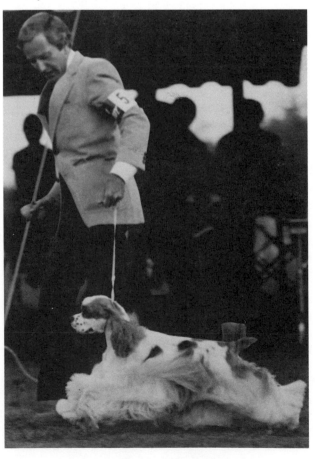

Joan Brearley's Black Crest Charcoal Champion, the author's first Cocker Spaniel. "Charky" was whelped in 1946 and was sired by Ch. Found out of Black Crest's Ebony Lady.

The author with her first Cocker Spaniel puppy. "Charcoal" was whelped in 1946 and was from the Black Crest Kennels in New Jersey.

The Lawlock Kennels in Noroton, Connecticut were showing Ch. Amanda of Lawlock in 1937. Amanda was Tip Coe breeding on both sides, Rip Van Winkle being the sire and Senorita her dam.

The Marjolear Kennels in Pittsburgh (not to be confused with the Mardormere Kennels) also bred to Ch. Found and bred Aileen Arion of Marjolear, a lovely black.

The Windridge Kennels in Everett, Washington produced a Canadian Champion in their Windridge Gold Dust. Gold Dust when bred to their Windridge Rosita gave them yet another winner in Windridge Serenade.

The list of Mepal Kennel's winning dogs over the period of several decades cannot be denied. In 1938 Mepal's Jester, sired by Orthodox Dickory Dock ex Mepal's Jessica was a top dog at the kennels in New Marlboro, Massachusetts. The Cassilis Kennels used Mepal's Sir Knight as stud to Pam of Cassilis and produced Dark Knight of Cassilis that same year.

By 1938 the My Rhythm Kennels in Milton Junction, Wisconsin were advertising their four generations of winning Cockers. B-Gae Kennels in Fallon, Nevada were winning with Ch. B-Gae's Pride O'Mee. And in New Jersey the Curtwin Kennel's Navigator, sired by Ch. Found out of Cedarbrook Skysaid was whelped in 1939 as was their Ch. Curtwins Cavalier.

Other great dogs were Ch. Nonquitt Notable's Pride, Ch. Freeland's Farmer, Ch. Mariquita Cavalier, Ch. Argyll's Enchantress and Ch. Argyll's Archer, Ch. Hadley's Trumpeter, Ch. MacRae's Molly and the remarkable Dual Ch. Miller's Ewauire, C.D.X., all whelped during the decade of the 1930's which many Cocker fanciers refer to as the Golden Decade in our breed.

In 1933 Ch. Windsweep Prudence was whelped. She was by Rees' The Guard ex Freeland's Lady Mildred. In Minneapolis at the Ivy Lane Kennels was Ch. Mariquita Cavalier. Shootingbox Kennels in Woodbury, Long Island whelped Shootingbox Hapenny in 1935 and Ch. Nonquitt Notable was making public appearances for "Dogs for Defense." Tokalon Perfection, Ch. Mardormere Winning Ways and International Ch. Live Oak Sand Storm were whelped in 1936. In 1937 Sir Gervais of King's Point and Ch. Captain Topper II were born.

Other kennel names that were making news were Charmarel in Great Neck, Long Island; Brookside; Heartsease Kennels in Stamford, Connecticut; Kay Emm's in California; Ramblelot in Rockford, Illinois; High Hampton in South Carolina; Philsworth in Rhode Island; and The Kennels of Cogges Hall in Wantagh, Long Island. In 1939 a Canadian champion was also being shown named Chimney Sweep's Roamer.

Ch. Stockdale Gay Bobarene, C.D., owned by Irene Gaddy Zimmerman, is pictured winning Best of Opposite to Best of Breed at the 1949 Cocker Spaniel Club of Southern California Specialty show under judge Rev. William Walsh.

Otto's Golden Promise, blond charmer from the decade of the 1940's. Owned by Marguerite Richardson of Hackensack, Minnesota, and bred by Mrs. George Otto, Promise was sired by Ch. Pinehill First Edition out of Otto's Golden Nymph.

We can only wonder how many of the Cocker fanciers could imagine the effect that one little red dog was going to have on the breed that was destined to mark the decades of the 1930's and 1940's two of the most famous and significant in the history of the breed. That little dog was Ch. My Own Brucie, whelped in 1935. By the end of the 30's breeders were beginning to realize the potential he provided, and it was brought home to everyone when he started off the decade of the 40's with two consecutive Best in Show wins at Madison Square Garden, the prestige show in the dog world.

THE 1940's

The effect that Ch. My Own Brucie had on Cocker Spaniels was such that has seldom been seen before or since in the breed.

The fame that surrounds every dog that wins Best in Show at "the Garden" automatically catapults that particular breed to the top of the list of purebred dogs. Suddenly everyone wants "a dog just like that one!" This often leads to over-breeding and results in a glut on the market. In some breeds down through the years it has actually been "the kiss of death" to good breeding when the demand exceeded the supply.

When Ch. My Own Brucie won the Westminster Kennel Club show in 1940 and again in 1941, as well as the American Spaniel Club top award in '41, some very excellent breedings took place as several sincere breeders incorporated his lines into their breeding programs. Whelped in 1935, Brucie was also valued for the direct line of descent through his father, Red Brucie. Mr. H. E. Mellenthin, a top dog man, realized this fully and Brucie was used at stud during the second half of the thirties and through the 1940's.

It is acknowledged that Brucie brought the Cocker Spaniel breed to the peak of its popularity during the 1940's. It was at this time that the American Kennel Club registrations for Cockers led all other breeds and established a place in this list of Top Ten favorite breeds which they never relinquished. By 1946 Cocker Spaniels were the #1 breed in rank with 75,242 registrations. In 1950 they were still in the #1 spot though registrations had dropped to 61,259. While registrations continued to drop, the breed itself maintained its popularity with dog fanciers.

Even in 1942 when the American Kennel Club made the distinction between the English

Cocker Spaniel and the American Cocker Spaniel varieties the interest did not decline. Each of them held its own as each assumed its individual identity in the show rings, and Ch. My Own Brucie continued to charm all comers to the breed.

The Windsweep Kennels in Sharon, Connecticut had used Brucie at stud in the late 1930's, well before his Garden success, and whelped Ch. Windsweep Repeat out of their Windsweep Diana. They had also recognized the quality and used Red Brucie, his sire, in the early 1930's on their Ch. Cordova Clare, and came up with their Ch. Windsweep Ladysman. In 1941 the name Red Brucie turned up once again. The Greenwich, Connecticut Pinefair Kennels bred Pinefair Red Brucie, sired by Walida Red Brucie ex Damsel of Pinefair.

It was also the decade of many famous names in the breed in addition to the continuing successes of kennels such as Knebworth, Stockdale, Nonquitt, and Try-Cob. Lucille Burgess, C. B. Van Meters, Ferne Mitchell, Mrs. Sara Higgs, and Myrtle Smith were advertising top dogs and/or puppies for sale. Kennel names appeared in great numbers such as Silver Maple Farms, Bobb's, Benbow, Lawrabee, Florister, Oak Manor, Woodlane, Claythorne, Strathmore, Sill's, Leo Goodman's Belden Kennels, Echo Ridge, Bar-Nan, Orchardlawn, Besswell, Wynnehaven, Mahaska, Gildran, Rural, Molinero, Marianna, Klyru, Lindaire, Southfair, Dalecarlia, Cottespur, Cap Mar, Rosajo, Thurlyn Acre, Downsbragh, Dungarvan, Sogo, Ivy Hill, Dutchtown, Merry Hill, and Biggs were just a few of those advertising and exhibiting in the rings during this exciting decade.

The complete list of all those contributing to the breed is too lengthy to include here, but an excellent record can be had in the Breeders' Directory and Index in the 1946 65th Anniversary Yearbook of the American Spaniel Club.

In the 1940's the Darlingdale Kennels in Adrian, Michigan advertised themselves as the "home of Better Reds" with show, field, and breeding stock for sale.

John R. Andrews, whose kennel name was Ditan, was a nationally known Cocker enthusiast, particularly around Houston, Texas, where he resided. In addition to his admiration for the breed, Mr. Andrews was renowned for ownership of one of the largest private collections of Cocker data in this country at the time. He used a great deal of this information as head of the Ditan Pedigree and Book Service and made considerable contributions to the fancy in published articles during the 1940's and 1950's.

Ch. Dream Boy of Chalburn, bred by Clint Callhan was a Best in Show winner under judge Ralph Craig at the New York American Spaniel Club in 1948. His owner was Mrs. Chalmers Burns.

Roy Cowan's Ch. Mariquita Miss Muffet was a top bitch whelped in 1940. She was sired by Ch. Mariquita Cavalier ex Lady Midge of Milroy. Virginia Muller of San Diego and the Myroy Kennels in Fresno were names noted in show catalogues on the West Coast in the early 1940's, as was the name Cha Ra in Eureka.

On the East Coast at Rockville Center, Long Island, the Hodges' Ch. Hodges' Honey Cloud was whelped in 1940 while further north in New York State the Try-Cob Kennels in Nanuet were showing their Ch. Try-Cob's Candidate. This lovely black was sired by Glidmere Buzz ex Ch. Brightfield Delight.

Stockdale Prince Royal started off the '40's for the Stockdale banner when Ch. Stockdale The Great came along in 1941. Ch. Topflite The Brat was the 1940 hopeful for Topflite Kennels in Minneapolis.

Mrs. Milo G. Vickery in California was the owner of Vickery's Gaming Acres, Maid O'War and Marmilo's Golden Lady. Wins made by these and other top dogs were reported by Dorothy W. Telfer, a popular columnist for *Kennel Review* magazine during the '40's. Out California way, Harry Sangster's County Gossip, a lovely black and tan son of Stockdale Town Talk, was also making the columns.

Dr. and Mrs. L. C. Henderson were showing Charson's Dutchess, Agnes Reichar had brought

The Cocker Spaniel as created by artist Carol Moorland Marshall of Santa Ana Heights, California. This magnificent rendering of the red and white Cocker exemplifies the fine style and quality of this artist whose work has been featured in many art shows and was sold in Abercrombie and Fitch for many years.

One of the early foundation dogs at the Roland Petts' Kennels was the beautiful Pett's Palladium. Photograph by Gunderson.

PETTS

Roland and Dorothy Pett started their Pett's Cockers Kennel in 1947. Now located at Dennis Port, Massachusetts, they can still boast of being a small kennel, based on sound stock, that has produced outstanding winners year after year and are still going. They have finished 52 champions and over 12 Canadian and foreign champions bearing the Pett prefix.

The Petts love the breed and consider it a beautiful small sporting dog that also fills the bill when one requires a dog that makes a happy loving family pet.

While the Petts are known mostly for buff-colored Cockers, their original foundation bitch was a black with a buff recessive. Her name was Pett's Cinderella. She was from a litter that produced three champion bitches, one being Ch. Elder's So Lovely, the dam of the great black dog, Ch. Elderwood Bangaway.

Pett's Special Reserve, the first show dog for the Roland Petts' Kennels, was out of their first homebred litter. Unfortunately, he died when just a little over a year old (with 10 points toward championship); but fortunately he sired pups and was the grandsire of Ch. Kingsley's Moonflower.

out her Areus Marius, and the Monterey Kennels in El Monte, California were showing Ch. Rocky Point Rob Roy.

One of the Ch. My Own Brucie winners in the early '40's was Mrs. Arthur F. Richardson's Ch. Covered Brook Buccaneer. The dam was Argyll's Dark Secret. Alderbrook Kennels' Ch. Alderbrook Tiger was being shown at this time, as was Ch. Stonelea Soldier.

The Nonquitt Kennel prefix was well-known for many champions and for many decades. Dogs such as Ch. Nonquitt Nola's Candidate, and her dam Ch. Nonquitt Nola were two of the better known, as was Nonquitt Niantic's Bill, not to mention International Ch. Nonquitt Nob's Bob whelped in 1942. His sire was Ch. Nonquitt Nobadeer ex Ch. Bob Jacks Only One.

During the 1940's the Stockdale Kennel name was appearing on a lot of red Cockers, not just the blacks. Stockdale Copper Count was one of them, whelped in 1943. The sire was Ch. Stockdale Mornin' Judge out of Adams' Black Linda. Aerolite Red Admiral whelped in 1944 was sired by Ch. Stockdale Town Talk by Stormalong's Racy Raven. Ch. Stockdale Town Talk was also the sire of Ch. Stockdale Red Rocket.

From their first litter out of Cinderella came their buff male, Pett's Special Reserve. Reserve died at 14 months before finishing his championship but the Petts were fortunate enough to be able to purchase a daughter of his named, appropriately enough, Pett's Happy Memory. She carried on the line by producing their Pett's Kingsley's Moonflower, finished before she was 11 months old.

By this time another buff male, Glo's Gay Echo arrived but was lost in a hurricane on Cape Cod. His daughter, Pett's Ragtime Rhythm, has been sold to Ruth Pusey, and came to fame by producing the famous great Ch. Artru Hot Rod. Both his show and stud record are Cocker history.

Some of their outstanding show dogs include Ch. Pett's Gentleman Jim, Golden Eagle, Yachtsman, Golden Key, Calendar Girl, Bamboo Biege, Coral Vision, Right Time, Daddy's Mink, and Pamper, the queen of the Pett Kennels—all champions and all bearing the famous Petts prefix. Surely Ch. Pett's Daddy's Mink will be remembered if only for the familiar notion his name implies!

Through the years the Petts have used professional handlers to show their dogs to their best advantage in the show rings. Norman Austin, Ted Young, Ruth Kraeuchi and Ron Fabis have piloted their beautiful dogs to their show wins. Recognized as perhaps their greatest show dog was Ch. Pett's Gentleman Jim, a Best in Show dog in the 1960's. "Frankie" sired many champions in most all colors, and two of his sons produced over 20 champions each.

Some of their other top-producing stud dogs were Ch. Pett's Yachtsman, sire of 24 champions, Ch. Pett's Golden Eagle, sire of 27 Champions, and Ch. Pett's Broker's Tip, sire of nine champions, to name just a few. A few of their top-producing brood bitches were Ch. Pett's Calendar Girl, dam of six champions; Pett's Lady Laurel, dam of six champions, plus a Canadian and a South American champion; Ch. Pett's Bit O'Pamper; Ch. Pett's Golden Eve, dam of five champions; and Pett's Imp of White Satin, dam of Ch. Hob-Nob-Hills Tribute, a sire of 54 champions.

There was a great deal of discussion during the early 1940's about the ideal weight minimums

Ch. Pett's Susie Snowflake is another superb show bitch from the 1950's, owned by Mr. and Mrs. Roland Pett of Dennis Port, Massachusetts. Gunderson photo.

Ch. Pett's Flashy Couquette, top show bitch from the 1950's, is pictured winning under judge Dr. John Eash at the Silver Jubilee show of the West Coast Cocker Spaniel Club Specialty. C.B. Van Meter of Stockdale Kennel fame presents the trophy. Norman Austin handled for owners Mr. and Mrs. Roland Pett of Dennis Port, Massachusetts. Ludwig photo.

and maximums. Many breeders were of the opinion that a 30-pound dog was ideal and needed to carry that weight to successfully handle a rabbit or pheasant in the tall grass, and that the dogs in and around the 18-pound class were good for nothing but serving as house pets and companions. Still others were firm in their opinion that no Cocker Spaniel should go below the 18-pound requirement. This problem seemed to be resolved when the American Kennel Club divided them into two varieties and settled the matter at that time.

THE 1950's

The decade of the Fifties was an exciting time in the dog fancy. Irene Phillips Khatoonian introduced her famous Phillips System in *Popular Dogs* magazine, and it became a major goal for every show dog in the nation to strive for a place in the Top Ten. Gail Hockman bred a marvelous black dog named Gail's Ebony Don D, and he was destined to become the first top Cocker Spaniel to grace the Phillips System.

Owned by Natalie Goldstein of Palm Beach, Florida, Don D not only was the #1 Cocker Spaniel in 1956 but #3 of all breeds during the first year the Phillips System was compiled. Year by year results of Phillips System are recorded in our chapter on statistics, but another mention of this remarkable little dog's show record bears repeating.

Another little black Cocker made it in the sporting division in 1956. His name was Ch. Baliwick Banter. And an ASCOB was close on his heels with major show wins and was called Ch. Eufaula's Dividend.

By 1958 Ch. Artu Hot Rod was on a winning streak that put him in the #4 position in the Top Ten ratings all-breeds, and in 1959 Ch. Clarksdale Capital Stock was #9 in the all-breed Top Ten, which made breeder-owners Leslie E. and Elizabeth C. Clark proud.

The 1950's were also the years when Ch. Hickory Hill Hi Jack, Ch. Wilco's Little Barney and Ch. Mel Lar's Prince Frederick were riding high, along with Ch. Windjammer's Passkey.

The Fifties saw many of the famous kennels of the past still continuing to show and breed, and many prominent newcomers that would continue in the fancy for many years to come.

Helen Shute and Knebworth

It is difficult to decide in which decade to recall the glories and contributions made by Helen Shute and the Knebworth Kennels since every decade finds the Knebworth name on the pedigrees of top dogs in the breed. At the time of her death in April, 1967 Helen had already celebrated over 50 years of breeding some of the greatest winning Cocker Spaniels in the history of the breed.

After her marriage to Dick Shute in 1910, her Knebworth dogs could be found at their kennels in California standing at stud or with puppies being sold to help establish other kennel lines around the country. Richard Shute died in 1933, but Helen carried on their illustrious Knebworth line. After her death her good friend and associate of many years' standing, Irene Gaddy Zimmerman, inherited and maintained the Knebworth Kennels producing many additional champions. In spite of ill health Mrs. Zimmerman continues to be interested in and associated with the breed in the 1980's, and more about her association with Helen Shute as well as her own many and varied contributions to the dog fancy can be found in the section on the 1970's.

Knebworth Knectarine is pictured winning Winners Bitch at the 1965 American Spaniel Club show, owner-handled by Irene Gaddy Zimmerman of Sun Valley, California. Knectarine was the first Cocker Spaniel in California to win points at a big show and "broke the ice" for the other Cockers that came along to establish the breed on the West Coast.

Best of Variety at the 1958 American Spaniel Club Specialty show was Ch. Artru Hot Rod, bred and owned by Mr. and Mrs. Arthur Benhoff of California. Judge Mrs. Myrtle Twelvetrees, a breeder of Cockers, presented the award to this famous ASCOB. Dr. Samuel Draper, another California Cocker Spaniel breeder, stewarded at this Cocker classic at the Roosevelt Hotel in New York City.

Myrtle Twelvetrees

Myrtle Twelvetrees was another famous Cocker Spaniel breeder with a kennel in California during the 1950's. Mrs. Twelvetrees was also a noted Cocker judge and officiated at many top Cocker Spaniel events during the course of her show ring career. It was Mrs. Twelvetrees who put up the famous Ch. Artru Hot Rod as the Best of Variety winner at the 1958 American Spaniel Club Show, held at the Roosevelt Hotel in New York City that year.

Dr. Samuel Draper

Samuel Draper was another well-known name in the Cocker circles during the mid-1950's. The breed held special appeal for him and he co-owned Ch. Knebworth Yankee Pasha with another famous California dog man, Joel Marston. Pasha was handled for them by Porter Washington who piloted the dog to top wins

after he completed his championship in 1957.

Pasha was sired by Roy Nelson's Ch. St. Andrea's Rain Maker who was sired by another famous champion, Landcaster Landmark, who traced his lines back to such famous kennel names as Nonquitt, Pinefair, Myroy, Mariquita, and Stockdale bloodlines. Pasha's dam was descended from Ch. Heather's Mister Chips and the Holmeric, Torohill, My Own, Argyll, and Stockdale lines.

Dr. Draper left California to become a Columbia University instructor and to hold other teaching positions, and has been honored many times for his achievements in the teaching field. He is a Non-Sporting Group judge and hopes to extend his judging assignments to include the Cocker Spaniel breed.

It is also interesting to note that both Dr. Draper and Joel Marston have become especially successful in the breeding and showing of top winning Chow Chows.

Trojan

Alice Kaplan started her Trojan line in 1956 in Magnolia, Texas. Breeding has always been on a small scale with just one or two litters a year; however, in spite of the small operation they can boast of having bred or owned 33 champions, starting with a homebred in 1958.

The first six of their champions were finished by professional handlers, but the fun and enjoyment of showing their own dogs soon saw them showing in the ring themselves.

Trojan's Aileen won the first leg on her C.D. title at just eight months of age, and Ch. Trojan Maxie Tan started his show career by being Best ASCOB Futurity puppy at an American Spaniel Club national Specialty show.

Two Trojan champions finished for their titles undefeated. Ch. Trojan's Oh Henry did it in six shows and Trojan Trimarron in just five shows. Ch. Trojan's Intandescent, a multiple Group winner was a #5 ASCOB bitch in 1971 and moved up to the #3 position in 1973. Ch. Trojan Ginny Lou was a multiple Variety winner with numerous Group placings and was #1 Parti bitch for 1971. Ch. Trojan's Evening Herald was a Group winner also.

Their stud dogs were champions Tagalong, Maxie Tan, and Tocayo, and outstanding brood bitches included Ch. Trojan Katy-Do, Ch. Trojan Tangelic, Ch. Trojan Katrina, Ch. Trojan's Mavourneen, Ch. Trojan Terri, and Trojan Sindhi.

Abbi's

Mrs. Harry Reno's Abbi Cockers have been bred for quality since the establishment of her kennels in 1958. Breeding Cockers has always been a hobby with her and she has always shown and finished her own dogs until recently.

Perhaps her first outstanding show dog was American and Canadian Ch. Abbi's Adored Mister A.O.K. He won seven Bests in Show and two Cocker Specialties before his demise at five and a half years of age.

His grandson, American and Canadian Ch. Abbi's Mister Shadow Boy, his grandson American and Canadian Ch. Abbi's Secret Service, and American and Canadian Ch. Abbi's Secret of Charity and Secret Shadow were to carry on the reputation of the Abbi Cockers.

Ch. Trojan's Ginny Lou, bred and owned by the Trojan Kennels, Magnolia, Texas, was shown during the 1970's.

Alice Kaplan and her Ch. Trojan Tocayo pictured winning Best of Variety.

Above: Ch. Trojan's Evening Herald, 1966 show winner from Alice Kaplan's Trojan Kennels, Magnolia, Texas.

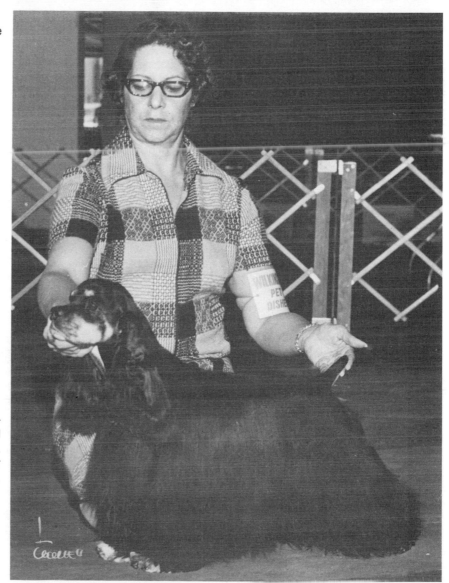

Right: Ch. Trojan's Intandescent is pictured at a 1970's show. Breeder-owner-handler is Alice Kaplan.

Three Abbi's Cockers ready for the show ring! All bred and owned by Mrs. Harry Reno of Port Huron, Michigan.

Am., Can. Ch. Abbi's Mister Shadow Boy is pictured winning under the late judge Winifred Heckmann. Owner-handled by Mrs. Harry Reno of Port Huron, Michigan.

Am., Can. Ch. Abbi's Adored Mister AOK bred, owned, and handled by Mrs. Harry Reno, Port Huron, Michigan.

American and Canadian Champions Abbi's Catch You and Fancy Little Nancy were the outstanding bitches at the Abbi Kennels in Port Huron, Michigan. Catch You, shown by Norman Austin, was highest winning bitch in 1966 at just ten months of age.

The challenge of the obedience ring did not escape Mrs. Reno during the years of breeding top dogs. Her Madamozelle Cherie earned her C.D., C.D.X., and U.D. titles in short order.

Corwin

Helen A. Rice started her Corwin Kennels in 1958 with black Cockers. Her first was a beautiful black bitch, Ch. Viking Tulla's Treat, which she obtained from the Erdahls. Tulla produced a champion son, Ch. Corwin Bo Jet. Tulla was followed by a black and white bitch, Ch. Nor Mar's Nice 'n Neat from Mari Doty's breeding and produced ten champions during her lifetime. Two of Nice 'n Neat's champion bitch daughters were Ch. Corwin Con-t-rite, a lovely tri-color and Ch. Corwin Diamond Lil, who was also a top producer.

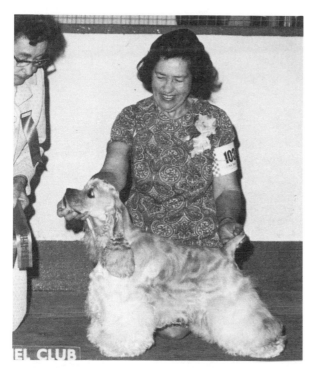

Left: American, Canadian and Bermudian Ch. Abbi's Secret Service is pictured winning Best of Variety at just 10 months of age at the Sarnia Kennel Club.

Above: Am., Can. Ch. Abbi's Fancy Little Nancy is pictured winning Best of Variety at the 1974 Berrle Kennel Club show under judge Raymond Beale. Bred, owned, and handled by Mrs. Harry Reno, Port Huron, Michigan.

Ch. Corwin Color Me Cindy is owned by Mr. and Mrs. Jack Frazier. This lovely daughter of Ch. Corwin Con-t-rite was bred by Helen Rice.

When Nice 'n Neat was bred to the famous Sinbad she produced two more outstanding bitches. These were Ch. Corwin Calico and Ch. Corwin My Cheri. In 1980 Cheri was still alive and ruling the roost at Corwin Kennels. In two litters Calico produced four champions for the Corwin line, and when bred to Ch. Camby's Dynamo, they produced Ch. Corwin Chances Are, a dog which won many Group placings and sired 15 champions. Two of the most outstanding of his champion get were Ch. Bondales Willie Thompson and Ch. Willwyn's With Style of Nosowea, a Best in Show winner.

The Corwin Cockers were handled to their show wins by Ray McGinnis, but Cheri and Calico were shown and finished to their championships by handler Mrs. Frank Wood. Other Corwin dogs were Ch. Corwin Ginger Bread Boy, Ch. Corwin Command Performance and Ch. Corwin Color Me Cindy.

Essanar

While the Essanar Kennels was founded in the late 1950's—1959 to be exact—it was during the 1960's that their breeding made its mark in the show ring. During the nine years of the kennel's existence ten litters were bred. The quality of these breedings was proven when 20 champions earned their titles from their original two bitches

Bringing home the silverware! Ch. Corwin Diamond Lil wins big at the West Coast Specialty show under judge Derek Rayne. Lil is owned by Mr. and Mrs. Frank Wood. Schley photograph.

of the Shandyvale line. Many others were pointed as well. These two bitches produced Champions Early Autumn, Enchanting Meadow, Edge of Night, and Ebb Tide, all bearing the Essanar prefix. Ch. Shandyvale's Gay Clown was another of their outstanding dogs.

Ch. Ebb Tide, bred back into the Shandyvale line, produced Essanar Escapade. While Escapade never became a champion, she became a strong influence in Hansi Rowland and Pat Segar's plans for their Essanar breeding program. She was only bred three times, and in her first litter to Ch. Nor-Mar's Newbeetee she produced three champions. One was Ch. Essanar El Bandido, American and Mexican Ch. Essanar Eden Rock, a Best in Show and Group winner in both countries, and American, Mexican, and Canadian Ch. Essanar Expectation, a Group winner in all three countries.

Their Ch. Mijo's Martini, a beautiful and extremely typy buff became the sire of 11 champions. He was bred to their black bitch, Escapade, and their litter produced two cham-

pions, Essanar Extra Dry and American and Mexican Ch. Essanar Early Times. Another acquisition was Har-Dee's Heartbeat, a black that when bred to Martini produced Ch. Essanar Espresso, East Side, Encore, and Elite. Their last litter was sired by Ch. Essanar East Side out of Eskimo Kiss, and she whelped a promising litter of six.

Ken and Bette Miller's Ch. Willowood Wampum started off the 1950's with some nice wins, as did Ch. Elderwood Bangaway. The Steward Elder's Ch. Elders So Lovely won a Specialty show during this decade also. Before the end of the fifties, Ch. Hollyrock Harvester, owned by Janet and Betty McEnany had been heard from and Ch. Dau-Han's Dan Morgan was doing his share of winning. He was owned by his breeder, Muriel Lauerbach, and handled for her by Pat Vincent Craig of California. Pat later gained fame as breeder-owner-handler of the nation's top-winning Norwegian Elkhounds and continued her winning ways with them at shows across the nation into the 1980's.

Ch. Milru's Tansation, whelped April 1960 and sired by Ch. Shady Hill's Bit O' Copper ex Milru's Cheery Cherub, U.D. During his show ring career, Tansation was handled by Ted Young, Jr., for owners Ruth and Milton Muller of Huntington, Long Island, New York.

Winner of the 1957 Ken-L-Ration Eastern Division Award for the most Group wins during the year was Ch. Gail's Ebony Don D, pictured with her owner and the winners in the other divisions.

KEN-L-RATION
1957 BENCH SHOW AWARD WINNER
SOUTHERN DIVISION
Int. Ch. Chik Tsun of Caversham

KEN-L-RATION
1957 BENCH SHOW AWARD WINNER
PACIFIC COAST DIVISION
Ch. Adastra Magic Fame

KEN-L-RATION
1957 BENCH SHOW AWARD WINNER
MIDWESTERN DIVISION
Ch. Palilyn's MacDuff

KEN-L-RATION
1957 BENCH SHOW AWARD WINNER
EASTERN DIVISION
Ch. Gail's Ebony Don D

THE 1960's

The Sixties could not have gotten off to a more auspicious start than to have a Cocker Spaniel named Top Dog in the Nation. The dog was the beautiful ASCOB Ch. Pinetop's Fancy Parade, and together with his extraordinary handler, Norman Austin, they went straight to the top of the list with 16,032 points for the title. Co-owners Mrs. Rose Robbins and William J. Laffon, Jr. couldn't have been more delighted when their dog headed the Top Ten list for 1960 over all-breed competition and emerged as #1.

Ch. Clarkdale Capital Stock and Ch. Holly Tree High Knight were also high up in the Top Ten Sporting Dogs category but none could best Parade's record of 28 Bests in Show, nine specialties and 63 Group Firsts in a single year.

It was a decade for "dream" dogs and "dream" kennels as well.

Dreamridge

Since 1961 when Thomas F. O'Neal established his Dreamridge Cocker Spaniel Kennel in Woodstock, Illinois, he has bred over 63 champions. He was named Cocker Spaniel Breeder of the Year for 1969, 1970, 1971, 1974, and tied for 1975. His Ch. Dreamridge Dominoe, the top living sire in the breed, has produced 98 champions. He was Top Sire in the breed for 1971, 1972, and 1973. Mr. O'Neal has served as President of the American Spaniel Club, Chairman of the Standard Committee for the American Spaniel Club, and is a past President of The Cocker Spaniel Club of the Midwest.

Other outstanding show dogs which bear the Dreamridge prefix are Ch. Dreamridge Delegate, a Best in Show winner at Crufts (in England) and an outstanding gundog, Ch. Dreamridge Dinner Date with 16 Specialty Bests of Breed, Ch. Dreamridge Dandiman, a Best in Show Winner at the American Spaniel Club, and Ch. Dreamridge Don Juan, a Group winner. Dreamridge dogs have distinguished themselves in the show rings of foreign countries also. Ch. Dreamridge Debonair was a Best in Show winner in Brazil, Ch. Dreamridge Demijohn is a champion in Colombia and Venezuela and Best in Show winner in both countries, and American Ch. Dreamridge Domineer is also a Scandinavian champion having won the title in Finland.

Dreamridge Pink Champagne earned a C.D.X. title with highest scoring dog in trial awards along the way.

A typical Dreamridge puppy, owned and bred by Tom O'Neal of the Dreamridge Kennels, Woodstock, Illinois.

The bitches at Dreamridge made a substantial contribution to the breed by producing quality puppies which made their championships in the show rings. Dreamridge Double Date was the dam of five champions, Dreamridge Party Doll produced four champions, and Champions Dreamridge Design and Daphne, three champions each. Dominoe tops their stud list with 98 champions, Dandiman with 13, Don Juan with 11, Drambuie, 10 and Drawing Card, six.

Tom O'Neal with Dreamridge Debonair in the trophy room at his Dreamridge Kennels in Woodstock, Illinois.

Ging

Bill Gorodner and Lloyd Alton, partners in the Ging's Kennels of Ridgewood, New Jersey, both got started in dogs in the 1950's but formed their partnership in the 1960's.

Bill's first dog show was the 1950 American Spaniel Club show at the Hotel Roosevelt in New York City, and as his enthusiasm for the breed grew, he acquired offspring of Ch. Sugarbrook Counterpoint, Ch. Carmor's Rise and Shine, Ch. Norbill's Fancy Vagabond and Blue Boy's Sand Storm II, and Ch. Champagne's Mr. Champagne.

Lloyd, an executive with Quotron in New York, also became interested in dog shows in the 1950's and when the partnership was formed in the 1960's became active in many club activities and handled most of the Ging Cockers in the show rings.

Ch. Trojan Tagalong, a son of Ch. Begay's Tanman put Ging's on the parti-color map. "Tags" reliably produced his own elegant type, and a lasting friendship between Bill, Lloyd, and Allie Kaplan of Trojan Kennels grew through their first sharing Tagalong and later sharing knowledge of the dog fancy.

In the success of the Ging Kennels, credit is due to Kaplan's Ch. Trojan Tocayo, Trojans Buttons (a favorite at Ging's and the dam of champions), Ch. Recycled Genes and Ch. Frandee's Declaration daughters, Ch. Ging's Phoebe Fireworks, Ch. Ging's Heller On Wheels, and Ch. Ging's Yankee Doodle Dee-Dee.

Their Ch. Begay's Huckleberry Friend is Tanman's only living brother. The success of the Declaration X Buttons breeding has prompted Ging's to line breed to the great Ch. Frandee's Declaration, and Chocolate Partis are also contemplated for the future.

Ging's line breeds carefully and uses outcrosses to assure parti-color quality and favors the Frandee and Rexpointe lines in their gene pool. The results of this careful planning has paid off, and the proof positive was witnessed at a recent Danbury show when judge Frank Fiore awarded ASCOB Winners Dog for a major win

Ch. BeGay's Huckleberry Friend and his daughters Ging's Welcome Wagon Lady (tri-color) and Ging's Jean Bubbly (b/w), owned by Bill Gorodner and Lloyd Alton of Ging's Kennels.

to Ging's Recycled Genes, Parti-color Winners Dog and Best of Winners to Ging's Wilmerding, and Parti-color Winner's Bitch to Ging's Phoebe Fireworks.

Memoir

Anita Roberts' Memoir Cockers began in 1962 with her first champion, Ch. Memoir's Dinah Midas. A natural show dog, she started her ring career as a six-month-old puppy. She was shown by Anita's son, Randy Roberts, and was the first of several champions shown under the Memoir prefix.

During the years, the Roberts have lived on both coasts of the United States and in Hawaii, so they have been "exposed" to the fancy over the years and preside over what they consider to be a small, quality kennel. Some of their winners were Ch. Memoir's Billy Hilder, Ch. Memoir's

Lovely head study of Ch. Memoir's Marc In The Dark, bred and owned by Anita Roberts.

Ch. Memoir's Dinah Midas is a black and tan bitch that came out of retirement to win over top-winning bitches with her handler Charles R. Roberts, son of breeder-owner Anita Roberts of Novato, California.

Ebony Keepsake, Ch. Memoir's Marc In The Dark, and on the distaff side, Memoir's New Raven Beautee, and Memoir's More Charm.

Roblen

The 1960's also saw the presentation of the excellent Cockers bred by Robert A. and Helen L. Johnston under their Roblen prefix. In 1980, twenty years after their getting into the breed, the Johnstons are still keen on Cockers and run a boarding facility they refer to as a "guest home for dogs" offering extra special care for all breeds. The Roblen Kennels are located in Central Point, Oregon where the Johnstons are still breeding quality puppies for show or for companionship. One of their more recent winners is Ch. Westland's Princess Elizabeth.

Cambys

In the 1960's Judy and Bob Covey's Ch. Camby's Dynamo was riding high in the ratings for the nation's top show dogs. This glorious parti-color was the product of the major outstanding bloodlines available during the sixties and produced many champion get. By 1963 three of his offspring, Ch. Merikay's Dynamite, Ch. Nosowea's Spring Nosegay, and Ch. Mausel's Majorette, accounted for the majority of the honors for the top-winning parti-colors of the year and the top-winning bitches in the nation for 1963.

"Dan's" sire was Ch. Dau-Han's Dan Morgan ex Ch. Camby's Carla of Wycar.

The story of Dynamo actually began in 1958 at the Liberty Bell Cocker Spaniel Club Specialty when the Coveys were looking for a stud for

One of the great show bitches in the breed, Ch. Camby's Susan owned by Mrs. Byron A. Covey of Arcadia, California. Susan was the top-winning bitch of her time with a Best in Show win and many Group firsts to her credit. She was also a granddam of the well-known Ch. Camby's Contribution.

Ch. Camby's Contribution pictured winning Best of Winners at the ASC Specialty show in 1966 on the way to his championship. Owner is Mrs. Byron A. Covey of Arcadia, California. Shafer photograph.

their top-winning black and white bitch, Ch. Camby's Carla of Wycar. It was at this show that they first spotted Dan Morgan and their search was ended. The get from their litter produced the champions Ch. Camby's Susan, top-winning Cocker bitch of all time (as of 1965), and their adored Dynamo.

Danny finished with six Bests of Variety and Group placements in top competition. When shown as a Special, he accumulated 16 Varieties and the title of one of the Top Ten parti-colors of 1960.

Bobwin

Mrs. Winnie Vick of Suisun, California started her Bobwin Kennels in 1965. Since that time she has been successful at breeding champion Cockers which have been show winners in

Am., Can. Ch. Ramrod Real McCoy is handled here by Rod Mathies for owners Robert and Helen Johnston, Roblen Kennels, Central Point, Oregon.

Ch. Bobwin's Fasmar Fascinator winning Best of Opposite Sex over Specials at a recent show. The sire was Bobwin's Sir Charles ex Ch. Tan-My Artru Fascination. Owned and shown by Winnie Vick, Suisun, California.

this country and in other countries around the world. Bobwin's Bangaway of Memoir was sold to Jean and Bill Gillies in New Zealand and had championship titles in America, England, Australia, and New Zealand. Bobwin's High Hopes was an American and Mexican champion and owned by Gabriel Marquez. Bobwin's Temptor of Whisborne was an American and Norwegian champion. This dog, sold to A. and H. Ulltugit-Moe was Top Spaniel of the Year in 1979 and #7 all-breeds in 1980. Bobwin's Billy the Kid went to Japan and had both American and Japanese champions. Owned by Mr. Shuiti Nakayama, he had multiple Bests in Show in Japan with his handler, Masao Tashimo.

A total of 45 Cocker champions have been bred at Bobwin; the dogs are owner-handled, and Winnie Vick is also an American Kennel Club approved judge of Cocker Spaniels. Her American and Canadian Ch. Bobwin's Boy Eagle was #2 in the nation in 1974. Ch. Bobwin's Sir Ashley was another show winner and her top-producing bitch, Ch. Bobwin's Thumbelina, produced seven champions out of a total of 14 puppies.

Tabaka

In 1964 in Seattle, Washington, Ruth Tabaka started her line of famous Cocker Spaniels. In the ensuing years there were several top show and obedience dogs that were to bear the Tabaka

name, and all within a very limited breeding program. Ruth Tabaka made it a practice not to keep stud dogs—choosing to go outside for stud service—but her brood bitches managed to produce (as of 1980) 14 champions, seven of which have obedience titles as well. Included on this list was the first mother-daughter champion and U.D. title holders in breed history.

From 1969 to 1973 Ruth Tabaka had Cockers in the Top Five ranking in obedience circles, with her Tammy Tan Toes, U.D.T., being the top obedience Cocker for 1971. Ch. Tabaka's Tidbit O'Wynden, C.D.X., had a remarkable career with 16 Bests in Show, 18 Specialty Bests of Breed, and three Bests of Opposite Sex at Specialties. She won a total of 176 Best of Variety wins during her four-year reign in the show ring and placed in the groups 75% of the time she was shown. In 1978 she was the #1 Cocker Spaniel in the nation and also on the Top Ten Sporting Dogs list.

American and Canadian Ch. Tabaka's Tan Treat finished undefeated in four shows and has had several Bests of Breed at Specialties in the States and in Canada as well as several Canadian Bests in Show. "Treat" was also the #2 Cocker Spaniel in Canada for two years with his owner-handler Diane Lilley.

Ruth Tabaka is also an obedience judge and, as of July 1980, a provisional Utility judge.

Ch. Tabaka's Tidbit O'Termite is pictured winning Best Puppy In Sweepstakes at the Cocker Spaniel Club of Central Ohio under judge Thomas Wessels. Owned and bred by Ruth Tabaka of Seattle, Washington.

Frandee

Frank and Dee Dee Wood established their Frandee Kennels in 1964 with parti-colors. Their first litter was whelped in June 1966, and three of those puppies finished from that first litter including one sold as a pet. As of 1980 Frandee had bred 43 champions, 35 partis and eight solid colors. All of the solids are Variety winners or better, as are 14 of the partis.

Out of Ch. Frandee's Celebration, their biggest winner, are many puppies winning in the show rings. Celebration is a fourth-generation Top Producer in the Cocker listings.

At the beginning of the 1980's Frank and Dee Dee were concentrating on the possibilities of brown and white parti-colors. Their black bitch, Frandee's Fictitious, bred to Alice Swiderski's black male, Ch. Rexpointe Black N' Fancy, produced two brown and whites in a litter of five. They have kept the brown and white male, Frandee's Aristocrat, and he was to be shown starting in the Fall of 1980.

Ch. Corwin Diamond Lil, their foundation bitch purchased from Helen Rice's Corwin Kennels, was the #2 Top Winning parti bitch in 1966, owner-handled. She was sired by Helen Rice's top-producing bitch, Ch. Nor-Mar's Nice n' Neat and sired by Ch. Gin-Di's Tri By Jiminy.

American and Mexican Ch. Frandee's Susan, a black and white daughter of Ch. Corwin Diamond Lil and Sonata's Holiday Caper, finished for her title at 14 months with many wins from the Puppy Class. After four litters she was specialed at six years of age, at which time she finished her Mexican championship undefeated in just four shows. At one time she was the #8 Top Winning parti bitch in the nation. In 1978 she won Veteran Bitch class and was pulled out in the Variety competition along with a son and daughter and grandson who had won the points from the Puppy Class. She was only defeated by her daughter for Best Opposite to Variety.

Other outstanding Frandee Cocker Spaniels were American and Canadian Ch. Frandee's Miss Independence, and American, Canadian, Mexican, Colombian, and International Ch. Frandee's Marquis. Owned by Pat Jones in Mission Viejo, California, this black is one of the two most titled Cockers in the country to date. He is litter brother to Ch. Frandee's Sundowner, the #2 Top Winning ASCOB on the West Coast in 1978 and #8 nationally. Sundowner is owned by Julie and John Wolfe of Cypress, California and was owner-handled.

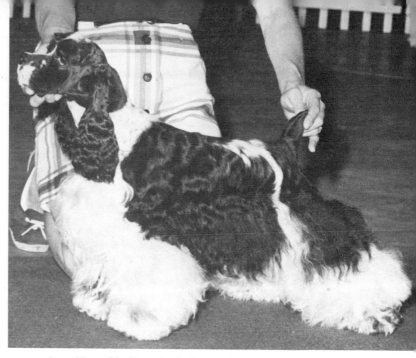

Am., Mex. Ch. Frandee's Susan finished her championship in 1970 at the Golden Gate Kennel Club show. Breeder-owners are Mr. and Mrs. Frank Wood of Norco, California.

Frandee Kennels are also known for Ch. Frandee's Sargent Pepper, Ch. Frandee's Freelancer and Ch. Frandee's Fly Me, shown by Julie Wood Wolfe for owners Ron and Becky Thomson. Ch. Frandee's Declaration, a black and white son sired by Ch. Pett's Handsome Harry ex Ch. Frandee's Declaration had produced 16 champions by 1980, with others pointed, bringing the total to around 25 by the end of that year.

Hall-way

Barbara and Tad Duncan of Edmonds, Washington were the proud owners of the parti-color Ch. Hall-way Fancy Free. She was bred by Mr. and Mrs. James Hall, noted for their wonderful parti-colored Cockers. "Spook" as she was called (and which all will agree is a highly questionable nickname for a show dog) produced five litters, and while four weeks pregnant with her first litter by Ch. Clarkdale Calcutta, took Best of Opposite Sex at the 1965 Skyline Cocker Spaniel Club Specialty under judge Mrs. Will Judy and handled by Norman A. Austin. She was also winner of the Brood Bitch Class at the 1965 Fall Specialty of the Washington State Cocker Spaniel Club under judge Byron A. Covey.

Shadowridge

Pensacola, Florida is the location of Dr. Cheryl A. McNeils' Shadowridge Kennels, established in 1965. Shadowridge is a small hobby kennel begun just before Cheryl entered veterinary college. While relatively inactive during those college years, she managed to find time to show a few Cockers, and even today the Shadowridge dogs are usually owner-handled.

While an active practice manages to keep her busy, she has racked up an impressive record in both show and obedience rings. Her Ch. Tallylyn Cassandra has numerous Group placings and was #6 bitch, all-varieties in 1977. Echo Valley's Star Sin-sation, finished for a C.D.X. title with scores of 198, 198, and 199 with high in trial awards. Her tri-bitch, Ch. Karavan's Cartoon Character, is the dam of three champions in one litter with another pointed.

Cheryl won the George Foley Scholarship award in 1969 and shared it again in 1970.

Ch. Shadowridge Follow Me, C.D., is owned by Miss Pam Burrows, who as a 15-year-old handled this dog to a majority of her points. Bred by Dr. Cheryl McNeil and Nancy Jones, sired by Ch. Pett's Brokers Tip ex Ch. Karavan's Cartoon Character.

As a veterinarian and a breeder of Cocker Spaniels, Dr. McNeil is concerned with the inherited defects, primarily cataracts, which afflict the breed and which breeders are most concerned about and it is the loving disposition, beauty, and intelligence that keep her interested in the breed today.

Ch. Karavan's Cartoon Character, pictured above as a three-month-old puppy, is also shown a little older below while finishing for her championship. Bred by Gail and Karen Gordon, owned by Dr. Cheryl McNeil and Nancy Jones, she is the dam of three champions at the time of this writing.

Merribark

Elane Poole established her Merribark Cocker Kennels in 1966 in Placentia, California. After a false start with a bitch that developed cataracts, she began anew with a parti-colored bitch, Granada's Tanya Lee, and a chocolate male, Windridge Chocolate Baron. Tanya proved not to be show quality after all, but her pedigree indicated good breeding potential. The chocolate dog was Windridge Chocolate Baron

Ch. Windridge Chocolate Baron, C.D., owned and trained by the Merribark Kennels, Placentia, California.

and he became a show champion and an obedience titlist at the same show. Later he was to become the first chocolate Cocker Spaniel to earn a Mexican championship and the first chocolate to earn a European title. "Baron" was sold to Madame Ruffer at six years of age, and she finished him to his title.

Before leaving the United States Baron sired a champion son, Ch. Merribarks Mr. Brown. He was Elaine Poole's first home-bred champion in October 1973. Mr. Brown, handled by Mrs. Pat Smith, became a consistent Variety winner with Group placements and was in the Top Ten winners for three of the four years he was specialed.

Mr. Brown's first champion son, Ch. Merribark's Carbon Copy, W.D.X., was one of the first Cockers to receive the Working Dog Excellent certificate from the American Spaniel Club. He was bred by Norma Cole and owned by Miss Nancy L. Ray.

Pryority

The May 1975 cover of the *American Cocker Review* featured Ch. Pryority's Patriot, Marilyn Pryor's pride and joy. This lovely black dog was third generation out of Bill and Marilyn Pryor's first champion bitch.

It had not been their intention to have a Specials dog. They would have settled (back in 1968) for a homebred champion they could point to with pride. But in April of 1968 they finished their first champion, Ch. Pryority's Prom Miss. By the end of that year two other Cockers, Poppy and Presentation, were finished and they left for Europe content to know they had three bitches to form the foundation of a small breeding program.

By 1970 they had a house in the country in the Madison, Wisconsin area and a few litters were planned. Their bitch, Parisienne, produced two champions for them in her first litter, and in the second litter they found Patriot. Patriot finished at just over one year of age with three Bests of Variety over Specials. "Ike" was handled by Ron Fabis, who handled all of the Pryority Cockers, and campaigned Patriot for the Pryors during the early 1970's.

Travel on

Lynn and Barbara White of Columbiana, Ohio established the Travel On Cocker Spaniel Kennels in 1968. Since then they have bred over 20 champions, many of which were top-winning dogs and all of which produced champions themselves. Perhaps their most famous was the black male, Ch. Travel On Jackson, winner of many Groups and Specialties who had over 70 Group placings before winding up his show ring career.

Ch. Leelon the Minstrel at 12 years of age is the sire of 10 champions, including the top-winning Ch. Travel On Jackson.

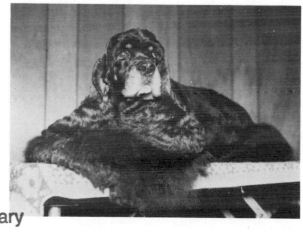

Ch. Travel On Jackson, owned by Dr. J. S. Evans, is pictured winning the Group at the Waterloo Kennel Club show under judge Bob Wills.

Jackson was the sire of the Group winning Ch. Wagtime David, also black. Other show dogs at Travel On were Ch. Travel On Albird, Ch. Travel On Castle Shannon, and their brood bitch was Ch. Travel On Graffiti, dam of four champions. Their "Danny" is the sire of 10 champions. Both Lynn and Barbara are also professional handlers.

THE END OF THE OLD TIMERS GROUP

In 1942 Will Judy, head of the dog publishing empire, founded a rather unique club he called "The Oldtimers of the Kennel World." Headquarters for the group was in Chicago, where Judy published books and edited his *Dog World Magazine* and served as the National Chairman. Each member had a lifetime membership and proudly displayed or wore the gold and white button issued to them if they qualified for membership.

Eligibility was based on 10 years of activity in some phase of the dog field; later it was raised to 15 years of active service to the fancy, then 20 years, and finally to a quarter of a century. The strict enforcement of requiring active participation in the dog fancy kept the roster of members to a minimum, and by the mid-sixties membership still remained under 500.

The purpose of this non-profit organization represented and provided a wealth of information and experience for newcomers who were graciously urged to take advantage of their counsel and advice so they could maintain the highest possible sportsmanship for the fancy.

The great versatility of the membership was clearly seen when the published directory for the club indicated that many of the Cocker Spaniel people were equally knowledgeable in other breeds. Leonie Boehmer had Staffordshires and Brussels Griffons sharing the spotlight at her de Tourney Kennels in Prospect Heights, Illinois. Ben and Kathryn Colton had Beagles and Keeshonden that they were showing along with their Cockers in the state of Washington. Mrs. E. Albert Eastman had Bostons and Pekingese, and Mary Ambler had Pekingese and Chihuahuas as well.

Chihuahuas and Chows kept quarters at Connie Eby's Kennels in Pinellas Park, Florida, and R. A. Moseley had Setters and Cockers at his Bobsday Kennels in Tallahassee. Jay Essenbager had Wires and Cockers, and Dr. B. Kater McInnes had Scottish Terriers at his Marymack Kennels in Charleston, South Carolina. Sara Phillips also bred Poodles at Philsworth Kennels in Batesville, Arkansas, and at Irwin Backman's Merry-Way Kennels in Wisconsin there was more than one breed.

Other members of the club that stuck strictly to Cockers were Mr. and Mrs. Robert W. Biggs, Fairhaven, Mass.; Oscar and Gertrude Hughes, Ossie's Kennels in Ohio; Carl and Violet Johnson, Vi-Jon's Kennels in Youngstown, Ohio; Mrs. Robert J. Kinney, Marbo Kennels, Fresno, California; Mr. and Mrs. Lee C. Kraeuchi, Silver Maple Farm, St. Louis, Missouri; Mr. and Mrs. Herman Kress, Kresshingham Kennels in Hingham, Massachusetts; Pamela Mack in Canada; Myrtle Twelvetrees, Kern City, California; George Miller, Duckwin Kennels, New Kensington, Pennsylvania; Ramona Wilcox, Wilmarray Kennels in Greensboro, North Carolina; and the well-known Harry P. Saunders, breeder of both English and American Cocker Spaniels at his Sporting Dog Kennels in Alberta, Canada that also included Brittany and Springer Spaniels.

It is regrettable that the mid-sixties saw the end to this club whose membership roster included so many of dogdom's elite that were so willing and generous to give their time. The value of such a group would be appreciated by many newcomers to the fancy today.

Michael Allen's drawing of the Dam and Get Trophy, Cocker Spaniel Club of Dallas, 1960.

THE 1970's

During the decade of the seventies registrations for all breeds of dogs with the American Kennel Club hovered around the one million mark. Dobermans were moving up to replace the German Shepherds and by 1977 our Cocker Spaniels moved up from 5th to 4th place on the charts. While the Cocker had been one of the most popular breeds until the mid-fifties, the seventies saw them making it to the top again with a definite increase in popularity. It was 1952 when the Cocker was #1 with 46,823 registered that year, though in their peak year, 1947, there were 78,507 registered. In 1976 when they were in 5th place there were 17,778 registrations, while the 19,369 figure for 1977 moved them up into the #4 spot. In 1979 at the end of this important decade there were still over 5,000 Cockers being registered each month.

It is gratifying to know that once again the marvelous disposition and temperament of the Cocker Spaniel helped establish this breed with the dog-loving public. But credit must also be given to the breeders of the marvelous little dogs that came before the public and proved themselves as all-around family dogs. The magnificent show dogs that were campaigned during the seventies certainly helped to show just how beautiful they could be.

A great deal of this credit can be given to Michael Allen who had at least one dog or bitch in the Top Ten Parti-colored Cockers for six straight years—1972 through 1977.

The multi-talented Michael Allen is well known in the dog fancy and has been for many

Ch. Dreamridge Dinner Date and Ch. Dreamridge Dominoe, two famous showdogs and sires, captured on canvas by famous artist Michael Allen.

Michael Allen's magnificent drawing of Ch. Windy Hill Delayed Action.

years. While her first show dog was a Chihuahua, she has had close associations with many breeds in both the show ring and at her drawing board. Her marvelous drawings of the famous and great dogs of the past and present, and we daresay, future, have been reproduced on covers of all the major dog publications.

Michael bred her first litter of puppies in 1960 but finished her first champion in 1953. Out of a total of nine litters to date, each contained at least one champion—which is quite a credit for a person who considers herself a hobby breeder. Michael usually handles her own dogs in the ring and uses the prefix Baliwick, adopted from Norman Austin when he gave it up.

In 1974 Michael had the #1 parti-color Cocker Spaniel in the nation, the dog which also won the Variety at the Garden and had multiple Groups and Specialties to his credit. His record still stands as the top-winning owner-handled Cocker in breed history.

Michael's interests extend to other animals as

well, having been involved with varieties of wild cats, horses, exotic fish, and breeding and exhibiting Peruvian cavies. She has raced sports cars, has had exhibitions of her work at various art shows and has memberships in Beta Sigma Phi and the Parachute Club of America.

A graduate of Texas Abilene College, she is currently president of Michael Enterprises, a graphic design and publishing company established in 1976 with headquarters in Costa Mesa, California. She is an accredited commercial artist and recently designed the official medallion for the 1981 Centennial Year for the American Spaniel Club and is also illustrating the new American Spaniel Club booklet. Little wonder that Michael Allen rates a listing in the book, *Who's Who in the West.*

The early 1970's were also the years of the brilliant show career of the beautiful buff bitch, Ch. Sagamore Toccoa, who was bred by Theodore J. and Lillian Klaiss. Her owner, Peggy Westphal had the great good sense to put Toc-

Ch. Signature's Solitaire captured on canvas by owner Michael Allen of Costa Mesa, California. Miss Allen is the owner of Michael Enterprises, Graphic Design and Publishing Company and editor of *The American Cocker Review*.

coa into the expert hands of handler Ted Young, Jr., and together they went straight to the top of the rainbow. While Toccoa was whelped in November of 1968, she was in full bloom those first years of the decade of the '70's and was a popular favorite in the dog-show rings. By 1972 she was #1 in the nation, all-breeds.

In fact, there were three Sagamore dogs in the list of Top Ten ASCOBs during the early 1970's. Ch. Sagamore Sprite, owned by N. Block, and Ch. Sagamore Colleen were also right up there with the wins.

Many of the kennel names we heard about in the sixties were also seen in the winner's circles.

Names like Seenar, Shardeloe, Forjay, Stonehenge, Har-Dee, Nor-Mar, HiJack Ramrod, to name a few—not to mention the #1 Cocker Spaniel for 1976, Ch. Rexpointe Kojak, many times Best in Show winner and equally as famous as his television namesake.

Joyce Scott Paine's Ch. Ancram's Simon was another great show dog of the '70's. Simon became the all-time top-winning Cocker Spaniel in the U.S.A. during his reign and ended up as the top Cocker Spaniel for 1969, 1970, and 1971. His champion offspring went over 17 during his winning years.

Ch. Feinlyn By George, handled by his owner,

Al Davies (co-owned with his wife Annette), was another Best in Show dog during the 1970's, which gave credence to the headline they used in their advertisements "By George, He's Got it!"

Fred and Margaret Gray had a couple of buff entries during the 1970's. Their Challenger prefix included champions John Schohr and Man With a Plan.

Hugh Campbell's Cockers enjoyed "colorful" careers during the 1970's, including Ch. Campbell's Color Me Cute, C.D., Ch. Campbell's Color Me Quaint, and Campbell's Rhapsody in Blue. Success was also achieved by the lovely black contender of Elizabeth Durland and David Kittredge in Ch. Dur-Bet's Prudential, the black and tan American and Canadian Ch. Dur-Bet's Tiger Paws, and Ch. Tartan.

Black-and-whites were also riding high in the '70's. Flintridge breeding produced the American, Bermudian and Canadian Ch. Flintcrest Farmers Dotter and Front and Center. Ch. Frandee's Declaration was another flashy black

One of top-winning show bitches in the breed, Ch. Sagamore Toccoa, is pictured going Best in Show over an entry of over 1600 dogs at the 1971 Staten Island Kennel Club show. Ted Young, Jr. handled for owner Peggy Westphal of Bedford, New York. Larry Downey was the judge. Dr. Bernard McGivern, club president and show chairman, presents the trophy.

and white dog and American and Mexican Ch. Frandee's Susan was an outstanding representative in the black-and-white bitch class. Another in the bitch class was Ch. Kamp's Kopy Girl, owned by Mai Wilson and sired by the great Ch. Rexpointe Kojak.

International, Mexican and American Ch. Kapewood Prince Matchebelli was a buff dog owned by Rune and Robin Enos Nilsson of Texas who also campaigned their Ch. Three Crown's Prince Charles, a silver-buff sired by their International winner. And when mentioning multiple champions, you must include Ruth Tabaka's and Laura O'Connor's American and Canadian Ch. Tabaka's Tidbit O'Wynden, who also earned her C.D.X. title.

Gladys Van Horn was breeding Cockers in Vancouver, Washington, and Gay Ernst was

The windblown Am., Can. Ch. Tabaka's Tidbit O'Wynden, C.D.X., is owned by Ruth Tabaka and Laura Watt O'Connor, Seattle, Washington.

Am., Can. Ch. Tabaka's Tidbit O'Wynden, C.D.X., is shown finishing for her C.D.X. at the Seattle Kennel Club show on the same day that she won her 21st Group First. She is co-owned by Ruth N. Tabaka and Laura Watt O'Connor and pictured here with Ruth Tabaka.

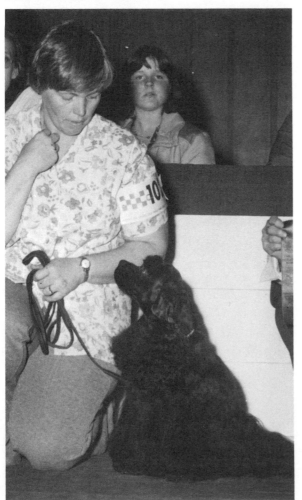

Ch. Frandee's Flurry, bred and owned by Frank and Dee Dee Wood, Norco, California, was sired by Ch. Rexpointe Shazam ex Ch. Frandee's Susan.

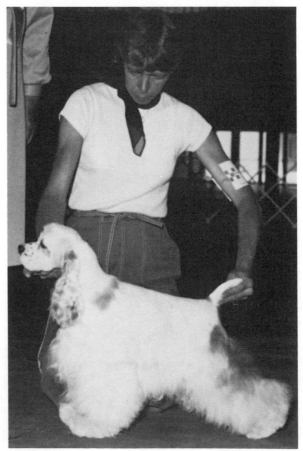

concentrating on chocolates at her Begay Kennels in East Hampton, New York. The 1970's saw several breeders concentrating harder and harder on attaining perfection with this color. Needless to say, this category includes the showy chocolates and whites also.

Doggone Kennels

John and Julie Wolfe started their Doggone Kennels in 1970 and are active in the show and field aspects of the dog fancy. Their ultimate goal is to have their dogs be dual champions. Their Ch. Frandee's Sundowner was the top winning ASCOB for 1978 and at the 1980 American Spaniel Club their Ch. Marquis Peter Pucker was Best of Variety in the Futurity. Their Doggone Liberty Belle has a W.D.X. title and is the first parti bitch to win a Working Dog Excellent award.

Julie is a daughter of the Frank Woods, owners of the famous Frandee Kennels, and consequently was brought up with dogs. It seems only natural that her years of experience would result in the breeding of excellent Cockers which excel in both field and show.

Monteverde

After 20 years of merely enjoying Cocker Spaniels, Mr. and Mrs. T. Richard Monteverde of Auburn, California went straight to the top with a real winner. Their Ch. Monteverde's Innkeeper, a product of the last planned breeding of judge Byron Covey, had three majors and 12 points by the time he was 10 months old during his first five times out in the Open classes. Their first showdog, Audie Merry, was only bred once and produced this one very special puppy whose line went back to the famous Ch. Scioto Bluff's Sinbad breeding. The sire was Ch. Dreamridge Dominoe ex Ch. Greenhill's Audacious Merry, and in the words of Maggie Monteverde, who said of Innkeeper, ". . . tamed by Mona Cantrell from a pompous baby hooligan to her adoring lamb in the show ring," Innkeeper was the cover dog for the March 1971 issue of the *American Cocker Review.*

Spirit

In the first five years that the Spirit Kennels of Susan Kelley of Sunnyvale, California were in existence, she had earned honors with her dogs in both the show ring and obedience. Her Ch. Bobwins Trace of Spirit was #5 ASCOB in the nation and was pointed in Canada as well. Her

Olympian Gorgeous George, C.D.X., and his owner-trainer, Susan Kelley, take time out for a rest between obedience trials at the Golden Gate Kennel Club.

Olympian Gorgeous George had a C.D.X. title and was working for a U.D. when hip problems prevented his jumping and forced him into retirement.

Susan Kelley also teaches conformation and obedience classes on occasion.

Ch. Kaplars Royal Kavalier was an American Spaniel Club Best in Show winner in 1977, and in 1978 Jean Van Patten was showing Ch. Twyneff Just Right, a black dog, after finishing Ch. Twyneff Just Jill, a black bitch. The Windridge Kennels in California were showing two top chocolates, Ch. Windridge Chocolate Comment and Chocolate Bonanza, sired by their Windridge Chocolate Royal. Needless to say the Windy Hill Kennels of Edna Anselmi were also in the ring with champion dogs of several colors. Milru and MeTu's cockers were also much in evidence and in the ribbons at the shows.

Ch. Forjays Winterwood, a lovely ASCOB, was among the Top Ten winners in the Sporting Group for 1975, and Merribark's Mr. Brown, C.D., was Elane Poole's chocolate contender in the ring.

Frederick and Nancy Ray, owners of the Cal-Ore Cockers in Brooks, Oregon, have been involved with the breed since 1970. Breeding only

Young owner-handler Monique Ray is with her Cal-Ore's Whispering Wind, lovely golden buff Cocker Spaniel sired by Am., Can. Ch. Westland Lord Snowden ex Cal-Ore's Satan's Mistress. The Cal-Ore Kennels are located in Brooks, Oregon.

three litters between 1973 and 1976 and keeping only one puppy from each litter, they have still managed to place promising show puppies in show homes. Their home-bred Cal-Ore's Chocolate Treat is a fourth-generation champion on his sire's side. The Rays are concentrating on the chocolates for the future but quality champions in the other colors as well.

The Ray children composed a fitting tribute to their buff Cocker, Lady Beverly Boots, when she died after 10 years of active field work with the family. It read: "In memory of Lady Beverly Boots, June 19, 1969, Summer of 1979. We miss you, Boots, on our Easter egg hunts and we hope the birds in Heaven aren't driving you as crazy as they did here on Earth. Love, Fred, Nancy, Lisa and Monique, and Grandpa and Grandma Ray."

The ultimate testimony of the camaraderie of children and dogs—or more specifically—children and Cockers.

White Deer Center

Doris Fink, owner of the White Deer Kennels in Tuckerton, New Jersey, is also the owner and breeder of Ch. White Deer's Scotch Guard. Scottie had sired five champions by the beginning of the 1980's with more litters on the way. He was among the Top Producers for 1979 and was sired by Ch. Dur Bet's Tartan ex Ch. White Deer's Love Letters.

Ch. Dur Bet's Tartan, owned by Doris Fink and bred by Betty Durland of the famous Dur Bet Cockers, finished his championship at a Syracuse Kennel Club show. "Scottie" was tied for Top-Producing Dog all-breeds in 1979, with 19 champions for that year and a total of 27 as of October 1980. His sire was Ch. Champagne's Dynamic ex Ch. Dur Bet's Tantalizer and is a seventh generation of consecutive Top Producers. He has won many Bests of Variety and won Best of Breed at an Upstate Cocker Spaniel

Club Specialty show, and he had eight Group Placements to his credit by the end of 1980. He will be campaigned during the eighties.

Louise Post

The name of Louise Post is almost synonymous with Cocker Spaniels. In the 1970's Louise was marking 30 years of activity and dedication to dogs. Serving the breed both inside and outside the rings, the name C. Louise Post has appeared as an officer of the Kennel Club of Northern New Jersey, the Ramapo Kennel Club, the Stewards Club of America, and the Cocker Spaniel Club of New Jersey. She has also been on the Board of Governors of the American Spaniel Club, served as the Futurity Chairperson for many years and as Show Chairperson for the 100th Anniversary Show. She has also judged at many Match Shows and Sweepstakes over the years, in addition to breeding and exhibiting her own line of Cocker Spaniels.

Louise is typical of the dedicated breeders and exhibitors that have persisted in the breed, whose accomplishments span several decades, and who have brought the breed along to the point of excellence in which we find it as we enter the decade of the eighties. We can be grateful for their work and interest and the foundation they have laid for an even more promising future for our breed.

KNEBWORTH MARCHES ON

It is wonderful to see Irene Gaddy Zimmerman carrying on in the fancy as we head into the eighties. It was Irene Gaddy Zimmerman whose path crossed with that of Richard and Helen Shute in December of 1949, and a life-long partnership

Windridge Chocolate Cyclone, sired by Ch. Windridge Chocolate Classic, is owned by the Cal-Ore Kennels of Nancy Ray, Brooks, Oregon.

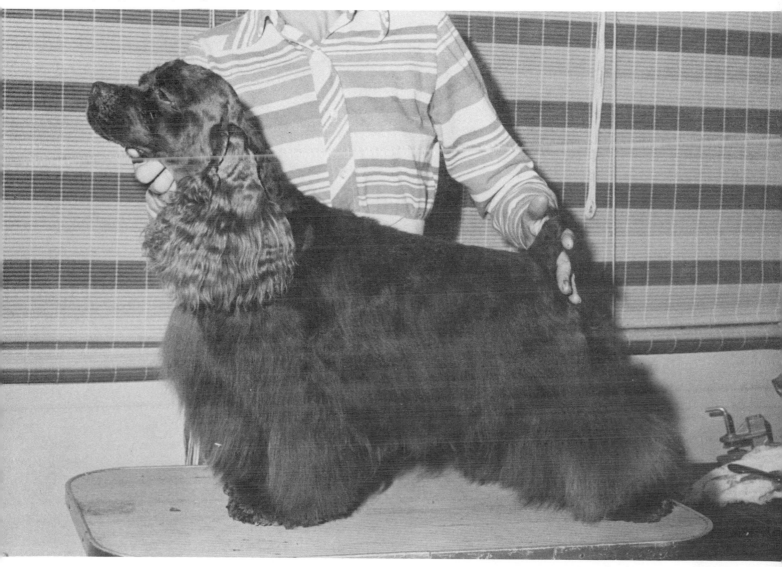

was formed that lasted until Helen's death on April 9, 1967. Helen and Richard started their Knebworth Kennels after their marriage on November 2, 1910 in the beautiful San Fernando Valley in California. Over the intervening years many a champion was bred and shown along with some Fox Terriers and Pekingese.

Dick Shute, before his death on May 5, 1933, and Helen were founders of the Cocker Spaniel Club of Southern California. Started in 1931, this club celebrated its 50th anniversary Specialty Show in September, 1979. 1931 was also the year that Helen Shute participated in the 1931 Olympic Games, held at the Coliseum in Los Angeles, with several of her dogs representing the breed with an impressive display of silver trophies won by the Knebworth dogs.

Irene Gaddy lived in New York, practically around the corner from "the Garden" where it was inevitable that she would attend the Westminster Kennel Club shows from 1931 through 1938 and got the "bug" to get into dogs. Two Pekingese were her passion then, though she had strong leanings towards Cockers even in those early days. Marriage to a member of the United States Coast Guard prevented her from establishing a kennel until 1947 when she acquired a

Ch. Knebworth Kayo's Korker, winning a West Coast show when he was about a year old was not shown again until he was over six years old and finished that same year with his final major under judge Vincent Perry in February 1973. Owned by Ida E. Fritsch of Phoenix, Arizona.

The excellent Ch. Knebworth Yankee Pasha, ASCOB co-owned by Dr. Samuel Draper and Joel Marston and bred by the legendary Helen Shute, made his championship in 1957 in California with his handler Porter Washington. The sire was Roy Nelson's Ch. St. Andrea's Rain Maker ex Knebworth Flirtatious.

black and tan Cocker bitch, Ch. Stockdale Gay Bobarene, C.D.; then she realized that Cockers were to play a major part in her life.

Her little bitch got off to a royal start, beginning with her championship in 1949, her Companion Dog title, and important show wins right away. Actually it was the obedience work that was Irene's primary interest in dogs at first and she later became one of the founders of the Oakland (California) Dog Training Club and was its first Life Member.

In 1949 she became the protegé of Helen Shute and the associate with Knebworth was cemented. Their involvement with the dogs also included Poodles, because of their friendship with Ernie Ferguson of Estid Poodles fame. Irene whelped, conditioned, and boarded all of Ernie Ferguson's Poodles, and when he died she acquired his two foundation bitches who lived out happy lives with her.

From 1950 through 1969 Irene held a Handler's License and piloted many breeds of dogs through their ring careers, not only Cocker Spaniels and Poodles of all three varieties, but Pekingese, Keeshonden, Bassett Hounds and Basenjis. She used whatever spare time she had teaching grooming and handling classes, and keeping active with dog club activities.

Some of the Knebworth Cockers that come to mind when Irene recalls past victories are Ch. Knebworth Yankee Pasha and his brother Ch. Knebworth Burnished Blade, two lovely black and tans; Ch. Knebworth Knectarine, a glorious golden bitch; Ch. Knebworth Knockout, another golden dog, and his black son, Ch. Knebworth Kayo's Korker; and American, Canadian and Mexican Champion Junkin Chochosan, a blonde bitch owned by Dr. Owen Young of Kekko Kennels fame.

"Korky," owned by Mr. and Mrs. Joseph Fritsch, Missieler Cockers, was the last Cocker champion for Knebworth since ill health has forced Irene to halt her breeding activities and to restrict herself to her presidency of the Cocker Spaniel Club of Southern California and as an interested and dedicated member of the American Spaniel Club.

THE 1980's

The 1980's got off to a fantastic start with the American Spaniel Club's 100th Anniversary celebration. The festivities and galas which marked this elaborate centennial will long be remembered, along with the dogs which made history during their first 100 years in this country.

Other landmark statistics were recognized at the start of this decade also. On March 10, 1981 the American Kennel Club announced the 25 millionth dog registration during a special ceremony during their annual meeting at the Biltmore Hotel in New York City. The A.K.C. —the world's largest animal registry for the second oldest sport's governing body—reached their first milestone in 1935 when registrations hit the one million mark. In 1970 they revealed another milestone when one million dogs had been registered during that single year. Then in 1981 they reached a total of 25 million dog registrations.

While that 25 millionth dog happened to be a Scottish Terrier, there is no denying the important place Cocker Spaniels have achieved on the list of popular favorites in the 126 breeds recognized by the American Kennel Club. The first year of the decade of the '80's found our Cocker Spaniels as #3 on the list with over 76,000 registrations for that year. Cockers were #3 for 1979 also with over 65,000 registrations, proof positive that this wonderful breed is continuing to enjoy popularity in the dog world. Heading the list of goodwill ambassadors for the breed was a glorious red-and-white dog named Ch. Kamp's Kaptain Kool.

"Kappy," bred by Harriet Kamp and owned by Cameron Covey and Mai Wilson, was the winner of the American Spaniel Club Specialty Show in January 1981. He is the top-winning parti-color Cocker Spaniel of all time, and the top-winning parti-color male of all time, topped only by the top-winning bitch for the breed, Ch. Sagamore Taccoa. In 1980 Kappy was also the top-winning Sporting Dog in the country.

Kappy is handled for his owners by Ted Young, Jr., and continues to rack up wins from coast to coast against all comers.

Mrs. Covey and her late husband, Byron A. Covey, were also the owners of Ch. Camby's Susan, the top-winning bitch in her time. She was a Best in Show winner and had many Group Firsts and placements to her credit. A great producer, she whelped Ch. Camby's Candlelight, the Covey's top-winning and Top-Producing Dog, Ch. Damby's Contribution. Contribution finished for his championship at an American Spaniel Club Specialty and returned the following year to win Best American-bred in Show and won Best of Variety the year after that.

Unfortunately, the Coveys lost Contribution when he was only four years of age, but during his brief life span he was responsible for producing 25 champions. These fabulous dogs are behind many of the top parti-colors in the breed today, including Kaptain Kool.

While Kappy continues his winning ways, he is by no means the only outstanding winning Cocker to flash across the horizon in the current decade. In fact, the number of top-winning dogs is so great that any accurate or complete list is next to impossible to include in a book of this kind. However, the pages of the various dog and Cocker Spaniel magazines bear testimony to their wins and current ratings and foretell glorious futures for them. Those interested in becoming involved in our breed would do well to keep up with the records of the breeders, kennels, and show wins through their various publications and membership in one or more dog clubs whose members are both active and informed. The carefully planned breeding programs, expert care, and scientifically researched nutrition have provided a "bumper crop" of magnificent dogs that assure Cocker fanciers great enjoyment and promise for those who love our breed during the decade of the '80's—and beyond.

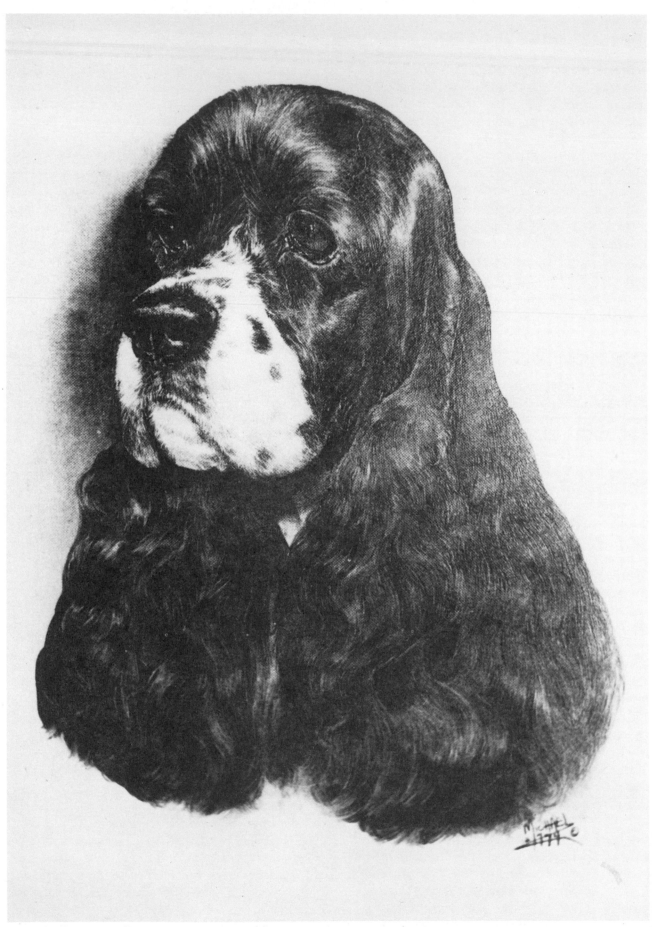

Magnificent true-to-life drawing by artist Michael Allen portraying Am., and Mex. Ch. Corwin Diamond Lil. Drawing and dog are owned by Frank and Dee Dee Wood of Norco, California, who commissioned the artist.

Right: Littermates Ch. Frandee's Celebration went Best of Breed and Ch. Frandee's Bill of Rights won Winners Dog and Best of Winners at the 1978 Cocker Spaniel Club of Southern California. **Below:** Ch. Frandee's Sundowner, owned by Julie Wood Wolfe, was top-winning ASCOB for 1978. Bill Francis photo.

Above: Ch. Pett's Twinkling Valerie pictured winning on the way to her championship at a 1974 show. Owned and bred by Mr. and Mrs. Roland Pett, Dennis Port, Massachusetts.

Opposite: Ch. Pett's Coral Vision, Winners Bitch from the Classes. Handled by Ron Fabis for owner-breeder Mrs. Roland A. Pett of Dennis Port, Massachusetts.

Above: Ch. Shadowridge Liberation pictured winning with handler Charles Self at a 1979 show on the way to championship. Liberation was sired by Ch. Frandee's Declaration ex Karavan's Dixie Pixie, bred by Dr. Cheryl McNeil and is owned by Venetia Friend and Dr. McNeil.

Opposite: Ch. Corwin Triumph is pictured winning under judge Myrtle Winsop at the 1972 Central Wyoming Kennel Club show. Owned by the Peter Moreys. Francis photo.

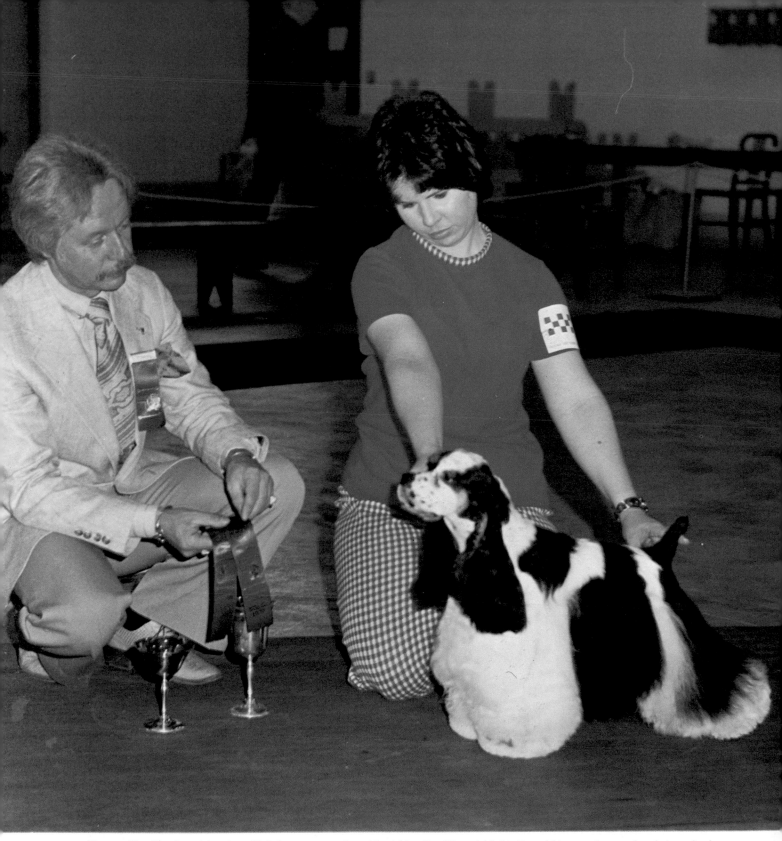

Above: Ch. Shadowridge Ima Rainbow, owned and bred by Dr. Cheryl McNeil and Nancy Jones, is pictured winning under judge Harlan Hoel. Sire was Ch. Pett's Broker's Tip ex Ch. Karavan's Cartoon Character. Dr. McNeil is a veterinarian in Pensacola, Florida.

Opposite: Ging's Integrated Circuit, tri-color dog, went Best of Winners for two points from the Puppy Class at the Rockland County Kennel Club show. Bred and owned by Lloyd Alton and Bill Gorodner, and handled by Mr. Alton. William Gilbert photograph.

Ch. Ging's Phoebe Fireworks and Ging's Wilmerding handled by breeder-owners Lloyd Alton and Bill Gorodner to Winners Dog and Winners Bitch at the same show. Ging Kennels was in Ridgewood, New Jersey. William Gilbert photo.

Mirko

74

Above: Ch. Bobwin's Persuasion is pictured taking Winners Bitch on the way to her championship at the 1978 Sacramento show. Bred and owned by Winnie Vick, Bobwin Acres, Suisun, California. The sire was Ch. Piner's Point of View ex Ch. Bobwin's Temptation.

Opposite: Ch. Bobwin's Trace of Spirit, owned by Susan Kelley of Sunnyvale, California.

Above: Cal-Ore's Mystic Time, black and tan bitch, is shown going Best of Opposite Sex to Best Adult in Match. Owned by Gladys Von Horn of Vancouver, Washington.

Opposite: This is the glorious chocolate Cal-Ore's Chocolate Treat, bred by Nancy Ray and owned by Glyn Petty, San-D-Glyn Cockers, Myrtle Creek, Oregon. The sire was Ch. Merribark's Brown N' Fancy ex Cal-Ore's Satan's Mistress.

Above: Ch. Memoir's Marc In The Dark, winning Best Opposite in the Mission Valley Cocker Spaniel Club Sweepstakes. Owned by Anita Roberts.

Opposite: Ch. Memoir's Ebony Keepsake, Best Bred by Exhibitor in Show at the summer American Spaniel Club National Specialty show. Owned and bred by Anita B. Roberts. Missy Yuhl photo.

Ch. Juban's Georgia Jazz, handled by Bob Covey for owners Charles and Jacquelyn Rowe, Rowingdale Cockers, La Mesa, California, is shown taking Group 2 at the 1980 Southern Oregon Kennel Club show.

CHAPTER FOUR

The American Spaniel Club

A Spaniel portrayed in oil on canvas, signed and dated 1796 by artist Henry Barrend Chalong (1770-1849), clearly illustrates the typical conformation at that period in time.

The American Spaniel Club was one of the very first of all American dog clubs devoted to one breed of dogs—the sporting Spaniels.

The American Spaniel Club came into existence in January 1881 when two devoted young Spaniel enthusiasts put their heads together to thrash out the details of just such a group of sportsmen getting together for the betterment and advancement of the breed. It was in A. Clinton Wilmerding's New York City office that James Watson first presented his idea. At that time it was to be called the American Cocker Spaniel Club and within a month of that memorable January day the organization meeting was held to lay down the rules and regulations of the club. The drawing up of a Standard was one of the first considerations of those who wished to differentiate the American Cocker from the Field Spaniels.

Several distinguished dog men attended that first February meeting. In addition to James Watson and A. Clinton Wilmerding, other charter members were J. Otis Fellows, M. P. McKoon, A. E. Goddefroy, Dr. J. S. Cattanack, Dr. J. S. Niven, E. Tinsley, Dr. J. L. Morrill, A. McCollom, A. H. Moore, C. B. Cummings, J. H. Whitman, J. F. Kirk and George D. McDougall, the latter being James Watson's partner in the Lachine Kennels. All were active in the sport of dogs from the New York, Philadelphia, and southeastern Canada area.

Mr. A. H. Moore of Philadelphia was elected President by a management committee on which Messrs. Cummings, Fellows, Kirk, McDougall, McKoon, Whitman, Moore, Tinsley and Morrill served. George McDougall became the first secretary.

In spite of the keenest efforts and desires of the members of the Club, it wasn't until 1905 that the American Kennel Club established and maintained separate stud books for Cocker and Field Spaniels. While championships were recorded separately for each breed, all registrations were entered in the same stud book. Once the distinction was made, the club changed its name from the American Cocker Spaniel Club to the American Spaniel Club, a name which it is known by today, a century later.

Five other Spaniel breeds were admitted to the club since most members, including Mr. Wilmerding, hunted over more than one breed. The American Spaniel Club was soon offering sterling silver challenge cups for breed winners at many of the all-breed shows. These could be won only by members of the American Spaniel Club and had to be won five times for permanent possession. The ultimate goal for members was to win the sterling silver challenge cup known as the American Field Trophy. This was offered for the first time at the Westminster Kennel Club show in 1892 and awarded to the Best American-bred Spaniel. Dr. N. Rowe of Chicago was the donor of this valuable American Field Trophy valued at one hundred dollars.

Puppy Sweepstakes were started as early as 1887, and in 1923 became an annual event called the Futurity. In the beginning the entry fee was set at $3, a far cry from today's.

FIELD TRIALS

In 1892 Mr. Wilmerding was appointed chairman of a committee to look into the possibility of the American Spaniel Club's sponsorship of field trials. Unfortunately, the idea never came to fruition. In 1906, with a continued lack of enthusiasm or support, the committee was dissolved, and by 1911 when Mr. Wilmerding resigned as Chairman, the Executive Committee ended the discussion entirely.

One of today's field performers is Sterling Silver Beau, W.D.X., owned and trained by Dennis Blake of Orange, California.

THE A.S.C. VERSUS THE A.K.C.

In 1887 the American Kennel Club was firmly established as both a governing body in the fancy and as a registry for all breeds of purebred dogs. In 1887 it issued a ruling that was to quickly affect breeders and exhibitors all over the country, a ruling that made the registration of dogs in their stud books a necessity and prerequisite for showing and breeding.

At the January 1888 meeting of the American Spaniel Club, members took exception to this ruling. A resolution was passed by the Executive Committee that it was their belief that compulsory registration was not in the best interests of dog breeding. The action of this committee resulted in the first mail vote to determine if the A.S.C. should withhold funds from shows that required dogs to be registered with the A.K.C. The objection was upheld by the club's members with 44 returned ballots indicating 35 agreed.

By the 1889 meeting of the A.S.C. it was deemed a lost cause and the club members voted to apply to the American Kennel Club for admission for the American Spaniel Club. By August of the same year James Watson was appointed as the club's first delegate to the American Kennel Club.

With their official affiliation with the acknowledged governing body of dogdom, the American Spaniel Club membership began to increase noticeably and the important kennels, people, and dog shows were to become part of the history of the dog show world. By 1894 the American Spaniel Club was ready to hold its first Specialty Show.

THE FIRST SPECIALTY

Strangely enough, it was not a member of the American Spaniel Club who dreamed up the idea of a Specialty Show but rather the Vice President of the American Kennel Club at the time whose interests included the staging of other animal events at New York's Madison Square Garden. A dog show at the same time they were holding other animal competitions and events was thought, by Thomas H. Terry, to be an excellent way of bolstering admissions. He made contact with several breed clubs including the A.S.C., the St. Bernard, Collie, Bulldog, and Fox Terrier clubs and suggested his plans. The clubs jumped at the idea when all they would

have to do was to select their own judges and Mr. Terry would foot the bills for all else which needed to be supplied for the May first through the fourth event.

The American Spaniel Club chose Ed Oldham for their judge. He was a long-time member of the A.S.C. and bred both Cocker and Field Spaniels. For various reasons, however, many of the members of the A.S.C. did not exhibit, but both Canada and the United States did exhibit, as was their custom, for the prestigious Westminster show, in spite of the long and difficult traveling in those olden times. While there is no known record of individual breed wins at this first show, the five clubs which were invited to participate accounted for an entry of 464 dogs.

Winners at this event can be found in the Anniversary Books of the American Spaniel Club, published in 1981. But the Specialty Show planned by Mr. Terry for the following year never came about. Members of the American Spaniel Club had to wait until 1903 before their next show was held in Atlantic City, New Jersey. There is no denying that several of the winners at that very first Specialty were highly influential in the future breeding lines of Cocker Spaniels known at the turn of the century.

Ch. Black Duke, who was judged Best Cocker Spaniel when bred to top winner Baby Ruth in the Black Open Bitch Class, would be known for years as the foundation behind the famous Mepal Kennels. The exhibits list included names such as Laidlaw, Foster, Keasbey, Brook, Luckwell, Douglas, and E. W. Fiske, to name a few—and, of course, the name of Mrs. H. E. Smyth, the first woman member of the club and the successful breeder and exhibitor of the Swiss Mountain Cockers.

In 1931, when Mr. Wilmerding wrote a brief history of the American Spaniel Club, he commented that none of the original members of the club were living, except himself, to enjoy the "golden anniversary" of the club and to reflect on its growth in the dog fancy. But those who know of him are able to remember, with respect and admiration, his many contributions to the club and to the fancy through his many roles as President, Secretary-Treasurer, and especially as "peace maker" during the club's many differences and policy changes. There are many Cocker fanciers who can attest to the fact that it was largely through the efforts of this great gentleman that the club survived to serve the breed in this country. And there are those who can remember his contribution to the breed by his breeding of his dogs Ch. Doc, the black dog whelped in 1885, and his Ch. Black Prince, a Field Spaniel. His first Cocker was a granddaughter of the first Cocker registered by the A.K.C. and purchased from James Watson and George McDougall. Her name was Madcap. Mr. Wilmerding during his lifetime owned all breeds of Spaniels and had a few bench champions though his main interests lay in the training and working of Spaniels in the field.

Mr. Wilmerding died at the age of 93 on December 12, 1953. Gone, but not forgotten, by all of us who love the breed.

REVISION OF THE STANDARD

In 1943 the Standard for the breed was finally revised, but only after years of discussions and variations on the theme. It was the aim of A.S.C. to more clearly define the American-type Cocker in both color and markings. A committee was formed, with representation from all parts of the country, and a new Standard was finally accepted by the American Spaniel Club, after which it was submitted to the American Kennel Club for approval.

In due process the American Kennel Club gave approval after two changes were made. One change had to do with the percentage of solid color in a parti-color Cocker and the second change required the changing of the word "disqualification" to "penalty" regarding the matter of weight "under twenty-two pounds or over twenty-eight pounds."

At the January 1944 annual meeting the Constitution and By-Laws of the Club were greatly revised after review by the members. These changes were due and greatly helped the proper functioning of the club in serving the great number of breeders and exhibitors that had enlarged the ranks during the decade of the thirties and early forties.

All breeds of Spaniels were increasingly popular and it became evident that individual breed organizations or governing bodies would be necessary to watch over each breed. The English Springer Spaniel was the most evident example of this and the American Spaniel Club transferred its jurisdiction over this breed to another club devoted to this breed exclusively. The American Kennel Club gave it their blessings and the English Springer Spaniel Field Trial Association was incorporated. However,

the A.S.C. reserved their right to include classes for this breed at the American Spaniel Club Specialties, and this also came to be. It was shortly after this that the English Cocker Spaniels were admitted to the Sporting Group.

The success of English Springer Spaniel negotiations and the registrations of Cocker Spaniels numbering in the twenty-odd thousands during a single year led to the formation of Specialty clubs for all of the other Spaniel breeds as well. The American Spaniel Club retained jurisdiction over Cocker Spaniels only. It was only during their annual American Spaniel Club Specialty Shows that all of the Spaniel breeds met and competed. This tradition still holds true today.

COLOR JURISDICTIONS

There is no doubt that the favorite and most dominant color in the breed since its introduction in this country was black. There were other colors on the scene as well, including the white dog, Simcoe Purity, whelped in 1904, heavily line-bred to the Obo line, but the blacks were in the majority. It was during the 1930's and 1940's that the Cockers were given a third variety in the Sporting Group—blacks, the reds-blacks-and-tans, and the parti-colors. And it was this distinction that prompted the 1943 approval of the new Standard which put additional emphasis on color and markings.

Little wonder with all the new changes and innovations that S.Y. L'Hommedieu decided it was time to bring out another Year Book, commemorating the 65th anniversary of the American Spaniel Club. He and George Greer had put together the 1930 Year Book, and L'Hommedieu had also issued a supplement to it in 1933, but by 1946 L'Hommedieu had nothing but praise for the efforts put forth to produce another.

A.S.C. YEAR BOOKS

In 1906 the American Spaniel Club decided enough material had been gathered and statistics had been compiled to warrant their becoming a matter of permanent record. It was decided to publish a hardcover book to commemorate its 25th silver anniversary and to augment the Jubilee Show. Well supported by the club members with paid advertising, the book did not appear as scheduled—due to a printers strike—and copies of the book are unknown.

In 1909 another book was published, equally well supported by the A.S.C. membership, and showed a profit of one hundred dollars. Another Yearbook was not to appear until the club celebrated its 50th anniversary in 1931. There was a Year Book published in 1946, the 65th anniversary of the A.S.C., which included *The Cocker Spaniel Pictured* by famous artist Paul Brown. It has also been distributed in booklet form because of its excellence in both quality and accuracy, and mentioned earlier.

Ch. Carlyn's Temptress to Gladyan is pictured winning at the American Spaniel Club's 1st summer National Specialty. Jerry Moon handled for owner Gladys Von Horn to this win under judge Dr. William Field.

Ch. Pett's Golden Key—one of the greats of yesteryear. Owned and bred by Mr. and Mrs. Roland Pett. Photo by Gunderson.

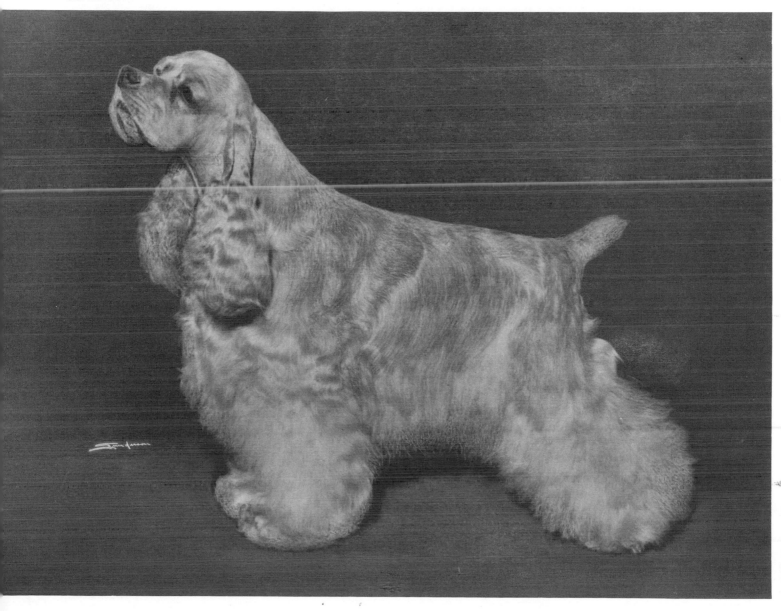

Ch. Frandee's Cat's Meow is the foundation bitch for the Frandee Kennels brown and white breeding program. She is a Ch. Frandee's Susan daughter sired by Ch. Kane Venture the Cat. This photo is of a five-point major win at a 1974 show. Owners are Frank and Dee Dee Wood with Dee Dee handling.

THE CENTENNIAL BOOKS

In 1981, the anniversary of the American Spaniel Club's first one hundred years was celebrated in part by the publication of *A Century of Spaniels*, The American Spaniel Club from 1881-1981. Editor-in-Chief Frances Greer produced in two magnificent volumes the entire history of this worthy organization in a most accurate and entertaining form. The capable staff reads like a "Who's Who" in Spaniels and each and every one is to be congratulated on a job well done. Anything you've ever wanted to know about Cockers can be found within its pages, ranging from ancient history and Cockers from countries around the world to modern times, with show and field and obedience records as well as the leading dogs and kennels active in the breed a century after the club's earliest days. Chock-full of photographs, many in full color, these books are a valuable part of any Cocker Spaniel enthusiast's library. Information on the purchase price of these two volumes may be had by writing to the Secretary of the American Spaniel Club whose current address may be obtained from the American Kennel Club, 51 Madison Avenue, New York, New York 10010.

At the 100th Anniversary Show, Frances Greer, Ph.D., received a standing ovation from the crowd when William Cobb, A.S.C. President, escorted her into the ring just prior to the Best in Show judging and presented her with a gift and certificate from the A.S.C. for the excellence of these books. At the same time copies of *A Century of Spaniels* were presented to William F. Stifel, President of the American Kennel Club for the library. Together, Mrs. Greer and Mr. Stifel cut the 100th Anniversary cake, provided by Jean Peterson, to celebrate the occasion.

Am., Can. Ch. Pett's Fire and Ice, pictured winning at the 1970 Rhode Island Cocker Specialty, is handled here by Ron Fabis for owner-breeders Mr. and Mrs. Roland Pett of Dennis Port, Massachusetts.

Ch. Pett's Golden Eagle represents the 34th champion in 21 years for the breeders, Mr. and Mrs. Roland Pett of Dennis Port, Massachusetts. "Bucky" was sired by Ch. Neffs Country Lad ex Pett's Moon Kist and was whelped in November 1968. This photograph was the cover picture on the April 1970 *American Cocker Review* magazine which included the illustrious story of the Petts' Cockers.

Ch. Blue Bay's Ring Leader, handled to a Best of Variety win by Art Benhoff for owner Mrs. Robert Fellows of Clarks Summit, Pennsylvania. "Ringer" is both a grandson and great grandson of the noted Ch. Scioto Bluff Sinbad.

Frances Greer and her late husband, George Greer, have been active in Spaniels for many years, with Mr. Greer having served as a past President. These books represent over a decade of research and gathering of material from many sources, for Frances Greer and her infinite knowledge of the breed, the club, and all available information cannot be denied. And fitting and proper, perhaps when it is remembered that it was her husband who was instrumental in the publishing of the 1930 Year Book.

THE A.S.C. CENTENNIAL CELEBRATION

The Rye Town Hilton Ballroom in Port Chester, New York on January 9, 10, and 11, 1981 was the site of the 100th Anniversary Show of the American Spaniel Club. Show Chairman Louise Post, and her assistant, Ron Merson, together with Obedience Chairman Stephan Jewell, spent over two years preparing for this "show of shows." The club literally took over an entire wing of the hotel for this major event, including the Ballroom for the show and sleeping quarters and meeting rooms to cover all of the club's annual activities.

Gorgeous head study of a Cocker owned by Irene Gaddy Zimmerman.

THE FUTURITY

One hundred fifty Cockers were entered in the Futurity Classes for judge Mildred Seger who chose Triannon's Wilma P. the winner. Wilma P. was bred by Wilma Parker and is owned by James M. Green. Handler Mike Kinchsular piloted the lovely parti-color to the top spot from the 9-12 month class. Best of Opposite Sex was from the ASCOB variety, Kaplar's Kruisin' Mi'Way, bred by Carol Ann Mills and Laura Henson and owned by Harold and Laura Henson. Mr. Henson handled the dog.

On Saturday all Puppy Classes were judged and Rudolph Merkel judged 54 obedience entries. All Flushing Spaniels were represented at the show for a total entry of 735. James Edward Clark judged the English Cocker Spaniels, while Fred Hunt judged all the remaining breeds.

By the end of the third day, the Best in Show had been awarded to Mrs. Cameron Covey and Mai Wilson's red-and-white dog, Ch. Kamp's Kaptain Kool, bred by Harriet Kamp. "Kappy" went on to win the Sporting Group at the Westminster Kennel Club the following February. A black-and-tan bitch, Ch. Lurola's Sara B., owned by David and Joanne Pulitzer, bred by Robert Lake and Mike Kinchsular, her handler, won the ASCOB variety. Black variety went to Jean and William Petersen's Ch. Rinky Dink's Socko, who also bred the dog. Charles Self handled for the Petersens. There were 11 finalists in the ring for the top award when just before 9 P.M. judge Roling pointed to Kappy for the top spot at this history-making 100th anniversary gala.

It is interesting to note that the entire event was captured on video tapes which were made available in part or whole to any club or individual who wished to own it for viewing in all the years to come.

JUNIOR SHOWMANSHIP

As usual, the youngsters participated in the activities sponsored by the A.S.C. 17 junior handlers competed for the title of Best Junior Handler, won by Lee Ann Symmonds and her ASCOB under judge Brady.

On the Thursday before the Friday Futurity, for those who wished to arrive early, Dr. Alvin Grossman conducted a six-hour judges workshop for over 25 interested participants.

TROPHIES

Adelaide Arnsten provided a trophy table with donations representing nine countries. Waterford crystal and Steiff pewter went to the winners.

CATALOGS

Drawings by Michael Allen decorated the dividers in the 800 catalogs that were snapped up in the early hours of the show and have by now become collectors' items.

BREEDER OF THE CENTURY

In addition to the honors bestowed upon Frances Greer for her *A Century of Spaniels* books, a plaque commemorating Ruth Benhoff as the Breeder of the Century was presented to her by Norman Austin on behalf of the club.

American and English Champion Sundust Bleuaire's Repercussion, Sundust Something Special and Ch. Sundust Extra Special owned by Yvonne Knapper, Sundust American Cockers, Dorset, England, exquisitely sketched by famous dog artist Michael Allen.

Am., Can. Ch. Abbi's Catch You is a buff bitch going Best of Opposite Sex to Best of Breed at a 1966 Specialty show. Catch You was the winning ASCOB bitch for 1966 at just 10 months of age. She is pictured here handled by Norman Austin for owner Mrs. Harry Reno, Port Huron, Michigan.

Mrs. A. H. Benhoff, Jr. was also honored in the centennial book for "the most Cocker Spaniel champions produced by a breeder in the first century of The American Spaniel Club." The number was 71—indeed a record to be proud of.

In his tribute to Mrs. Benhoff, Mr. Austin declared her to be a woman who "embodies the true spirit of the dedicated Cocker Spaniel breeder." How fortunate for all of us that Mrs. Benhoff chose our breed.

THE SECOND HUNDRED YEARS

By midnight most of the cars and vans had pulled away from the Hilton, the fond farewells had been said, and everyone was contemplating what the second one hundred years had in store for Cocker Spaniels and the American Spaniel Club . . .

Ch. Artru Action, producer of 53 champions as of 1979. Action was #3 in the Top Ten producing ASCOB sires in 1979, is #10 in the Top Ten producing sires in Cocker history to date, and is #4 in the Top Ten living sires in the history of the breed to date. Owner, Gay Ernst, BeGay Cockers, East Hampton, New York.

CHAPTER FIVE

The Cocker Spaniel as a Breed

The lovely red and white, Ch. Trojan Tagalong, bred by Alice Kaplan and Norman Austin. Owners are Lloyd Alton and Bill Gorodner of Ridgewood, New Jersey.

THE AMERICAN KENNEL CLUB

The American Kennel Club is the registering body for the dog fancy in the United States. Litter and breed registrations are recorded and stud books maintained for all purebred dogs. Located at 51 Madison Avenue in New York City, the A.K.C., as it is commonly referred to, recognizes over 125 of the approximately 400 breeds of dogs in the world. Their system of classifying the individual breeds is followed in the entire Western hemisphere. The breeds eligible for registration in the stud books of the A.K.C. may compete at bench shows and at obedience and field trials held under their license and approval.

The American Kennel Club also approves judges for judging at championship dog shows and at obedience and field trials and approves the scheduling of dog shows held by member kennel clubs. They maintain a Dog Show Plans department and offer instruction to member kennel clubs in the staging of dog shows, and they give final approval on the breed Standards submitted by Specialty clubs.

WHAT ARE BREED STANDARDS?

Breed Standards are written descriptions of the "ideal" dog in conformation and appearance in each of the individual breeds. Standards are written by a Standards Committee, a panel of experts chosen by the members of each breed's parent club, and are then submitted to the American Kennel Club for approval.

It is these Standards that judges use to evaluate dogs in the show ring and which serve as a guide to breeders and buyers of purebred dogs.

STANDARD FOR THE COCKER SPANIEL

General Appearance: The Cocker Spaniel is the smallest member of the Sporting Group. He has a sturdy, compact body and a cleanly chiseled and refined head, with the over-all dog in complete balance and of ideal size. He stands well up at the shoulder on straight forelegs with a topline sloping slightly toward strong, muscular quarters. He is a dog capable of considerable speed, combined with great endurance.

Above all he must be free and merry, sound, well balanced throughout, and in action show a keen inclination to work; equable in temperament with no suggestion of timidity.

Head: To attain a well-proportioned head, which must be in balance with the rest of the dog, it embodies the following:

Skull: Rounded but not exaggerated with no tendency toward flatness; the eyebrows are clearly defined with a pronounced stop. The bony structure beneath the eyes is well chiseled with no prominence in the cheeks.

Muzzle: Broad and deep, with square, even jaws. The upper lip is full and of sufficient depth to cover the lower jaw. To be in correct balance, the distance from the stop to the tip of the nose is one half the distance from the stop up over the crown to the base of the skull.

Teeth: Strong and sound, not too small, and meet in a scissors bite.

Nose: Of sufficient size to balance the muzzle and foreface, with well-developed nostrils typical of a sporting dog. It is black in color in the blacks and black and tans. In other colors it may be brown, liver or black, the darker the better. The color of the nose harmonizes with the color of the eye rim.

Eyes: Eyeballs are round and full and look directly forward. The shape of the eye rims gives a slightly almond-shaped appearance; the eye is not weak or goggled. The color of the iris is dark brown and in general the darker the better. The expression is intelligent, alert, soft and appealing.

Ears: Lobular, long, of fine leather, well feathered, and placed no higher than a line to the lower part of the eye.

Neck and Shoulders: The neck is sufficiently long to allow the nose to reach the ground easily, muscular and free from pendulous "throatiness." It rises strongly from the shoulders and arches slightly as it tapers to join the head. The shoulders are well laid back forming an angle with the upper arm of approximately 90 degrees which permits the dog to move his forelegs in an easy manner with considerable forward reach. Shoulders are clean-cut and sloping without protrusion and so set that the upper points of the withers are at an angle which permits a wide spring of rib.

Body: The body is short, compact and firmly knit together, giving an impression of strength. The distance from the highest point of the shoulder blades to the ground is fifteen (15%) per cent or approximately two inches more than the length from this point to the set-on of the tail. Back is strong and sloping evenly and slightly downward from the shoulders to the set-on of the docked tail. Hips are wide and quarters well rounded and muscular. The chest is deep, its lowest point no higher than the elbows, its front sufficiently wide for adequate heart and lung space, yet not so wide as to interfere with the straightforward movement of the forelegs. Ribs are deep and well sprung. The Cocker Spaniel never appears long and low.

Tail: The docked tail is set on and carried on a line with the topline of the back, or slightly higher; never straight up like a terrier and never so low as to indicate timidity. When the dog is in motion the tail action is merry.

Legs and Feet: Forelegs are parallel, straight, strongly boned and muscular and set close to the body well under the scapulae. When viewed from the side with the forelegs vertical, the elbow is directly below the highest point of the shoulder blade. The pasterns are short and strong. The hind legs are strongly boned and muscled with good angulation at the stifle and powerful, clearly defined thighs. The stifle joint is strong and there is no slippage of it in motion or when standing. The hocks are strong, well let down, and when viewed from behind, the hind legs are parallel when in motion and at rest.

Ch. Pleasant Valley Swinger, ivory male bred by Kathleen Guyer and owned by Lindy Hay of Bakersfield, California. The sire was Ch. Artru Sandpiper ex Ch. LaMar's Ivory Cameo.

Feet: Compact, large, round and firm with horny pads; they turn neither in nor out. Dewclaws on hind legs and forelegs may be removed.

Coat: On the head, short and fine; on the body, medium length, with enough undercoating to give protection. The ears, chest, abdomen and legs are well feathered, but not so excessively as to hide the Cocker Spaniel's true lines and movement or affect his appearance and function as a sporting dog. The *texture* is most important. The coat is silky, flat or slightly wavy, and of a texture which permits easy care. Excessive or curly or cottony textured coat is to be penalized.

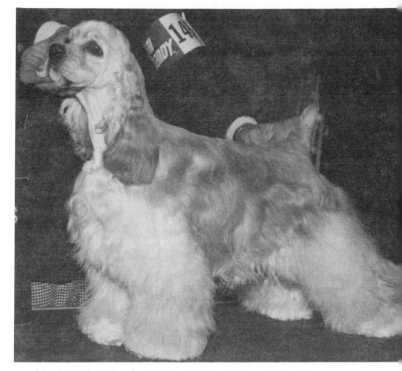

Ch. Sunshine's Summer Song, Best of Variety, ASCOB at the American Spaniel Club Futurity at the 1979 show. Summer Song finished for her championship at just 12 months of age. Bred and owned by Steve and Cindy Dennehy, Sunshine Kennels, Muskogee, Oklahoma.

Ch. Mar-Jac's Frandee Folly, black bitch which is the foundation bitch for the Frandee Kennels' black line, is pictured here at just 10 months of age going all the way to Best of Opposite Sex from the puppy classes over Specials at a 1972 show. Handled by Dee Dee Wood. J. H. Boyd, judge.

Color and Markings:

Black Variety: Solid color black, to include black with tan points. The black should be jet; shadings of brown or liver in the sheen of the coat is not desirable. A small amount of white on the chest and/or throat is allowed, white in any other location shall disqualify.

Any Solid Color Other Than Black: Any solid color other than black and any such color with tan points. The color shall be of a uniform shade, but lighter coloring of the feather is permissible. A small amount of white on the chest and/or throat is allowed, white in any other location shall disqualify.

Ch. Pett's Pamper, beautiful buff bitch and a show winner at the 1959 Cocker Spaniel Club of Virginia Specialty show on the way to her championship, is handled by Ted Young, Jr., for owners Roland and Dorothy Pett of Dennis Port, Massachusetts.

Parti-Color Variety: Two or more definite, well-broken colors, one of which must be white, including those with tan points; it is preferable that the tan markings be located in the same pattern as for the tan points in the Black and ASCOB varieties. Roans are classified as parti-colors, and may be of any of the usual roaning patterns. Primary color which is ninety percent (90%) or more shall disqualify.

Tan Points: The color of the tan may be from the lightest cream to the darkest red color and should be restricted to ten percent (10%) or less of the color of the specimen, tan markings in excess of that amount shall disqualify.

In the case of tan points in the Black or ASCOB variety, the markings shall be located as follows:

(1) A clear tan spot over each eye
(2) On the sides of the muzzle and on the cheeks
(3) On the undersides of the ears
(4) On all feet and/or legs
(5) Under the tail
(6) On the chest, optional, presence or absence not penalized

The magnificently full-coated Reverie Reminisce, owned by Pam Burrows, Gainsville, Florida.

Tan markings which are not readily visible or which amount only to traces, shall be penalized. Tan on the muzzle which extends upward, over and joins shall also be penalized. The absence of tan markings in the Black or ASCOB variety in each of the specified locations in an otherwise tan-pointed dog shall disqualify.

Movement: The Cocker Spaniel, though the smallest of the sporting dogs, possesses a typical sporting dog gait. Prerequisite to good movement is balance between the front and rear assemblies. He drives with his strong, powerful rear quarters and is properly constructed in the shoulders and forelegs so that he can reach forward without constriction in a full stride to counterbalance the driving force from the rear. Above all, his gait is coordinated, smooth and effortless. The dog must cover ground with his action and excessive animation should never be mistaken for proper gait.

Height: The ideal height at the withers for an adult dog is 15 inches and for an adult bitch 14 inches. Height may vary one-half inch above or below this ideal. A dog whose height exceeds 15½ inches or a bitch whose height exceeds 14½ inches shall be disqualified. An adult dog whose height is less than 14½ inches or an adult bitch whose height is less than 13½ inches shall be penalized.

Note: Height is determined by a line perpendicular to the ground from the top of the shoulder blades, the dog standing naturally with its forelegs and the lower hind legs parallel to the line of measurement.

DISQUALIFICATIONS

Color and Markings—
   Blacks—White markings except on chest and throat.
   Solid Colors Other Than Black—White markings except on chest and throat.
   Black and Tans—Tan markings in excess of ten (10) percent; tan markings not readily visible in the ring, or the absence of tan markings in any of the specified locations; white markings except on chest and throat.
   Parti-Colors: Ninety (90) percent or more of primary color; secondary color or colors limited solely to one location.
   Height—Males over 15½ inches; females over 14½ inches.

COCKER SPANIEL COLORS

One of the most beautiful features of our breed is the wide array of colors and color combinations available to us. Such was not the case in the beginning. As far as we can determine the first "Spanyels" were red and red-and-white. We must remember that we could in no way consider that the "red" color of that time could be the same as the reds we see today. The "red" could better be described as being more of a yellow or dun color and not the rich red mahogany shade we see in the show rings during more recent years.

Those ancient Irish Red Spaniels, or "Modder Rhu" as it was called in Gaelic, was a different color indeed.

There were some objections to the self-colored "reds." A chief objection was the danger that their color would fade into the surrounding brush, resulting in their being hard to follow by the hunters and a danger of their being shot in the fields. The red-and-whites made spotting them easier for the hunter but also it made it easier for the game to spot the dogs! There was also the danger of losing the dogs in the field,

Ch. Corwin Gandy Dancer, son of Ch. Corwin My Cheri, is owned by Mr. and Mrs. Dennis Hart. This striking black and white was bred by Helen Rice of Stanton, California, and is pictured winning under judge Mrs. Harvey.

and those who were concerned sometimes tied a piece of white cloth around their dogs' necks to make them stand out against the field.

However, all colors were seen at the time that the breed became established, and there is no denying that while all colors could be seen, certain periods saw certain colors come into vogue. In the early days of the breed in this country the majority of dogs were red or red-and-white. By the 1940's a succession of really good blacks brought a sudden prominence to them that would assure their future in the fancy. The black-and-tans enjoyed a new popularity during the 1940's and 1950's because of the outstanding dogs of that color during these decades. Wide use of these colors for stud service was bound to create a trend for the future which would see all colors enjoying equal billing in the show rings.

During the 1950's the flashy black-and-whites saw a sudden trend when Norman Austin was campaigning Mackey Irick's dog in the rings. As we enter the 1980's there is more and more interest in breeding the browns and brown-and-whites once again, remembering that Chloe II, the first bitch to come to this country, carried brown genes.

Unlike so many other breeds where color and color patterns are severely restricted, we are most fortunate to be able to enjoy our dogs in such a wide spectrum of colors.

Ging's Phoebe Fireworks, red and white bitch bred and owned by Lloyd Alton and Bill Gorodner of Ridgewood, New Jersey.

Michael's Murmer, a well-marked "Fharkel" with good pigment, was sired by Ch. Baliwick Blotter and owned by Michael Allen of Costa Mesa, California.

Ch. Travel On Thunderbird is pictured winning the breed at a 1979 kennel club show. This lovely black and tan is owned and bred by Barb White, Travel On Kennels, Columbiana, Ohio.

Frandee's Fight On, tri-color Cocker Spaniel dog, is pictured winning under judge Pat Seger. Fight On is owned by Mary Wooley of California.

A BREED SURVEY

Along with the over 500 invitations to submit photographs of the leading Cocker Spaniels to be included in this book, a random selection of questionnaires were included in the envelopes to secure a sampling of information on our breed.

Among the questions were two that everyone took much time and thought to answer. Those two questions were: "What do you believe are the outstanding characteristics of the breed today?" and "What do you feel are the major faults in the breed today?"

Without quoting exact percentages, the answer to the first question was unanimous in putting excellent temperament and beauty as the most desirable characteristics. The Cockers' desire to please and the profusion of coat ranked high in these decisions.

Oddly enough this profusion, or as some put it, excess of coat, was also one of the criticisms that many other breeders had considered a fault. They felt too much emphasis was being put on coat today. Several suggested "a happy medium" could be reached which would suit both pet and show dogs. One respondant remarked, "Ask any veterinarian or dog groomer about those matted ears!"

Matted ears and excess coat seem to go hand in hand where Cockers are concerned. But let's face it, if a Cocker owner really cares about his dog, he knows enough to keep those ears brushed and combed.

While coat and grooming were mentioned repeatedly in the responses, more significant replies were made on more serious threats to the breed. Almost everyone's main concern was eye disease; namely cataracts and PRA. Eye diseases, which are prevalent in most all breeds, rank especially high on our list in spite of the great advancements in research on diseases of the eyes.

Three serious anatomical changes were mentioned as faults. Efforts to further shorten the muzzle in recent years came under considerable criticism, along with too much slope on the topline and over-angulation in the hindquarters. Hip dysplasia was also mentioned.

It was interesting to note that while the percentages were almost unanimous on the outstanding characteristics of the breed, the percentages on muzzle, topline and over-angulation were almost evenly divided and hovered below the 50% mark. However, concern over eye disease was over 80% and profusion of coat below 25% and mostly from owners of one-dog families or owners whose dogs were active in the field.

While questionnaires, polls, and surveys never prove anything 100%, sometimes they do give an indication of what is on the minds of the breeders who are dedicated to continuing to try to breed better dogs. For that reason, if no other, we would do well to get other opinions to add to our own and to stimulate our thinking.

YOUR ZOOLOGICAL CHART

In completely identifying your dog you can use the following chart:

Kingdom: Animalia
Phylum: Chordata
Class: Mammalia
Order: Carnivora
Family: Canidae
Genus: *Canis*
Species: *Familiaris*

Chuck and Billie Ballantine's Ch. Rinky Dink's Tis Kismet, sired by Ch. Rinky Dink's Sir Lancerlot ex Chess King's Rinky Dink Too. This lovely bitch champion was photographed by William Kohler.

COCKER SPANIEL PUBLICATIONS

The most popular and the oldest single breed publication in America is the *American Cocker Review*, a magazine dedicated to our breed. The Cocker Review was started in 1957 and has passed through several owners and editors. Starting in 1981 the editorship has been given over to the capable abilities of Frances Greer, who was editor-in-chief of the American Spaniel Club's two-volume publication, *A Century of Spaniels*. These books, published in 1981 to commemorate the 100th Anniversary of the American Spaniel Club, are "required reading" for all Cocker Spaniel enthusiasts.

Along with Kate Romanski, Managing Co-editor, and Bill Gorodner, the Assistant Editor, these two books constitute one hundred years of information and photographs of Cocker history that will be treasured in the breed forever. An outstanding Editorial Board, chaired by Norman A. Austin and Statistics Chairperson Margaret M. Saari, D.V.M. have put on record facts and figures found in no other place or so readily available. Advertising Chairperson Laura Watt O'Conner presents a photo gallery of today's great dogs which delights the eyes and brings the history of the breed up-to-date with all of the old-timers pictured in the text.

Countries of the world are represented with their histories with much thanks to International Coordinator Owen L. Young, Ph.D., and photographs and information on other dogs which represent the other Spaniels are a delight to see and read about. Information on how to purchase these books can be had by writing to the American Spaniel Club.

The editors and staff of *A Century of Spaniels*, 1881-1981, are to be complimented on a superb job of presenting our breed for posterity.

Over the years there have been other publications that featured Cocker Spaniel information. The American Spaniel Club has also published their 5th Annual Health Registry. A 65-page, soft-cover volume priced at four dollars was published under the direction of The Hereditary and Congenital Defects Committee of the A.S.C. and they have complied the medical records of over 1,000 Cockers covering four major life-threatening defects: cataracts (CAT), progressive retinal atrophy (PRA), Factor 10 (FAC 10), and hip dysplasia (HD).

Anyone who wishes to buy and/or breed a Cocker would do well to consult this booklet and to use it for constant reference.

Two Torchlite Cocker Spaniels pictured at ten months of age: Torchlite Temptation on the left and Torchlite Tempting on the right. Tempting is the dam of one champion and the granddam of several champions. Their sire was Ch. Artru Red Baron out of Ch. Caramel's Cozette. Bred by Margaret M. Saari, D.V.M., of New York City.

EARLIEST RECORDS

Earliest news about the breed was undoubtedly included in a newspaper-type publication called the *American Stock-Keeper*. There also have been magazine-type publications, usually issued on a monthly basis, such as *The Cocker Spaniel Visitor*, a national breed magazine published by Bart and Kay King in Minneapolis, and another called *The Cocker Spaniel Spokesman*. General information on the breed could be garnered from columns in magazines featuring all breeds. These were the *American Kennel Gazette*, *Popular Dogs* magazine, *Dog World*, and others.

Copies of most of these can be seen in libraries today which feature dog publications—and especially in the excellent library at the American Kennel Club.

Ch. Frandee's Sargent Pepper, parti-color dog, and littermate to Ch. Frandee's Susan, pictured at a win. Owners and breeders are Frank and Dee Dee Wood. Nicholas Kay, judge.

Ch. Pett's Gentlemen Jim, bred and owned by the Roland Petts of Dennis Port, Massachusetts, was a top show-winner in the 1960's.

CHAPTER SIX

Cocker Spaniel People and Places

Ch. Pett's Gentleman Jim, owned and bred by Mrs. Roland Pett of Dennis Port, Massachusetts, is pictured here winning at the Hiawatha Cocker Spaniel Specialty show in 1966 on the way to his championship. Handled for owner by Ron Fabis under judge Eugene Gaynor, Sr. Olson photo.

TOP TEN BREEDERS IN THE HISTORY OF THE BREED

While the phrase "Top Ten" became known when the Phillips System came into being in 1956, quite naturally there has always been a listing of the "top" contenders in any breed, whether it's Top Ten winners or Top Ten anything when a list of accomplishments is being made. So it was in the early days of the breed when breeders and exhibitors began compiling records on the progress of their dogs in breed history.

Names like W. T. Payne, H. E. Mellenthin, H. K. Bloodgood, O.B. Gilman, the George Greers, George Douglas, Louise Hering, Mrs. L'Hommedieu, O.B. and W.G. Hark, and F. J. McGauvran fit this Top Ten category in those early days when it came to breeding champions, show winners, and contributing time and effort to all phases of breed history. The Top Dogs belonged to their kennels and made history.

By 1981 when the American Spaniel Club celebrated its 100th Anniversary, the list of Top Ten Breeders in Cocker Spaniels still included many of the breeders that were active for many years. When homage was paid to the leading breeders in the first one hundred years of the breed, the name of Mrs. Arthur H. Benhoff, Jr., headed the list. Her Artru kennel name was behind 71 champions of note. The Silver Maple Kennels of Mr. and Mrs. Lee Kraeuchi were close behind, having produced 70 champions.

The Stockdale Kennels of C.B. Van Meter and Myrtle Smith produced 67 champions, followed by Thomas O'Neal's Dreamridge Kennels with 64. Betty Durland's Dur-Bet and Marion Bebeau's Maribeau bred 52 and 51 champions respectively, and Clarence A. Smith's Heyday produced 49. The Roland Petts account for 48 champions. To round out today's list of Top Ten Breeders to an even 10 we must also include Harlan Hoel and A.T. Stimpfig's Harlanhaven Kennels with a total of 47, and Beatrice Wegusen's Honey Creek with 44.

The list of kennels that produced 20 or more champions during this first one hundred year period is amazingly long and attests to a record of which the old timers and the newcomers can be proud.

OWNERS AND HANDLERS

In any compilation of facts and figures in a breed as popular and prolific as Cocker Spaniels, it is next to impossible to compose a list including *every* dog worthy of mention. The same holds true for their human counterparts, and we regret any omissions in this book. The names of so many people who have made a contribution—large or small—boggles the mind, especially when so many of them serve in many capacities as breeders, exhibitors, owners, judges, authors, columnists, kennel owners or managers, club officers, show managers and so on.

During the early days in Cockers there were several important professional handlers who were responsible for the campaigning of important dogs that set the pace for the breed. Many of them owned and worked their own dogs as well as represented the prominent kennels of the day in the show rings. Names like Clint Callahan, Bain and Ken Cobb, and Lee Kraeuchi immediately come to mind, as readily as Mellenthin, Townshend Scudder, John Bailey Charles, Jack Gleason, or Mildred Vogel Imrie. Needless

to say, the contributions and supreme handling talents of Norman Austin over the decades is legend.

Could anyone speak of the show ring success of the great dogs of the past without mentioning Ted Young Sr.? Not only did he achieve success in the show ring but he was lauded as a breeder, trainer, exhibitor, and competitor in the field. In the same breath when mentioning Ted Young, Sr., one automatically calls to mind his son, Ted Young, Jr., who, to coin a phrase, followed in his father's illustrious footsteps to make a career of his own—a career which has reached the heights and continues in the fancy today.

Others that come to mind when we talk about deft handling are Parley Larabee from the 1950's, Michael Kinchsular, the late Bill Ernst and Pedro Rivero, Irene Gaddy Zimmerman, Ron Fabis, Howard Reno, and Dee Dee Wood, to name just a few of those fortunate enough to show dogs as well as to breed and own them.

Breeder-owner-handlers are also a very special group of fanciers whose dedication to the breed is to be commended. But for those Cocker fanciers, who for any reason whatsoever cannot handle their own dogs in the show rings, the expertise of our professional handlers is to be appreciated.

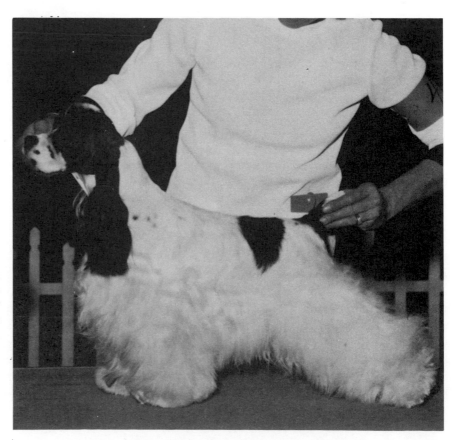

Ch. Frandee's Windswept, bred and owned by Frank and Dee Dee Wood of Norco, California, is litter sister to Ch. Frandee's Declaration.

Film star Rita Hayworth poses with her brown and white Cocker Spaniel, "Pookles," in this Columbia Pictures photo.

COCKER SPANIEL TALES

The great beauty of the Cocker Spaniel has always attracted dog lovers. Those soft brown eyes have captured the hearts of many famous people, including several motion picture stars. Who doesn't remember the glamorous publicity photos of the famous Margarita Cansino—better known as Rita Hayworth—with her adorable red Cocker Spaniel?

Another glamorous film and stage star, Lauren Bacall, was the proud owner of "Droopy" and his daughter "Puddles," and they travelled all over the country with her. The great affection she had for them (in spite of the names she gave them!) is clearly evident in her autobiography, *Lauren Bacall By Myself*, wherein she writes of the death of Droopy and the injury to his puppy when they were hit by a car.

Basil Rathbone was another dog lover whose public appearances included adulation for Cockers. A lovely red Cocker named "Peter" appeared with TV personality Arlene Francis in various promotions for Sergeant's Dog Care Products. It was also a pedigreed Cocker Spaniel that was presented one year to an Easter Seal Society's poster-boy on the Don McNeil Breakfast Club radio show.

The famous Captain Eddie Rickenbacker poses with two Cocker Spaniel puppies from the Merrylee Kennels of Mr. and Mrs. Leon Blair. The occasion was the Navy Charity Carnival in Key West, Florida.

Glamorous television star Arlene Francis with "Butch," the famous Cocker Spaniel that has appeared on over 125 national magazine covers. Butch is the model for his artist-owner, Albert Staehle. This photograph was taken at a fourth birthday party in 1954. Photo by Hollander.

NEWSWORTHY COCKER SPANIELS

Cocker Spaniels have not only proven themselves as being photogenic but have certainly distinguished themselves in the news media. A red Cocker named "Rusty" always went along with his owner, Tom Blacke, a world-champion surfer each time he chose to ride the waves. They were a familiar sight on the beaches of Waikiki, Hawaii whenever the waves were of the proper height. Rusty had become such a legend that he and his master appeared in a full-page picture in the September 1944 issue of the *National Geographic* Magazine.

Across another ocean in Copenhagen, Denmark to be exact, Niels Larsen's Cocker Spaniel kept his master out of jail! When sentenced to spend 20 days in jail, Mr. Larsen showed up with his 12-year-old Cocker Spaniel explaining that if he and the dog were to be separated, the dog would die. The jail, which had no facilities for inmates with dogs, referred Mr. Larsen back to the judge who promptly dismissed the charges for the duration of the dog's life. We can rest assured that that Cocker Spaniel was to enjoy the good life from that day forward.

SELF SERVICE

An Associated Press report out of Kohler, Wisconsin in the 1970's reported on the unusual habit of "Scamp" who really loved apples. From the day that one first fell off an apple tree and landed in front of him—tempting him to take a bite—Scamp has constantly been trying to lead his owners, Elmer and LaVerne Bridson, down to the apple grove when he can't jump and pull the fruit off the lower branches himself. When apples aren't in season, Scamp also dives for articles tossed into three feet of water or puts money into a piggybank. The photo which accompanied the news report shows Scamp, with his ears flying, leaping several feet off the ground for the choicest apples. Mrs. Bridson claims Scamp "always goes for the best apples." "I don't know how he does it," she says.

"Scarlet," a Cocker Spaniel owned by Mrs. Katheryn Williams of Lancaster, Texas, prefers the company of "Henrietta," the duck in her dog house. Henrietta came to the family as an Easter duckling, but now full grown she vies for equal space in the dog house.

We have no doubts that Scarlet will make the necessary adjustment just as easily as "Laddie," a Cocker Spaniel owned by Phil Savage, adjusted to using a hearing aid when his hearing became impaired.

Dog owners frequently are amazed at the resourceful behavior of their dogs. The Gaines Research Center in White Plains, New York, recently highlighted the story of a Cocker Spaniel in Cornwall, England, discovered dropping bones down an abandoned mine shaft to feed her puppy that had fallen into it.

We were all touched to learn that "Shadow" (part Cocker Spaniel and part Lhasa Apso) owned by Kevin Cleary and his mother of Oak Forest, Illinois, had their dog returned to them by some people from Texas after it had been taken from their backyard in Iran. This was during the time the Americans had been taken hostage. It is still not known how the dog got to Texas, but after 15 months the dog was returned to the Clearys in Illinois.

The Peter Chapin Memorial at William and Mary College is a memorial to a black Cocker Spaniel of that name, presented by his owners. This Peter Chapin collection at the Swem Library was donated by Mr. and Mrs. Howard Chapin of Providence, Rhode Island, in 1937. The collection includes books about every breed recognized by the American Kennel Club and in

Ch. Milru's Cheery Cherub, U.D., painted by Bob Hickey for owner Ruth Muller of Centerport, New York.

1937 received wide acclaim for the magnificent Pug dog exhibit which featured all sizes of Pug figurines and memorabilia.

If we wanted to continue name dropping we would have to include the newest celebrity to gain popularity in the press. We refer to our 1981 Vice President George Bush who still enjoys the company of his aging Cocker Spaniel, "Fred."

While many famous Cocker Spaniels have shared the spotlight in the dog show, obedience, and field circles, a new dimension has been added to the dog fancy. "Frisbee" competitions are now a popular sport and are enjoying widespread competition. "Raisin," was the name of the Cocker Spaniel that won the 1977 Frisbee Fetch and Catch competition in Central Park, New York.

While most of the ancient masterpiece paintings of dogs feature hunting scenes with the various sporting and hound breeds, we do have a few representations of Cocker Spaniels by more modern artists that choose, if not favor, our breed. The greatest selection can be researched at the American Kennel Club library. Important too are the marvelous anatomical and numbered drawings by Paul Brown (for the various Year Books) of the "good" and "bad" points of our breed. Gaines Dog Research Center also circulated a booklet of these drawings which has met with tremendous interest over many years.

THE COCKER SPANIEL IN ART

Perhaps the most famous of our current artists who devotes so much time and talent to capturing the beauty of the Cocker on canvas or paper is Michael Allen. An outstanding breeder of Cockers, she would naturally be creatively attuned to the beauty of our breed and is extensively represented by her work in this volume. To own a Michael Allen drawing of your own dog is a treasure indeed.

The hallways of the American Kennel Club feature famous artists' paintings of dogs. Three Spaniels by W.E. Turner painted in 1868 is one of them. Many more famous paintings of dogs of all breeds are to be found in the private collections of the dog fanciers and it is hoped will eventually be given to the American Kennel Club for permanent preservation and for the enjoyment of the myriads of people who visit the A.K.C. every year.

Ch. Torchlite Tantalizin', bred and owned by Margaret Saari, D.V.M., of New York City, is seen in a magnificent drawing by Michael Allen.

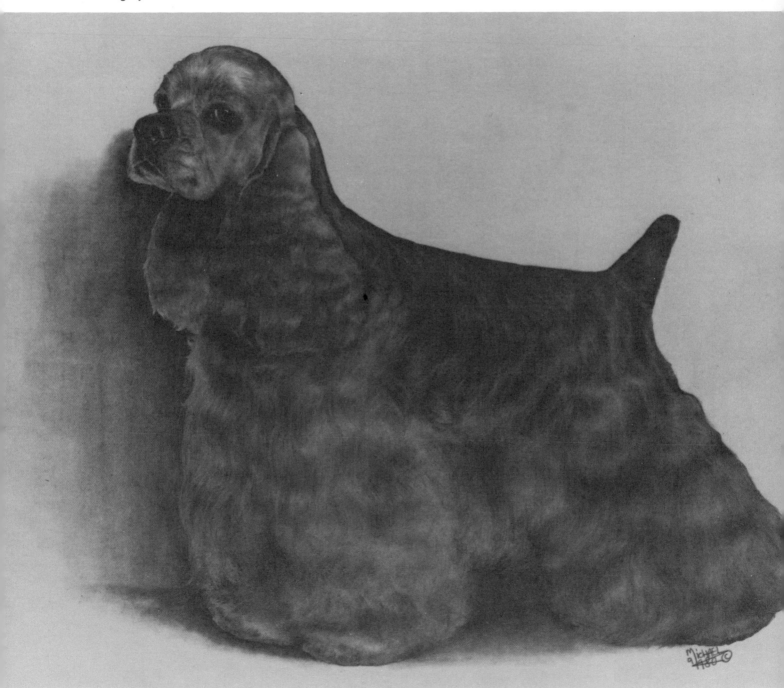

In 1969 a Cocker Spaniel bitch with a basketful of her puppies was featured on a plate by Bing and Grondahl. Entitled "Dog and Puppies," the plate originally sold for $9.75. The present day value is in excess of $500. Collector's Plates have become a popular art form for all animal lovers, and many times these pieces can be picked up at auctions and flea markets for a mere fraction of their value. "Dog and Puppies" was the first in a series painted by artist Henry Thelander, and each plate features a mother (animal) with her young in the traditional cobalt blue underglaze on bas-relief porcelain.

Ch. Dreamridge Dominoe, sire of 98 champions to date. This fabulous drawing by Michael Allen was the June cover picture for one of the leading Cocker magazines. Owner is Tom O'Neal, Dreamridge Kennels, Woodstock, Illinois. Among Dominoe's other credits is top living Cocker Spaniel sire.

Trojan's Thomas At Court, shown in a pastel done by Jean Brodhagen for owner Alice Kaplan of Magnolia, Texas.

THE COCKER SPANIEL IN LITERATURE

In many books, especially those written to delight youngsters, we have all noticed illustrations of medium-sized, floppy-eared, fuzzy-footed, and sad-eyed dogs which we could easily reckon as being at least "part Cocker Spaniel." Their temperament is such that they are easily paired with children.

However, one of the most famous of all Cocker Spaniels in literature has to be the renowned "Flush," beloved companion of the famous author, Elizabeth Barrett Browning. A biography of Flush was written by Virginia Woolf, which eventually was issued as a paperback in 1961 from the original manuscript copyrighted in 1933. It is a charming story and

anyone who is at all interested in the charm and companionship of a Cocker Spaniel must read it. Just be sure to have a box of tissues handy if you read through to the sad ending.

Elizabeth Barrett Browning wrote to many of her friends about her dog Flush as the years passed and they grew old together. But perhaps her most lasting tribute to her dear little dog was the dedication which read, "To Flush, My Dog," in her book, *Poems*, written at her home on Wimpole Street, and the book for which she became so well-known. Norma Shearer portrayed Elizabeth Barrett Browning in the motion picture, "The Barretts of Wimpole Street" in which Flush had a major role.

Ch. Trojan's Intandescent, captured in a pen and ink sketch by Peggy Bang for owner Alice Kaplan, Trojan Kennels, Magnolia, Texas.

Am., Can. Ch. Windy Hill's Delight O'Calypso, owned by Tom and Laurie Acklin and Edna Anselmi, is pictured here in a pencil portrait by Lynn Drew. Delight's sire was Ch. Windy Hill's Tis Demi's Demon ex Windy Hill's Tis Fanci Eaglet.

COCKER SPANIELS IN POLITICS

We have previously mentioned Vice President George Bush's Cocker Spaniel, "Fred," and we are aware that President Nixon had an Irish Setter named "King Timahoe" while he occupied the White House during better days. But actually it was a Cocker Spaniel named "Checkers" that brought political fame to the then vice presidential candidate.

Nixon refused to withdraw from the election because of criticism over his acceptance of a gift of a dog after Pat had mentioned on a radio show that their two children wanted a dog. A man in Texas sent the Nixon children a black-and-white spotted Cocker Spaniel which the girls promptly named Checkers and as Nixon stated to the press emphatically, ". . . the kids love that dog and I just want to say this right now, that regardless of what they say about it, we're going to keep it."

Ch. Dreamridge Dominoe, pictured again In a drawing by Michael Allen for the June 1977 cover story in a leading Cocker Spaniel magazine.

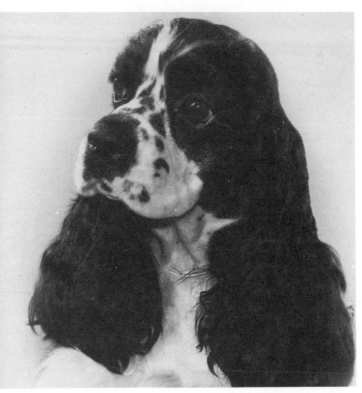

Ch. Dreamridge Dinner Date is owned by Thomas O'Neal, Dreamridge Kennels, Woodstock, Illinois. Dinner Date has 16 Best of Breed Specialty wins to his credit and has sired several champions including Ch. Dreamridge Don Juan, a Group winner; Ch. Dreamridge Debonair, a Best in Show winner in Brazil; and Ch. Demijohn, a champion in Colombia and Venezuela, and a Best in Show winner in those countries as well. He is also the sire of American and Scandinavian Ch. Dreamridge Domineer.

He further stated that he would withdraw if the nation wished him to and suggested the public wire or write the National Republican Committee with their opinion. Over 300,000 letters, wires, and petitions were received in the affirmative, and Richard Nixon stayed on the ticket and won. There are many who firmly believe that after what is now referred to as his "Checkers speech" Nixon couldn't lose. It was a turning point in his career, and Checkers became a national celebrity with the most prestigious address in town!

COCKER SPANIELS IN FOREIGN LANDS

It was really after World War II that Cocker Spaniels were seen in any great numbers in foreign countries. They had reached Japan by the mid-forties, as pets of military personnel in that country, and had spread as far south as Mexico by the late 1940's. Of course, several specimens of the breed were seen in both Australia and New Zealand as early as the 1920's and had arrived there via England. The lengthy quarantine—in the case of a United States import, a dog had to go by way of English rules and could remain as long as a year and a half in quarantine—so few were purchased from this country.

Some Dreamridge Kennel Cockers being shown at a Japanese dog show in 1976.

After World War II they reached the Netherlands and parts of Germany, France by 1956, and Denmark in 1965. South American countries were importing by the 1950's with Argentina and Brazil establishing impressive kennels in those countries.

Colombia had Cocker Spaniels by the mid-1960's; Venezuela saw its first import in 1964. Finland imported its first in the late 1960's, and Switzerland not until 1974.

Oddly enough, Spain, the country from which the Cocker Spaniel derived its name and "origin," had very few before 1975 and most of them were bred on the European continent, not directly imported from America.

The appeal of the Cocker Spaniel continues to spread abroad as it has in this country. Those kennels that have maintained the breed in foreign lands have done a superb job of breeding quality dogs and keep close contact with American breeders to insure quality and standards. One need only observe photographs of foreign winners to know that the breed is in good hands around the world as well as in the United States, the land that claimed them for their very own.

Ch. Bobwin's High Hopes is pictured winning Group 2 in San Juan del Rio. In this 1977 show "T. J." finished for his Mexican championship. Owned by Mrs. Winnie Vick, Bobwin Kennels, Suisun, California. Mrs. Thelma Von Thaden, judge.

Ch. Dreamridge Dinner Date, a Best in Show winner in Caracas, Venezuela.

Famed dog photographer Joan Ludwig caught this darling picture of three of Michael Allen's puppies: future champions Baliwick Barrymore, Born Free and The Impecabl' Frekl.

The first chocolate to win Best of Breed at a Specialty Show, Ch. BeGay's Archie B. Hershey, is pictured winning at the 1975 Upstate Cocker Spaniel Club Specialty in 1975. Archie is owned by Gay Ernst of East Hampton, Long Island, New York, owner of the BeGay Cocker Spaniels.

Henry

114

Above: Ch. Bouley's London Jewel, red bitch, pictured winning a five-point major under judge Ellen Strang. Jewel was the 2nd top-winning ASCOB bitch for 1977. Sired by Ch. Lamar's London ex Ch. McEnroe's Mystique. She was handled to this Best of Variety win from the Classes by Dee Dee Wood for owners Bill and Mary Bouley.

Opposite: Ch. Vista G. Altair, #1 parti-color in the United States in 1974, a Multiple Group and Specialty winner, and the top winning owner-handled parti in breed history as of 1980. Bred and owned by Shirley Galassi and co-owned by the handler, Michael Allen of Costa Mesa, California. The sire was Ch. Baliwick Blotter ex Ar-Gyle Tartan Tam.

Ch. Memoir's Licorice Lady, a black bitch, wins Best of Variety over nine Specials from the Classes to finish for her championship at the Southern California Specialty show under judge Everett Dean. Owned by Anita B. Roberts, Memoir Kennels, Novato, California. Bergman photo.

Ging's Wilmerding, tri-color dog bred and owned by Lloyd Alton and Bill Gorodner of Ridgewood, New Jersey, is pictured on the way to his championship. Ashbey photo.

Ch. Baliwick Bricklayer, black and white male, bred by Michael Allen and co-owned with her by Lindy Hay. The sire was Ch. Baliwick Barrymore, sire of five champions to date, and the dam was Ch. Bizzmar Bon Bon, a Best in Show winning bitch from the Classes. Henry Schley photograph.

Ch. Artru Jan-Myr Entertainer is a glorious buff color Cocker Spaniel owned by Charles Rowe, Rowingdale Cockers, La Mesa, California.

Above: Ch. Trojan's In Earnest, black and white dog, being shown by owner Alice Kaplan to a Sporting Group Second win from the Classes at the Calcasieu Kennel Club show under judge Tom Rainey.

Opposite: Ch. Merribark's Mr. Brown, chocolate Cocker, is pictured winning at a show. Owned by Elane Poole of Placentia, California.

Ging's Star Spangled Romeo, red and white dog owned by Neil Poquette and Jim Smith. "Spinner" is being handled by Jean Flynn to a win at the 1976 San Joaquin Kennel Club show in California on the way to his championship. Bred by Lloyd Alton and Bill Gorodner. Jayne Langdon photo.

Merribark's Mocha Motion, the foundation bitch for solid chocolates and blacks at the Cal-Ore Kennels in Brooks, Oregon. Owners of Mocha are Nancy L. and Lisa L. Ray. Here, Mocha wins under judge Langdon Skarda at the Golden Gate Kennel Club.

Above: The lovely chocolate bitch, Ch. BeGay's Sauce C. Hershey, owned by Gay Ernst of East Hampton, New York. Saucey's show career included a five-point major win at the Cocker Spaniel Club of New Jersey Specialty show in 1980.

Opposite: Ch. Kaplar's Kopper Key, red dog shown winning Best of Variety and Group 3rd from the 9-12 month Class. Handled by Julie Wood Wolf, bred by Kap and Laura Henson, and owned by Chris Richter.

Above: Ch. Pett's Patty Cake, beautiful buff dam of Ch. Pett's Right Time. Bred and owned by Dorothy and Roland Pett.

Opposite: Ch. Merribark's Mr. Brown, eight-and-a-half-year-old chocolate, is pictured winning the 1980 Summer National Specialty at Tampa, Florida. Owned by Elane Poole, Merribark Kennels, Placentia, California.

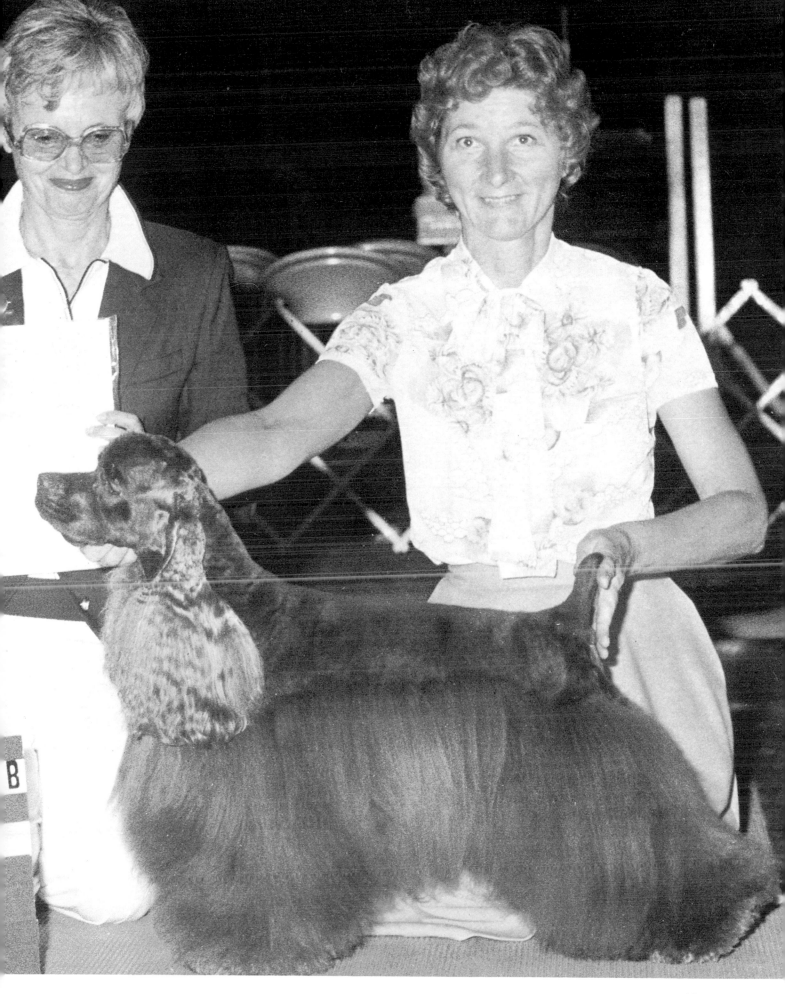

The ultimate in color coordination—Ch. Baliwick The 'Impecabl Frekl and his daughter, Ch. The 'Insufrabl Frekl, with matching mice. Photograph submitted by Michael Allen through the courtesy and infinite patience of the photographer.

CHAPTER SEVEN

Buying Your First Cocker Spaniel Puppy

Mrs. Harry Reno is holding one of her typey Abbi's Cocker Spaniels.

In searching for that special puppy, there are several paths that will lead you to a litter from which you can find the puppy of your choice. If you are uncertain as to where to find a reputable breeder, write to the parent club and ask for the names and addresses of members who have puppies for sale. The addresses of Cocker Spaniel breed clubs can be obtained by writing directly to the American Kennel Club, 51 Madison Avenue, New York, N.Y. 10010. They keep an up-to-date, accurate list of breeders from whom you can seek information on obtaining a good, healthy puppy. The classified ad listings in dog publications and the major newspapers may also lead you to that certain pup. The various dog magazines generally carry a monthly breed column which features information and news on the breed that may aid in your selection.

It is advisable that you become thoroughly acquainted with the breed prior to purchasing your puppy. Plan to attend a dog show or two in your area at which you can view purebred dogs of just about every breed at their best in the show ring. Even if you are not interested in purchasing a show-quality dog, you should be familiar with what the better specimens look like so that you will at least purchase a decent

representative of the breed for the money. You can learn a lot from observing the show dogs in action in the ring, or in a public place where their personalities can be clearly shown. The dog show catalogue is also a useful tool to put you in contact with the local kennels and breeders. Each dog that is entered in the show is listed along with the owner's name and address. If you spot a dog that you think is a particularly fine and pleasing specimen, contact the owners and arrange to visit their kennel to see the types and colors they are breeding and winning with at the shows. Exhibitors at the dog shows are usually more than delighted to talk to people interested in their dogs and the specific characteristics of their breed.

Once you've decided that the Cocker Spaniel is the breed for you because you appreciate its exceptional beauty, personality, and intelligence and you have a place in your home for a Cocker Spaniel, it is wise to thoroughly acquaint yourself by reading some background material on owning the breed. When you feel certain that this puppy will fit in with your family's way of life, it is time to start writing letters and making phone calls and appointments to see some puppies.

Trojan Pretty Patty, whelped in 1976 at the Trojan Kennels, was sired by Ch. Trojan Tagalong ex Ch. Trojan's Mavourneen. Patty is pictured here at seven weeks old.

Some words of caution: don't choose a kennel simply because it is near your home and don't buy the first "cute" puppy that romps around your legs or licks the end of your nose. All puppies are cute, and naturally some will appeal to you more than others. But don't let preferences sway your thinking. If you are buying your Cocker Spaniel to be strictly a family pet, preferences can be permissible. If you are looking for a top-quality puppy for the show ring, you must evaluate clearly, choose wisely, and make the best possible choice. Whichever one you choose, you will quickly learn to love your Cocker puppy. A careful selection, rather than a "love at first sight" choice will save a disappointment later on.

To get the broadest idea of what puppies are for sale and the going market prices, visit as many kennels as possible in your area and write to others farther away. With today's safe and rapid air flights on the major airlines, it is possible to purchase dogs from far-off places at nominal costs. While it is safest and wisest to first see the dog you are buying, there are enough reputable breeders and kennels to be found for you to take this step with a minimum of risk. In the long run, it can be well worth your while to obtain the exact dog or bloodline you desire.

It is customary for the purchaser to pay the shipping charges, and the airlines are most willing to supply flight information and prices upon request. Rental on the shipping crate, if the owner does not provide one for the dog, is nominal. While unfortunate incidents have occurred on the airlines in the transporting of animals by air, the major airlines are making improvements in safety measures and have reached the point of reasonable safety and cost. Barring unforeseen circumstances, the safe arrival of a dog you might buy can pretty much be assured if both seller and purchaser adhere to and follow up on even the most minute details from both ends.

Future champion Trojan's Erin, pictured at just nine weeks old, was bred by Trojan Kennels, Magnolia, Texas.

A trio of quality Cocker puppies, bred and owned by Ruth Muller, Centerport, Long Island, New York.

WHAT TO LOOK FOR IN A COCKER SPANIEL PUPPY

Anyone who has owned a Cocker Spaniel as a puppy will agree that the most fascinating aspect of raising the pup is to witness the complete and extraordinary metamorphosis that occurs during its first year of maturing. Your puppy will undergo a marked change in appearance, and during this period you must also be aware of the puppy's personality for there are certain qualities visible at this time that will generally make for a good adult dog. Of course, no one can guarantee nature and the best puppy does not always grow up to be a great dog. However, even the novice breeder can learn to look for certain specifics that will help him to choose a promising puppy.

Should you decide to purchase a six- to eight-week old puppy, you are in store for all the cute antics that little pup can dream up for you! At this age, the puppy should be well on its way to being weaned, wormed, and ready to go out into the world with its responsible new owner. It is better not to buy a puppy that is less than six weeks old; they simply are not ready to leave their mother or the security of the other puppies. By eight to twelve weeks of age you will be able to notice much about the behavior and ap-pearance of the dog. Cocker puppies, as they are recalled in our fondest childhood memories, are amazingly active and bouncy—as well they should be! The normal puppy should be alert, curious, and interested, especially about a stranger. However, if the puppy acts a little reserved or distant, don't necessarily construe these acts to be signs of fear or shyness. It might merely indicate that he hasn't quite made up his mind whether he likes you as yet! By the same token, though, he should not be openly fearful or terrified by a stranger—and especially should not show any fear of his owner!

In direct contrast, the puppy should not be ridiculously over-active, either. The puppy that frantically bounds around the room and is never still is not especially desirable. And beware of the "spinners"! Spinners are the puppies or dogs that have become neurotic from being kept in cramped quarters or in crates and behave in an emotionally unstable manner when let loose in adequate space. When let out they run in circles and seemingly "go wild." Puppies with this kind of traumatic background seldom ever regain full composure or adjust to the big outside world. The puppy which has had the proper exercise and appropriate living quarters will have a normal, though spirited, outlook on life and will do its utmost to win you over without having to go into a tailspin.

A bevy of beauties from Anita Roberts' Memoir Kennels in Novato, California.

If the general behavior and appearance of the dog thus far appeal to you, it is time for you to observe him more closely for additional physical requirements. First of all, you cannot expect to find in the Cocker puppy all the coat he will bear upon maturity. That will come with time and good food, and will be additionally enhanced by the many wonderful grooming aids which can be found in pet shops today. Needless to say, the healthy puppy's coat should have a nice shine to it, and the more dense at this age, the better the coat will be when the dog reaches adulthood.

Look for clear, dark, sparkling eyes that are free of discharge. From the time the puppy's eyes open until the puppy is about three months old the eyes might have a slight blue cast to them. The darker the blue, the better are the chances for a good dark eye in the adult dog.

It is important to check the bite. Even though the puppy will cut another complete set of teeth somewhere between four and seven months of age, there will already be some indication of how the final teeth will be positioned. Too much of an overshot bite (top teeth are positioned too far *over* the bottom teeth) or too much of an undershot jaw (bottom teeth are positioned too far out *under* the top teeth) is undesirable as they are considered faults by the breed Standard.

Puppies take anything and almost everything into their mouths to chew on, and a lot of diseases and infections start or are introduced in the mouth. Brown-stained teeth, for instance, may indicate the puppy has had a past case of distemper, and the teeth will remain that way. This fact must be reckoned with if you have a show puppy in mind. The puppy's breath

A typical quality Frandee puppy.

should be neither sour nor unpleasant. Bad breath can be a result of a poor mixture of food in the diet, or of eating meat of low quality, especially if fed raw. Some people say that the healthy puppy's breath should have a faint odor vaguely reminiscent of garlic. At any rate, a puppy should never be fed just table scraps, but should be raised on a well-balanced diet containing a good dry puppy chow and a good grade of fresh meat. Poor meat and too much cereal or fillers tend to make the puppy grow too fat. Puppies should be in good flesh, but not fat from the wrong kind of food.

Needless to say, the puppy should be clean. The breeder that shows a dirty puppy is one to steer away from. Look closely at the skin. Make sure it is not covered with insect bites or red, blotchy sores and dry scales. The vent area around the tail should not show evidences of diarrhea or inflammation. By the same token, the puppy's fur should not be matted with excretion or smell strongly of urine.

True enough, you can wipe dirty eyes, clean dirty ears, and give the puppy a bath when you get it home, but these things are all indications of how the puppy has been cared for during the important formative first months of its life, and can vitally influence its future health and development. There are many reputable breeders raising healthy puppies that have been reared in proper places and under the proper conditions in clean housing, so why take a chance on a series of veterinary bills and a questionable constitution?

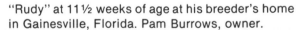

"Rudy" at 11½ weeks of age at his breeder's home in Gainesville, Florida. Pam Burrows, owner.

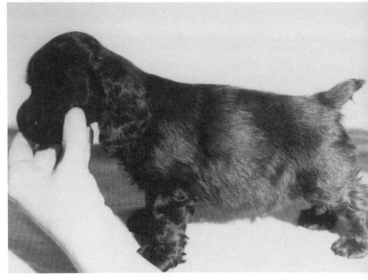

Future champion Memoir's Mannix, pictured at seven weeks of age, was sired by Ch. Hob Nob Hill's Tribute ex Memoir's New Raven Beautee. Mannix's breeder-owner is Anita Roberts, Memoir Kennels, Novato, California.

MALE OR FEMALE?

The choice of sex in your puppy is also something that must be given serious thought before you buy. For the pet owner, the sex that would best suit the family life you enjoy would be the paramount choice to consider. For the breeder or exhibitor there are other vital considerations. If you are looking for a stud to establish a kennel, it is essential that you select a dog with both testicles evident, even at a tender age, and verified by a veterinarian before the sale is finalized if there is any doubt.

The visibility of only one testicle, known as monorchidism, automatically disqualifies the dog from the show ring or from a breeding program, though monorchids are capable of siring. Additionally, it must be noted that monorchids frequently sire dogs with the same deficiency, and to introduce this into a bloodline knowingly is an unwritten sin in the fancy. Also, a monorchid can sire dogs that are completely sterile. Dogs with undescended testes called cryptorchids and are sterile.

An additional consideration in the male versus female decision for the private owners is that with males there might be the problem of leg-lifting and with females there is the inconvenience while they are in season. However, this need not be the problem it used to be—pet shops sell "pants" for both sexes, which help to control the situation.

THE PLANNED PARENTHOOD BEHIND YOUR PUPPY

Never be afraid to ask pertinent questions about the puppy, as well as questions about the sire and dam. Feel free to ask the breeder if you might see the dam; the purpose of your visit is to determine her general health and her appearance as a representative of the breed. Ask also to see the sire if the breeder is the owner. Ask what the puppy has been fed and should be fed after weaning. Ask to see the pedigree, and inquire if the litter or the individual puppies have been registered with the American Kennel Club, how many of the temporary and/or permanent inoculations the puppy has had, when and if the puppy has been wormed, and whether it has had any illness, disease, or infection.

You need not ask if the puppy is housebroken . . . it won't mean much. He may have gotten the idea as to where "the place" is where he lives now, but he will need new training to learn where "the place" is in his new home! And you can't really expect too much from puppies at this age anyway. Housebreaking is entirely up to the new owner. We know puppies always eliminate when they first awaken and sometimes dribble when they get excited. If friends and relatives are coming over to see the new puppy, make sure he is walked just before he greets them at the front door. This will help.

The normal time period for puppies (around three months of age) to eliminate is about every two or three hours. As the time draws near, either take the puppy out or indicate the newspaper for the same purpose. Housebreaking is never easy, but anticipation is about 90 per cent of solving the problem. The schools that offer to housebreak your dog are virtually useless. Here again the puppy will learn the "place" at the schoolhouse, but coming home he will need special training for the new location.

A reputable breeder will welcome any and all questions you might ask and will voluntarily offer additional information, if only to brag about the tedious and loving care he has given the litter. He will also sell a puppy on a 24-hour veterinary approval basis. This means you have a full day to get the puppy to a veterinarian of your choice to get his opinion on the general health of the puppy before you make a final decision. There should also be veterinary certificates and full particulars on the dates and types of inoculations the puppy has been given up to that time.

Ch. Baliwick Bricklayer and his 10-week-old daughter, Classic's Coming Attraction. Coming Attraction was bred by owner Lindy Hay who co-owns the sire with Michael Allen.

"You stay out of this" might be an appropriate title for this picture of two Cocker puppies.

PUPPIES AND WORMS

Let us give further attention to the unhappy and very unpleasant subject of worms. Generally speaking, most puppies—even those raised in clean quarters—come into contact with worms early in life. The worms can be passed down from the mother before birth or picked up during the puppies' first encounters with the earth or their kennel facilities. To say that you must not buy a puppy because of an infestation of worms is nonsensical. You might be passing up a fine animal that can be freed of worms in one short treatment, although a heavy infestation of worms of any kind in a young dog is dangerous and debilitating.

The extent of the infection can be readily determined by a veterinarian, and you might take his word as to whether the future health and conformation of the dog has been damaged. He can prescribe the dosage and supply the medication at this time and you will already have one of your problems solved.

VETERINARY INSPECTION

While your veterinarian is going over the puppy you have selected to purchase, you might just as well ask him for his opinion of it as a breed as well as the facts about its general health. While few veterinarians can claim to be breed-conformation experts, they usually have a good eye for a worthy specimen and can advise you where to go for further information. Perhaps your veterinarian could also recommend other breeders if you should want another opinion. The veterinarian can point out structural faults or organic problems that affect all breeds and can usually judge whether an animal has been abused or mishandled and whether it is oversized or undersized.

Out for a stroll—Wendy Ernst with a litter of parti-colors, all owned by Gay Ernst, BeGay Cockers, East Hampton, New York.

A charming trio of black and tan Cockers, pictured at five months of age, include from left to right Shadowdance Goodness Gracious, Shadowdance Goodness Sake and Shadowdance Thank Goodness. They were sired by Ch. Chess King's Board Boss ex Ch. Dur Bet's Surely Goodness, C.D.X. Photographed for owner Jean Barney of Scottsdale, Arizona, by William Kohler.

I would like to emphasize here that it is only through this type of close cooperation between owners and veterinarians that we can expect to reap the harvest of modern research in the veterinary field.

Most reliable veterinarians are more than eager to learn about various breeds of purebred dogs, and we in turn must acknowledge and apply what they have proved through experience and research in their field. We can buy and breed the best dog in the world, but when disease strikes we are only as safe as our veterinarian is capable—so let's keep them informed breed by breed, and dog by dog. The veterinarian can mean the difference between life and death!

THE CONDITIONS OF SALE

While it is customary to pay for the puppy before you take it away with you, you should be able to give the breeder a deposit if there is any doubt about the puppy's health. You might also (depending on local laws) postdate a check to cover the 24-hour veterinary approval. If you decide to take the puppy, the breeder is required to supply you with a pedigree, along with the puppy's registration papers. He is also obliged to supply you with complete information about the inoculations and American Kennel Club instructions on how to transfer ownership of the puppy to your name.

Puppy love! Owners of all three are Mr. and Mrs. Robert Vick of Suisun, California.

Some breeders will offer buyers time payment plans for convenience if the price on a show dog is very high or if deferred payments are the only way you can purchase the dog. However, any such terms must be worked out between buyer and breeder and should be put in writing to avoid later complications.

You will find most breeders cooperative if they believe you are sincere in your love for the puppy and that you will give it the proper home and the show ring career it deserves (if it is sold as a show quality specimen of the breed). Remember, when buying a show dog, it is impossible to guarantee nature. A breeder can only tell you what he *believes* will develop into a show dog . . . so be sure your breeder is an honest one.

Jenny and Caleb are pictured at eight and a half weeks of age in July 1977. Owned by Mrs. Nancy L. Ray of Brooks, Oregon.

Also, if you purchase a show prospect and promise to show the dog, you definitely should show it! It is a waste to have a beautiful dog that deserves recognition in the show ring sitting at home as a family pet, and it is unfair to the breeder. This is especially true if the breeder offered you a reduced price because of the advertising his kennel and bloodlines would receive by your showing the dog in the ring. If you want a pet, buy a pet. Be honest about it, and let the breeder decide on this basis which is the best dog for you. Your conscience will be clear and you'll both be doing a real service to the breed.

Four-week-old silver puppy dog, Gladyan Moonraker.

BUYING A SHOW PUPPY

If you are positive about breeding and showing your Cocker, make this point clear so that the breeder will sell you the best possible puppy. If you are dealing with an established kennel, you will have to rely partially, if not entirely, on their choice, since they know their bloodlines and what they can expect from the breeding. They know how their stock develops, and it would be foolish of them to sell you a puppy that could not stand up as a show specimen representing their stock in the ring.

However, you must also realize that the breeder may be keeping the best puppy in the litter to show and breed himself. If this is the case, you might be wise to select the best puppy of the opposite sex so that the dogs will not be competing against one another in the show rings for their championship title.

THE PURCHASE PRICE

Prices vary on all puppies, of course, but a good show prospect at six weeks to six months of age will usually sell for several hundred dollars. If the puppy is really outstanding, and the pedigree and parentage is also outstanding, the price will be even higher. Honest breeders, however, will all quote around the same figure, so price should not be a strong deciding factor in your choice. If you have any questions as to the current price range, a few telephone calls to different kennels will give you a good average. Reputable breeders will usually stand behind the health of their puppies should something drastically wrong develop, such as hip dysplasia, etc. Their obligation to make an adjustment or replacement is usually honored. However, this must be agreed to in writing at the time of the purchase.

Am., Can. Ch. Abbi's Adored Mister AOK is pictured at 10 months of age with his breeder-owner Mrs. Harry Reno, Abbi's Cockers, Port Huron, Michigan.

THE COST OF BUYING ADULT STOCK

Prices for adult dogs fluctuate greatly. Some grown dogs are offered free of charge to good homes; others are put with owners on breeders' terms. But don't count on getting a "bargain" if it doesn't cost you anything! Good dogs are always in demand, and worthy studs or brood bitches are expensive. Prices for them can easily go up into the four-figure range. Take an expert with you if you intend to make this sort of investment. Just make sure the "expert" is free of professional jealousy and will offer an unprejudiced opinion. If you are reasonably familiar with the Standard, and get the expert's opinion, you can usually come to a proper decision.

Two little Abbi's Cocker Spaniel puppies sired by American, Canadian, and Bermudian Ch. Abbi's Secret Service ex Abbi's Hiyouall are from a litter bred in 1980 by Mrs. Harry Reno, Port Huron, Michigan.

A handsome trio of two littermates with their dam, owned and bred by Mrs. Harry Reno, Abbi's Cockers, Port Huron, Michigan. Am., Can. Ch. Abbi's Adored Mister AOK; Am., Can. Ch. Darji's Abigail Lee; and Can. Ch. Abbi's Adorable Crumpet.

Juban's By Jingo is pictured at four and a half months of age. Owned by Kathy and Gary Nishi and Ann M. Smith.

Darling three-month-old puppy, Trojan's Buttons, owned by Lloyd Alton and Bill Gorodner of Ridgewood, New Jersey. Alice Kaplan was the breeder of this red and white bitch.

Heads up! These tri-color puppies, pictured at eight weeks of age, are owned by Gladys Von Horn of Vancouver, Washington.

Memoir's Jay R, owned by Anita Roberts of Novato, California.

Shadowridge Parkwood Morgan poses for the camera at just three and a half months of age. This darling young hopeful was bred by Cheryl McNeil and Frances Watson and is owned by Dr. McNeil of Pensacola, Florida. The sire was Shadowridge Go For Broke ex Ch. Pett's Fanciful.

One of the old-time winners, Ch. Knebworth Gloriana, whelped February 27, 1923. Gloriana started her show career at just over a year old. She whelped a litter sired by Ch. Knebworth Cyclone, a Best in Show dog. The litter included Ch. Knebworth Buddie. Gloriana was a Group winner as well.

CHAPTER EIGHT

Eleven-and-a-half-week-old Justin on his way to the grooming table. Even at this tender age Justin seems to know what is in store for a longhaired show dog. Owner Pam Burrows, Gainsville, Florida.

Grooming Your Cocker Spaniel

Anyone who admires the beautiful coats on today's Cocker Spaniels must surely realize that a lot of grooming time is responsible for those flowing coats. In fact, anyone who considers owning a Cocker Spaniel must also consider whether they will have the time to properly groom their dog to keep it looking like a respectable specimen of the breed.

In addition to the time required there is a certain "knack" to grooming properly so that the dog always appears to be in full bloom. The moment a grooming chapter was planned for this book it became evident that an expert would be required to explain the true and proper way to present a dog, and my first thought, of course, was of the well-known Cocker man, Bill Gorodner. Bill has been "in Cockers" for years and there is no denying that his dogs have always been represented in the ring in magnificent coat and condition.

In our discussion of the basics required for this grooming chapter, Bill had the following to say:

"Grooming a Cocker Spaniel is more than using clippers, scissors, and brushes. One works as an illusionist to help mold the dog at hand into what the Standard calls for."

Bill commented on the fact that Cockers, being the smallest of all the sporting dogs, must be groomed to perfection to show off the compact body, the long neck, and clean shoulders. Proper grooming can make the most of a good front, showing the feet turning neither in nor out and displaying a rear end with well bent stifles and a proper tail set.

The unique American Cocker Spaniel head is a thing of beauty when correctly shaped to show the well developed skull, low ear set, the chiselling under the eyes, well-defined stop, and the deep soft muzzle. Who would want to distract from those dark expressive eyes!

The coat should enhance the dog's over-all picture of beauty and purpose with the coat flat to slightly wavy against its sturdy body.

GROOMING EQUIPMENT

1. A clipper, such as the Oster Azoras, with #10, #15, #8½, and #5/8 inch blades
2. A pinbrush
3. A wire slicker brush
4. A 7½ inch steel comb
5. A flea comb, or a furrier's mink comb
6. Single-edge thinning shears
7. Large, heavy, straight shears (the kind especially designed for scissoring Poodles)
8. A hand or floor blow dryer
9. A good shampoo
10. Anti-static spray
11. An Oliver rake
12. Rounded shears
13. Nail clipper

If the names of these utensils sound strange to the newcomer to dog grooming, simply consult with pet shop owners who sell dog supplies and they will not only have them for sale but can advise you on the best to buy and how to care for them for ultimate satisfaction and wear.

Full show coat in the true sense of the word is exemplified by Mrs. Harry Reno's gorgeous Am., Can. Ch. Abbi's Adored Mister AOK, ready for the show ring.

BATHING YOUR COCKER SPANIEL

While a gentle brushing a few times a week will help keep the mats out of the coat, every once in awhile it will be necessary to groom your dog a little more thoroughly. This will mean giving the dog a bath as well.

Before actually putting the dog in the tub, give the dog a thorough brushing. This will help get rid of most of the surface dirt and will prevent the shampoo from gathering in the mats or tangles if they are left in the coat. It will be a great help if you teach your dog to lie on his side and on his back while you groom so that you can reach all areas of the body. Tangles have a way of forming under the elbows and in the groin, and they will be much easier to get at if the dog is relaxed and you are able to move its legs while you groom.

The secret of success is to get your dog to enjoy the grooming time from an early age. If he thinks you are happy "doting" on him, he will be more apt to relax and make it easy for you to accomplish what you set out to do. If your dog pulls away or whimpers or just plain fights you every minute, perhaps you are being too rough or holding on to him too tightly. Be gentle, but be firm. Talk to the dog while you work. Keep food or other distractions at a minimum, and don't groom for too long a time while you are learning or when the dog is very young. A tidbit as a reward when you are through can be an incentive at times also. It just takes patience and practice!

After you have removed all the tangles from the coat, you might want to place cotton in the dog's ears, or perhaps a drop of mineral oil in the eyes to prevent the eyes from tearing. Most shampoos sold today do not burn so this may not be necessary.

Place the dog in a tub of very warm—but not hot—water high enough to cover the legs. Use a cup or small bowl to pour the water over the entire body until the entire coat is thoroughly saturated. Save the head until last so the dog gets used to the feel of the water, and so the younger dogs do not panic when they first get a little water in their eyes. Hold the head back by placing your hand under the chin and pour the water down off the back of the head and down the front of the throat and chest from under the mouth.

Once the dog is thoroughly soaked, give two complete soapings and two or three complete rinsings. The complete rinsings cannot be emphasized enough! Any shampoo left in the coat will make it sticky or gummy and will tend to dry the skin with a sort of dandruff condition resulting. These white flakes do not add to your dog's appearance! After the thorough rinsings let the dog "drip dry" for a few minutes, gently squeezing the excess water out of the coat with your hands before placing a large turkish, or absorbent towel over it.

Some groomers like to use this drip dry time to cut the toenails. If the nails are cut too short and bleed, the blood does not soil the coat since the water can be run over the feet while they are still in the tub. Once the dog is used to having his nails cut, such measures may not be necessary. But if they do bleed, use a touch of vaseline on wet cotton pressed to the edge of the nail. This should stop the bleeding. Some prefer to use the styptic pencils that men use when they cut themselves while shaving.

Once the drip dry process has been completed in the tub, lift the dog in a towel out of the tub and onto a grooming table. Make sure the table is clean and free of any powder or discarded hair. The same applies to your brushes and combs. They should be cleaned before being used on the freshly bathed dog. But before you begin your drying process, pat the dog as dry as possible with the towels. *Never* rub a Cocker's coat or the friction will cause mats to form.

While you are patting the dog dry, turn on your dryer so that the air has a chance to warm up and you don't suddenly hit the dog with a blast of cold air when he is just out of a warm tub. When you are ready to begin grooming, use the slicker brush and work it gently in the area where the warm air is hitting the coat. Also, take care not to groom constantly in one spot so that the dog is finished in one place and still wet over the rest of the body. Keep the pattern of air and grooming moving over the entire body in a slow and relaxed manner.

If the dog gets restless you might be grooming too roughly or too long in one spot, and if the dog pants heavily, the air might be too hot. Offer a little drink of water if you see that the dog is getting overheated. Also, give him a pat on the head or a good scratch behind the ears now and then along with a kind word to let him know you do not consider this a torture treatment but rather your kind attention to make him look his very best. Grooming can be a traumatic experience for both of you or it can be a time of great satisfaction and benefit for both.

Once the dog is dry all over, with each hair seemingly hanging independent of the other and looking full, soft, and shiny, it is time to consider the clipping and trimming.

CLIPPING AND TRIMMING YOUR DOG

Let us state right at the beginning that dog grooming is an art. To the beginner, it is essential to learn how to groom by reading everything you can get your hands on about it, and by first watching someone else do it and listening to their advice about the best methods. If they can show you on your own dog, so much the better. Practice will be necessary if you are to become proficient. And if you wish to show your dog, it will take even longer to perfect your technique to the point where your dog will look as professionally groomed as those competing in the ring with you. There is no reason why (with the proper equipment and plenty of practice) you cannot keep your Cocker Spaniel looking well-groomed and in proper pattern for you to be satisfied and proud of your own work.

Once you have mastered the clipping and trimming requirements, you may wish to improve on your dog's outline by grooming him and shaping him to more correctly adhere to the Standard. Before beginning the clipping and trimming, put your hands on the dog. Go over the entire dog. Make a mental picture in your mind of the photograph which often accompanies the Standard, or compare the dog with photographs you have seen of the top show dogs. If your dog is inclined to be long in body perhaps you might shape the feathering on the hind legs to change the image slightly. True, this shaping requires an expert eye but it can make a difference in the general picture you wish to present to make your dog a true representative of the breed.

GROOMING THE HEAD

To achieve the true alert and expressive look of the Cocker Spaniel, you will need to use the #10 blade on the clippers. The entire head piece is essential to this look and you can start by clearing the throat. Lift the ears up with one hand, and starting at the point under the ear, shave slowly down against the grain toward the cheek and lips with a feather-light motion, holding the blade of the clipper away from the muzzle.

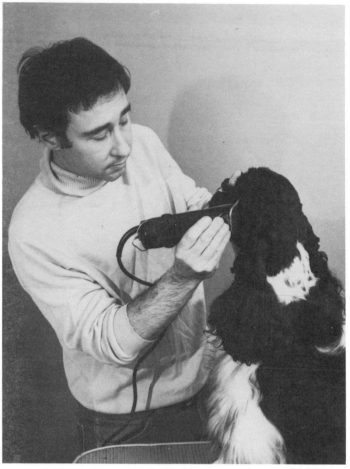

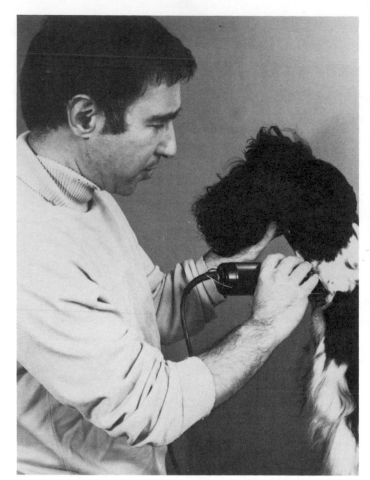

1. To clean up the face and bring out the chizzling under the eyes, use the clipper against the grain of the fur and out away from the eyes.

2. Clip throat down the breastbone, with clipper strokes pointing toward the table.

3. Blend the hair on the skull with single-edged thinning shears.

4. To continue your neat line, thin hair on the back of neck with single-edged thinning shears.

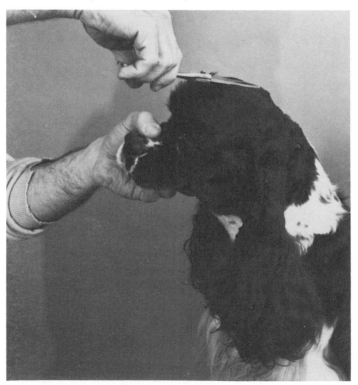

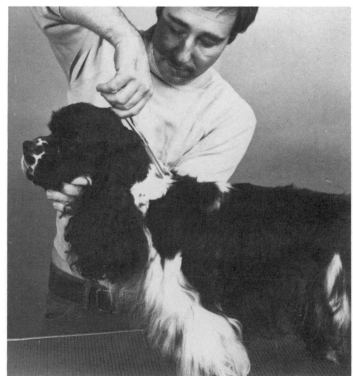

Under the chin you will also go against the grain, working from the chin downward all around, evening the lip line and carefully trimming away all the hair from the dog's flews. Cut all the way down to the breast bone, using the dog's ears as a guide. Also trim the tops of the ears about a quarter of the way down the ear leather to show a clean well-set ear.

Next, with the #15 blade, very carefully trim away under the eye. Make sure the blade is directed toward the nose when doing this and not pointed toward the eye. Use the #5/8 inch blade to trim between the eyes to show the correct degree of stop. If the dog is inclined to be a little shy in stop, use the thinning shears. The more hair left in a deficient stop, the more impression of depth you will create.

Using the #8½ blade, trim the back part of the skull to where the neck crests. Lightly trim the sides of the neck also and under the dog's tail. So much for the clippers . . .

THE COMBING

Using the flea or mink comb, carefully comb through the hair on the back. The idea is to get the hair to lie as flat as possible to show the proper topline. Next, use the thinning shears on the sides of the neck. Trim off any long hairs until

the area looks smooth and clean. Very carefully thin out the hair on the tail also. Be sure to leave a bit of fullness in front of the tail to show the proper set.

With the steel comb and anti-static spray lightly cover the entire dog with a fine mist of the spray and comb through until dry. Comb out the hair on the feet between the toes, clip the nails if you haven't already done so, and with the rounded shears shape the feet. They should be rounded to resemble powder puffs. Not pancakes, mind you, but full powder puffs. And cut out the hair between the toes on the under side of the foot.

With the thinning shears thin out the belly coat so that it lies against the body. Spray once again with the anti-static spray and brush through the coat, paying particular attention to the ears.

Right about now it is time to take a step backward and get an idea of the over-all picture of the dog. Use the heavy shears to get rid of any stray hairs which might distract from that perfect silhouette!

We can all be grateful to Bill Gorodner for making good grooming seem as easy as it does when he explains it. Just be sure to remember his two key words to success . . . patience and practice!

5. Because the hair on the ears is long it requires frequent grooming with a pin brush. Check also for tangles and mats which might also require a comb to remove all the tangled hair.

6. When brushing ears, a forward motion with the pin brush will prevent the ear fur from getting mixed in with the fur on the body.

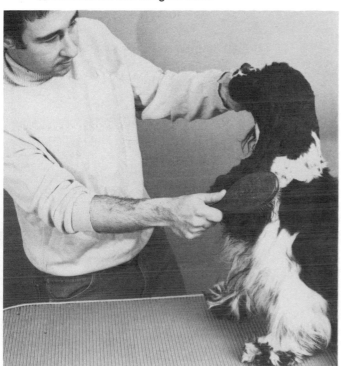

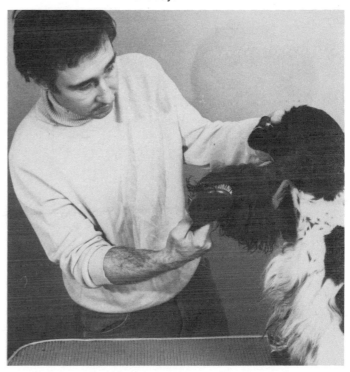

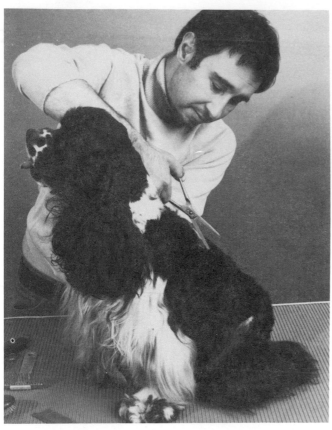

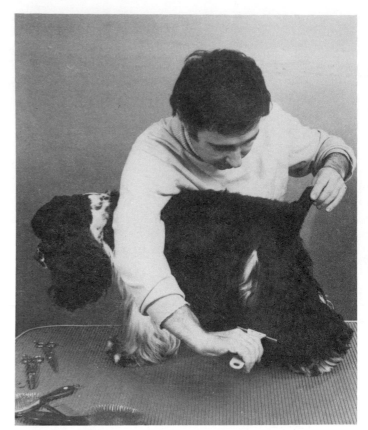

7. After the head and back of the neck are shaped and thinned, use only thinning shears to trim the back. On reds and buff-colored Cockers a "skip-stone" may be substituted for thinning shears.

8. With gentle strokes and your wire rake, go over the entire coat, stopping when you hit a tangle or mat. Pull the mat apart with your fingers and then gently brush through with the rake until all the hair blends in.

9. Make sure all four legs are brushed out completely before starting to shape the feet.

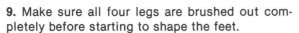

10. All four feet should be evenly rounded, always keeping in mind that they should resemble "puffs" not "pancakes."

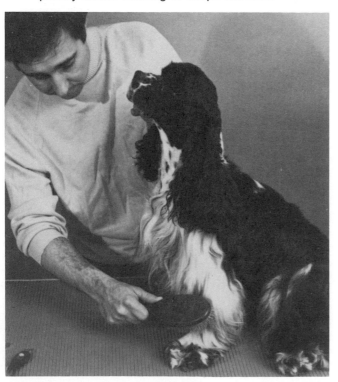

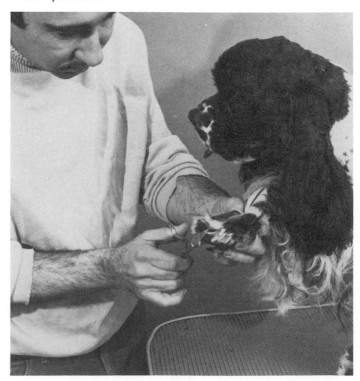

11. After shaping the feet rebrush hair on legs and feet to see that all the hair blends in together. Take a step backward to check the overall blending and silhouette that you are trying to attain.

12. Using your thinning shears, thin out the hair on the tail very carefully. Remember to leave "fill" in front of the tail so that you do not create a "low" tail set. The topline should appear to be a straight line from the withers to the end of the tail.

GROOMING SHOPS

While grooming and clipping the Cocker Spaniel may become a relatively simple matter after practice, there may be those who do not feel they could do it to their satisfaction or who do not wish to do it themselves at all. For those who do not enjoy grooming their dogs, there is an alternative.

Grooming shops can be located in the yellow pages of the telephone book and a schedule can be set up with one of them to have your Cocker groomed on a regular basis. Costs vary from area to area, and shop to shop, so when you call to make your first appointment, make sure you ask the price once you have told them exactly what you wish to have done. Some shops will pick up and deliver, but there is usually an additional charge for this. Besides, it is best to go directly to

the shop when making your first appointment so that you can check to see if the shop and groomers are clean, whether they use the best equipment, and if the dogs are treated kindly by the personnel.

Some grooming parlors will want to tranquilize a dog that "acts up" or is excessively fearful or aggressive. *Make sure you explain that you do not want this for your dog*, and take it elsewhere if they choose not to handle your dog without this unnecessary precaution.

If you are in doubt about the price of the services, make a few telephone calls or visits to various shops before making your decision. You will find that most shops in your area are usually charging the same fees for the same service and are willing to discuss them with you. Remember, word of mouth is their best advertising and they will want to please both you and your dog.

The exquisite Merribark's Brown and Fancy pictured with breeder Elane Poole of the Merribark Kennels. Brown and Fancy later went to live with Alice Swiderski. Henry Schley photograph.

CHAPTER NINE

The Dog Show World

Gladyan Kharisma, seven-month-old puppy bitch, took Best Puppy in Match under judge Mrs. Frank Wood. "Carrie" also won points as Winners Bitch when she was just six months and five days old. Jerry Moon is handling for owner Gladys Von Horn.

Let us assume that after a few months of tender loving care, you realize your dog is developing beyond your wildest expectations and that the dog you selected is very definitely a show dog! Of course, every owner is prejudiced. But if you are sincerely interested in going to dog shows with your dog and making a champion of him, now is the time to start casting a critical eye on him from a judge's point of view.

There is no such thing as a perfect dog. Every dog has some faults, perhaps even a few serious ones. The best way to appraise your dog's degree of perfection is to compare him with the Standard for the breed, or before a judge in a show ring.

MATCH SHOWS

For the beginner there are "mock" shows, called match shows, where you and your dog go through many of the procedures of a regular dog show, but do not gain points toward championship. These shows are usually held by kennel clubs, annually or semiannually, and much ring poise and experience can be gained there. The age limit is usually reduced to two months at match shows to give puppies four months of training before they compete at the regular shows when they reach six months of age. Classes range from two to four months, four to six months, six to nine months, and nine to

twelve months. Puppies compete with others of their own age for comparative purposes. Many breeders evaluate their litters in this manner, choosing which is the most outgoing, which is the most poised, the best showman, etc.

For those seriously interested in showing their dogs to full championship, these match shows provide important experience for both the dog and the owner. Class categories may vary slightly, according to number of entries, but basically include all the classes that are included at a regular point show. There is a nominal entry fee and, of course, ribbons and usually trophies are given for your efforts as well. Unlike the point shows, entries can be made on the day of the show right on the show grounds. They are unbenched and provide an informal, usually congenial atmosphere for the amateur, which helps to make the ordeal of one's first adventure in the show ring a little less nerve-wracking.

POINT SHOWS

It is not possible to show a puppy at an American Kennel Club sanctioned point show before the age of six months. When your dog reaches this eligible age, your local kennel club can provide you with the names and addresses of the show-giving superintendents in your area who will be staging the club's dog show for them, and where you must write for an entry form.

The forms are mailed in a pamphlet called a premium list. This also includes the names of the judges for each breed, a list of the prizes and trophies, the name and address of the show-giving club and where the show will be held, as well as rules and regulations set up by the American Kennel Club which must be abided by if you are to enter.

A booklet containing the complete set of show rules and regulations may be obtained by writing to the American Kennel Club, Inc., 51 Madison Avenue, New York, N.Y., 10010.

When you write to the dog show superintendent, request not only your premium list for this particular show, but ask that your name be added to their mailing list so that you will automatically receive all premium lists in the future. List your breed or breeds and they will see to it that you receive premium lists for specialty shows as well.

Unlike the match shows where your dog will be judged on ring behavior, at the point shows he will be judged on conformation to the breed Standard. In addition to being at least six months of age (on the day of the show) he must be purebred for a point show. This means he and both of his parents are registered with the American Kennel Club. There must be no alterations or falsifications regarding his appearance. Females cannot have been spayed and males must have both testicles in evidence. No dyes or powders may be used to enhance the appearance,

and any lameness or deformity or major deviation from the Standard for the breed constitutes a disqualification.

With all these things in mind, groom your dog to the best of your ability in the specified area for this purpose in the show hall and *exercise your dog before taking him into the ring!* Too many Cocker Spaniel owners are guilty of making their dogs remain on their crates so they do not get dirty, and the first thing the animals do when they start to show is stop to empty themselves. There is no excuse for this. All it takes is a walk *before* grooming. If your dog is clean, well groomed, *empty*, and leash trained you should be able to enter the show ring with confidence and pride of ownership, ready for an appraisal of your dog by the judge.

The presiding judge on that day will allow each and every dog a certain amount of time and consideration before making his decisions. It is never permissible to consult the judge regarding either your dog or his decision while you are in the ring. An exhibitor never speaks unless spoken to, and then only to answer such questions as the judge may ask—the age of the dog, the dog's bite, or to ask you to move your dog around the ring once again.

However, before you reach the point where you are actually in the ring awaiting the final decisions of the judge, you will have had to decide in which of the five classes in each sex your dog should compete.

Best Stud Dog and Best Brood Bitch in Show at the 1975 West Coast Cocker Spaniel Club Specialty show were Ch. Kane Venture The Cat, owned by Diana Kane, and Am., Mex. Ch. Frandee's Susan, owned by Frank and Dee Dee Wood. Their nine-and-a-half-month-old sons are Ch. Frandee's Free N' Easy (tri), Mex. Ch. Frandee's Fat Cat (b/w) and Ch. Frandee's Tycoon (r/w). The judge is Dr. Alvin Grossman.

Am., Can. Ch. Ramrod Real McCoy pictured winning the Stud Dog Class at the 1976 Washington State Cocker Spaniel Club Specialty under breeder-judge Mrs. Cameron Covey. McCoy is pictured winning with his two champion daughters, Am., Can. Ch. Westland's Princess Desiree, tri-color bitch, and Am., Can. Ch. Westland's Princess Elizabeth, red and white bitch. These littermates were bred by Georgia Westland. McCoy is owned by Robert and Helen Johnston, Roblen Kennels, Central Point, Oregon.

POINT SHOW CLASSES

The regular classes of the A.K.C. are: PUP-PY, NOVICE, BRED-BY-EXHIBITOR, AMERICAN-BRED, OPEN; if your dog is undefeated in any of the regular classes (divided by sex) in which it is entered, he or she is *required* to enter the Winner's Class. If your dog is placed second in the class to the dog which won Winner's Dog or Winner's Bitch, hold the dog or bitch in readiness as the judge must consider it for Reserve Winners.

PUPPY CLASSES shall be for dogs which are six months of age and over but under twelve months, which were whelped in the U.S.A. or Canada, and which are not champions. Classes are often divided 6 and (under) 9, and 9 and (under) 12 months. The age of a dog shall be calculated up to and inclusive of the first day of a show. For example, a dog whelped on January 1st is eligible to compete in a puppy class on July 1st, and may continue to compete up to and including December 31st of the same year, but is not eligible to compete January 1st of the following year.

THE NOVICE CLASS shall be for dogs six months of age or over, whelped in the U.S.A. or Canada which have not, prior to the closing entries, won three first prizes in the Novice Class,

a first prize in Bred-by-Exhibitor, American-bred or Open Class, nor one or more points toward a championship title.

THE BRED-BY-EXHIBITOR CLASS shall be for dogs whelped in the U.S.A. which are six months of age and over, which are not champions and which are owned wholly or in part by the person or by the spouse of the person who was the breeder or one of the breeders of record. Dogs entered in the BBE Class must be handled by an owner or by a member of the immediate family of an owner, i.e., the husband, wife, father, mother, son, daughter, brother, and sister.

THE AMERICAN-BRED CLASS is for all dogs (except champions) six months of age or over, whelped in the U.S.A. by reason of a mating that took place in the U.S.A.

THE OPEN CLASS is for any dog six months of age or over, except in a member specialty club show held for only American-bred dogs, in which case the class is for American-bred dogs only.

WINNERS DOG and WINNERS BITCH: After the above male classes have been judged, the first-place winners are then *required* to compete in the ring. The dog judged "Winners Dog" is awarded the points toward his championship title.

RESERVE WINNERS are selected immediately after the Winners Dog. In case of a disqualification of a win by the A.K.C., the Reserve Dog moves up to "Winners" and receives the points. After all male classes are judged, the bitch classes are called.

BEST OF BREED OR BEST OF VARIETY COMPETITION is limited to Champions of Record or dogs (with newly acquired points, for a 90-day period prior to A.K.C. confirmation) which have completed championship requirements, and Winners Dog and Winners Bitch (or the dog awarded Winners if only one Winners prize has been awarded), together with any undefeated dogs which have been shown only in non-regular classes; all compete for Best of Breed or Best of Variety (if the breed is divided by size, color, texture, or length of coat hair, etc.).

BEST OF WINNERS: If the WD or WB earns BOB or BOV, it automatically becomes BOW; otherwise they will be judged together for BOW (following BOB or BOV judging).

BEST OF OPPOSITE SEX is selected from the remaining dogs of the opposite sex to Best of Breed or Best of Variety.

OTHER CLASSES may be approved by the A.K.C.: STUD DOGS, BROOD BITCHES, BRACE CLASS, TEAM CLASS; classes consisting of local dogs and bitches may also be included in a show if approved by the A.K.C. (special rules are included in the A.K.C. Rule Book).

The MISCELLANEOUS CLASS shall be for purebred dogs of such breeds as may be designated by the A.K.C. No dog shall be eligible for entry in this class unless the owner has been granted an Indefinite Listing Privilege (ILP) and unless the ILP number is given on the entry form. Application for an ILP shall be made on a form provided by the A.K.C. and when submitted must be accompanied by a fee set by the Board of Directors.

All Miscellaneous breeds shall be shown together in a single class except that the class may be divided by sex if so specified in the premium list. There shall be *no* further competition for dogs entered in this class. Ribbons for 1st, 2nd, 3rd, and 4th shall be Rose, Brown, Light Green and Gray, respectively.

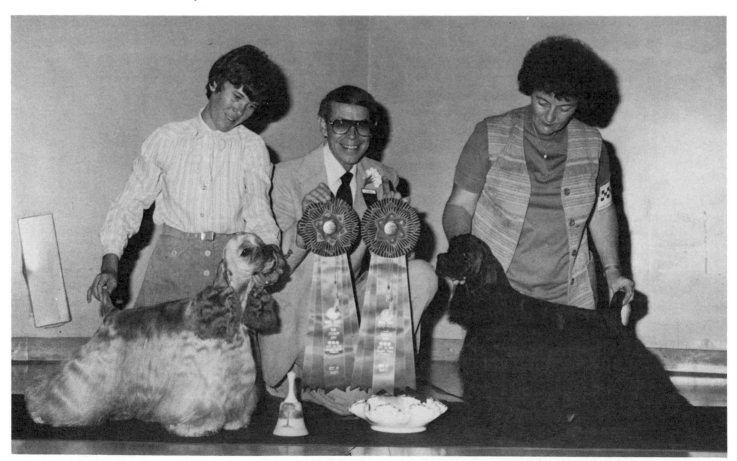

At the Washington State Cocker Spaniel Club Specialty in 1980 under judge George Koskey were Ch. Flairhaven's Sire Duffington and his sire Ch. Bobwin's Sir Ashley. "Duffy" was Best of Variety ASCOB and Ashley was Best of Variety Black. Owned by Mrs. Winnie Vick, Bobwin Acres, Suisun, California.

Ch. Dreamridge Dandiman, Best in Show winner at the 1975 American Spaniel Club show. He is pictured here winning Best of Breed at the Cocker Spaniel Club of Central Ohio show under judge Mark Davis. Owned by Tom O'Neal, Dreamridge Kennels, Woodstock, Illinois.

OBEDIENCE TRIALS

Some shows also offer Obedience Trials, which are considered as separate events. They give the dogs a chance to compete and score on performing a prescribed set of exercises intended to display their training in doing useful work.

There are three obedience titles for which they may compete: First, the Companion Dog or C.D. title; second, the Companion Dog Excellent or C.D.X.; and third, the Utility Dog or U.D. Detailed information on these degrees is contained in a booklet entitled *Official Obedience Regulations* and may be obtained by writing to the American Kennel Club.

JUNIOR SHOWMANSHIP

Junior Showmanship competition is for boys and girls in different age groups handling their own dogs or ones owned by their immediate family. There are four divisions: Novice A (10 to 12-year-olds) and Novice B (13 to 16-year-olds) for competitors with no previous Junior Showmanship wins, Open A (10 to 12-year-olds) and

Open B (13 to 16-year-olds) for competitors with one or more JS awards.

As Junior Showmanship at the dog shows increased in popularity, certain changes and improvements had to be made. As of April 1, 1971, the American Kennel Club issued a new booklet containing the Regulations for Junior Showmanship which may be obtained by writing to the A.K.C. at 51 Madison Avenue, New York, N.Y. 10010.

DOG SHOW PHOTOGRAPHERS

Every show has at least one official photographer who will be more than happy to take a photograph of your dog with the judge, ribbons, and trophies, along with you or your handler. These make marvelous remembrances of your top show wins and are frequently framed along with the ribbons for display purposes. Photographers can be paged at the show over the public address system, if you wish to obtain this service. Prices vary, but you will probably find it costs little to capture these happy moments, and the photos can always be used in the various dog magazines to advertise your dog's wins.

Ch. Juban's Jorgey Girl, bred and owned by Ann and Julian Smith, winning at the April 1980 Combined Specialties of Atlanta show.

TWO TYPES OF DOG SHOWS

There are two types of dog shows licensed by the American Kennel Club. One is the all-breed show which includes classes for all the recognized breeds, and groups of breeds; i.e., all terriers, all toys, etc. Then there are the specialty shows for one particular breed which also offer championship points.

BENCHED OR UNBENCHED DOG SHOWS

The show-giving clubs determine, usually on the basis of what facilities are offered by their chosen show site, whether their show will be benched or unbenched. A benched show is one where the dog show superintendent supplies benches (cages for toy dogs). Each bench is numbered and its corresponding number appears on your entry identification slip which is sent to you prior to the show date. The number also appears in the show catalogue. Upon entering the show you should take your dog to the bench where he should remain until it is time to groom him before entering the ring to be judged. After judging, he must be returned to the bench until the official time of dismissal from the show. At an unbenched show the club makes no provision whatsoever for your dog other than an enormous tent (if an outdoor show) or an area in a show hall where all crates and grooming equipment must be kept.

Benched or unbenched, the moment you enter the show grounds you are expected to look after your dog and have it under complete control at all times. This means short leads in crowded aisles or getting out of cars. In the case of a benched show, a "bench chain" is needed. It should allow the dog to move around, but not get down off the bench. It is also not considered "cute" to have small tots leading enormous dogs around a dog show where they might be dragged into the middle of a dog fight.

IF YOUR DOG WINS A CLASS

Study the classes to make certain your dog is entered in a proper class for his or her qualifications. If your dog wins his class, the rule states: *You are required* to enter classes for Winners, Best of Breed and Best of Winners (no additional entry fees). The rule states, "No eligible dogs may be withheld from competition." It is not mandatory that you stay for group judging. *If your dog wins a group,* however, *you must stay for Best In Show competition.*

Ch. Frandee's Board Broad finished with a four-point major under judge Paul C. Hipsley, Sr., at the West Coast Cocker Spaniel Club show. This was her fifth major. Bred and owned by Dee Dee and Frank Wood, she was shown to her championship by Dee Dee in June 1980.

THE PRIZE RIBBONS AND WHAT THEY STAND FOR

No matter how many entries there are in each class at a dog show, if you place first through fourth position you will receive a ribbon. These ribbons commemorate your win and can be impressive when collected and displayed to prospective buyers when and if you have puppies for sale, or if you intend to use your dog at public stud.

All ribbons from the American Kennel Club licensed dog shows will bear the American Kennel Club seal, the name of the show, the date and the placement. In the classes the colors are blue for first, red for second, yellow for third and white for fourth. Winners Dog or Winners Bitch ribbons are purple, while Reserve Dog and Reserve Bitch ribbons are purple-and-white. Best of Winners ribbons are blue-and-white; Best of Breed, purple-and-gold; and Best of Opposite Sex ribbons are red-and-white.

In the six groups, first prize is a blue rosette or ribbon, second placement is red, third yellow and fourth white. The Best In Show rosette is either red, white and blue or incorporates the colors used in the show-giving club's emblem.

Ch. Pett's Pampered Pearl won a five-point major at a Kentucky Specialty. Ron Fabis handled for owner Mrs. Virginia H. Kinnane, N. Swansea, Massachusetts. Ken Miller, judge.

QUALIFYING FOR CHAMPIONSHIP

Championship points are given for Winners Dog and Winners Bitch in accordance with a scale of points established by the American Kennel Club based on the popularity of the breed in entries, and the number of dogs competing in the classes. This scale of points varies in different sections of the country, but the scale is published in the front of each dog show catalogue. These points may differ between the dogs and the bitches at the same show. You may, however, win additional points by winning Best of Winners, if there are fewer dogs than bitches entered, or vice versa. Points never exceed five at any one show and a total of 15 points must be won to constitute a championship. These 15 points must be won under at least three different judges, and you must acquire at least two major wins. Anything from a three to five point win is a major, while one and two point wins are minor wins. Two major wins must be won under two different judges to meet championship requirements.

PROFESSIONAL HANDLERS

If you are new in the fancy and do not know how to handle your dog to his best advantage, or if you are too nervous or physically unable to show your dog, you can hire a reliable professional handler who will do it for you for a specified fee. The more successful or well-known handlers charge slightly higher rates, but generally speaking there is a pretty uniform charge for this service. As the dog progresses with his wins in the show ring, the fee increases proportionately. Included in this service is professional advice on when and where to show your dog, grooming, a statement of your wins at each show, and all trophies and ribbons that the dog accumulates. Any cash award is kept by the handler as a sort of "bonus."

When engaging a handler, it is advisable to select one that does not take more dogs to a show than he can properly and comfortably handle. You want your dog to receive his individual attention and not be rushed into the ring at the last moment because the handler has been busy with too many other dogs in other rings. Some handlers require that you deliver the dog to their establishment a few days ahead of the show so they have ample time to groom and train him. Other handlers will accept well-behaved and

trained dogs that have been groomed from their owners at ringside, if they are familiar with the dog and the owner. This should be determined well in advance of the show date. NEVER expect a handler to accept a dog at ringside that is not groomed to perfection!

There are several sources for locating a professional handler. Dog magazines carry their classified advertising. A note or telephone call to the American Kennel Club will also put you in touch with several in your area.

Ch. Rainbow's Summer Breeze, double Sweepstakes winner, finished for her championship with three major wins. Bred by Mike Garrigan and Barbara Deffenbaugh, she is handled by Ron Fabis for owners Steve and Cindy Dennehy, Sunshine Kennels, Muskogee, Oklahoma. She is the dam of Ch. Sunshine's Shannon, Ch. Sunshine's Summer Song and other pointed get.

DO YOU REALLY NEED A HANDLER?

The answer to that question is sometimes yes, sometimes no! However, the answer that must be determined first of all is, "But can I *afford* a professional handler?" or, "I want to show my dog myself. Does that mean my dog will never do any big winning?"

Do you *really* need a handler to win? If you are mishandling a good dog that should be winning and isn't because it is made to look bad in the ring by its owner, the answer is yes. If you don't know how to handle a dog properly, why make your dog look bad when a handler could show it to its best advantage?

Some owners simply cannot handle a dog well and still wonder why their dogs aren't winning in the ring, no matter how hard they try. Others are nervous and this nervousness travels down the leash to the dog and the dog behaves accordingly. Some people are extroverts by nature, and these are the people who usually make excellent handlers. Of course, the biggest winning dogs at the shows usually have a lot of "show off" in their nature, too, and this helps a great deal.

THE COST OF CAMPAIGNING A DOG WITH A HANDLER

At present many champions are shown an average of 25 times before completing a championship. In entry fees at today's prices, that adds up to over $250. This does not include motel bills, traveling expenses, or food. There have been dog champions finished in fewer shows, say five to ten shows, but this is the exception rather than the rule. When and where to show should be thought out carefully so that you can perhaps save money on entries. This is one of the services a professional handler provides that can mean a considerable saving. Hiring a handler can save money in the long run if you just wish to make a champion. If your dog has been winning reserves and not taking the points and a handler can finish him in five to ten shows, you would be ahead financially. If your dog is not really top quality, the length of time it takes even a handler to finish it (depending upon competition in the area) could add up to a large amount of money.

Campaigning a show specimen that not only captures the wins in his breed but wins Group and Best in Show awards gets up into the big money. To cover the nation's major shows and rack up a record as one of the top dogs in the nation usually costs an owner between 10 and 15 thousand dollars a year. This includes not only the professional handler's fee for taking the dog into the ring, but the cost of conditioning and grooming, board, advertising in the dog magazines, photographs, etc.

There is great satisfaction in winning with your own dog, especially if you have trained and cared for it yourself. With today's enormous entries at the dog shows and so many worthy dogs competing for top wins, many owners who said "I'd rather do it myself!" and meant it became discouraged and eventually hired a handler anyway.

However, if you really are in it just for the sport, you can and should handle your dog if you want to. You can learn the tricks by attending training classes, and you can learn a lot by carefully observing the more successful professional handlers as they perform in the ring. Model yourself after the ones that command respect as being the leaders in their profession. But, if you find you'd really rather be at ringside looking on, then do get a handler so that your worthy dog gets his deserved recognition in the ring. To own a good dog and win with it is a thrill, so good luck, no matter how you do it.

Ch. Baliwick Behold, bred by Michael Allen, finished with four majors at 10 months of age with three Best of Variety wins over numerous other winning male Specials in 1978. The sire was Ch. Baliwick The Impecabl Frekl ex Ch. Regalia's One-Sided Affair.

Ch. Corwin Clean Sweep, sired by Ch. Corwin Chances Are ex Ch. Nor Mar's Nice N' Neat and owned by Helen A. Rice of Stanton, California. Bennett Associates photo.

Ch. Baliwick Barrymore, owned by Michael Allen of Costa Mesa, California.

Above: Ch. Baliwick The 'Nsuffrable Frekl finished for his championship with a Sweepstakes win and a Best of Variety over Males Special. Owned by Debbie Schnabel and Michael Allen, pictured handling.

Opposite: Ch. Frandee's Miss Independence pictured winning at a show with a four-point major on the way to her championship. She is the dam of Ch. Frandee's Declaration and is bred and owned by Frank and Dee Dee Wood of Norco, California.

Left: Ch. Pett's Angel Touch pictured winning Best of Variety under judge Ellsworth Gamble. Ron Fabis handled for owner-breeders Mr. and Mrs. Roland Pett of Dennis Port, Massachusetts. **Below:** Ch. Travel On Castle Shannon, sired by Ch. Travel On Jackson ex Bahari Billow, is pictured finishing at the Western Reserve Kennel Club. Handled and owned by Barb White of Columbiana, Ohio. **Opposite:** Marjorie Bond's Ch. Bondale's Harriet, pictured with her handler Ray McGinnis. Alfred Stillman photograph.

164

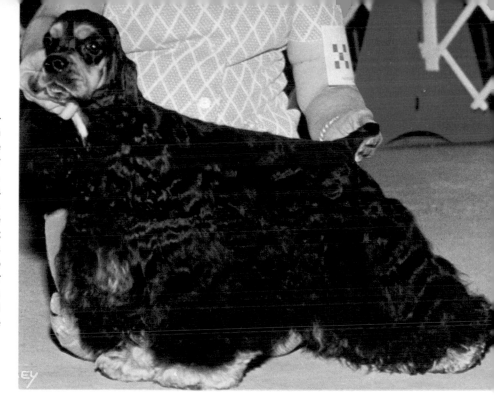

Opposite: Ch. McEnroe's Mystique, top-winning ASCOB bitch for 1975. Handled by Dee Dee Wood for owners Bill and Mary Bouley. Francis photo. **Right:** Ch. Trojan Maxie Tan finishes with a third major for his championship. Handled by breeder-owner Alice Kaplan. Twomey photo. **Below:** Ch. Frandee's Diamond Lil goes all the way from Winners Bitch to Best of Opposite Sex over Specials at the 1980 American Spaniel Club show. Bred and owned by Frank and Dee Dee Wood.

Ch. Tam-Crest Summertime Promise is pictured taking Winners Bitch, Best of Winners, and Best of Opposite Sex at the Olympia Kennel Club show. Owned by Steve and Joyce Johnson and handled by Debbie Von Horn.

Ch. Frandee's Tycoon pictured winning with her handler Diana Kane. Owned by Frank and Dee Dee Wood, Norco, California.

Opposite: Bobwin's Sir Charles, pictured winning Best of Variety over Specials under judge Robert Walters at the 1979 Sacramento Kennel Club, is owned by Bobwin Kennels, Suisun, California. **Right:** Ch. Canterbury's Archbishop, owned by the Rowingdale Kennels, La Mesa, California, is pictured winning Best of Variety. Bill Francis photo. **Below:** Ch. Torchlite Tantalizin', bred and owned by Margaret M. Saari, D.V.M., was sired by Ch. Ashley's Golden Rule ex Ch. Caramel's Cozette.

Above: Ch. Branridge Semi-Tough pictured going Best Adult in Match under judge Dee Dee Wood. Owned and handled by Jerry Moon.

Opposite: Ch. Memoir's Marc In The Dark finishes at the 1979 Houston Kennel Club show. Owned by Anita Roberts, Novato, California. Ashbey photo.

Above: Ch. Marquis Peter Pucker, owned by Julie and John Wolfe, is pictured winning at the Santa Ana Valley Kennel Club show.

Opposite, above: Ch. Ging's Recycled Genes pictured winning at the 1980 Pocono Mountain Kennel Club show with handler Ted Young. Breeder-owners are Lloyd Alton and Bill Gorodner, Ridgewood, New Jersey. **Below:** Ch. Frandee's Celebration wins Best of Variety at the 1978 American Spaniel Club Specialties show. Bred and owned by Frank and Dee Dee Wood, Norco, California.

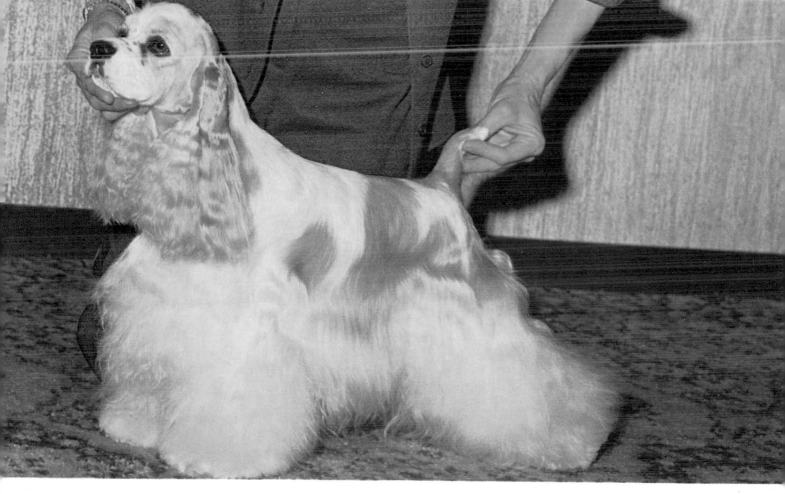

Am., Can. Ch. Butch's Kountry Boy wins Best of Breed at the Washington State Cocker Spaniel Club Specialty show under judge Harlan Hoel. Jerry Moon handled for owner Gladys Von Horn of Vancouver, Washington.

CHAPTER TEN

Showing and Judging the Cocker

Ramrod Shirley Muldowney, tri-color bitch sired by Am., Can. Ch. Ramrod Lakeside Lucifer, is pictured winning at a 1977 show. This five-point major finished her championship. Handled by Rod Mathies for breeder-owners Helen Johnston and Cherie Mathies.

Ever since I started judging dogs in 1961, I never enter a show ring to begin an assignment without thinking back to what the late, great judge Alva Rosenberg told me when we discussed my apprentice judging under his watchful eyes. His most significant observation I find still holds true for me today—that a judge's first and most lasting impression of a dog's temperament and bearing will be made the moment it walks into the ring.

It has always been a source of amazement to me the way so many exhibitors ruin that important first impression of their dog before the judge. So many are guilty of dragging their dogs along behind them, squeezing through the ringside crowds and snapping at people to get out of their way, just to arrive in the ring with a dog whose feet have been stepped on by people pushing to get closer to ringside and whose coat has been ruined by food and cigarette ashes. After all this, the dog is expected to turn on its charm once inside the ring, fascinate the crowds, captivate the judge, and bring home the silverware and ribbons! All this on a day that invariably is either too hot or too cold—or too rainy—not to mention the hours of standing rigidly on a crate, being sprayed in the face and

all over their bodies with a grooming substance that doesn't smell or taste too good, and then brushed and trimmed until dry to their handler's satisfaction. Add this to the lengthy bath and grooming session the day before the show and the bumpy ride to the show grounds, and, well Alva Rosenberg had a point! Any dog that can strut into the ring after what it regards as a 48-hour torture treatment *DOES* have to have an excellent disposition and a regal bearing. How fortunate we are that so many of our flashy little Cockers do have such marvelous temperaments in spite of our grooming rituals!

There is no reason an exhibitor cannot allow sufficient time to get to ringside with a few minutes to spare, in order to wait calmly somewhere near the entrance to the ring. They need only walk directly ahead of the dog, politely asking the people along the way to step aside with a simple statement to the effect that there is a "dog coming through." It works. I have seen spectators promptly step aside, not only to oblige this simple request when politely stated, but also to observe the beauty of the show dog passing by. Those who prefer to carry their dogs, and know how to do it without disturbing the coat, can make the same request for the same result.

The short waiting period at ringside also allows time for the dog to gain his footing and perspective and gives the exhibitor time to get his armband on securely so it won't drop down the arm and onto the dog's head during the first sprint around the ring. These few spare moments will also allow a great deal of the "nervousness" that travels down the lead to your dog to disappear as the realization that you have arrived at your class on time occurs to you, and you and your dog can both relax.

Ch. Milru's Fancy Free is pictured in proper show stance. Owner, Ruth C. Muller, Milru Cockers, Centerport, New York.

ENTERING THE RING

When the ring steward calls out the numbers for your class, there is no need for you to try to be first in the ring. There is no prize for being first. If you are new at the game, you would do well to get behind a more experienced exhibitor or professional handler where you can observe and perhaps learn something about ring behavior. The judges will be well aware of your presence in the ring when they make a small dot or a small check mark in their judge's book, as you enter. The judges must also mark all absentees before starting to evaluate the class, so you can be sure no one will be overlooked as they "count noses."

Simply enter the ring as quickly and calmly as possible with your dog on a loose lead, and at the first opportunity make sure you show your armband to the judge. Then take a position in the line-up already forming in the ring (usually at the opposite side from the judge's table). Set your dog up in the show pose so that once the judge has checked in all the dogs in the class he will have an immediate impression of the outline of your dog in show stance. This is also referred to as "stacking" your dog.

The judge will then go up and down the line of dogs in order to compare one outline with another, while getting an idea of the symmetry and balance of each profile. This is the time when you should see that your dog maintains the show stance. Don't be nervously brushing your dog, constantly adjusting his feet, tilting his head, primping his tail, etc. All of this should have been done while the judge was walking down the line with his eyes on the other dogs in the class.

By the time the judge gets to your dog it should be standing as still as a statue, with your hands off it if at all possible. Far too many exhibitors handle show dogs as if they were puppets with strings attached to all the moving parts. They are constantly pushing them in place, prodding them to a desired angle for the judge to see, placing the head and tail and feet according to their idea of perfection. More often than not their fingers are covering the dog's muzzle or they are employing their thumbs to straighten out a topline, or using a finger to tilt a tail to the proper angle. Repeatedly moving a dog's feet tends to make the judge believe the dog can't stand correctly by itself. If a dog is standing incorrectly the judge might assume that it just happened to be standing incorrectly at that moment and that the exhibitor couldn't imagine such a thing and therefore never noticed it!

Fussing over a dog only calls attention to the fact that the exhibitor either has to do a lot to make the dog look good or is a rank amateur and is nervously mis-handling the dog. A free, natural stance, even when a little "off base," is still more appealing to the judge than a dog presented with all four feet barely touching the ground. All Cocker Spaniels are beautiful on their own and unnecessary handling can only be regarded as a distraction, not as indulgence on the part of the exhibitor. Do not get the mistaken idea that if the judge thinks you are working hard with your dog you deserve to win.

MOVE THEM OUT

Once the judge has compared the outlines (or profiles) of each dog he will ask the exhibitors to move the dogs around the ring so that he might observe the dogs in action. This usually means two complete circles of the ring, depending on the size of the ring and the number of dogs competing in it. This is the time when the judge must determine whether the dog is moving properly or if it is limping or lame. The judge will check out the dog for proper gait and observe if the dog is moving freely on its own—not strung up on the end of a lead with the handler holding the head high.

Be careful not to hamper your dog in any way in the limited time and space you have to show the judge how your dog moves. This means gaiting on a loose lead. Move next to your dog at a safe distance to the side so that you do not step on it going around corners or pull it off balance on turns. You must also keep in mind that you should not get too close to the dog ahead of you and that you must keep far enough ahead of the dog behind you so that your dog doesn't get spooked—or that you don't break the gait.

Once the judge has had the time to observe each dog in motion, the signal will be given to one person to stop at a specific spot in the ring, forming the line-up for closer inspection of each dog individually. At the judge's discretion the individual evaluation can be done either in place or on a small table placed in the ring. Whether the judge chooses to evaluate each dog on the ground or on a table, the judge must go over the dog completely in order to evaluate it in accordance with the Standard for the breed.

JUDGING THE HEAD

As the judge approaches your dog, he will get his first close look at the expression. The judge will want to see the dark eye, will check the stop, the muzzle, the occiput, ear leather and set, and the head in its entirety for excellence. During this examination the exhibitor must make sure the dog remains perfectly still and in correct show stance. Since the dangers of the various virus infections and contagious diseases that can be passed from dog to dog at the shows has been made known to us, it is hoped the judge will ask that you show your dog's bite. It is permissible, however, for the judge to open the dog's mouth to check out the bite, especially if the judge has

Ch. Frandee's Celebration is pictured winning at the 1978 Santa Barbara Kennel Club show. Celebration is owned and bred by Frank and Dee Dee Wood, Norco, California. Callea photo.

reason to believe there is a fault.

The judge will also evaluate the head from straight on as well as in profile.

Next the neck and shoulders will be checked. The judge will lift up the ears to see just how long the neck really is and how well placed the shoulders are. Shoulders play an important part in the proper placement of the front legs and pasterns. Running his hands down the front leg, the judge will go all the way to the foot, picking it up and checking the foot pads and nails, and paying particular notice to whether the dog puts its foot down correctly in place when released.

The judge will check the brisket and the tuck-up as well as the topline. At this point, with his hands going over the dog, the judge can determine the proper texture of the coat, the profusion of feathering, and the general weight of the dog. Tail length and carriage are to be considered as well. Judging the hindquarters should prove the dog's legs are sturdy and well placed and strong enough to provide the strength for proper gait and movement. This is also the time when the judge will check to see that on male dog both testicles are present and descended.

Ch. Malady's Merry Fellow finished for championship with four major wins. Bred by Mrs. Robert Fellows, the sire was Ch. Fellows Highland Fling ex Malady Rose. Handler was David Lowe under judge Clark Thompson.

Ch. Malady Canniable Sam, owned by Mrs. Robert Fellows and handled to this 1970 Specialty Show win by David Lowe, was sired by Ch. Fellows Highland Fling ex Malady Morning Glory. Breeder was Mrs. Fellows. Shafer photo.

Once the judge has gone over the dog completely he will usually take a step or two away from the dog to give it a final over-all view, keeping a complete picture of it in his mind to make the comparison with the dog he has judged just before and will judge after yours. This is the time you must still keep your dog "on his toes" so that when the judge glances ahead or behind, your dog is not sitting down, chasing butterflies, or lifting his leg on the number markers. Remember, training is done at home—*performance* is required in the show ring at all times.

INDIVIDUAL GAITING

Once the judge has gone over each dog individually, he will go to the end of the ring and ask each handler to gait his dog. It is important at this point to pay strict attention to the judge's instructions as to how this is to be done. Some judges require the "T" formation, others the half-triangle. Further observation of your dog may bring a request for you to repeat the pattern, especially if your dog did not show well during the first trip. It is important that you hear whether the judge wants you to repeat the entire exercise or merely to gait your dog "down and back" this time.

When each dog has been gaited, the judge will want a last look at all of them lined up together before making his final decisions. Usually the procedure will be to once again present the left side of your dog as the judge weaves in and out of the line to check once more the fronts or rears or other individual points of comparison. Some dogs may be asked to gait a third time or to gait side by side with one of the other dogs should the judge want to "break a tie" as to which dog is the better mover. Because such deciding factors cannot be predicted or anticipated, it is necessary for the handler to always be ready to oblige once the request is given by the judge.

After the decisions are made, the judge will point to his four placements and those four will set their dogs up in front of the designated number markers on the side of the ring. Be ready at this point to show the numbers on your armband so that the judge can mark his judge's book. The judge then will present the winners with the appropriate color ribbons and any trophies won, and you may leave the ring.

Contrary to popular opinion it is not necessary or even correct to thank the judge for the ribbon.

It is to be assumed that the dog *deserved* the ribbon or the judge would not have awarded it. Handing you the ribbon is part of the procedure and does not warrant a thank-you. The club, not the judge, is responsible for the donation of the trophies. It is not called for that the exhibitor speak to the judge, but if the win is significant enough so that you feel compelled to say *something*, a simple and not overly exuberant "I'm so pleased that you like my dog," or something similar is still more than is necessary.

The "thank-you" for the ribbon has on occasion become what some exhibitors like to think of as a "weapon." At ringside you can sometimes hear words to the effect that, "I didn't even thank him for that rotten red ribbon!" As if the judge had even noticed! However, it *is* expected that you take with you from the ring a ribbon of *any color*. To throw it on the ground or leave it behind in the ring so that the steward is obliged to call you back into the ring for the judge to hand it to you again is most unsportsman-like. You must play the game according to the rules. Your entry fee is to obtain the opinion of your dog by the judge. You must take the opinion and behave accordingly. If you do not like it, do not give them another entry, but you owe the judge the courtesy of respect for that title.

After this judging procedure is followed in the five classes for dogs, and Winners Dog and Reserve Winners Dog have been determined, the bitches are judged in this same manner. After Winners Bitch and Reserve Winners Bitch awards have been made, the Best of Breed judging follows. Class procedures here are discussed elsewhere in this chapter. Once the judge has completed his assignment and signed his judge's book, it is permissible to request any photographs that you may wish to have taken of your wins. At this time it is also permissible to ask the judge his motives in his judging of *your* dog. If you wish to, it should be done in a polite and calm manner. It must be remembered that the judge is not going to make comparisons rating one dog against another, but can, if he chooses, give a brief explanation as to how he evaluated your dog.

It is helpful to remember that "no one wins them all." You will win some and lose some no matter how good your dog is. Judges are human and, while no one is perfect, they have earned the title of "judge" for some mighty good reasons. Try to recall that this is a sport and it should be fun—tomorrow is another day.

THE GAMES PEOPLE PLAY

If you are new to the game of dog-show exhibiting there are a few things you should know about, such as how to protect yourself and your dog so that you do not get too discouraged and disillusioned right at the start.

There may be an occasion where your dog is winning a great deal and jealousy will arise from others competing in the ring with you. It has been known that some of these bad sports will try to get between you and the judge so the judge cannot see your dog at his best. Others may try stepping on your dog, breaking his gait so that he cannot be adequately judged, bringing bitches in season into the ring, throwing bait around to distract your dog, and so on. Needless to say, most judges are aware of these nasty tricks people play and will not tolerate them. Just be on your guard. Do not leave your dog alone or leave it in the care of others. Thefts have been known at dog shows, as well as poisoning and physical abuse.

Ch. Calypso's Double Delight, owned and bred by Tom and Laurie Acklin of Tonawanda, New York. The sire was Ch. Windy Hill's Makes-Its-Point ex Ch. Windy Hill's Delight O'Calypso. Delight, on the way to championship, is pictured winning under judge Robert Wills.

CHILDREN IN THE SHOW RING

No one is more approving than I of children learning to love and to care for animals. It is beautiful to see a child and an animal sharing complete rapport and companionship or performing as a team in the show ring. Those of us who have been around dog shows for any length of time have all been witness to some remarkable performances by children and their dogs. Junior Showmanship is one example; dogs caring for or standing guard over babies and infants is another example.

Tami Lee and her Lady of Ebony's Carbon Copy, pictured at home in Bothell, Washington.

However, there is nothing "cute" about a child being allowed to handle a dog where the welfare of both the child and the general public are in danger. Dogs have been known to pull children to the ground with resulting injury to either child or dog, or both. I have seen frightened children let go of leashes or become tangled up in them in the middle of dog fights that left all three participants injured.

If a child shows the natural desire to exhibit a dog after having attended handling classes where they are taught how to properly show a dog, they must also be taught ring procedure. It is not fair to expect other exhibitors to show patience while a judge or the steward informs the child where to stand or waits for them to gait the dog several times before they do it in the formation requested. Lack of knowledge or repeated requests delay the judging, look bad to the ringside crowds, and certainly don't make the dog look good.

If necessary, parents might stay after the dog-show judging and actually train the child in an empty ring. Parents should also sit ringside with the children to explain the judging procedures to them so they will know what to expect when they enter the ring. Many match show appearances should precede any appearance in a point show ring also. Certainly no parent could possibly expect a judge to give them a win just because they are a cute pair—even though they are!

BAITING

No matter how one feels about baiting a dog in the ring, we must acknowledge that almost everyone at one time or another has been guilty of it. Certain breeds are particularly responsive to it, while others show little or no interest with so much going on all around them.

There is no denying that baiting can be an aid to basic training. But in the show ring some judges consider it an indication that the training of the dog for the show ring is not yet complete. It becomes obvious to the judge that the dog still needs an incentive to respond to what other dogs are doing in the name of performance and showmanship.

Frequently, squeaky toys will work as well. Using conversation and pet nicknames in trying to encourage the dog is equally inappropriate.

DOUBLE-HANDLING

You can be sure the competent judge becomes aware of any double-handling to which some of the more desperate exhibitors may resort.

Double-handling is both distracting and frowned upon by the American Kennel Club. Nonetheless, some owners go to all sorts of ridiculous lengths to get their apathetic dogs to perform in the ring. They hide behind trees or posts at ringside or may lurk behind the ringside crowd until the exact moment when the judge is looking at or gaiting their dog and then pop out in full view perhaps emitting some familiar whistle or noise or wave a hat or whatever in hopes that the dog will suddenly become alert and express a bit of animation.

Don't be guilty of double-handling. The day may come when you finally have a great show dog, but the reputation of an owner guilty of double handling lives on forever! You'll be accused of the same shady practices and your new show dog is apt to suffer for it.

APPLAUSE, APPLAUSE!

Another "put-on" by some of our less secure exhibitors is the practice of bringing their own cheering section to applaud vigorously every time the judge happens to cast an eye on their dog.

The judge is concentrating on what he is doing and will not pay attention to this or will not be influenced by the cliques set up by those trying to push their dogs to a win, supposedly by popular approval. The most justified occasions for applause are during a Parade of Champions, during the gaiting of an entire Specialty Best of Breed Class or during the judging awards for Stud Dog, Brood Bitch, and Veterans Class. At these thrilling moments the tribute of spontaneous applause—and the many tears—are understandable and well received, but to try to prompt a win or stir up interest in a particular dog during the normal course of class judging is amateurish.

If you have ever observed this practice, you will notice that the dogs being applauded are sometimes the poorest specimens whose owners seem to subconsciously realize they cannot win under normal conditions.

SINS WHEN SHOWING DOGS

* DON'T forget to exercise your dog before entering the ring. Do it before grooming if you are afraid the dog will get wet or dirty after getting off the grooming table.

* DON'T ever take a dog into the show ring that isn't groomed the very best you know how.

* DON'T take a dog into the ring if you have any indication it is sick or not *completely* recovered from a communicable disease.

* DON'T drag the dog around the ring on a tight lead that destroys its proud carriage or disposition or chances of becoming a show dog in the future if not that particular day.

* DON'T talk to the judge in the ring. Watch the judge closely and follow instructions carefully. Don't speak to those at ringside, or to your dog in an excessive or loud manner.

Three-month-old Trojan British Sterling. "Silver" is a typical quality puppy from the Trojan Kennels, Magnolia, Texas.

* DON'T strike or in any way abuse your dog before, during, or after the judging. The time and place for training and discipline is at home, not in public. Always use the reward system, not punishment, for the most successful method of training a dog.

* DON'T be a bad loser. You can't win 'em all, so if you win today, be gracious; if you lose, be happy for the dog who won.

* DON'T shove your dog in a crate or leave him on the bench alone until it's time to leave the show grounds. A drink of water or something to eat and a little companionship will go a long way toward making dog shows more enjoyable for him so that he will show even better the next time.

183

Ch. Scioto Bluff's Sinbad is pictured at 12 years of age. Sinbad was the sire of 118 champions, was a top-producing Cocker Spaniel and was the Best in Show winner at the 1963 American Spaniel Club show. Shafer photograph.

CHAPTER ELEVEN

Statistics and the Phillips System

Ch. Caramel's Cozette, owned by Margaret M. Saari and bred by C. and M. Keytor, was sired by Ch. Kahdas Kegooligom ex Caramel's Contrary Mary.

As Cocker Spaniels continued to grow in popularity it was only natural that the entries at the dog shows continued to swell and competition was keen. The larger the entries, the more coveted the wins. In 1956 when Irene Phillips created her Phillips System of evaluating show dogs, Cocker Spaniel fanciers fell right in line with her point system and began keeping records of their dogs' wins to compare them not only with other Cocker Spaniels, but with other Sporting dogs, and even other dogs of all breeds.

At the beginning of the 1980's, a quarter of a century later, dog fanciers are still keeping score on the top winners in the breeds, and while many a "system" of making it to the top of a winner's list has been recorded and publicized, there is no denying that they are all based on the most popular, fairest, and most recognized of all systems for naming the top winning dogs in the country.

True, records are made to be broken, and we can all look forward to the day when another magnificent Cocker Spaniel will come on the show scene and cut a path through the crowds of show dogs to triumph as the newest top-winning dog in our breed. There is always room for another great dog to bring additional glory to the Cocker Spaniel and just as naturally as night follows day, we all hope that extra special specimen will be our own.

As this book goes to press at the beginning of the eighties, we have a remarkable list of sensational dogs that can already claim fame as being at the top of the list of all-time show winners in the history of the breed, to date. This book would be less than complete if it did not pay tribute in both word and picture to those dogs that have earned their titles by accumulation of Phillips System points, the first and most fairly compiled system of achievement for the nation's top dogs.

WHAT IS THE PHILLIPS SYSTEM?

In the mid-fifties Mrs. John Phillips, a woman famous for her Haggiswood Irish Setter Kennels and a judge of many breeds, devised a point system based on show records published in the *American Kennel Gazette* to measure the wins of the nation's show dogs.

As in all sports, competition and enthusiasm in the dog fancy run high, and Irene Phillips—now Mrs. Harold Schlintz—came up with a simple, yet certainly true, method of measuring wins for this competition, which over the years has provided many thrills for dog lovers interested in the good sportsmanship so essential to a competitive sport.

***Note:** Beginning on page 307 of this book are "Cocker Spaniel Statistics" listing the top Cockers in breed history as well as on a year-by-year basis.*

The Phillips System, which Mrs. Phillips not only devised but also compiled during the early years, was sold as an annual feature to *Popular Dogs* magazine, whose editor at that time, Mrs. Alice Wagner, did much to make it the most important rule of success for a show dog. Later, when I took over as editor of *Popular Dogs* in 1967, I carried on the tradition and did the compiling of the figures as well. For the five years I was tallying the finals for the Phillips System, it was a constant source of enjoyment for me to watch the leading dogs in this country, in all breeds, climb to the top. Because I knew so many others felt the same way, and since the competition increases with each passing year, I felt that a healthy sampling of the Cocker Spaniels which have achieved honors should be represented in this book so that they may become a matter of permanent record.

HOW THE SYSTEM WORKS

The Phillips System was designed to measure, with fairness, the difference between a dog-show win scored over many dogs and one scored over just a few dogs. For example, a Best In Show win over 1,000 dogs should obviously have more significance than a Best In Show scored over 200 dogs. The Phillips System acknowledged this difference by awarding points in accordance with the number of dogs over which the win was scored. Points were awarded for Best In Show and Group Placings only. Best of Breed wins did not count.

The Best in Show dog earned a point for each dog in actual competition; absentees or obedience dogs were not counted. The first place winner in each of the six Groups earned a point for each dog defeated in his Group. The dog that placed second earned a point for each dog in the Group less the total dogs in the breed that were first. Third in the Group earned a point for each dog in the Group less the total of the breeds that were first and second. Fourth in the Group earned a point for each dog in the Group less the total of the breeds that were first, second, and third.

Sources for the count were the official records for each dog-show as published each month in the *American Kennel Gazette* magazine, the official publication for the American Kennel Club. An individual card was kept on each dog and every dog that placed in the Group or won a Best in Show during the entire year. Figures were

tallied for publication at the end of each 12-month period, and a "Special Issue" of *Popular Dogs* magazine was devoted each year to presenting the Top Ten Winners in each breed.

In the beginning only a few of the top dogs were published, but by 1966 the phrase "Top Ten" was firmly established in dog-show jargon and the system had captured the imagination of dog fanciers all over the nation—many striving to head the list of the top-winning dog in the country for that year.

The published figures included the total number of points (or number of dogs defeated), the number of Bests in Show, and the number of Group Placements. It is extremely interesting to note that as each year passed there was a tremendous increase in the amount of points accrued by the big winners. There is proof positive of the amazing success and increase in the number of entries at the dog-shows from the mid-fifties when the System was first created by Irene Phillips to the mid-seventies, when it became a matter of record that the #1 dog in the nation amassed over 50,000 points to claim the title of Top Show Dog in the United States that year.

1956 AND CH. GAIL'S EBONY DON D

Our Cocker Spaniels did well for themselves in that very first year of the Phillips System. Not only did Ch. Gail's Ebony Don D top the list of Cocker Spaniels, but Don D placed third on the list for all breeds, having amassed a grand total of 9.077 points for winning 13 Bests in Show, five Specialties, 33 Sporting Group Firsts, and eight other Group Placements.

Another black Cocker Spaniel, Ch. Baliwick Banter, placed as #7 in the Top Ten Sporting Dogs and an ASCOB, Ch. Eufaula's Dividend, was #8 with 2,880 and 2,792 points respectively. Banter had won three Bests in Show, Dividend had one, and each had seven Specialty wins to their credit. Banter was handled by Norman Austin for owner Mrs. Rose Robbins, and Ted Young, Jr. handled Dividend for C.E. Dimon.

IN 1957 IT'S CH. GAIL'S EBONY DON D AGAIN

While Ted Young and Don D racked up 9,448 points during the 1957 show season, it rated Don D a #4 spot for the Top Ten Dogs in the Nation for that year. Ten Bests in Show and two Specialty wins were included in the show record along with 30 Group Firsts and 17 Group Placements. Owners Alan and Natalie Goldstein of Chestnut Hill, Massachusetts were delighted when Don D also won the Quaker Oats Award for having won the most Sporting Group Firsts for that year, including the Sporting Group at Westminster, with his agent-handler Norman Austin.

The ASCOB Cocker Ch. Artru Hot Rod ranked in fourth place in the Top Ten Sporting Dogs for that year with 4,158 points. Two Bests in Show and 12 Specialties helped add to the tally with eight Group Firsts and 18 Group Placements. Number 10 place on the Sporting Group list went to Ch. Hickory Hill Hi Jack, a black, with 2,033 points; one Best in Show, three Specialties, two Group Firsts, and eight Group Placements rounded out his record. Owned by Mrs. Robert Mauchel, and handled by Ted Young, one of Jack's Group wins included the Morris and Essex Kennel Club event over a huge entry.

Ch. Artru Hot Rod was handled by Everett Dean, Jr. who piloted him to a Best in Show at the 1958 American Spaniel Club event for owner Mrs. Arthur H. Benhoff, Jr.

IN 1958 CH. ARTRU HOT ROD MAKES IT TO THE TOP

1958 was Ch. Artru Hot Rod's turn to be listed among the Top Ten in the all-breed ranks. He ended up #4 with 8,045 points. His #1 position in the Sporting Dogs category included nine Bests in Show, 14 Specialties, 26 Group Firsts, and 18 Group Placements. Positions #2 and #3 were also won by Cockers. Number 2 was the Parti-color Ch. Wilco's Little Barney. Owned by Carol Ann and Robert L. Martin, he had a total of 5,425 points as a result of his three Bests in Show, 23 Group Firsts, and 26 Group Placements. First shown in June 1957, in the following year and a half he had won 76 Best of Varieties with his handler George Sangster.

In the #3 position was the black Cocker, Ch. Clarkdale Capital Stock owned by Leslie and Elizabeth Clark. At just two years of age he managed to earn 3,820 points for his four Bests in Show, five Specialties, and 11 Group Firsts. A dozen Group Placements finished out his wins.

The #7 spot went to the top-winning particolor in the country for 1958, Ch. Mel-Lar's Prince Fredrick. Owned by Melvin and Lorine Kessler and handled by Ruth Kraeuchi, "Freddy" had 2,845 points for his one Best in Show, three Specialties, nine Group Firsts, and 21 Placements.

Ch. Milru's Kismet Too, owned by Ruth C. Muller of Centerport, New York.

Ch. Baliwick Blotter, owned by Michael Allen, is an excellent example of a true "fharkel" face.

1959 AND CH. CLARKDALE CAPITAL STOCK

Number 9 in the Top Ten Dogs for 1959 was the Black Cocker, Ch. Clarkdale Capital Stock. Only ranking #3 in the Sporting Dog category for 1958, Capital Stock came up to the #1 spot in Sporting Dogs and #9 for all-breeds, with 7,688 points. He had won seven Bests in Show that year as well as 11 Specialties, 21 Group Firsts, and 20 placements. When just three years old "Cappy" went on to win Best in Show at the 1960 American Spaniel Club Show and was the sire of several champions at this early age. Harry Reno was his handler.

Sharing Top Ten Sporting Dog honors with Cappy that year were three other excellent Cockers, and all new additions to the Top Ten lists. In the #3 position for Sporting breeds was Ch. Pinetops Fancy Parade, a lovely ASCOB with 6,220 points for five Bests in Show, 10 Specialties, 22 Group Firsts, and 28 Placements. Whelped in January 1958, he went on to win the Sporting Group at Westminster in 1960. Norman Austin was his handler, and William J. Laffoon and Mrs. Rose Robbins were his co-owners.

Number 6 in the 1959 Sporting Group was Ch. Holly Tree High Knight, a black male whelped in December 1957 and owned by the Sea Swing Kennels in Meriden Connecticut. Handled by Ted Young, Jr., he won 3,403 for his two Bests in Show, two Specialty wins, four Groups, and eight Placements.

Close on High Knight's heels in the #8 position was yet another black dog, Ch. Windjammer's Passkey with 3,062 points. Passkey had also won two Bests in Show, six Group Firsts, and six Group Placements.

1960 AND THE "DOG OF THE YEAR" IS CH. PINETOP'S FANCY PARADE

The decade of the 1960's started off with a bang for Cocker Spaniels. During 1960 Ch. Pinetop's Fancy Parade who ranked only third in the Sporting Dogs finals last year surged ahead to capture the #1 position for all breeds. Fancy, a glorious ASCOB, won the most Bests in Show of any dog in the nation to win the *Popular Dogs* magazine "Dog of the Year" title. Handled by Norman A. Austin for co-owners William J. Laffon, Jr. and Mrs. Rose Robbins, Fancy's total was 16,032 points for his 28 Bests in Show, nine Specialty wins, 63 Group Firsts,

and 12 Group Placements—a truly amazing record. No other dog of any breed even came close. The dog in the #2 all-breed category was just less than 5,000 points behind. The #2 ranking Sporting Dog was just less than 10,000 points behind.

Number 2 Sporting Dog was Ch. Clarkdale Capital Stock, who had held the #1 spot for the previous year and finished up the year with 5,525 points, five Bests in Show, eight Specialties, 20 Group Firsts, and 11 Placements. Number 6 was Ch. Holly Tree High Knight, who was also #6 the previous year. 3,935 points were amassed by his winning four Bests in Show, 11 Specialties, 14 Group Firsts, and 14 Group Placements.

1961 AND THE NEWCOMERS

Oddly enough, there were no Cocker Spaniels in the Top Ten Dogs all-breeds for 1961, even though a Cocker, Ch. Pinetop's Fancy Parade, had held the #1 spot in 1960. When the 1961 points were counted there were none of the "old familiar faces" on the list, just three newcomers to the ranks and none higher than the #5 position in the Top Ten Sporting Dogs section.

Ch. Whitefield's Why Certainly made a good showing in the #5 position with 4,217 points for his four Bests in Show, 10 Group Firsts, and seven Group Placements. Top-ranking Cocker, all varieties for this year, was owned by Mr. and Mrs. William L. Randall and handled by Porter Washington.

Number 8 position went to Ch. Silver Maple Jimmy Stardust, an ASCOB, with 2,866 points for one Best in Show, two Specialty wins, 16 Group Firsts, and 20 Placements. Number 9 was another black, Ch. Har-Dee's Hell Bender II, with 2,837 points for three Bests in Show, two Specialty wins, seven Group Firsts, and 15 Group Placements.

1962

Nineteen hundred sixty-two was another disappointing year for Cocker Spaniel show winners. Ch. My Ida Ho Promise to Maryville was #8 Sporting Dog but only ranked #32 in all-breed competition. 3,822 points was the final tally for the three Bests in Show, 18 Specialties, and 13 Group Placings. Additionally, Promise was the only Cocker Spaniel of any variety to place in the Sporting Dog Group. On a list of the Top Fifty Dogs of 1962, compiled by Mrs. Evelyn P. Sidewater for *Popular Dogs* and published in the April 1963 issue, Ch. Silver Maple Jimmy Stardust ranked 43rd and Ch. Fraclin Colonel Caridas #50. While the representation for 1961 and 1962 did not quite meet that of 1960, it is impressive all the same when it is remembered that the #1 dog in the nation for 1962, Ch. Tedwin's Top Billing, a Miniature Poodle, defeated 15,471 competitors

to earn that title, and Ch. Pinetop's Fancy Parade defeated 16,032!

1963

No Cocker Spaniels qualified for either the Top Ten all-breed winners or the Top Ten Sporting Dog awards. While show wins were short of these two high categories, the quality of the dogs and bitches being shown still ran high and the top three winners in each variety were

Ch. Pett's Bamboo Beige is pictured winning Best of Opposite Sex at a Hiawatha Cocker Spaniel Club Specialty under judge B. Buding. Owner is Mrs. R. A. Pett.

published in *Popular Dogs* magazine. The three top winners in the blacks went to three newcomers to the breed. They were Ch. Lurola's Leading Issue, Ch. Flo Bob's Noble Knight (more about him later), and Ch. Greenbriar's Jimmy Cricket. Leading Issue had a Best in Show win to his credit and 2,614 points. He had won 10 Group firsts and had 16 Placements as well. Noble Knight had 1,319 points, 4 Group firsts, and 13 Placements. Cricket had 863 points and 7 Group Placements.

In the ASCOB division Ch. Biggs Snow Prince, Ch. Artru Johnny Be Good, and Ch. Har Ken's Tee Vee Tony were the leaders. Prince had 2,713 points, three Bests in Show, eight Group Firsts, and eight Placements; while Johnny had 1,064 points, two Groups, and 12 Placements. Tee Vee Tony racked up 943 points in competition that year with six Group Placements.

A top-winning Cocker in the early 1960's was Ch. Pett's Bit O'Pamper, pictured here winning at the 1961 Baltimore County Kennel Club show. Bred and owned by R. A. Pett; shown here with handler Ted Young, Jr.

In the Parti division Ch. Merikay's Dynamite, Ch. Fraclin Colonel Caridas, and Sciota Bluff's Sinbad headed the list. Dynamite had 1,354 points for having won two Groups and 10 Group Placements. Colonel Caridas won four Groups and seven Placements for a total of 843 points, and Sinbad also won 843 points for two Group Firsts and nine Group Placements.

The lack of representation in the Top Ten for the breed was surprising since in both 1962 and 1963 Cocker Spaniels retained their #8 position in the listing of American Kennel Club registrations for those years with 14,509 and 14,791 respectively.

MOVING UP IN 1964

There were three Cockers—ASCOBS—in the Top Ten Sporting Dog category. Heading the list was Ch. Biggs Snow Prince with 8,478 points. In the #7 position was Ch. Forjay's Sundown with 4,440 and #10 Ch. Hi Boots Such Brass won 3,303. Described as a silver-buff dog, "Pops" was winner of the American Spaniel Club Specialty in 1964 under the late Dr. Joseph Redden and had 11 all-breed Bests in Show, nine Specialties, 33 Group Firsts, and 24 Group Placements to his credit for the #1 spot in the Sporting Dog tally. Owned by Mrs. H. Terrell Van Ingen of Greenwich, Connecticut, Pops was handled to the top spot by Ted Young, Jr.

One of the top show dogs from the Trojan Kennels in the 1960's was Ch. Trojan Topper, bred, owned and handled by Alice Kaplan.

Ch. Bondale Ann E. Will is pictured winning a five-point major on the way to championship. This winner in the 1960's was handled by Ray McGinnis for owner Marjorie Bond, Bondale Kennels, Eugene, Oregon.

1965

There were no all-breed winners in our breed for 1965 either, but the #7 and #10 dogs from 1964 moved up. Ch. Forjay's Sundown moved into the #1 position and Ch. Hi Boots Such Brass held on to the #10 position. Sundown was 9,571 points and Brass totaled 4,305. Ch. Biggs Snow Prince dropped to the #3 spot in ASCOBs this year with 2,213 points.

In Black Cocker Spaniel competition Ch. Mijo's Momentum was #1 in his color category. He had won 12 Groups and 11 Group Placings in just eight months of showing during 1965. In

Partis it was Ch. Orient's Pleasing You, Ch. Scioto Bluff's Sin Bahr, and Ch. Stonewalk Squareshooter, named as the top three. All nine dogs had over 1,500 points to reach the top of their color varieties.

1966

The second half of the decade of the sixties found Ch. Pinefair Password as the #6 Sporting Dog in the country. 9,319 points for his three Bests in Show, 12 Group Firsts, and 30 Group Placements had this lovely black in the Top Ten listings.

Ch. Corwin Contrite, a 1965 show winner owned by Helen A. Rice of Stanton, California, is pictured here winning at the 1965 San Joaquin Valley Cocker Spaniel Club Specialty show.

Ch. Corwin's Streak-O-Lightnin' is pictured winning Best of Variety at the 1966 Riverside Kennel Club show. Lightnin' is owned by Mr. and Mrs. Bill Ryan. Henry Schley photo.

Ch. Pett's Pink Ice, an important winner in the 1960's, is pictured here on the way to her championship at the 1967 Cocker Spaniel Club of the Middle West Specialty show. Breeder-owners are Mr. and Mrs. Roland Pott.

Ch. Trojan Tangelic is pictured winning at the 1966 Cocker Spaniel Club of the Middle West Specialty show. "Angel," a black and tan, was bred, owned and handled by Alice Kaplan, Trojan Kennels, Magnolia, Texas.

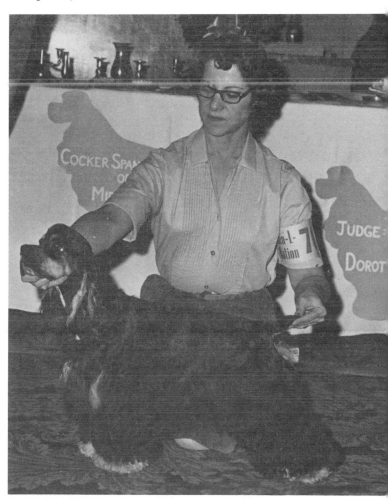

1967

In 1967 there were no Cocker Spaniels listed in the Top Fifty Dogs of all breeds in total number of points won. In the Sporting Group two black Cockers took the #7 and #8 spots. Ch. Dream Echo Magic Touch had 5,232 points for his two Bests in Show, 13 Group Firsts, and 28 Group Placements. Magic Touch was owned by Mr. and Mrs. J. L. Juelich. Number 8 was Ch. Treasure Hill Masterpiece, owned by M. and J. Ferrero, and won 4,018 points for his Best in Show, nine Group Firsts, and 21 Group Placements.

1968

Show results from the 1968 show season listed Ch. Hugomar Headliner as the #6 ranking Sporting Dog in the nation. Owned by Al Siekierski, this strikingly marked Parti-Cocker earned 7,796 points that year with two Bests in Show, 15 Group Firsts, and 23 Group Placements. Handled by Ted Young, Jr., "Chum" was Top-winning Cocker, all colors, for 1968 and had two Specialty show wins to his credit as well.

Ch. Treasure Hill Masterpiece headed the list of Black Cockers for 1968 with 3,893 points for one Best in Show, five Group Firsts, and 23 Group Placements. Heading the list for the ASCOBs was Ch. Heyday Hobbit with 3,274 points for one Best in Show, four Group Firsts, and 21 Group Placements. Masterpiece was owned by M. Ferrero and Hobbit by Dr. C. Smith.

1969

Silver Maple Kennels and Oren O. Jones's parti-color Cocker, Ch. Bursons Blarney was #9 Sporting Dog in 1969. 5,496 points were earned for one Best in Show, 15 Group Firsts, and 20 Group Placements. Number 1 ASCOB Cocker in 1969 was Ch. Silver Maple Star Performer owned by Miss V. Gillett. 1,895 points represent four Bests in Show, six Group Firsts, and 24 Group Placements. The #1 Black that year was R. and P. St. John's Ch. Hi Fi's Show Stopper with 2,308 points for one Best in Show, four Group Firsts, and 14 Group Placements.

THE DECADE OF THE 1970's

There were no Cocker Spaniels in either the all-breed Top Ten or in the Sporting Group for 1970, but those that were #1 in their varieties are worthy of mention.

Ch. Pett's Country Charmer was a show winner for the Petts' Kennels in the late 1960's.

In Blacks Ch. Newton's Speedy Gonzales, owned by M. and J. Ferrero was credited with 3,060 points. Six Group Firsts and 17 Group Placements earned him the top spot. In Parti-color category Ch. Burson's Blarney was #1 with a total of 5,431 points. Blarney had won two Bests in Show, eight Group Firsts, and 18 Group Placements. In the ASCOB division we see the #1 spot went to Ch. Sagamore Toccoa, marking the beginning of her illustrious career, and making owner Peggy Westphal proud.

1971

The beautiful buff Cocker Ch. Sagamore Toccoa managed to climb to the #4 spot in the Top Ten Sporting Dogs in 1971 with 15,886 points. She won eight Bests in Show during '71 and 14 Group Firsts. She and her handler, Ted Young, Jr., also won 25 Group Placements along the way. She was to go on to even bigger and better wins before she reached the end of her show-ring career.

The top black Cocker Spaniel was Ch. Seenar's Alibaba, owned by J. and D. Sedgwick, and finished the year with 3,526 points. In the Parti-color variety it was Ch. Ramrod Sherman, owned by W. N. Bloch, that was ranked #1. His points totaled 3,859 with one Best in Show, eight Group Firsts, and 13 Placements.

1972 IS THE YEAR OF TOCCOA

Number 1 dog in the nation in the Phillips System for 1972 was the beautiful ASCOB Ch. Sagamore Toccoa with over 50,000 points to her credit. Toccoa, beautifully handled and presented to perfection by Ted Young, Jr., was always a popular favorite with the crowd and a beautiful show girl. Owned by A. and P. Westphal, she won 30 Bests in Show with 27 Group Firsts, and 15 Group Placements for a total of 50,063 points. A truly remarkable record and only the second Cocker Spaniel in the history of the Phillips System to take the #1 spot. Not since 1960 when Ch. Pinetop's Fancy Parade had won the Dog of the Year honors had a Cocker nailed the first place honors.

The top black Cocker for 1972 was Ch. Shardeloe's Selena owned by Dr. C. A. Smith. Selena finished with 5,118 points for her Best in Show, eight Group Firsts, and 17 Group Placements. Number 1 in the Parti-Cocker division was Ch. Regalias Snowdrifter, with 4,067 points. Drifter had two Bests in Show, four Group Firsts, and 10 Placements. The owner was C. Laubecker.

Nineteen hundred seventy-one marked the end of my compiling the records for the Phillips System for *Popular Dogs* magazine. The 1972 statistics were compiled by Marty and Bobby Rothman. The last issue I received of the magazine was the February 1974 issue. Since the Phillips System final statistics were published in the July issue, we can only assume that the 1973 and 1974 ratings were lost to the fancy. The Top Ten results for American show dogs next appeared in *Showdogs* magazine in April 1975, listed as the "Showdogs Rating System" and naming the Top Twenty Dogs all-breeds and the Top Ten in each group and breed. No compiler was named for the system so we cannot know who spent the hundreds and hundreds of hours required to tally all the wins to complete such a system for the fancy. We regret that the winning dogs cannot be credited.

Am., Mex. Ch. Corwin's Command Performance, owned by Ralf Reveley and Wayne Simpson and handled for them by Joe Waterman, is pictured winning at a 1973 show. This stunning son of Ch. Corwin Calico was bred by Helen A. Rice.

Tri-color bitch, bred and owned by Ging's Kennels, Ridgewood, New Jersey, Ch. Ging's Calico Swatches is pictured winning at a 1973 show.

There were no Cocker Spaniels on the list of the Top Twenty Dogs all-breeds in 1975; however, there was an ASCOB in the #6 spot, Ch. Forjay's Winterwood, with a total of 14,270 points. The 1975 tallies also showed Ch. Tabaka's Tidbit O'Wynden moving up in the polls as well.

Following the records based on the original rules of the famous Phillips System which appeared in other publications, but to assure consistency and specific wins, it is best to consult the records kept by the members of the fancy; many of these included the Best of Variety wins for their winners.

Cal-Ore's Coal Dust took Sporting Group 2nd at a match show early in his career. Bred and owned by Nancy L. Ray, Coal Dust is handled here by Debbie Von Horn at the 1978 event.

TOP SIRES AND DAMS

In 1962 *Popular Dogs* magazine published a statistical survey on the Top Producers of the Year compiled by Robert Graham, Jr. In the 107 breeds covered in the survey it was reported that 2,861 dogs sired 3,824 champions, for the year 1961.

We are pleased to note that the dog heading the list of America's Top Sires for 1961, all-breeds, was the ASCOB Cocker Spaniel Ch. Crackerbox Certainly with 16 champions to his credit that year, and a total of 43 to that date. Bred and owned by Bob and Betty Graham, Crackerbox Kennels, Greensboro, North Carolina, Crackerbox was photographed by Tauskey for his recognition in the magazine and stood at stud at Ted Young, Jr.'s well known Tedwin Kennels in Connecticut.

We can be equally proud to note that two other—and interesting to see one from each color variety—Cocker Spaniels were included in the Top 12 Sires for all-breeds. Number 3 was the Parti Ch. Dau-Han's Dan Morgan with 10 champions to his credit for the year 1961. Number 4 was Ch. Clarkdale Capital Stock, a black, with nine champions for that same year.

The records showed that in the Sporting Dog Group 538 dogs sired 771 champions and Cocker Spaniels contributed 234 titles by 123 sires. An impressive tally, to be sure.

In the breakdown of the Sporting Group Top Twelve, only two other dogs, an Irish Setter and an English Setter, were on the list. All the others were Cocker Spaniels. After Capital Stock with his nine champion offspring for 1961 were Ch. Artru Ambassador with six champions, Ch. Norbill's Fantabulous with six, Ch. Hall-Way Hoot Mon with five, Ch. Merryhaven Strutaway, Ch. Valli-Lo Flashaway, Ch. Hickory Hill High Catch, Ch. Norbill's Naturally, and Ch. Taylor's Dark Knight, each with five champions to their credit for 1961.

"LES GIRLS"

Topping the list of Top Producing Dam of 1961 was the black Ch. Palmwood Ace Hi Pattern who produced five champions in that single year. No other bitch of any breed produced more than five champions during that year. Ch. Kromwell Kid Gloves was right behind with four champion get, and Ch. Hickory Hill High Night, Ch. Pinetop's Certainly Fancy, and Yamtown Scotchbroom all produced three champions each.

A pair of six-month-old puppies sired by Ch. Daybreak Dubonnet and owned by the Dreamridge Kennels.

TOP PRODUCING SIRES AND DAMS FOR 1962

Robert Graham's statistical survey for 1961 produced such interest that *Popular Dogs* published the results of the 1962 survey in April 1963.

Ch. Crackerbox Certainly, the top living sire in the breed at that time with 60 champions to his credit to this date was again #1 all-breed winner for having sired 18 champions during 1962. Little wonder this enviable record prompted Mr. Graham to compile the statistics that revealed our top sires and dams.

Ch. Clarkdale Capital Stock was second in the Sporting Group with 16 champions; Ch. Scioto Bluff's Sinbad was third with 12. Ch. Merryhaven Strutaway and Ch. Valli-Lo's Flashaway each accounted for six champions. Ch. Dau-Hans Dan Morgan, Ch. Norbill's Naturally, and Ch. Pinetop's Fancy Parade sired five champions each.

On the distaff side, bitches were required to have whelped three or more champions to make the list of Top Producing Dams of 1962. Four Cocker bitches qualified with three or four champions that year. Ch. Misty Mornin' Motif whelped four champions in 1962 while Ch. Chuck O'Luck's Calliope, Nor-Mar's Nicolette, and Southerndown Midnight Magic each produced three.

Five hundred twenty-seven Sporting dogs sired 770 champions during 1962 of which Cocker Spaniels accounted for 226 champions out of 122 dogs.

Sundust Johan Frisco, photographed at two and a half years of age. The sire was American Ch. Dur Bets Knight to Remember ex English and American Ch. Windy Hill's Dur Bet Tis Patti of Sundust. Owned by Yvonne Knapper of Dorset, England.

1965

During 1965, Mrs. Irene Phillips began keeping statistical records of the Top Sires and Dams and her compilations were published in the May 1966 issue of *Popular Dogs*. According to her statement in that article, she regretted Mr. Graham's ending his tally with the 1963 results and took it upon herself to continue the system as a contribution to our Top Producers. She made the requirements stand at five or more champions for the sires and three for the dams. Needless to say, her study attracted much interest and enthusiasm.

In 1965, six Cocker Spaniels qualified for her list of sires. Ch. Maindale's Mr. Success and Ch. Artru Available each sired 10 that year to head the list of Cockers, with Ch. Artru Johnny Be Good contributing nine champions. Ch. Jo-Be-Glen's Bronze Falcon, Ch. Merryhaven Strutaway, Ch. Orient's It's A Pleasure, and Ch. Scioto Bluff's Sinbad each had eight. Ch. Bigg's Snow Prince and Ch. Maticours Monogram sired seven each, and Ch. Baliwick Baghdad accounted for six. Ch. Hall-Way Hoot Mon, Ch. Pinetop's Fancy Parade, Ch. Silver Maple Sharp Tri-Umph, Ch. Stonewalk Sharpshooter, and Ch. Winsom Ways' Tob racked up five champions each.

TOP PRODUCING DAMS FOR 1965

Two Cocker Spaniel dams produced four champions during the year to qualify. They were Ch. Chalimoor Gum Drop and Ch. Hall-Way Fancy Free. They were both the top winners in the Sporting Group with no dam of any breed having more than four champions. There were three other Cocker bitches that qualified, each with three champions for 1965. They were Ch. Pioneer Peek-A-Boo, Ch. R-Fun's Fun Loving, and Tucky-Ho Artrunet.

OTHER TOP PRODUCER STATISTICS

Records of the Cocker Spaniel Top Sires and Dams were published in magazines such as the *American Cocker Review* and the aforementioned. Dr. Marge Saari was the compiler for the yearly recordings and articles on the breed's prominent contenders for these titles.

GREAT SHOW DOGS OF AMERICA

In May 1976, *Showdogs* magazine began a six-part series of articles featuring the great show dogs of America from 1955 through 1966 as compiled by Irene Phillips, now Mrs. Harold Schlintz. Each month a specific group was featured and the results of the six groups were published originally in book form.

Irene Phillips again called upon her successful Top Ten rating system broken down into groups. Six Cocker Spaniels were represented in the Sporting Group of great show dogs of America. They were: for 1960, Ch. Pinetop's Fancy Parade and Ch. Gail's Ebony Don D; for 1956 and 1957, Ch. Artru's Hot Rod; for 1958, Ch. Wilco's Little Barney; and Ch. Clarkdale Capital Stock for 1959.

Others listed under the Cocker Spaniel breed heading in addition to the above were Ch. Baliwick Banter, Ch. Eufaula's Dividend, Ch. Hickory Hill High Jack, Ch. Mel-Lar's Prince Frederick, Ch. Holly Tree High Knight, Ch. Windjammer's Passkey, Ch. Whitefield's Why Certainly, Ch. Silver Maple Jimmy Stardust, Ch. Har-Dee's Hell Bender II, Ch. My-Ida-Ho Promise to Maryville, Ch. Bigg's Snow Prince, Ch. Forjay's Sundown, Ch. Hi-Boots Such Brass, and Ch. Pinefair Password.

We can be grateful to Mrs. Irene Phillips Schlintz for her many, many hours of dedicated work in the compilation of these statistics over so many years.

OUR WESTMINSTER WINNERS

It was 1921 when William T. Payne's Cocker Spaniel, Ch. Midkiff Seductive won Best in Show at the Westminster Kennel Club show. The show which was held on February 10, 11, and 12 at Madison Square Garden, had 1,754 dogs representing 2,725 entries that year as compared to 1,177 dogs for their first Westminster show in 1877 at Gilmores Garden. The Cocker entry was 91 for judge C.F. Neilson.

In 1935 Miss Alice A. Dodsworth's brace of Cocker Spaniels won the rosette for Best Brace in Show at the Garden, but it wasn't until the 1940 Westminster show that another Cocker Spaniel won Best in Show, a win he repeated in 1941. The dog was Ch. My Own Brucie, owned by H. E. Mellenthin, and he was to give new impetus to the breeding of Cocker Spaniels. The entries were 2,738 and 2,548 respectively.

In 1954, Mrs. Carol E. Morgan's Ch. Carmor's Rise and Shine won the coveted #1 win at this most prestigious of all American dog shows and it has not seen a Cocker in that top spot since. Rise and Shine topped an entry of 2,572 dogs.

WESTMINSTER GROUP WINNERS

After My Own Brucie's Best in Show win, it wasn't until 1945 that a Cocker topped the Sporting Group at Westminster. Ch. Stockdale Town Talk, owned by C. B. Van Meter, was the dog. The next was Rise and Shine in 1954, and Ch. Gail's Ebony Don D, owned by Mr. and Mrs. R. O. Fraser, in 1957. In 1960 Laffoon and Robbins' Ch. Pinetop's Fancy Parade won the Sporting Group and in 1961 it was Mrs. Clinton Bishop's Ch. Fraclin Colonel Caridas. 1973 saw Peggy Westphal's beautiful buff bitch, Ch. Sagamore Toccoa, win it and in 1981, Mrs. Byron Covey and Mai Wilson's gorgeous Kamp's Kaptain Kool thrilled the spectators with his Sporting Group win.

MARGARET SAARI AND HER STATISTICS FOR THE AMERICAN SPANIEL CLUB

By 1959 the national standings for Cocker Spaniels in the show rings was producing interest, and Dr. Margaret Saari, D.V.M., was encouraged to start keeping records of her own. These yearly standings were first published in *The American Cocker Review* in 1959 and have been published ever since.

Dr. Saari not only compiled a list of the Top Ten Winners for each year since that time, but she has devoted further compilation of records concerning the Top Thirty Cocker Studs and Bitches in the history of the breed as well as the Top Living Sires and Dams today. Such valuable statistics should be made a written record and preserved for future breed enthusiasts. Dr. Saari's tabulations, some of which have not been published elsewhere before, present a slightly different result from the Phillips System final awards. They are presented on pages 307-319 of this book as a tribute to her years of dedication to facts and figures. Every serious Cocker Spaniel exhibitor will find them invaluable.

The author is particularly grateful that Dr. Saari offered her statistics for inclusion in this book to present them as a permanent record for dog show enthusiasts.

THE DECADE OF THE 1980's

Since it is our intention to publish a Cocker Spaniel breed book each decade from now on, we feel it important to record the top-producing sires and dams for 1980 as this book goes to press. For those interested in having their dogs represented in the next volume for wins accrued during the 1980's, it is suggested that photographs be collected along with the winning records for publication in the 1990 edition. In addition to giving the top show dogs of the '80's their "claim to fame," it will be of interest for comparison with these great dogs who contributed so much to the breed during the previous decades.

Shadowridge Anticipation, bred by Dr. Cheryl McNeil of Pensacola, Florida, and owned by Joy and George Kirkland. Sire was Ch. Frandee's Declaration ex Karavan's Dixie Pixie.

Susan Kelley's fabulous Gorgeous George, C.D.X., during an obedience trial. Well known in Cocker obedience circles in California, George was a successful and willing worker—even after suffering a stroke at six years of age.

CHAPTER TWELVE

Cocker Spaniels in Obedience

Pam Burrows and parti-color Ch. Shadowridge Follow Me, C.D., wait while Mismark Midnight Cinda, C.D.X., goes over the jump. Pam, "Mia" and Cinda were photographed at obedience practice in 1977.

Dogs shows and conformation classes had a big head start on obedience. It was in 1933 that the first obedience tests were held in Mount Kisco, New York. It was Mrs. Helene Whitehouse Walker who inaugurated these initial all-breed obedience tests that she had brought from England. Along with her kennel maid at that time, Blanche Saunders, they were responsible for the staging of the first four obedience tests held in the United States.

Obedience training and tests for dogs were an immediate success from the moment those first 150 spectators saw the dogs go through their paces.

Mrs. Walker was instrumental in getting the American Kennel Club to recognize and even sponsor the obedience trials at their dog shows, and her discussions with Charles T. Inglee (then the vice president of the A.K.C.,) ultimately led to their recognition. In 1935 she wrote the first published booklet on the subject called simply "Obedience Tests." These tests were eventually incorporated into the rules of the A.K.C. obedience requirements in March 1936. It developed into a 22-page booklet that served as a manual for judges, handlers, and the show-giving clubs. The larger version was called "Regulations and Standards for Obedience Test Field Trials."

Mrs. Walker, Josef Weber (another well-known dog trainer), and Miss Saunders added certain refinements and basic procedures and exercises and these were published in the April 1936 issue of the *American Kennel Gazette.*

On June 13th of that same year, the North Westchester Kennel Club held the first American Kennel Club licensed obedience test in conjunction with their all-breed dog show. The exercises for Novice and Open classes remain virtually unchanged today—almost half a century later. Only Tracking Dog and Tracking Dog Excellent have been added in the intervening years.

At that very first show there were 12 entries for judge Mrs. Wheeler H. Page.

By June of 1939 the A.K.C. realized obedience was here to stay and saw the need for an advisory committee. One was established and chaired by Donald Fordyce with enthusiastic members from all parts of the country willing to serve on it. George Foley of Pennsylvania was on the board. He was one of the most important of all men in the fancy, being superintendent of most of the dog shows on the Eastern seaboard. Mrs. Radcliff Farley, also of Pennsylvania, was on the committee with Miss Aurelia Tremaine of Massachusetts, Mrs. Bryand Godsell of California, Mrs. W. L. McCannon of Massachusetts, Samuel

Blick of Maryland, Frank Grant of Ohio, as well as Josef Weber and Mrs. Walker. Their contribution was to further tighten and standardize judging procedures and utility exercises.

A little of the emphasis on dog obedience was diverted with the outbreak of World War II, when talk switched to the topic of dogs serving in defense of their country. As soon as peace was declared, however, interest in obedience reached new heights. In 1946, the American Kennel Club called for another Obedience Advisory Committee, this time headed by John C. Neff. This committee included Blanche Saunders, Clarence Pfaffenberger, Theodore Kapnek, L. Wilson Davis, Howard P. Calussen, Elliott Blackiston, Oscar Franzen, and Clyde Henderson.

Under their leadership, the obedience booklet grew to 43 pages. Rules and regulations were even more standardized than ever before and there was the addition of the requirements for the Tracking Dog title.

In 1971, an obedience department was established at the American Kennel Club offices to keep pace with the growth of the sport and for constant review and guidance for show-giving clubs. Judge Richard H. D'Ambrisi was the director until his untimely death in 1973, at which time his duties were assumed by James E. Dearinger along with his two special consultants L. Wilson Davis for Tracking and Reverend Thomas O'Connor for Handicapped Handlers.

Ar-Gyle Coco of San-D-Glyn, C.D.X. "Coke" is ready to try for his U.D. title and is believed to be the first chocolate Cocker Spaniel to earn the C.D.X. title. His owner is Glyn Petty of Myrtle Creek, Oregon. The sire was Ch. Ar-Gyle Coco Caravelle ex Ar-Gyle Coco Caramel.

The members of this 1973 committee were Thomas Knott of Maryland, Edward Anderson of Pennsylvania, Jack Ward of Virginia, Lucy Neeb of Louisiana, William Phillips of California, James Falkner of Texas, Mary Lee Whiting of Minnesota, and Robert Self of Illinois, co-publisher of the important *Front and Finish* obedience newspaper.

While the Committee functions continuously, meetings of the board are tentatively held every other year, unless a specific function or obedience question comes up, in which case a special meeting is called.

During the 1975 session, the Committee held discussions on several old and new aspects of the obedience world. In addition to their own ever-increasing responsibilities to the fancy, they discussed Seminars and Educational Symposiums, the licensing of Tracking clubs, a booklet with suggested Guidelines for obedience judges, Schutzhund training, and the aspects of a Utility Excellent Class degree.

Through the efforts of succeeding Advisory Committee members, the future of the sport has been insured, as well as the continuing emphasis on the working abilities for which dogs were originally bred. Obedience work also provides novices an opportunity to train and handle their dogs in an atmosphere that provides maximum pleasure and accomplishment at minimum expense—which is precisely what Mrs. Walker intended.

When the Advisory Committee met in December 1980 many of the familiar names were among those listed as attending and continuing to serve the obedience exhibitors. James E. Dearinger, James C. Falkner, Rev. Thomas V. O'Connor, Robert T. Self, John S. Ward, Howard E. Cross, Helen F. Phillips, Samuel W. Kodis, George S. Pugh, Thomas Knott, and Mrs. Esme Treen were present and accounted for.

As we look back on almost a half century of obedience trials, we can only surmise that the pioneers—Mrs. Helene Whitehouse Walker and Blanche Saunders—would be proud of the progress made in the obedience rings.

THE OBEDIENCE RATING SYSTEMS

Just as the Phillips System mushroomed out of the world of show dogs, it was almost inevitable that a "system" or "systems" to measure the successes of obedience dogs would become a reality.

By 1974, Nancy Shuman and Lynn Frosch had established the "Shuman System" of recording the Top Ten all-breed obedience dogs in the country. They also listed the Top four in every breed if each dog had accumulated a total of 50 points or more according to their requirements. Points were accrued in a descending scale based on their qualifying scores from 170 and up.

No Cocker Spaniel qualified for All-breed of Sporting Group in 1974, but there were four Cockers that rated in their breed. Topping the list was Mary Lee Whiting's Kiss O'Blarney, U.D.; M.B. and W.H. Reusch's Sherry Flip, U.D., second; E.C. Gilbert's Breamrid Pink Champagne, third; and Bronze Classy Mr. Casey, U.D., owned by I. Smithwick, fourth.

1975 OBEDIENCE WINNERS

Front and Finish, the dog trainers' newspaper also publishes the Delany System for the Top Ten Obedience Dogs, compiled by Kent Delaney, which rates the dogs in a different manner from the Shuman System.

In the Delaney System, points are awarded for High in Trial or for class placements only and based on the published results in the *American Kennel Gazette*. High in Trial winners get a single point for each dog in competition. First place in the class earns a point for each dog competing in that class. Second place in the class earns a point for each dog competing in the class less one. Third place in the class earns a point less two, and the fourth place winner in the class earns a point for each dog competing less three.

In 1975 no Cocker Spaniel made it to the Top Ten all-breed or Sporting Group lists, but there were 10 that qualified for the Top Ten Cocker Spaniels. Mary Lee Whiting's Mar Lee's Folly O'Blarney, C.D.X. was #1 with E.R. Lang's Butch's Athena, C.D.X. in the #2 spot. K and R Steele's Lady Peggy Lucky Ace of Hearts was #3; B. Hoel and B. McGowan's Ch. Handsome Beelzebub, C.D. was #4; J. Jacobson's Par Fra's Captain Jamoree, #5; J. Hayes's Chesterfield's Amazing Grace, #6; Mrs. S. Petty's Teddy Bear of Roxie Rogue, #7; Juniper's Jamborette owned by L. Smithwich, #8; Bloom's Buzzin Honeybee owned by R. and P. Bloom, #9; and Sargeant Pepper Lonely Heart, owned by R. Pennix was #10.

Ch. Tabaka's Tres Jolie, U.D., with her offspring winning the Brood Bitch Class at the 1970 Washington State Cocker Spaniel Club Specialty show. Four of the five pictured went on to finish their championships. Owned and bred by Ruth N. Tabaka of Seattle, Washington.

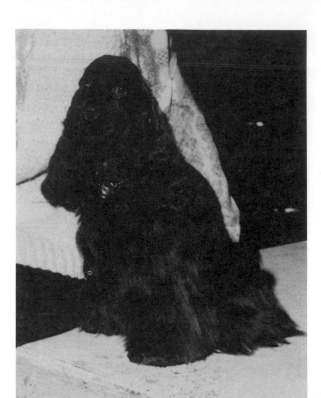

San-D-Glyn's Choclit Cenderela earned her C.D. title in three shows, with her lowest score being 194. Cindy was sired by Ar-Gyle Coco of San-D-Glyn ex Golden Copper.

1976 WINNERS

In 1976, Mary Lee Whiting's Folly O'Blarney once again was #1 in the Top Ten Cocker Spaniels in obedience, in the Delaney System, as published in *Front and Finish*, and once again Butch's Athena repeated the 1975 win in the #2 position. Reusch's Sherry Flip tied for the #5 and #6 spots with M. Dupree's Mighty Mac West Oak. In the #3 listing was Ch. Dalmarkei's Bo Jangles owned by M. Keith; Shelby 11 owned by S. Tramp was #4. S. and T. Smith's Misty Dawn of Sugar Hill was #7, C. and K. Wilson's Frosted Freckled Faerie was #8, F. and S. Hammond's Lord Hanzel of Canterbury was #9, and R. and N. Beam's Black Shadow was #10 on the list.

The Top Four Cocker Spaniels in 1976 saw Ch. Mar Lee's Folly O'Blarney, U.D., and Butch's Athena in the first and second positions respectively for the third consecutive year. Number 3 listing was Cue's Midnight Cinderella owned by T. and J. McCue, and #4 was E. and A.B. Hoversen's Crestwood Black Mischief, U.D. There were no Cocker Spaniels in the Shuman System for all-breeds or Top Sporting Dogs for 1976.

1977

The 1977 Shuman System winners were once again familiar names in obedience circles. For the fourth year in a row Ch. Mar Lee's Folly O'Blarney U.D. held the #1 spot. Butch's Athena dropped to the #3 position while Reusch's Sherry Flip moved up to #2. Cue's Midnight Cinderella, U.D. tied for third with Athena.

1978

In 1978 *Front and Finish* published the top obedience award winners compiled as the Delaney System, and the Top Ten Dogs were listed for all breeds, groups, and individual breeds. The Cocker Spaniel list was topped by Ch. Mar Lee's Folly O'Blarney, U.D. for an incredible fifth year in a row! Two through 10 were listed as follows: Reusch's Gin & Sin, C.D.X., #2; Dreamridge Beautiful Dream, C.D. owned by D. Prueske was #3; Raintree Libby Libby Libby owned by D. and J. Wilson was #4; Reusch's Sherry Flip, U.D., owned by M. and W. Reusch was #5; Roz's Stormy Knight owned by R. Boyer was #6; Reusch's Mickey Finn Lea Lad owned by M. Reusch and L. Harrington was #7; Our Shana Bagel owned by S. Kornhaber was #8; Nuggets' Golden Buff, C.D. owned by D. Zimmerman was #9; and Val's Little Krisegg owned by V. Wilmot was #10.

Gladyan Voodoo Dahl, pictured in September 1979, is owned by J. Prouty of Canada. Dahl is a Canadian champion and earned a Canadian C.D.X.

Top Four Cocker Spaniels in the 1978 Shuman System were Reusch's Sherry Flip, U.D. in the #1 position with the 5-year #1 dog, Ch. Mar Lee's Folly O'Blarney dropping to #2. Reusch's Gin and Sin was #3 and Dreamridge Beautiful Dreamer was #4.

1979

The Top Ten in the '79 Delaney System was topped by Mrs. B. Baker's Em's Bakers Bartered Goods. In the #2 spot was Mary Lee Whiting with yet another top O'Blarney Cocker. This time it was Mar Lee's Jopa O'Blarney. Number 3 was Smarti Parti Rellin's Topaz, C.D. owned by D. Miller. Number 4 was M. Wilson's Willow Hill's Tuckerton Rick; #5 was Midnight Star In The Sky owned by M. Wilhelm; #6 was Cypress Bayou's Mardi Gras owned by R. Logrie; #7 was Ch. Karlyle's Midnight Sun owned by D. and R. Jones, #8 was Dreamridge Beautiful Dream, C.D.X. owned by Mrs. D. Prueske; #9 was Lea Lad's Touch of Class owned by D. and D. Miller, and #10 was D. Jay's Pepe Bundle of Fun owned by C. Strom.

The Shuman System for the same year named the Top Four Cocker Spaniels as: #1, Dreamridge Beautiful Dream; #2, Reusch's Gin and Sin; and #3 and #4 with an equal score was Meri-Knol's Marmalade, U.D., and Sieben's Misty Girl.

Tom O'Neal and future Dreamridge champions whelped in 1977. DanDee, Democrat, and Dare-Me became show winners.

Echo Valley's Star Sin-sation, C.D.X., owned by Dr. Cheryl McNeil and Alyce M. Rhodes, was bred by Bud and Carole Obriecht. Star was sired by Ch. Scioto Bluffs Sin-Bahr ex Ch. Mar-Geo's Star Brite.

1980

The 1980 Delaney System winners were headed by Belgium Buff Earl of Pearl, owned by S. and S. Bergen. The Gilbert's Gilhaven's Gypsy Girl, M.B. Reusch's Gin & Sin, and H. Robinson's Yukon's Buffed Gold Nugget were second, third, and fourth respectively. Number 5 was E. O'Neal's Rusty Rum of Radclif, and #6 went to yet another of Mary Lee Whiting's Cockers, Mar Lee's Bridie O'Blarney. Number 7 was D. Jay's Pepe Bundle of Fun, C.D., owned by C. Strom, and J & A Regan's Almajon's Dream O'Shannon was #8. Number 9 was Call Me Jayson Michael, C.D., owned by C. Knauss, and the #10 spot was filled by Lady Mara, owned by C. Strong.

By the end of the second quarter of 1980 a Cocker Spaniel named Em's Bakers Bartered Goods made it to the #14 position on the list of obedience Sporting Dogs according to the Shuman System, and Belgium Buff Earl of Pearl had captured the #14 position in the Delaney System as published in *Front and Finish*.

THE DOG OBEDIENCE CLASSICS

In March 1976 the Gaines' Dog Research Center, located in White Plains, New York began its sponsorship of the United States Dog Obedience Classic. Founded by the Illini Obedience Association in 1975 the first classic was held in Chicago.

Gaines' motive in the support of the regional events and the Classic was to emphasize to dog owners, both present and future, their belief that an obedience trained dog is a better citizen and an asset to any community. Their support was to offer rosettes, trophies, and plaques, as well as prize money for a series of regional competitions and for the Classic at the year's end. Prize money for the regional awards was almost $3,000 while the Classic prize money was in excess of $5,000. Each year the Classic is held in another region where a local obedience club plays host to participants from all over the country.

By 1978 when the two-day Classic was held in Los Angeles at their Sports Arena, people from 23 states exhibited with an entry well over the 180-dog limit with dogs going through their paces in eight rings. The top winner earns the title of Super Dog, and along with other prizes and money, takes home the sterling silver dumbbell trophy.

The Gaines' Dog Obedience Classic competition is open to all breeds and owners who qualify and enjoy the challenge of team work with their dogs.

Ch. Merribark's Carbon Copy, C.D.X., bred by the Merribark Kennels in California, is proudly exhibited by Nancy L. Ray, owner and junior handler.

THE GAINES' DOG OBEDIENCE "FIDO"

In 1980 Gaines began yet another award of recognition in the dog fancy. They started awarding a yearly "Fido" statue for outstanding achievement in the dog obedience field. Their first "Fido" was presented on November 22, 1980 in Denver, Colorado to Mary Lee Whiting of Minneapolis, Minnesota.

Gaines' Steve Willett, Director of their Professional Services, made the award for outstanding contributions to the advancement of obedience training and competition.

"Marley" is an American Kennel Club approved judge for all obedience classes and a member of the A.K.C.'s Obedience Advisory Committee. Marley trains over 275 dogs a week at her Canine College in Minneapolis. She is also a breeder of Cocker Spaniels and at the beginning of the 1980's was exhibiting her sixth generation of Cockers in both obedience and breed rings. She is one of the original supporters of the Illini Obedience Association and finished in the finals of both the 1975 and 1976 Classic finals. She has also authored a book entitled *From Cradle to College—Raising Your Puppy*.

Marley's Mar-Lee's Air O'Blarney, U. D. was also the Top Obedience Cocker Spaniel in 1967, was 3rd Highest Scoring Sporting Dog, and was number nine in the all-breeds category. He was Top Obedience Cocker in 1968 as well, a year when 106 Cockers earned obedience titles.

One of the first ladies of the obedience world, Mary Lee Whiting, was presented with the first Gaines Fido award in obedience. The statuette was presented by A. Steve Willett, Director of the Gaines Professional Services, before a crowd of hundreds of obedience people at the banquet marking the Gaines Obedience Classic in Denver, Colorado, in November 1980. The inscription cites Mary Lee for "outstanding contributions to the advancement of obedience training and competition." She is also an American Kennel Club approved judge for all obedience classes and was a member of the A.K.C.'s Obedience Advisory Committee. She is owner and trainer at her Canine College in Minneapolis.

Milru's Licorice Honey, U.D.T., whelped June 1951, and owned and trained by Ruth Muller of Centerport, New York. This incomparable worker was excellent at tracking and was always a high scorer in the trials. Her sire was Ch. Blue Gates Sky King ex Moretta's Gilaine.

MILRU—1930's

One of the oldest and best known names in Cocker Spaniels belongs to Ruth C. Muller who established her Milru Kennels back in the 1930's in Huntington Terrace, Long Island. A certificate from the litter registration department at the American kennel Club, dated June 26, 1939, registered a litter of two males and two females whelped June 6, 1939, sired by Brynwood Danny Boy out of Tinkle. That was a long time ago, and as we enter the decade of the 1980's Milru is still very much in evidence—especially in obedience circles.

In 1959, Milru's Cheery Cherub earned her U.D. title, and in addition to many other wins and trophies, was highest scoring dog in many shows along the way to winning the title. "Cherie" also entertains at various local hospitals with Mrs. Muller who puts her through her obedience exercises for their enthusiastic audiences.

In 1951, Milton and Ruth Muller had another U.D.T. dog, Milru's Licorice Honey, who retired the Bob Noerr Memorial Trophy for being highest scoring dog at the American Spaniel Club show two years in a row for 1956 and '57. Honey enjoyed every phase of training and showing, proving herself to be a "natural" in both field and water trials; she especially enjoyed tracking. She was always "in the ribbons" when working.

The Mullers were also the breeder-owners of Ch. Milru's Tansation, whelped April 1960, sired by Ch. Shady Hill's Bit o'Copper and out of Milru's Cheery Cherub, shown by Ted Young, Jr. in the show ring.

Milru's Cheery Cherub, U.D., owned by Ruth Muller of Centerport, New York. Cherub and her owner put on special obedience exhibitions at hospitals for mentally retarded children and delighted audiences by retrieving stuffed toys from them. Cherub is pictured here with one of her own favorite stuffed toys.

Ch. Kamps Kaptain Kool was one of the major Sporting Dog winners in 1980 and is top-winning male Cocker Spaniel of all times. He is also the top-winning parti-color of all times. This glorious photo of "Kappy" was taken by Missy Yuhl for co-owners Mrs. Byron A. Covey and Mai Wilson.

Above: Champion and O.T. Champion Mar Lee's Folly O'Blarney, the first O.T. Champion Cocker Spaniel in the breed. Owned and trained by Mary Lee Whiting, Minneapolis, Minnesota. Folly taking the jump with the dumbbell was photographed by Matt Phillips.

Opposite: American and Mexican Ch. Sharay's Sherbert Delight, C.D., W.D.X., was trained by Don Ploke for owner Sharon Landry of Las Vegas. "Sherb" is among the top three or four field Cockers in the country. He is also the first Cocker with a W.D.X. to produce an offspring, Sharay's Delight of My Luv, that also qualified for a W.D.X.

Above: Ch. Frandee's Amos Moses, C.D., owned by Sandy Smith and handled for her here by Dee Dee Wood. Photo by Henry Schley.

Opposite: Best Brace in the Sporting Group at the Portland Kennel Club show were Marquis Wild Firer and Ch. Tam-Crest Summertime Promise. Debbie Von Horn handled the brace owned by Gladys Von Horn and Joyce and Steve Johnson.

Above: Ch. Tallylyn Cassandra, a Specialty and Group-placing bitch, owner-handled by Dr. Cheryl McNeil, who co-owns her with John and Laura Sherrick. Sire was Ch. Heatherland Hillbilly, C.D., ex Tallylyn Tan Pizazz. The breeder was Barbara Bush. The judge was Dick Duding.

Opposite: Reverie Reminisce, bred by Robert and Eileen Schooley and owned by Joy Kirkland and Pam Burrows. This lovely, heavy-coated bitch was sired by Ch. Heatherland Hillbilly, C.D., ex Parksway's Chanson De La Soir. "Missy" is pictured here at the age of one year in 1979.

Above: American and Canadian Ch. Tabaka's Tidbit O'Wynden, C.D.X., Best In Show at the huge Trenton Kennel Club show in New Jersey under judge Robert Graham. Ted Young, Jr., handled for co-owners Ruth Tabaka and Laura Watt O'Connor, Seattle, Washington.

Opposite: American and Canadian Ch. Tabaka's Tan Treat, winner of four Bests in Show in Canada and winner of numerous Bests of Breed and Specialties. Treat is shown winning Best of Breed at the Washington State Cocker Spaniel Club Specialty under judge Howard Frailey. Bred by Ruth Tabaka and owned by Diane Lilley.

Above: American and Canadian Ch. Butch's Kountry Boy, multiple Best in Show and Best of Breed winner, is pictured winning the breed at the summer National Specialty show under judge Colonel Lamar Mathis. Handler is Jerry Moon for owner Gladys Von Horn of Vancouver, Washington.

Opposite: Canadian Ch. Calypso's Sparkling Burgundy, bred and owned by Tom and Laurie Acklin, pictured winning Best of Opposite at the Cocker Spaniel Club of Central Ontario show in 1978 under handler Martin Flugel. Sire was Ch. Windy Hill's Makes-Its-Point ex Calypso's Tanfastic Action.

Above: American and Canadian Ch. Schiely's Tar N Feathers, photographed in full show coat, is owned by Beverly Schiely of North Olmsted, Ohio.

Opposite: American, Mexican and Canadian Ch. O'Brien's Silver Challenge, silver dog bred by Mary Anne O'Brien and owned by Lindy Hay. The sire was Ch. LaMar's London Marc ex Our Sassy Irish Girl. Photo by Missy Yuhl.

221

Above: Best of Breed at the 1980 Bay Cities Cocker Spaniel Club show was Ch. Bobwin's Sir Ashley, owned and shown by Winnie Vick of Suisun, California. Miss Martha Jane Ablett, judge.

Opposite: International Champion Junkin Chochosan pictured winning Best Opposite Sex at the 1971 Cocker Spaniel Club of Southern California Specialty show. Carl Anderson handled and Irene Gaddy Zimmerman, Club President, presented the trophy.

223

Ch. The Nsufrabl Frekl, the April 1980 cover dog for the *American Kennel Club Gazette*. Owned and photographed by Michael Allen of Costa Mesa, California.

SAN-D-GLYN

Glyn Petty is the owner of Ar-Gyle Coco of San-D-Glyn, C.D.X. and is training with Coco for his U.D. title. "Coke" may prove to be the first chocolate Cocker to earn this title, beginning his training in 1980. Glyn is also the owner of Cal-Ore's Chocolate Treat, bred by Nancy Ray, and she is active in the show ring as well as in the field. She has three Cockers, all of which have earned their C.D. titles in just three shows, and Coke who won his C.D.X. in just five shows. All are happy, eager workers with scores in the 190's.

OBEDIENCE AND THE MOVIES

Three of William and Peggy Mellen's most famous Cocker Spaniels were Jet Job Astra's Red Bruce, U.D.T., Jet Job's Starfire, C.D.X., and Jet Job's Trace of Astra, C.D. They were famous because they were "movie dogs" and worked in several motion pictures. As Peggy Mellen sees it, the more obedience training a dog has, the better movie dog the animal will be. It isn't hard to understand the necessity for a dog being able to take instruction while working in front of a camera.

Mrs. Mellen, an A.K.C obedience judge, was the trainer in the late 1960's for the Hollywood Dog Obedience Club and was herself active in obedience circles as a breeder-owner-handler of many Cocker obedience titlists. She also held "Cinema Classes" for other dogs that were trained to perform in motion pictures. The curriculum was divided into two categories: required, basic obedience commands; and special tricks, which included yawning, sneezing, walking on hind legs, etc., all of which might be required performance in a movie.

William Koehler, the author of many books on obedience training, was also active in motion picture work. It was his job to train the dogs for the MGM production of *It's a Dog's Life*. Many dogs from the Orange Empire Dog Club had been trained by Mr. Koehler and were used in the picture.

And lest we forget, it was Carl Spitz's St. Bernard who starred in the adaptation of Jack London's *"Call of the Wild"* starring Clark Gable. Scott Roberts was another of the early dog trainers who worked with the motion picture companies.

OTHER OBEDIENCE ACTIVITIES

For those interested in the obedience sport there are many other activities connected with dog training.

There are Scent Dog Seminars, Hurdle races, World Series of Dog Obedience in Canada, the Association of Obedience Clubs and Judges, to name just a few. The best possible way to keep informed on activities on both a national and local scale is by membership in kennel or obedience clubs, and by reading dog magazines and newspapers published by obedience enthusiasts.

Front and Finish, the dog trainers' newspaper, is perhaps the leading publication of the Delany System and current subscription rates can be had by writing to H. and S. Publications, Inc., 113 S. Arthur Avenue, Galesburg, Illinois 61401. A. J. Harler and Robert T. Self are co-editors of this most worthy and informative publication.

LATEST OBEDIENCE RULES AND REGULATIONS

The American Kennel Club publishes the Obedience Regulations booklet and offers it free of charge when single copies are requested. A check or money order for fifteen cents per copy is required when ordering in quantities for clubs or organizations.

HOW TO UNDERSTAND AND ENJOY AN OBEDIENCE TRIAL

For those just getting into obedience work with their dogs, it is suggested that they obtain and read a booklet entitled "How to Understand and Enjoy an Obedience Trial" available free of charge by the Ralston Purina Company, Checkerboard Square, St. Louis, Missouri 63188.

TRAINING YOUR DOG

While the American Kennel Club will gladly send along the booklets with the rules and regulations for competition at the shows, you must be prepared to start "basic training" with your dog long before you start thinking about entering obedience trials. There are few things in the world a dog would rather do than please his master; therefore, obedience training—even the learning of his name—will be a pleasure for your dog. If taught correctly it will certainly make him a much nicer animal to live with the rest of his life.

EARLY TRAINING AT HOME

Some breeders believe in starting the training as early as two weeks of age. Repeating the puppy's name and encouraging the puppy to come when called is a good start, if you don't expect too much too soon. Some recommend placing a narrow ribbon around the puppy's neck to get him used to the feel of what will later be a leash. The puppy can play with it and learn the pressure of the pull on his neck before he is actually expected to respond to it.

If you intend to show your puppy, there are other formalities you can observe as early as four weeks of age that will also minimize the start of training. One of the most important points is setting him up on a table in show stance. Make it short and sweet; make it a sort of game, but repeatedly place the puppy in a show stance and hold him that way gently, giving him lavish praise. After a couple of weeks of doing this a few times each day, you will find the puppy takes to the idea of the "stand" and "stay" commands very readily.

WHEN TO START FORMAL TRAINING

Official training should not start until the puppy is about six months of age. Most obedience trainers will not take them in their classes much before this age. However, as the puppy grows along the way, you should certainly get him used to his name, to coming when he is called, and to the meaning of words like "no" and "come" and other basic commands. Repetition and patience are the keys to success since most dogs are not ready for a wide range of words in their rather limited attention span. If your dog is to be a show dog, it would be wise not to forget to concentrate on the "stand" and "stay" commands.

THE REWARD METHOD

The only acceptable kind of training is the kindness and reward method which will build a strong bond between dog and master. Try to establish respect and attention, not fear of punishment. Give each command, preceded by the dog's name, and make it "stick." Do not move on to another command or lesson until the first one is mastered. Train where there are no distractions at first and never when the dog is tired, right after eating, or for too long a period of time. When his interest wanes, quit until another session later in the day. Two or three sessions a day with a bright dog, increasing the time from, say, five minutes to fifteen might do. Each dog is different and you must set your own schedule according to your own dog's ability.

WHAT YOU NEED TO START TRAINING

The soft nylon show leads available at all pet stores are best for early training. Later, perhaps a choke chain can be used. Let the puppy play with the lead or even carry it around when you first put it on. Too much pressure pulling at the end of it is liable to get him off to a bad start. The collar shouldn't seem like a harness.

Three generations of U.D.-titled Cocker Spaniels, owned and trained by Mary Lee Whiting of Minneapolis, are (left to right) Marly's Harvest Queen, Mar Lee's Air O'Blarney, and Mar Lee's Wee Bit O'Blarney.

FORMAL SCHOOL TRAINING

The yellow pages of your phone book can lead you to dog training schools or classes for official training along with other dogs. Usually they are moderately priced and you might best start making inquiries when the puppy is about four months of age so you can be ready for the start of the training classes. If you intend to show your dog, training will make him easier to live with and will do credit to the breed, as well as to both of you.

OBEDIENCE DEGREES

There are several obedience titles recognized by the American Kennel Club that dogs may earn through a process of completed exercises. The Companion Dog, or C.D. degree, is divided into three classes: Novice, Open, and Utility, with a total score of 200 points. After the dog has qualified with a score of at least 170 points or better, he has earned the right to have included the letters "C.D." after his name and is eligible to compete in Open Class competition to earn a Companion Dog Excellent degree, or "C.D.X.", after his name. After qualifying in three shows for this title, he may compete for the Utility Dog title, or "U.D." initials after his name. There are also Tracking Dog and Tracking Dog Excellent titles that may be earned, the requirements for which may be obtained from the A.K.C.

OBEDIENCE TRIAL CHAMPIONSHIP TITLES

The Board of Directors of the American Kennel Club approved Obedience Trial Championship titles in July 1977. Points for these championship titles are recorded only for those dogs that have earned the U.D. title. Any dog that has been awarded the title of Obedience Trial Champion may continue to compete. Dogs that complete requirements receive an Obedience Trial Championship Certificate from the American Kennel Club and are permitted the use of the letters O.T. Ch. preceding their name.

There is great satisfaction for both owner and dog in earning those titles that can be earned, and when considering such training for your dog, you would do well to recall St. Mathilde's Prayer:

O, God,
Give unto me by grace
that obedience which thou hast
given to my little dog
by nature.

CHECK POINTS FOR OBEDIENCE COMPETITORS

* Do your training and have your lessons down pat before entering the show ring

* Make sure you and your dog are ready before entering a show

* Don't expect more than your dog is ready to give. Obedience work is progressive, not all learned in the first few lessons

* It's okay to be nervous, but try not to let your dog know it by over-handling or fidgeting

* Do not punish your dog in or out of the ring. If the dog doesn't work well, it is probably your fault, not his

* Pay attention to the judge and follow instructions exactly

* Pay attention to your own dog and don't talk to others

* Don't forget to exercise your dog before entering the ring

* Be a good loser. If you don't win today, you can try again another day.

* Have confidence in your dog's intelligence. His greatest desire in life is to please you if you have earned his respect and admiration

* If it isn't fun for you and your dog, stay out of the ring and try another sport

Sharay's Delight of My Luv, W.D.X., owned by Bob and Jeanne Boyd of Las Vegas and trained for them by Don Ploke, received his W.D.X. at a field test sponsored by the Cocker Spaniel Club of Orange County, California. Skippy is an offspring of Ch. Sharay's Sherbert Delight, C.D., W.D.X., and is the first offspring of a W.D.X. Cocker to receive the degree in recent times.

CHAPTER THIRTEEN

Cockers in the Field

Ch. Frandee's Fireworks, W.D., excels in the field as well as in the show ring. Bred and owned by Frank and Dee Dee Wood of Norco, California.

At the beginning of the 1980's there were over 7,000 field trials held in the United States, with slightly less than half of them held under the jurisdiction of the American Kennel Club. It is safe to assume that just about every weekend, in just about every state in the union, one can enter a dog in a field trial and become one of the more than a quarter of a million competitors in what is becoming one of America's most popular outdoor sports.

These events include trials for all Pointing dogs, Beagles, Hounds, and Retrievers as well as entries from the various Coon Dog Clubs as well. The Spaniel Trials for all of the accepted Spaniel breeds quite naturally include our Cockers, the smallest of all the sporting and flushing breeds. In the field trials Spaniels are required to cover the ground within distance of their master, to find game, to flush it, and then to stay until commanded to retrieve on land or in water.

IN THE BEGINNING

We know that field competitions have been a great sport ever since the first two men and their dogs appeared in a field together to see whose dog could run the game first; however, the first written record of hunting dogs being used for competitive sports appeared in the *London Gazette* in 1681. For the next one hundred years these hunting matches were made and came to be a regularly organized sporting event in British country life.

The written records indicate that these matches between various kennels were for the purpose of testing speed and endurance. The field trials as we know them today only began to resemble competitions around 1850 when Joshua Logan, a bird dog enthusiast of that era, made an appeal for officially recognized and organized events for sportsmen. He was not successful in the venture until after more than a decade of campaigning and editorializing in the sport journals of the day on behalf of himself and other hunting dog owners. He received additional support in 1857, when J. H. Walsh (the famous dog writer who used the pseudonym "Stonehenge") became editor of *The Field* and published many editorials calling for organized field trials.

In 1864, a Mr. John Douglas took it upon himself to stage the first officially recognized field trial. He wrote the rules, invited the judges, and put up all the prize money. It was the first positive step in the right direction. This first trial was held on Tuseday, April 18, 1865 at the Southill, Bedfordshire estate of Samuel White-

Champion Altair, in full coat, readily takes to the water and retrieves on his first day in the field at the age of seven years. Michael Allen, Costa Mesa, California.

bread. Sixteen bird dogs competed for judges Rev. Thomas Pearce and John W. Walker, and they were judged on the following point system:

Nose	40 points
Pace and Range	30 points
Temperament	10 points
Staunchness Before	10 points
Staunchness Behind	10 points

By May of 1866 the point count had been revised somewhat with the requirements as follows:

Pace and Range	20 points
Obedience	20 points
Style in Hunting	15 points
Game-finding Abilities	20 points
Style in Pointing	10 points

The first field trials just for Spaniels were held on January 3 and 4, 1899 and sponsored by the Sporting Spaniel Club in England. The winner was a 25-pounder named Stylish Pride. While the trials were said to have been satisfactory, apparently all the performances by the dogs were not. Mr. Arkwright, president of the club, commented: "All Spaniels were unsteady to shot and wing. All ran mute with the exception of one puppy." The second trial held in December of the same year found the club president making another pointed comment: "All winners quiet, mute, and too highly trained!"

"BREAKING" FOR THE FIELD

Before 1850, many of the prominent hunters of the day relied on dog dealers to field train or "break" their dogs or to supply their packs with dogs that had already been trained and broken. As time went by many of the owners had become so involved with field work that they actually preferred to break their own dogs—though the methods and procedures on just how to accomplish this were not common knowledge to everyone.

With the idea of doing their own training a brand new idea appeared in the spring 1858 edition of *The Field*. Certain basic rules and observations on how to accomplish this were published. It had become an expensive proposition to have dogs professionally trained, and the sportsmen came to the conclusion that they would rather spend the money set aside for training their dogs on buying quality puppies for their field work and doing their own breaking.

In the beginning many sought and required the assistance and advice of a keeper who had done breaking himself and who sometimes assisted the sportsmen in seeing to it that they secured only the best possible prospects at the outset.

ACTUAL TRAINING

Sportsmen hunted most frequently with a brace of dogs, the brace consisting of four dogs. And while the brace was always prepared for hunting in the field, there was a brace-and-a-half being trained to supplement the already existing pack. This also allowed for replacements in the existing group and allowed for drop-outs or defects in the dogs going through the training process. These specially chosen puppies were fed according to the best available diets known at the time and were carefully housed and observed as part of the training for the field.

Training commenced near the end of January each year and continued until each dog was ready to join a pack or was mustered out for lack of ability. The dogs were taken out on virtually empty stomachs in the belief that too much food affected their ability or desire to keep on the scent.

Puppies were "walked out" early and taught as soon as possible to learn their name and that each command would be preceded by their name; they learned to heel, to run forward, and to lie down and stay down on command, and they were taught strict adherence to orders. Occasionally guns were shot off over their heads to prevent their being gun-shy at maturity.

The trainers, also called "breakers," began teaching the puppies restraint by placing tidbits of food before them and restraining them with the word "toho." Restraint was an important part of the training so that later when they came upon the game in the field they would not damage or devour it, since the dog's instinct or desire for game should be greater than its appetite for food if it was going to be a good field dog.

This restraint was not as difficult to teach as might be imagined, unless the breakers went too far with the dietary limitations and the underfed dogs became ravenous. Just to be sure—if they had any doubts during the early training—they made use of a device known as a "puzzle-peg," though we do not know why it was called this. The puzzle-peg prevented the dogs from actually taking the game into their mouths. Its use was limited since training for the field was based upon voice commands. Since many puppies were taught, with the aid of a check-board to drop and stay down when guns were discharged, they could be reeled in should they seem to want to pick up the game. There is also no written account of one ever being used on a Cocker Spaniel, but they were in evidence during the early days of field training in England.

With the preliminaries mastered, the "range" was taught, which was the most difficult aspect of breaking. It is most desirable for a dog to hunt freely; he should range only when and where directed and should not depend on other dogs to find the scent or allow them to detract him from the scent. The younger dogs were taken into the fields with the older, more experienced dogs to learn this routine. Once they had learned the "follow the leader" idea, the younger dogs were hunted on their own until they were able to flush on their own. Then they were hunted in pairs and eventually became part of the brace of two or four.

This usually did not happen until they had also learned to "quarter" the ground with the dog being "down wind." This assured that the dog was learning to hunt on body scent as well as by foot scent. The good hunter who waited for orders with a competent master managed very well on both counts. But only the really proficient hunters were successful, for the instinct to hunt has to be bred into the dog. The master merely develops it and puts it to use.

Merribark's Moonshadow, C.D., bringing back the bird. Handled by John Ulrick who co-owns with Lorna Ulrick.

Even though almost every dog in the world loves to "fetch"—which is another word for "retrieve"—actual retrieving of game in early times was usually restricted to the special breeds of dogs, such as the Cockers, who were specially trained for this purpose. Then, as now, endless patience is required for field training, and many hours are required for the actual developing of the natural instincts to produce a capable hunting dog that will come anywhere near perfection in the pursuit of a field trial title.

While interest continues on a small but dedicated level in England today, it is a matter of fact that the English field trial enthusiasts almost always have to "take a back seat" when the Irish trainers come over to England for competition. Two field trials were held by the Irish Kennel Club in their first year, 1922.

The first book on the subject appeared in 1847. Its title was *Dog Breaking* and it was written by General W. N. Hutchinson. It sparked additional interest in field work at that time and for a long time afterward.

FIELD TRIALS AT THE TURN OF THE CENTURY

Field trials in England from the earliest beginnings up to the beginning of the 20th century increased from one and two a year to four or five a year. A record eleven field events were held in 1900. After World War II obedience and field trial work increased in popularity in England, though it could in no way be compared with the extensive competition we saw in this country after it first caught on in the mid-1930's.

Am., Mex. Ch. Sherbert Delight, C.D., W.D.X., is owned by Sharon Landry of Las Vegas. "Sherb" is shown retrieving a bird as he qualifies for his W.D.X. in Las Vegas in April 1980.

FIELD TRIALS IN AMERICA

P. H. Bryson of Memphis, Tennessee can be credited for starting the first combination dog show and field trial event in this country. He formed the Tennessee Sportsmen's Association and held the first dual event on October 7 and 8, 1874. Entries totaled 95 dogs to compete, and only Pointers and Setters vied for the Best in Show award, which oddly enough was won by Mr. Bryson's own dog. Fourteen of the show dogs competed the following day in the field trial won by an all-black setter, and the results of the event are recorded in the National American Kennel Club's Stud Book.

In the same year, the first issue of *The Sportsman's Newspaper of America* was published. This weekly became the "bible" of the field trial and hunting set. They opened a kennel registry for field dogs in March of 1876, and the first

three volumes were based on Arnold Burges's book, *The American Kennel and Sporting Field*, copies of which were later given to the American Kennel Club and became the basis of their stud book.

In 1900 the American Field established their own registry. Their *Field Dog Stud Book* specialized in the sporting breeds, and there are several million dogs listed in their files.

Under the jurisdiction of the Amateur Field Trial Clubs of America and the American Field, over a thousand trials are held each year with a championship title being awarded if an entry wins one of their championship stakes and fulfills their qualifying rules. Many hunters and field trialers prefer to compete under the rules of the F.D.S.B. rather than the American Kennel Club, while others maintain dual registrations on all their dogs so they can compete in the events of all organizations.

FIELD TRIALS TODAY

The chief deterrent to field trials today remains to be the locating of suitable grounds on which to hold them. Real estate prices have soared and most "estates" of dog breeders or sportsmen are either too small or non-existent. Locations for field trials are even more impossible to find in the metropolitan areas, and the increased costs of transportation getting to and from the trial sites has also taken its toll of entries.

The day of the family gathering in a picnic atmosphere with participants on horseback and the shouts of "Tally Ho!" are almost completely a thing of the past. However, some diehards have managed to keep the sport going and those fortunate enough to live in the vicinity of a field trial area are lucky indeed. The rest of us must depend on an occasional outing and the wherewithal to travel to and from the field locations whenever possible.

It is all the more amazing that we have as many entries as we do in Sporting dogs. We could only wish our Cocker Spaniels were more a part of it.

WORKING TITLES

With no A.K.C. or A.S.C. sponsorship of field trials for Cocker Spaniels for many years, field enthusiasts decided to take matters into their own hands and came up with a Working Test based on those created by the English Cocker Spaniel Club of America. These tests are not as rigid, nor do they require all the same performances as the ones held under A.K.C. jurisdiction, but they do test the dog's ability to flush live game while under the command of their owner or handler. They must seek game, flush it, mark it, and retrieve to hand—undamaged—on land and from the water. The W.D., or Working Dog, title can be followed by a W.D.X., or Working Dog Excellent title, which requires even more rigorous training procedures.

Frank Wood of the Frandee Kennels in Norco, California, has been Chairman of the A.S.C. Field Trials since 1977, and he is another of those enthusiasts working toward and hoping for resumption of licensed field trials for Cocker Spaniels on a nationwide basis again in the near future.

Lady Beverly Boots in first field day practice held in May 1975 at the Orange County Cocker Spaniel Club. Boots flushed and retrieved from the pond her first time out, and she worked well both off and on lead. Owned by Mr. and Mrs. Fredrick N. Ray, Cal-Ore Kennels, Brooks, Oregon.

Ch. Don's Dartanun, C.D., W.D.X., black, and Sterling Silver Beau, W.D.X., working in the field. Cockers take naturally to field work and are willing workers. This Don Ploke photo was taken in the field at a July 1980 test.

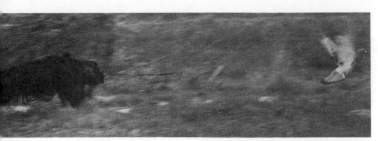

Ch. Don's Dartanun, C.D., W.D.X., flushes a bird during training with the Cocker Spaniel Club of Orange County California. He is owned by Don Ploke of Las Vegas, who photographs these remarkable dogs as they work in the field.

FINDING THE FACTS

For those who still enjoy a challenge and wish to compete in field trials, the American Kennel Club offers a free booklet entitled, *Registration and Field Trials Rules and Standard Procedures For Pointing Breeds, Dachshunds, Retrievers and Spaniels*. It is frequently amended to keep up with the very latest requirements and may be obtained by writing to the American Kennel Club, Inc., 51 Madison Avenue, New York, New York 10010.

The American Kennel Club has a Director of Field Trials on its staff who oversees the field trial activities for the events held under the jurisdiction of the American Kennel Club. Additional questions may be addressed to this department.

CHOOSING A FIELD DOG

The two vital points to bear in mind when buying a young dog for the field are the pedigree and the reputation of the kennel from which you purchase it. Many of the good and bad traits found in field dogs are definitely inheritable, so check the pedigree carefully before buying. Also check the performance record of the kennel. What is the ratio of field champions compared to the number of puppies actually started? How long have the owners been in the kennel business? Do they also train and work their dogs, or is the kennel operation just a breeding mill? Ask to see their record of wins. Above all, don't hesitate to ask to see some of the grown dogs work in the field.

There are advantages to buying young puppies, one being that you have a larger selection and can train the dog from start to finish yourself. Field dogs must be loyal creatures and must know just one master in the field, and bringing a dog up from a youngster offers this advantage.

BUYING THE OLDER FIELD DOG

Remember the old saying, "you can't teach an old dog new tricks"? Well, you can't break them of bad habits either so if you are buying an older field dog, be sure he doesn't have any bad habits! With the older dog be *sure* to watch him work in the field and be sure he would fit in with what you may be working with already. Ask the owner for a trial workout with the dog. Also, ask other hunters their opinion of the dog's past performances. Make sure the temperament of the dog is sound and that he is still somewhat trainable and not completely set in his ways, since you may have a few more things you want to teach him. And make sure the price is right. Good field dogs can command a lot of money—as much as, or perhaps even more in some cases— than show dogs. So ask for opinions and make comparisons with other dogs from other kennels as well as other prices on dogs from within the same kennel. Check out the pedigree once again before signing the final papers and the contract for purchase.

JOINING A FIELD TRIAL CLUB

Chances are that by the time you are considering buying your field dog you will have become involved with someone else interested in the sport who is a member of a field trial club. If he is truly a friend, he will not only help you to join the club but also will advise you on where to go to purchase a satisfactory dog for use in the field. Membership in these clubs can be just as valuable to you as the breed club is to those who exhibit their dogs at the bench shows. Club bulletins, the exchange of ideas and experiences at meetings, and the valuable information gained just by observing at one of these field trial events can be very helpful to newcomers in the sport with so much to learn.

Frandee's Heritage is off and running at the trials. Julie Wolfe handles for owner Dee Dee Wood.

KINDS OF FIELD TRIALS

There are three kinds of field trials. A *member field trial* is one at which championship points are awarded by the club if it is a member of the American Kennel Club. A *licensed field trial* is one at which championship points may be awarded, though the club is not a member of the A.K.C. but is licensed for this specific event. The third kind is called a *sanctioned field trial* and is a completely casual, informal trial with the dogs competing under regular rules but not for championship points. The club in this instance may or may not be a member of the A.K.C. but will have obtained A.K.C. sanction to hold the trial.

RIBBONS AND PRIZES

Clubs holding a licensed or member field trial shall offer five prizes in the form of ribbons or rosettes in the following colors at the regular stakes. First prize, blue; second, red; third, yellow; fourth, white; a special prize takes dark green. These ribbons are of regulation width and length and bear the name of the club, the trial date, and the facsimile of the seal of the American Kennel Club.

Ribbons and rosettes for sanctioned field trials, or in the non-regular stakes at licensed or member field trials, have different colors for winners. First prize is rose, second is brown, third is light green, fourth is gray, and the special prize is a combination of any of these colors. However, the ribbons must bear the words A.K.C. Sanctioned Field Trial but need not necessarily be of any certain size or design.

Money prizes, when offered, must be of a fixed amount or a percentage of the entry fee for each prize and shall be stated. The value for each prize must also be stated, and stud services are not permitted as prizes.

JUDGES

A field trial club may invite anyone who is in good standing with the American Kennel Club to judge at its trials. Those wishing to judge at trials, in other words, need not first obtain a license, but the A.K.C. must be informed as to exactly who will be officiating. Advertised judges, however, who wish to judge at licensed or member field trials must first sign an agreement certifying that they have a thorough knowledge of the rules, regulations, and procedures for the event and that they will judge in strict ac-

cordance with them. As in all other dog events, the decisions of the judges are final in regard to the performances of the dogs, and the judges have full discretionary power to withhold awards for lack of merit.

ENTERING A FIELD TRIAL

The premium lists that announce the holding of a field trial by the club will give the name and address of the field trial secretary, who will receive all written entries. These premium lists contain the rules and regulations under which the show will be held and will contain an entry form that you must fill out in order to enter your dog.

ELIGIBILITY FOR ENTRY

All dogs competing in a field trial must be individually registered with the A.K.C or be a part of a registered litter. If whelped outside this country, a foreign registry number must be obtained. There are variations on the rule as to time, etc., so if there is any doubt at the time of entry, it would be wise to check it out before entry deadline. Errors in entry forms are the responsibility of the owner. Check with a friend if you have any doubts. Don't arrive at your first trial and find that through a careless error or omission you are not able to compete.

Rules are strict about the health of the dogs competing also. Any dog that shows signs of infectious disease or has been exposed to another dog or dogs that are known to have infectious disease is ineligible and will be asked to leave the trial grounds. While a field trial committee may refuse your entry or ask that you leave, they cannot do so without cause and must file their complaint with the American Kennel Club. However, if you enter and attend, you must compete in *all* stakes in which you have entered, unless excused by the field trial committee at the trial after a consultation with the judge or judges.

SPECIAL AWARDS

At any licensed or member field trial the judges may make a "Judges' Award of Merit" in any stake to any unplaced dog for particularly excellent work. The name and registration number of each dog to which such an award is made shall be noted on the back page in the judge's book of the stake in which the award was made.

Championship certificates are issued to owners of dogs that have completed all requirements for this title. A field champion may be designated as "dual champion" if it has also been recorded as a bench show champion, though no certificate is issued for this.

THE VARIOUS KINDS OF STAKES

Classes for the official stakes at a Spaniel field trial are held for Puppy, Novice, Limit, Open All-Age, Qualified Open All-Age, and Amateur All-Age. Each class has its own qualifications so be sure to read the entry rules carefully before entering. At some trials there will also be a Novice Handler Stake for handlers who are just getting into the sport and have never handled a dog that has placed in an Open All-Age Stake in a licensed or member Spaniel trial. Unlike the show ring where a dog is considered a puppy until the day of his first birthday, in field trials a dog is a puppy until he has reached his second birthday. There are also Shooting Dog Stakes at field trials for dogs over six months of age.

NATIONAL CHAMPIONSHIP STAKES

There are National Championship Stakes for Cocker Spaniels over six months of age that become eligible under special rules approved by the A.K.C. based on previous wins. This stake can be run only once in any given calendar year by a parent club that is duly licensed by the A.K.C.

WHAT IS REQUIRED OF A FIELD CHAMPION

Field champions must have proven their ability to retrieve game from water, after a swim. Water tests during the field trials are left to the discretion of the Field Trial Committees of the show-giving clubs, but dogs competing must, if asked by the judge, take this test. Refusal will result in a disqualification. It must be a winner or have placements in Open All-Age or Qualified Open All-Age Stakes, the number being determined and fixed by the Board of Directors of the American Kennel Club.

Following instructions in the field is Lor-Jon's Hot Chocolate, owned by John and Lorna Ulrick and handled by John.

At present, to acquire a Field Championship a Cocker Spaniel must win a National Championship Stake or two Open All-Age Stakes or two Qualified Open All-Age Stakes or one Open All-Age Stake and one Qualified Open All-Age Stake at different trials with at least six starters in either stake.

THE GUNS

The gun to be used in a Spaniel field trial is required to be a double barrel, hammerless, 12-gauge. Further requirements in the A.K.C. booklet read: "No load less than 3¼ drams of powder and 1 1/8 ozs. of No. 5, No. 6, No. 7, or No. 7½ shot may be used. All shooting in other than Shooting Dog Stakes will be done by Guns appointed by the Committee. In Shooting Dog Stakes only, it is permissible to use any type 12-, 16-, or 20-gauge gun, provided not more than two shells are in the gun at any time."

JUDGING THE GAME

There are never more than two judges adjudicating at any one time, and they are both required to examine the game before making their decisions as to whether the dog has a hard mouth or a soft mouth. This means that the dog must not damage or mutilate the game when retrieving.

WEATHER CONDITIONS

Additional thought must be given to proper clothing if one is to be a field trial enthusiast. Get some hints for your outfit from friends who have learned the hard way about unfavorable weather conditions. Field trialers are apt to compete in all kinds of weather, but if conditions are so bad that the Field Trial Committee decides to postpone an event, they may do so only for three consecutive days following the last advertised day and providing it does not conflict with any other scheduled Spaniel field trial.

SOME OF THE FINER POINTS

No traps which release game are allowed. Game must be flushed in the open, and the judge may disqualify or turn out any dog that does not obey its handler's commands. By the same token, he may also turn out bitches in season. And of course as might be expected, handlers enter their dogs at their own risk and agree to abide by the rules.

There are many rules pertaining to the handler, or gunner, and what is required of the dog. The dog should flush the game confidently, on command, and should retrieve on command only. This will be in response to a command by the judge to the handler. The game should be delivered to the handler and the dog should sit or "hup" until given further orders.

THE "OLD" VERSUS THE "NEW"

Stonehenge in his book *On The Dog* states that all varieties of Spaniels were expected to give tongue on scent. As he put it centuries ago, "A spaniel possessing a musical but not noisy voice is all the more valuable if it distinguishes in its notes between various kinds of game." Today any Spaniel that yips or gives tongue on game in field trials is severely penalized.

PARTING SHOT

As we have mentioned before, while field trials are thriving all over the nation, the Cocker Spaniel's participation in them is small, if at all. The purpose of the space and information given in this chapter is with the hope that new interest may be stimulated and we can see our wonderful breed excelling and "doing what comes naturally!" If not now, then in the very near future . . .

DON PLOKE

In 1970 Don Ploke of Las Vegas, Nevada established his line of Cocker Spaniels that were to excel in the field. His Ch. Don's Dartanun, C.D., W.D.X., is one of top three or four field Cockers in the country today. In 1980 Dartanun turned nine years of age and is as active in field training as he ever was. From his brood bitches, Mar Jac Don's Cold Duck and Don's Allstarr, Don is breeding outstanding field and show dogs. Ch. Don's Drifter and Ch. Frandee's Co-Pilot are two others at his kennel. While Don Ploke is well aware of the beauty of the Cocker coat required for the show ring, he is equally aware that the heavier coats are tending to make Cockers less effective in the field. Their success in the field is paramount, since field work is what the Cocker was bred to do.

Don Ploke is an expert with a camera and has managed to capture many of the field Cockers in Nevada and surrounding areas at work in the field. We are pleased that many of them are featured in this chapter.

brent lindstrom

Ch. Tabaka's Tammy Tan Toes, U.D.T., finished her breed championship and U.D. title on the same weekend at just two years of age, which was a first in the breed. Tammy was bred and owned by Ruth N. Tabaka of Seattle, Washington.

CHAPTER FOURTEEN

Breeding Your Cocker Spaniel

Darling black puppy, sired by Am., Can. Ch. Peppygae Simeon of Somerset out of Lady of Ebony's Carbon Copy and whelped in 1979, is owned by Sharon Lee of Bothell, Washington.

Let us assume the time has come for your dog to be bred, and you have decided you are in a position to enjoy producing a litter of puppies that you hope will make a contribution to the breed. The bitch you purchased is sound, her temperament is excellent and she is a most worthy representative of the breed.

You have a calendar and counted off the 10 days since the first day of red staining and have determined the 10th to 14th day, which will more than likely be the best days for the actual mating. You have additionally counted off 60 to 65 days before the puppies are likely to be born to make sure everything necessary for their arrival will be in good order by that time.

From the moment the idea of having a litter occurred to you, your thoughts should have been given to the correct selection of a proper stud. Here again, the novice would do well to seek advice on analyzing pedigrees and tracing bloodlines for the best breedings. As soon as the bitch is in season and you see color (or staining) and a swelling of the vulva, it is time to notify the owner of the stud you selected and make appointments for the breedings. There are several pertinent questions you will want to ask the stud owners after having decided upon the pedigree. The owners, naturally, will also have a few questions they wish to ask you. These questions will concern your bitch's bloodlines, health, age, how many previous litters she's had, if any, etc.

THE POWER IN PEDIGREES

Someone in the dog fancy once remarked that the definition of a show prospect puppy is one third the pedigree, one third what you see and one third what you *hope* it will be! Well, no matter how you break down your qualifying fractions, we all quite agree that good breeding is essential if you have any plans at all for a show career for your dog. Many breeders will buy on pedigree alone, counting largely on what they themselves can do with the puppy by way of feeding, conditioning, and training. Needless to say, that very important piece of paper commonly referred to as the "pedigree" is mighty reassuring to a breeder or buyer new at the game or to one who has a breeding program in mind and is trying to establish his own bloodline.

One of the most fascinating aspects of tracing pedigrees is the way the names of the really great dogs of the past keep appearing in the pedigrees of the great dogs of today—positive proof of the strong influence of heredity and witness to a great deal of truth in the statement that great dogs frequently reproduce themselves, though not necessarily in appearance only. A pedigree represents something of value when one is dedicated to breeding better dogs.

To the novice buyer or one who is perhaps merely switching to another breed and sees only a frolicking, leggy, squirming bundle of energy in a fur coat, a pedigree can mean everything! To those of us who believe in heredity, a pedigree is more like an insurance policy—so always read it carefully and take heed.

For the even more serious breeder of today who wishes to make a further study of bloodlines in relation to his breeding program, the American Kennel Club library stud books can and should be consulted.

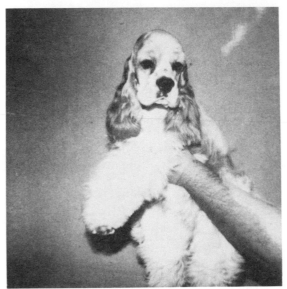

Future champion Frandee's Cat's Meow, pictured when five months old, is owned by Frank and Dee Dee Wood, Norco, California.

THE HEALTH OF THE BREEDING STOCK

Some of your first questions should concern whether the stud has already proved himself by siring a normal healthy litter. Also inquire as to whether the owners have had a sperm count made to determine just exactly how fertile or potent the stud is. Determine for yourself whether the dog has two normal testicles.

When considering your bitch for this mating, you must take into consideration a few important points that lead to a successful breeding. You and the owner of the stud will want to recall whether she has had normal heat cycles, whether there were too many runts in the litter and whether a Caesarean section was ever necessary. Has she ever had a vaginal infection? Could she take care of her puppies by herself, or was there a milk shortage? How many surviving puppies were there from the litter, and what did they grow up to be in comparison to the requirements of the breed Standard?

Don't buy a bitch that has problems in heat and has never had a live litter. Don't be afraid, however, to buy a healthy maiden bitch, since chances are, if she is healthy and from good stock, she will be a healthy producer. Don't buy a monorchid male, and certainly not a cryptorchid. If there is any doubt in your mind about his potency, get a sperm count from the veterinarian. Older dogs that have been good producers and are for sale are usually not too hard to find at good established kennels. If they are not too old and have sired quality show puppies, they can give you some excellent show stock from which to establish your own breeding lines.

WHEN TO BREED A GROWN BITCH

The best advice used to be not until her second heat. Today with our new scientific knowledge, we have become acutely aware of such things as hip dysplasia, juvenile cataracts, and other congenital diseases. The best advice now seems to be aimed at not breeding your dogs before two years of age when both the bitch and the sire have been examined by qualified veterinarians and declared—in writing—to be free and clear of these conditions.

THE DAY OF THE MATING

Now that you have decided upon the proper male and female combination to produce what you hope will be—according to the pedigrees—a fine litter of puppies, it is time to set the date. You have selected the two days (with a one day lapse in between) that you feel are best for the breeding, and you call the owner of the stud. The bitch always goes to the stud, unless, of course, there are extenuating circumstances. You set the date and the time and arrive with the bitch *and* the money.

Standard procedure is payment of a stud fee at the time of the first breeding, if there is a tie. For the stud fee, you are entitled to two breedings with ties. Contracts may be written up with specific conditions on breeding terms, of course, but this is general procedure. Often a breeder will take the pick of a litter to protect and maintain his bloodlines; this can be especially desirable if he needs an outcross for his breeding program or if he wishes to continue his own bloodlines if he sold you the bitch to start with, and this mating will continue his line-breeding program. This should all be worked out ahead of time and written and signed before the two dogs are bred. Remember that the payment of the stud fee is for the services of the stud—not for a guarantee of a litter of puppies. This is why is it so important to make sure you are using a proven stud. Bear in mind also that the American Kennel Club will not register a litter of puppies sired by a male that is under eight months of age. In the case of an older dog, they will not register a litter sired by a dog over 12 years of age, unless there is a witness to the breeding in the form of a veterinarian or other responsible person.

Many studs over 12 years of age are still fertile and capable of producing puppies, but if you do not witness the breeding there is always the danger of a "substitute" stud being used to produce a litter. This brings up the subject of sending your bitch away to be bred if you cannot accompany her.

The disadvantages of sending a bitch away to be bred are numerous. First of all, she will not be herself in a strange place, so she'll be difficult to handle. Transportation, if she goes by air (while reasonably safe), is still a traumatic experience. There is always the danger of her being put off at the wrong airport, not being fed or watered properly, etc. Some bitches get so upset that they go out of season and the trip—which may prove expensive, especially on top of a substantial stud fee—will have been for nothing.

If at all possible, accompany your bitch so that the experience is as comfortable for her as it can be. In other words, make sure before setting this kind of schedule for a breeding that there is no stud in the area that might be as good for her as the one that is far away. Don't sacrifice the proper breeding for convenience, since bloodlines are so important, but put the safety of the bitch above all else. There is always a risk in traveling, since dogs are considered cargo on a plane.

HOW MUCH DOES THE STUD FEE COST?

The stud fee will vary considerably—the better the bloodlines, the more winning the dog does at shows, the higher the fee. Stud service from a top winning dog could run up to $500.00. Here again, there may be exceptions. Some breeders will take part cash and then, say, third pick of the litter. The fee can be arranged by a private contract rather than the traditional procedure we have described.

Here again, it is wise to get the details of the payment of the stud fee in writing to avoid trouble.

THE ACTUAL MATING

It is always advisable to muzzle the bitch. A terrified bitch may fear-bite the stud, or even one of the people involved, and the wild or maiden bitch may snap or attack the stud to the point where he may become discouraged and lose interest in the breeding. Muzzling can be done with a lady's stocking tied around the muzzle with a half knot, crossed under the chin and knotted at the back of the neck. There is enough "give" in the stocking for her to breathe or salivate freely and yet not open her jaws far enough to bite. Place her in front of her owner, who holds onto her collar and talks to her and calms her as much as possible.

If the male will not mount on his own initiative, it may be necessary for the owner to assist in lifting him onto the bitch, perhaps even in guiding him to the proper place. Usually, the tie is accomplished once the male gets the idea. The owner should remain close at hand, however, to make sure the tie is not broken before an adequate breeding has been completed. After a while the stud may get bored, and try to break away. This could prove injurious. It may be necessary to hold him in place until the tie is broken.

Ch. Juban's Jorgey Girl, bred and owned by Ann and Julian Smith of Roswell, Georgia.

We must stress at this point that while some bitches carry on physically, and vocally, during the tie, there is no way the bitch can be hurt. However, a stud can be seriously or even permanently damaged by a bad breeding. Therefore, the owner of the bitch must be reminded that she must not be alarmed by any commotion. All concentration should be devoted to the stud and a successful and properly executed service.

Many people believe that breeding dogs is simply a matter of placing two dogs, a male and a female, in close proximity, and letting nature take its course. While often this is true, you cannot count on it. Sometimes it is hard work, and in the case of valuable stock it is essential to supervise to be sure of the safety factor, especially if one or both of the dogs are inexperienced. If the owners are also inexperienced, it may not take place at all.

Three-month-old Trojan Trionic, bred and owned by Alice Kaplan.

ARTIFICIAL INSEMINATION

Breeding by means of artificial insemination is usually unsuccessful, unless under a veterinarian's supervision, and can lead to an infection for the bitch and discomfort for the dog. The American Kennel Club requires a veterinarian's certificate to register puppies from such a breeding. Although the practice has been used for over two decades, it now offers new promise, since research has been conducted to make it a more feasible procedure for the future.

There now exists a frozen semen concept that has been tested and found successful. The study, headed by Dr. Stephen W.J. Seager, M.V.B., an instructor at the University of Oregon Medical School, has the financial support of the American Kennel Club, indicating that organization's interest in the work. The study is being monitored by the Morris Animal Foundation of Denver, Colorado.

Dr. Seager announced in 1970 that he had been able to preserve dog semen and to produce litters with the stored semen. The possibilities of selective world-wide breedings by this method are exciting. Imagine simply mailing a vial of semen to the bitch! The perfection of line-breeding by storing semen without the threat of death interrupting the breeding program is exciting also.

As it stands today, the technique for artificial insemination requires the depositing of semen (taken directly from the dog) into the bitch's vagina, past the cervix and into the uterus by syringe. The correct temperature of the semen is vital, and there is no guarantee of success. The storage method, if successfully adopted, will present a new era in the field of purebred dogs.

THE GESTATION PERIOD

Once the breeding has taken place successfully, the seemingly endless waiting period of about 63 days begins. For the first 10 days after the breeding, you do absolutely nothing for the bitch—just spin dreams about the delights you will share with the family when the puppies arrive.

Around the 10th day it is time to begin supplementing the diet of the bitch with vitamins and calcium. We strongly recommend that you take her to your veterinarian for a list of the proper or perhaps necessary supplements and the correct amounts of each for your particular bitch. Guesses, which may lead to excesses or insufficiencies, can ruin a litter. For the price of a visit to your veterinarian, you will be confident that you are feeding properly.

The bitch should be free of worms, of course, and if there is any doubt in your mind, she should be wormed now, before the third week of pregnancy. Your veterinarian will advise you on the necessity of this and proper dosage as well.

PROBING FOR PUPPIES

Far too many breeders are overanxious about whether the breeding "took" and are inclined to feel for puppies or persuade a veterinarian to radiograph or X-ray their bitches to confirm it. Unless there is reason to doubt the normalcy of a pregnancy, this is risky. Certainly 63 days is not too long to wait, and why risk endangering the litter by probing with your inexperienced hands? Few bitches give no evidence of being in whelp, and there is no need to prove it for yourself by trying to count puppies.

ALERTING YOUR VETERINARIAN

At least a week before the puppies are due, you should telephone your veterinarian and notify him that you expect the litter and give him the date. This way he can make sure that there will be someone available to help, should there be any problems during the whelping. Most veterinarians today have answering services and alternative vets on call when they are not available themselves. Some veterinarians suggest that you call them when the bitch starts labor so that they may further plan their time, should they be needed. Discuss this matter with your veterinarian when you first take the bitch to him for her diet instructions, etc., and establish the method that will best fit in with his schedule.

DO YOU NEED A VETERINARIAN IN ATTENDANCE?

Even if this is your first litter, I would advise that you go through the experience of whelping without panicking and calling desperately for the veterinarian. Most animal births are accomplished without complications, and you should call for assistance only if you run into trouble.

When having her puppies, your bitch will appreciate as little interference and as few strangers around as possible. A quiet place, with

Three-and-a-half-month-old Juban's Fire and Ice, bred by Ann and Julian Smith of Roswell, Georgia, and owned by Yvonne Smith.

her nest, a single familiar face, and her own instincts are all that is necessary for nature to take its course. An audience of curious children squealing and questioning, other family pets nosing around, or strange adults should be avoided. Many a bitch that has been distracted in this way has been known to devour her young. This can be the horrible result of intrusion into the bitch's privacy. There are other ways of teaching children the miracle of birth, and there will be plenty of time later for the whole family to enjoy the puppies. Let them be born under proper and considerate circumstances.

LABOR

Some litters—many first litters—do not run the full term of 63 days. So, at least a week before the puppies are actually due, and at the time you alert your veterinarian as to their expected arrival, start observing the bitch for signs of the commencement of labor. This will manifest itself in the form of ripples running down the sides of her body, that will come as a revelation to her as well. It is most noticeable when she is lying on her side—and she will be sleeping a great deal as the arrival date comes closer. If she is sitting or walking about, she will perhaps sit down quickly or squat peculiarly. As the ripples become more frequent, birth time is drawing near, and you will be wise not to leave her. Usually within 24 hours before whelping she will stop eating, and as much as a week before she will begin digging a nest. The bitch should be given something resembling a whelping box with layers of newspaper (black and white only) to make her nest. She will dig more and more as birth approaches, and this is the time to begin making your promise to stop interfering unless your help is specifically required. Some bitches whimper and others are silent, but whimpering does not necessarily indicate trouble.

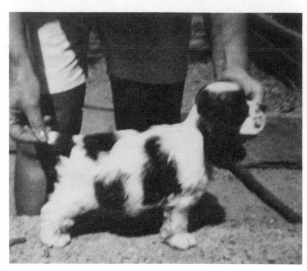

Future champion Pett's Broker's Tip, bred and owned by Dorothy and Roland Pett of Dennis Port, Massachusetts. Note perfect show stance even at this early age.

THE ARRIVAL OF THE PUPPIES

The sudden gush of green fluid from the bitch indicates that the water or fluid surrounding the puppies has "broken" and they are about to start down the canal and come into the world. When the water breaks, birth of the first puppy is imminent. The first puppies are usually born within minutes to a half hour of each other, but a couple of hours between the later ones is not uncommon. If you notice the bitch straining constantly without producing a puppy, or if a puppy remains partially in and partially out for too long, it is cause for concern. Breech births (puppies born feet first instead of head first) can often cause delay or hold things up, and this is often a problem that requires veterinarian assistance.

FEEDING THE BITCH BETWEEN BIRTHS

Usually the bitch will not be interested in food for about 24 hours before the arrival of the puppies, and perhaps as long as two or three days after their arrival. The placenta that she cleans up after each puppy is high in food value and will be more than ample to sustain her. This is nature's way of allowing the mother to feed herself and her babies without having to leave the nest and hunt for food during the first crucial days. In the wild the mother always cleans up all traces of birth so as not to attract other animals to her newborn babies.

However, there are those of us who believe in making food available should the mother feel the need to restore her strength during or after delivery—especially if she whelps a large litter. Raw chopped meat, beef bouillon, and milk are all acceptable and may be placed near the whelping box during the first two or three days. After that, the mother will begin to put the babies on a sort of schedule. She will leave the whelping box at frequent intervals, take longer exercise periods and begin to take interest in other things. This is where the fun begins for you. Now the babies are no longer soggy little pinkish blobs. They begin to crawl around and squeal and hum and grow before your very eyes!

It is at this time, if all has gone normally, that the family can be introduced gradually and great praise and affection given to the mother.

BREECH BIRTHS

Puppies normally are delivered head first; however, some are presented feet first or in other abnormal positions, and this is referred to as a "breech birth." Assistance is often necessary to get the puppy out of the canal, and great care must be taken not to injure the puppy or the dam.

Aid can be given by grasping the puppy with a piece of turkish toweling and pulling gently during the dam's contractions. Be careful not to squeeze the puppy too hard; merely try to ease it out by moving it gently back and forth. Because even this much delay in delivery may mean the puppy is drowning, do not wait for the bitch to remove the sac. Do it yourself by tearing the sac open to expose the face and head. Then cut the cord anywhere from one-half to three-quarters of an inch away from the navel. If the cord bleeds excessively, pinch the end of it with your fingers and count five. Repeat if necessary. Then pry open the mouth with your finger and hold the puppy upside down for a moment to drain any fluids from the lungs. Next, rub the puppy briskly with turkish or paper toweling. You should get it wriggling and whimpering by this time.

If the litter is large, this assistance will help conserve the strength of the bitch and will probably be welcomed by her. However, it is best to allow her to take care of at least the first few herself to preserve the natural instinct and to provide the nutritive values obtained by her consumption of one or more of the afterbirths as nature intended.

DRY BIRTHS

Occasionally the sac will break before the delivery of a puppy and will be expelled while the puppy remains inside, thereby depriving the dam of the necessary lubrication to expel the puppy normally. Inserting vaseline or mineral oil via your finger will help the puppy pass down the birth canal. This is why it is essential that you be present during the whelping—so that you can count puppies and afterbirths and determine when and if assistance is needed.

THE TWENTY-FOUR HOUR CHECKUP

It is smart to have a veterinarian check the mother and her puppies within 24 hours after the last puppy is born. The veterinarian can check the puppies for cleft palates or umbilical hernia and may wish to give the dam—particularly if she is a show dog—an injection of Pituitin to make sure of the expulsion of all afterbirths and to tighten up the uterus. This can prevent a sagging belly after the puppies are weaned and the bitch is being readied for the show ring.

FALSE PREGNANCY

The disappointment of a false pregnancy is almost as bad for the owner as it is for the bitch. She goes through the gestation period with all the symptoms—swollen stomach, increased appetite, swollen nipples—even makes a nest when the time comes. You may even take an oath that you noticed the ripples on her body from the labor pains. Then, just as suddenly as you made up your mind that she was definitely going to have puppies, you will know that she definitely is not! She may walk around carrying a toy as if it were a puppy for a few days, but she will soon be back to normal and acting just as if nothing happened—and nothing did!

CAESAREAN SECTION

Should the whelping reach the point where there is complication, such as the bitch's not being capable of whelping the puppies herself, the "moment of truth" is upon you and a Caesarean section may be necessary. The bitch may be too small or too immature to expel the puppies herself, her cervix may fail to dilate enough to allow the young to come down the birth canal, there may be torsion of the uterus, a dead or monster puppy, a sideways puppy blocking the canal, or perhaps toxemia. A Caesarean section will be the only solution. No matter what the cause, get the bitch to the veterinarian immediately to insure your chances of saving the mother and/or the puppies.

The Caesarean section operation (the name derived from the idea that Julius Caesar was delivered by this method) involves the removal of the unborn young from the uterus of the dam by surgical incision into the walls through the abdomen. The operation is performed when it has been determined that for some reason the puppies cannot be delivered normally. While modern surgical methods have made the operation itself reasonably safe, with the dam being perfectly capable of nursing the puppies shortly after the completion of the surgery, the chief danger lies in the ability to spark life into the puppies immediately upon their removal from the womb. If the mother dies, the time element is even more important in saving the young, since the oxygen supply ceases upon the death of the dam, and the difference between life and death is measured in seconds.

After surgery, when the bitch is home in her whelping box with the babies, she will probably nurse the young without distress. You must be sure that the sutures are kept clean and that no redness or swelling or ooze appears in the wound. Healing will take place naturally, and no salves or ointments should be applied unless prescribed by the veterinarian, for fear the puppies will get it into their systems. If there is any doubt, check the bitch for fever, restlessness (other than the natural concern for her young), or a lack of appetite, but do not anticipate trouble.

Ch. Travel On Dante at four months of age with breeder-owner Barb White, Travel On Kennels, Columbiana, Ohio.

EPISIOTOMY

Even though most dogs are generally easy whelpers, any number of reasons might occur to cause the bitch to have a difficult birth. Before automatically resorting to Caesarean section, many veterinarians are now trying the technique known as episiotomy.

Used rather frequently in human deliveries, episiotomy (produced E-PEASE-E-OTT-O-ME) is the cutting of the membrane between the rear opening of the vagina back almost to the opening of the anus. After delivery it is stitched together, and barring complications, heals easily, presenting no problem in future births.

SOCIALIZING YOUR PUPPY

The need for puppies to get out among other animals and people cannot be stressed enough. Kennel-reared dogs are subject to all sorts of idiosyncrasies and seldom make good house dogs or normal members of the world around them when they grow up.

The crucial age that determines the personality and general behavior patterns that will predominate during the rest of the dog's life are formed between the ages of three and 10 weeks. This is particularly true during the 21st and 28th day. It is essential that the puppy be socialized during this time by bringing him into family life as much as possible. Walking on floor surfaces, indoor and outdoor, should be experienced; handling by all members of the family and visitors is important; preliminary grooming gets him used to a lifelong necessity; light training, such as setting him up on tables and

The epitome of mother love! Ch. Milru's Lady Be Good is pictured being a good mother. Owned by Ruth Muller of Centerport, New York.

cleaning teeth and ears and cutting nails, etc., has to be started early if he is to become a show dog. The puppy should be exposed to car riding, shopping tours, a leash around its neck, children —your own and others—and in all possible ways relationships with humans.

It is up to the breeder, of course, to protect the puppy from harm or injury during this initiation into the outside world. The benefits reaped from proper attention will pay off in the long run with a well-behaved, well-adjusted grown dog capable of becoming an integral part of a happy family.

Ready for the outside world—out of the whelping box at Winnie Vick's Bobwin Kennels in Suisun, California.

REARING THE FAMILY

Needless to say, even with a small litter there will be certain considerations that must be adhered to in order to insure successful rearing of the puppies. For instance, the diet for the mother should be appropriately increased as the puppies grow and take more and more nourishment from her. During the first few days of rest while the bitch just looks over her puppies and regains her strength, she should be left pretty much alone. It is during these first days that she begins to put the puppies on a feeding schedule and feels safe enough about them to leave the whelping box long enough to take a little extended exercise.

It is cruel, however, to try to keep the mother away from the puppies any longer than she wants to be because you feel she is being too attentive or to give the neighbors a chance to peek in at the puppies. The mother should not have to worry about harm coming to her puppies for the first few weeks. The veterinary checkup will be enough of an experience for her to have to endure until she is more like herself once again.

The crucial period in a puppy's life occurs when the puppy is from 21 to 28 days old, so all the time you can devote to them at this time will reap rewards later on in life. This is the age when several other important steps must be taken in a puppy's life. Weaning should start if it hasn't already, and it is the time to check for worms. Do not worm unnecessarily. A veterinarian should advise on worming and appropriate dosage and he can also discuss with you at this time the schedule for serum or vaccination, which will depend on the size of the puppies as well as their age.

EVALUATING THE LITTER

A show puppy prospect should be outgoing, (probably the first one to fall out of the whelping box!) and all efforts should be made to socialize the puppy that appears to be the most shy. Once the puppies are about three weeks old, they can and should be handled a great deal by friends and members of the family.

During the third week they begin to try to walk instead of crawl, but they are unsteady on their feet. Tails are used for balancing, and they begin to make sounds.

Ch. Ging's Gammon and Ging's Backstage Baksheeh Gal photographed at three months of age by Cryzentia. Bill Gorodner and Lloyd Alton are owners and breeders of this treasure chest of puppy love.

Exercise and grooming should be started at this time, with special care and consideration given to the diet. You will find that the dam will help you wean the puppies, leaving them alone more and more as she notices that they are eating well on their own. Begin by leaving them with her during the night for comfort and warmth; eventually when she shows less interest, keep them separated entirely.

By the time the fifth week arrives, you will already be in love with every member of the litter and desperately searching for reasons to keep them all. They recognize you—which really gets to you!—and they box and chew on each other and try to eat your finger and a million other captivating antics that are special with puppies. Their stomachs seem to be bottomless pits, and their weight will rise. At eight to 10 weeks, the puppies will be weaned and ready to go.

SPAYING AND CASTRATING

A wise old philosopher once said, "Timing in life is everything!" No statement could apply more readily to the age-old question that every dog owner is faced with sooner or later . . . to spay or not to spay.

For the one-bitch pet owner, spaying is the most logical answer, for it solves many problems. The pet is usually not of top breeding quality, and therefore there is no great loss to the bloodline; it takes the pressure off the family if the dog runs free with children, and it certainly eliminates the problem of repeated litters of unwanted puppies or a backyard full of eager males twice a year.

But for the owner or breeder, the extra time and protection that must be afforded a purebred quality bitch can be most worthwhile—even if it

Ch. Echo Valley's Sinistar, pictured at five months of age, was bred by Leo and Carole Obriecht. Sinistar was sired by Ch. Dreamridge Drambuie ex Ch. Mar-Geo's Star Brite and is owned by Cheryl McNeil, D.V.M. Sinistar was the foundation bitch at Shadowridge and she was also that kennel's first owner-handled champion.

Ch. Frandee's Free N' Easy is pictured at work in the field at just four months of age. Owners are Frank and Dee Dee Wood, Norco, California.

is only until a single litter is produced after the first heat. It is then not too late to spay; the progeny can perpetuate the bloodline, the bitch will have been fulfilled—though it is merely an old wives' tale that bitches should have at least one litter to be "normal"—and she may then be retired to her deserved role as family pet once again.

With spaying, the problem of staining and unusual behavior around the house is eliminated, as is the necessity of having to keep her in "pants" or administering pills, sprays, or shots . . . which most veterinarians do not approve of anyway.

In the case of males, castration is seldom contemplated, which to me is highly regrettable. The owner of the male dog merely overlooks the dog's ability to populate an entire neighborhood, since he does not have the responsibility of rearing and disposing of the puppies. When you take into consideration all the many females the male dog can impregnate, it is almost more essential that the males rather than the females be taken

out of circulation. The male dog will still be inclined to roam but will be less frantic about leaving the grounds, and you will find that a lot of the *wanderlust* has left him.

STERILIZING FOR HEALTH

When considering the problem of spaying or castrating, the first consideration after the population explosion should actually be the health of the dog or bitch. Males are frequently subject to urinary diseases, and sometimes castration is a help. Your veterinarian can best advise you on this problem. Another aspect to consider is the kennel dog that is no longer being used at stud. It is unfair to keep him in a kennel with females in heat when there is no chance for him to be used. There are other more personal considerations for both kennel and one-dog owners, but when making the decision remember that it is final. You can always spay or castrate, but once the deed is done there is no return.

Ch. Trojan Tan Janette, pictured at just seven weeks of age, was bred by the Trojan Kennels, Magnolia, Texas.

CHAPTER FIFTEEN

Feeding and Nutrition

Mmmm-mmmm-good! A typical Abbi's Cocker Spaniel puppy expresses appreciation of a meal.

FEEDING PUPPIES

There are many diets today for young puppies, including all sorts of products on the market for feeding the newborn, for supplementing the feeding of the young, and for adding "this or that" to diets, depending on what is lacking in the way of a complete diet.

When weaning puppies it is necessary to put them on four meals a day, even while you are tapering off with the mother's milk. Feeding at six in the morning, noontime, six in the evening and midnight is about the best schedule since it fits in with most human eating plans. Meals for the puppies can be prepared immediately before or after your own meals without too much of a change in your own schedule.

6 A.M.

Two meat and two milk meals serve best and should be served alternately, of course. Assuming the 6 A.M. feeding is a milk meal, the contents should be as follows: goat's milk is the very best milk to feed puppies, but is expensive and usually available only at drug stores, unless you live in farm country where it could be readily available fresh and less expensive. If goat's milk is not available, use evaporated milk (which can be changed to powdered milk later on) diluted two parts evaporated milk and one part water, along with raw egg yolk, honey, or Karo syrup, sprinkled with high-protein baby cereal and some wheat germ. As the puppies mature, cottage cheese may be added or, at one of the two milk meals, it can be substituted for the cereal.

NOONTIME

A puppy chow that has been soaked in warm water or beef broth according to the time specified on the wrapper should be mixed with raw or simmered chopped meat in equal proportions with vitamin powder added.

6 P.M.

Repeat the milk meal—perhaps varying the type of cereal from wheat to oats, corn, or rice.

MIDNIGHT

Repeat the meat meal. If raw meat was fed at noon, the evening meal might be simmered.

Please note that specific proportions on this suggested diet are not given; however, it's safe to say that the most important ingredients are the milk and cereal, and the meat and puppy chow that forms the basis of the diet. Your veterinarian can advise on the portion sizes if there is any doubt in your mind as to how much to use.

Four Cocker puppies with their eating snoods on and ready for chow! Left to right are Memoir's More Charm, Ch. Windy Hill's 'Tis Joy O'Memoir, Memoir's Mimosa and Memoir's Merry Legs. All owned by Anita B. Roberts of Novato, California.

If you notice that the puppies are cleaning their plates, you are perhaps not feeding enough to keep up with their rate of growth. Increase the amount at the next feeding. Observe them closely; puppies should each "have their fill," because growth is very rapid at this age. If they have not satisfied themselves, increase the amount so that they do not have to fight for the last morsel. They will not overeat if they know there is enough food available. Instinct will usually let them eat to suit their normal capacity.

If there is any doubt in your mind as to any ingredient you are feeding, ask yourself, "Would I give it to my own baby?" If the answer is no, then don't give it to your puppies. At this age, the comparison between puppies and human babies can be a good guide.

If there is any doubt in your mind, I repeat: ask your veterinarian to be sure.

Many puppies will regurgitate their food, perhaps a couple of times, before they manage to retain it. If they do bring up their food, allow them to eat it again, rather than clean it away. Sometimes additional saliva is necessary for them to digest it, and you do not want them to skip a meal just because it is an unpleasant sight for you to observe.

This same regurgitation process holds true sometimes with the bitch, who will bring up her own food for her puppies every now and then. This is a natural instinct on her part that stems from the days when dogs were giving birth in the wild. The only food the mother could provide at weaning time was too rough and indigestible for her puppies; therefore, she took it upon herself to predigest the food until it could be taken and retained by her young. Bitches today will sometimes resort to this, especially bitches that love having litters and have a strong maternal instinct. Some dams will help you wean their litters and even give up feeding entirely once they see you are taking over.

WEANING THE PUPPIES

When weaning the puppies, the mother is kept away from the little ones for longer and longer periods of time. This is done over a period of several days. At first she is separated from the puppies for several hours, then all day, leaving her with them only at night for comfort and warmth. This gradual separation aids in helping the mother's milk to dry up gradually, and she suffers less distress after feeding a litter.

If the mother continues to carry a great deal of milk with no signs of its tapering off, consult your veterinarian before she gets too uncomfortable. She may cut the puppies off from her supply of milk too abruptly if she is uncomfortable, before they should be completely on their own.

There are many opinions on the proper age to start weaning puppies. If you plan to start selling them between six and eight weeks, weaning should begin between two and three weeks of age. (Here again, each bitch will pose a different situation.) The size and weight of the litter should help determine the time, and your veterinarian will have an opinion as he determines the burden the bitch is carrying by the size of the litter and her general condition. If she is being pulled down by feeding a large litter, he may suggest that you start at two weeks. If she is glorying in her motherhood without any apparent taxing of her strength, he may suggest three to four weeks. You and he will be the best judges. But remember, there is no substitute that is as perfect as mother's milk—and the longer the puppies benefit from it, the better. Other food yes, but mother's milk first and foremost for the healthiest puppies.

FEEDING THE ADULT DOG

The puppies' schedule of four meals a day should drop to three by six months and then to two by nine months; by the time the dog reaches one year of age, it is eating one meal a day.

The time when you feed the dog each day can be a matter of the dog's preference or your convenience, so long as once in every 24 hours the dog receives a meal that provides it with a complete, balanced diet. In addition, of course, fresh clean water should be available at all times.

There are many brands of dry food, kibbles, and biscuits on the market that are all of good quality. There are also many varieties of canned dog food that are of good quality and provide a balanced diet for your dog. But, for those breeders and exhibitors who show their dogs, additional care is given to providing a few "extras" that enhance the good health and good appearance of show dogs.

A good meal or kibble mixed with water or beef broth and raw meat is perhaps the best ration to provide. In cold weather many breeders add suet or corn oil (or even olive or cooking oil) to the mixture and others make use of the bacon fat after breakfast by pouring it over the dog's food.

Salting a dog's food in the summer helps replace the salt he "pants away" in the heat. Many breeders sprinkle the food with garlic powder to sweeten the dog's breath and prevent gas, especially in breeds that gulp or wolf their food and swallow a lot of air. I prefer garlic powder; the salt is too weak and the clove is too strong.

There are those, of course, who cook very elaborately for their dogs, which is not necessary if a good meal and meat mixture is provided. Many prefer to add vegetables, rice, tomatoes, etc., in with everything else they feed. As long as the extras do not throw the nutritional balance off, there is little harm, but no one thing should be fed to excess. Occasionally liver is given as a treat at home. Fish, which most veterinarians no longer recommend even for cats, is fed to puppies, but should not be given in excess of once a week. Always remember that no one food should be given as a total diet. Balance is most important; a 100 per cent meat diet can kill a dog.

THE ALL-MEAT DIET CONTROVERSY

In March of 1971 the National Research Council investigated a great stir in the dog fancy about the all-meat dog-feeding controversy. It was established that meat and meat by-products constitute a complete balanced diet for dogs only when it is further fortified.

Therefore, a good dog chow or meal mixed with meat provides the perfect combination for a dog's diet. While the dry food is a complete diet in itself, the fresh meat additionally satisfies the dog's anatomically and physiologically meat-oriented appetite. While dogs are actually carnivores, it must be remembered that when they were feeding themselves in the wild they ate almost the entire animal they captured, including its stomach contents. This provided some of the vitamins and minerals we must now add to the diet.

In the United States the standard for diets that claims to be "complete and balanced" is set by the Subcommittee on Canine Nutrition of the National Research Council (NRC) of the National Academy of Sciences. This is the official agency for establishing the nutritional requirements of dog foods. Most foods sold for dogs and cats meet these requirements and manufacturers are proud to say so on their labels, so look for this when you buy. Pet food labels must be approved by the Association of American Feed Control Officials (AAFCO) Pet Foods Committee. Both the Food and Drug Administration and the Federal Trade Commission of the AAFCO define the word "balanced" when referring to dog food as follows:

"Balanced is a term which may be applied to pet food having all known required nutrients in a proper amount and proportion based upon the recommendations of a recognized authority (The National Research Council is one) in the field of animal nutrition, for a given set of physiological animal requirements."

With this much care given to your dog's diet, there can be little reason for not having happy well-fed dogs in proper weight and proportions for the show ring.

Marquis Wild Firer, red and white bitch bred by Karen Marquez and owned by Gladys Von Horn.

OBESITY

As we mentioned before, there are many "perfect" diets for your dogs on the market today. When fed in proper proportions, they should keep your dogs in "full bloom." However, there are those owners who, more often than not, indulge their own appetites and are inclined to overfeed their dogs as well. A study in Great Britain in the early 1970's found that a major percentage of obese people also had obese dogs. The entire family was overfed and all suffered from the same condition.

Obesity in dogs is a direct result of the animal's being fed more food that he can properly "burn up" over a period of time, so it is stored as fat or fatty tissue in the body. Pet dogs are more inclined to become obese than show dogs or working dogs, but obesity also is a factor to be considered with the older dog since his exercise is curtailed.

A lack of "tuck up" on a dog, or not being able to feel the ribs, or great folds of fat that hang from the underside of the dog can all be considered as obesity. Genetic factors may enter into the picture, but usually the owner is at fault.

The life span of the obese dog is decreased on several counts. Excess weight puts undue stress on the heart as well as on the joints. The dog becomes a poor anesthetic risk and has less resistance to viral or bacterial infections. Treatment is seldom easy or completely effective, so emphasis should be placed on not letting your dog get FAT in the first place!

Rowingdales Resolution is in top condition. "Margi" was sired by Ch. Kapewoods Rowesbeau ex Ch. La Toka's Joy of Kapewood and was pointed from the Puppy Classes. Owners, breeders and handlers are Charles and Jacquelyn Rowe of La Mesa, California.

ORPHANED PUPPIES

The ideal solution to feeding orphaned puppies is to be able to put them with another nursing dam who will take them on as her own. If this is not possible within your own kennel, or a kennel that you know of, it is up to you to care for and feed the puppies. Survival is possible but requires a great deal of time and effort on your part.

Your substitue formula must be precisely prepared, always served heated to body temperature, and refrigerated when not being fed. Esbilac, a vacuum-packed powder, with complete feeding instructions on the can, is excellent and about as close to mother's milk as you can get. If you can't get Esbilac, or until you do get Esbilac, there are two alternative formulas that you might use.

Mix one part boiled water with five parts of evaporated milk and add one teaspoonful of dicalcium phosphate per quart of formula. Dicalcium phosphate can be secured at any drug store. If they have it in tablet form only, you can powder the tablets with the back part of a tablespoon. The other formula for newborn puppies is a combination of eight ounces of homogenized milk mixed well with two egg yolks.

You will need baby bottles with three-hole nipples. Sometimes doll bottles can be used for the newborn puppies, which should be fed at six-hour intervals. If they are consuming sufficient amounts, their stomachs should look full, or slightly enlarged, though never distended. The amount of formula to be fed is proportionate to the size, age, growth, and weight of the puppy, and is indicated on the can of Esbilac, or consult the advice of your veterinarian. Many breeders like to keep a baby scale nearby to check the weight of the puppies to be sure they are thriving on the formula.

At two to three weeks you can start adding Pablum or some other high protein baby cereal to the formula. Also, baby beef can be licked from your finger at this age, or added to the formula. At four weeks the surviving puppies should be taken off the diet of Esbilac and put on a more substantial diet, such as wet puppy meal or chopped beef; however, Esbilac powder can still be mixed in with the food for additional nutrition. The baby foods of pureed meats in jars make for a smooth changeover also, and can be blended into the diet.

HOW TO FEED THE NEWBORN PUPPIES

When the puppy is a newborn, remember that it is vitally important to keep the feeding procedure as close to the natural mother's routine as possible. The newborn puppy should be held in your lap in your hand in an almost upright position with the bottle at an angle to allow the entire nipple area to be full of the formula. Do not hold the bottle upright so the puppy's head has to reach straight up toward the ceiling. Do not let the puppy nurse too quickly or take in too much air and possibly get the colic. Once in awhile take the bottle away and let him rest a moment and swallow several times. Before feeding, test the nipple to see that the fluid does not come out too quickly, or by the same token, too slowly so that the puppy gets tired of feeding before he has had enough to eat.

When the puppy is a little older, you can place him on his stomach on a towel to eat, and even allow him to hold on to the bottle or to "come and get it" on his own. Most puppies enjoy eating and this will be a good indication of how strong an appetite he has and his ability to consume the contents of the bottle.

It will be necessary to "burp" the puppy. Place a towel on your shoulder and hold the puppy on your shoulder as if it were a human baby, patting and rubbing it gently. This will also encourage the puppy to defecate. At this time, you should observe for diarrhea or other intestinal disorders. The puppy should eliminate after each feeding with occasional eliminations between times as well. If the puppies do not eliminate on their own after each meal, massage their stomachs and under their tails gently until they do.

You must keep the puppies clean. Under no circumstances should fecal matter be allowed to collect on their skin or fur.

All this—plus your determination and perseverance—might save an entire litter of puppies that would otherwise have died without their real mother.

GASTRIC TORSION

Gastric torsion, or bloat, sometimes referred to as "twisted stomach," has become more and more prevalent. Many dogs that in the past had been thought to die of blockage of the stomach or intestines because they had swallowed toys or

Lovely head study of Marjorie Bond's Ch. Bondale's Mary Bridget. The Bondale Kennels are in Eugene, Oregon.

other foreign objects are now suspected of having been the victims of gastric torsion and the bloat that followed.

Though life can be saved by immediate surgery to untwist the organ, the rate of fatality is high. Symptoms of gastric torsion are unusual restlessness, excessive salivation, attempts to vomit, rapid respiration, pain, and the eventual bloating of the abdominal region.

The cause of gastric torsion can be attributed to overeating, excess gas formation in the stomach, poor function of the stomach or intestine, or general lack of exercise. As the food ferments in the stomach, gases form which may twist the stomach in a clockwise direction so that the gas is unable to escape. Surgery, where the stomach is untwisted counter-clockwise, is the safest and most successful way to correct the situation.

To avoid the threat of gastric torsion, it is wise to keep your dog well exercised to be sure the body is functioning normally. Make sure that food and water are available for the dog at all times, thereby reducing the tendency to overeat. With self-service dry feeding, where the dog is able to eat intermittently during the day, there is not the urge to "stuff" at one time.

If you notice any of the symptoms of gastric torsion, call your veterinarian immediately. Death can result within a matter of hours!

Charming head shot of Ch. Baliwick Bricklayer, owned by Linda Hay, Bakersfield, California. Photo by Michael Allen, the breeder.

Am., Can. Ch. Roblen's Tempawnee Princess, sired by Just Plain Pawnee and owned by Mrs. H. L. Johnston.

Lovely close-up of Am., Can. Ch. Ramrod Real McCoy, owned by Helen and Robert Johnston, Roblen Kennels, Central Point, Oregon.

Bleuaire's Repercussion and daughters. Repercussion is a champion in England and America. Photograph submitted by Michael Allen, Costa Mesa, California.

Lovely head study of Ch. White Deer's Scotch Guard, bred and owned by Doris Fink, White Deer Kennels, Tuckerton, New Jersey. In just two litters he sired five champions, with more litters of show age about to begin their ring careers. One of the top producers for 1979, he was sired by Ch. Dur Bets Tartan ex. Ch. White Deer's Love Letters.

Above: "Getting to know you . . ." Michael Allen of Costa Mesa, California, tries an introduction between Ch. Bizzmar Bon Bon and Fang, the ocelot. Ms. Allen is the editor and publisher of *American Cocker Review*, the prestige magazine for the breed.

Opposite, above: Ch. Sugarbrooks Most Happy Fellow, owned by Mrs. Robert Fellows of Clarks Summit, Pennsylvania. "Buster" finished his championship with five majors and two points from Puppy Classes. Sire was Ch. Artru Skyjack ex Sugarbrooks Artru Chicklet. Ashbey photo. **Below:** Ch. Willwyn Withstyle O'Nosowea, owned by the Willwyn Kennels. This Best in Show winner is a son of Ch. Corwin Chances Are. Photo by Twomey.

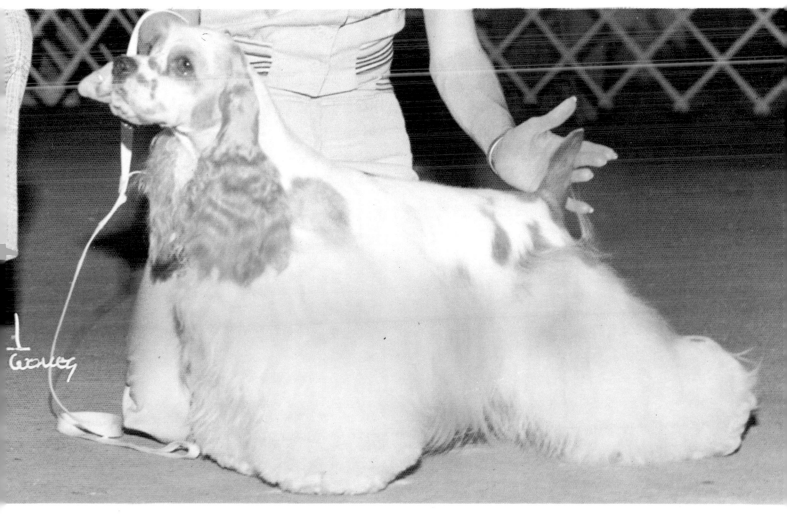

Above: Fi-Fo's Puff-a-Lore, pictured winning Best of Variety at the Del-Otse-Nango show, is handled by owner Mrs. Robert Fellows. The sire was Ch. Fi-Fo's Folklore ex Fi-Fo's Puff-o-Jene. Stephen Klein photo.

Opposite: Ch. Frandee's Declaration, pictured winning under judge Mrs. Winnie Vick. Declaration is the Frandee Kennels' top-producing stud dog. Owner-breeders are Frank and Dee Dee Wood, Norco, California.

Above: Ch. Dur Bets Tartan pictured finishing for championship at a 1976 show under judge Annett Davies. "Scottie" was tied for Top Producing Dog All-breeds for 1979. He had 19 champions in 1979 and a total of 27 to date. Bred by Betty Durland, he is pictured being handled by his owner Doris Fink, White Deer Kennels, Tuckerton, New Jersey.

Opposite: Four-month-old future champion Frandee's Free N' Easy, owned and bred by Dee Dee Wood, Norco, California.

On following pages: Two chocolate Cockers shown at the Clackamas Kennel Club Spring Fun Match in May 1980 were Cal-Ore's Tootsie Pop and the dog, Cal-Ore's Choclit Giacobazzi. The sire of this brother and sister was Cal-Ore's The Devil's Advocate ex Merribark's Mocha Motion. Breeder-owner-handler of Tootsie is Nancy L. Ray, and "Jock" is owned by Mrs. Mary A. Carpenter and handled by Lisa Ray. The judge was Noreen Gonce.

Left: Ch. Frandee's Prim N' Proper, daughter of Ch. Mar-Jac's Frandee Folly, is owned and handled by Frank Wood. Bergman photo. **Below:** Ch. Pett's Molly Pitcher, whelped in 1975, pictured winning at a 1976 Cocker Spaniel Club Specialty show. Sired by Ch. Candylane Cadet ex Pett's Charmer, Molly is owned by Dorothy and Roland Pett of Dennis Port, Massachusetts. **Opposite:** Milru's Mr. Good Fellow pictured winning at six months of age at the Buckhorn Kennel Club Match show in 1980. This darling black and tan was sired by Ch. Dur-Bets Tartan ex Ch. Milru's Tanandorable. Owned and handled by Mrs. Robert Fellows.

BEST OF OPPOSITE

TATHAM PHOTO

Left: Thomas F. O'Neal, owner of the famous Dreamridge Kennels in Woodstock, Illinois, with a bunch of Cocker puppies whelped at Dreamridge during 1978. **Below:** Eighteen-year-old Trojan Queen's Replica and her seventh generation descendant, Trojan June One, painted in 1973 by Peggy Bang for owner Alice Kaplan, Trojan Cockers, Magnolia, Texas. **Opposite:** Classic's Trifully Tri, pictured at seven and a half months of age, is a tri-color bitch, bred and owned by Lindy Hay of Bakersfield, California. The sire was Ch. Nor Mar's No Doubt II, a black and white, and the dam was Gam-b-line Raising Kane, a tri-color.

Above: Ch. Cobb's Moonglo, silver buff puppy bitch, is shown going Winners Bitch and Best of Opposite Sex under judge Langdon Skarda. Bob Covey handled for owner Gladys Von Horn of Vancouver, Washington.

Opposite: Six-week-old puppy sired by Ch. Frandee's Celebration ex Ch. Laurim's Super Star. This beautiful buff puppy was bred and is owned by Dee Dee Wood of Norco, California.

Ch. Ging's Charlie Chutney, beautiful tri-color dog, pictured here at eight months of age. Photographed by Cryzentia for breeder-owners Bill Gorodner and Lloyd Alton of Ridgewood, New Jersey.

CHAPTER SIXTEEN

The Blight of Parasites

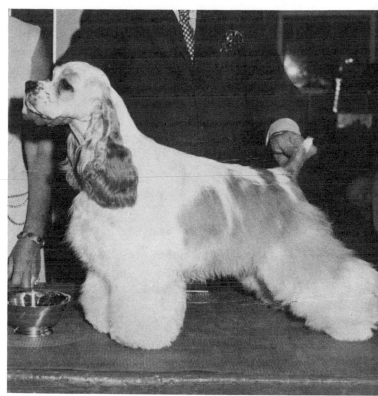

Ch. Pett's Yachtsman, bred by Roland A. Pett of Dennis Port, Massachusetts. Yachtsman was a show winner in the 1970's. Photo by Ritter.

Anyone who has ever spent hours peering intently at their dog's warm, pink stomach waiting for a flea to appear will readily understand why I call this chapter the "blight of parasites." It is that dreaded onslaught of the pesky flea that heralds the subsequent arrival of worms.

If you have seen even one flea scoot across that vulnerable expanse of skin, you can be sure there are more lurking on other areas of your dog. They seldom travel alone. So, it is now an established fact that *la puce*, as the French refer to the flea, has set up housekeeping on your dog! It is going to demand a great deal of your time before you manage to evict them—probably just temporarily at that—no matter which species your dog is harboring.

Fleas are not always choosy about their host, but chances are your dog has what is commonly known as *Ctenocephalides canis*, the dog flea. If you are a lover of cats also, your dog might even be playing host to a few *Ctenocephalides felis*, the cat flea, or vice versa. The only thing you can be really sure of is that your dog is supporting an entire community of them, all hungry and sexually oriented, and you are going to have to be persistent in your campaign to get rid of them.

One of the chief reasons fleas are so difficult to catch is that what they lack in beauty and eyesight (they are blind at birth, throughout infancy, and see very poorly if at all during adulthood), they make up for in their fantastic ability to jump and scurry about.

While this remarkable ability to jump—some claim 150 times the length of their bodies—stands them in good stead with circus entrepreneurs and has given them claim to fame as chariot pullers and acrobats in side show attractions, the dog owner can be reduced to tears at the very thought of the onset of fleas.

Modern research has provided a panacea in the form of flea sprays, dips, collars, and tags which can be successful to varying degrees. However, there are those who still swear by the good old-fashioned methods of removing them by hand, which can be a challenge to your sanity as well as your dexterity.

Since the fleas' conformation (they are built like envelopes, long and flat), with their spiny skeletal system on the outside of their bodies, is specifically provided for slithering through forests of hair, they are given a distinct advantage to start with. Two antennae on the head select the best spot for digging and then two mandibles penetrate the skin and hit a blood vessel. It is also at this moment that the flea brings into play his spiny contours to prop himself against surrounding hairs to avoid being scratched off as he puts the bite on your dog. A small projecting tube is then lowered into the hole to draw out blood and another tube pumps saliva into the wound; this prevents the blood from clotting and allows the flea to drink freely. Simultaneously, your dog jumps into the air and gets one of those back legs into action, scratching endlessly and in vain, and ruining some coat at the same time!

If you should be so lucky as to catch an itinerant flea as it mistakenly shortcuts across your dog's tomach, the best hunting grounds in the world are actually in the deep fur all along the dog's back from neck to tail. However, the flea, like every other creature on earth, must have water, so several times during its residency it will make its way to the moister areas of your dog's anatomy such as the corners of the mouth, the eyes, or the genital parts. This is when the flea collars and tags are useful. Their fumes prevent fleas from passing the neck to get to the head of your dog.

Your dog can usually support several generations of fleas, if it doesn't scratch itself to death or go out of its mind with the itching in the interim. The propagation of the flea is insured by the strong mating instinct and the well-judged decision of the female flea as to the best time to deposit her eggs. She has the rare capacity to store semen until the time is right to lay the eggs after some previous brief encounter with a passing member of the opposite sex.

When that time comes for her to lay, she does so without so much as a backward glance and moves on. The dog shakes the eggs off during a normal day's wandering, and they remain on the ground until hatched and the baby fleas are ready to jump back onto a passing dog. If any of the eggs have remained on the original dog, chances are that in scratching an adult flea, he will help the baby fleas emerge from their shells.

Larval fleas are small and resemble slender maggots; they begin their lives eating their own egg shells until the dog comes along and offers them a return to the world of adult fleas, whose excrement provides the predigested blood pellets they must have to thrive. They cannot survive on fresh blood, nor are they capable at this tender age of digging for it themselves.

After a couple of weeks of this freeloading, the baby flea makes his own cocoon and becomes a pupa. This stage lasts long enough for the larval flea to grow legs, mandibles, and sharp spines and to flatten out and in general become identifiable as the commonly known and obnoxious *Ctenocephalides canis*. The process can take several weeks or several months, depending on weather conditions, heat, moisture, etc., but generally three weeks is all that is required to enable the flea to start gnawing your dog in its own right.

And so the life-cycle of the flea is renewed and begun again. If you don't have plans to stem the tide, you will certainly see a population explosion that will make the human one resemble an endangered species. Getting rid of fleas can be accomplished by the aforementioned spraying of the dog, or the flea collars and tags, but air, sunshine and a good shaking out of beds, bedding, carpets, cushions, etc., certainly must be undertaken to get rid of the eggs or larvae lying around the premises.

Should you be lucky enough to get hold of a flea, you must squeeze it to death (which isn't likely) or break it in two with a sharp, strong fingernail (which also isn't likely) or you must release it *underwater* in the toilet bowl and flush immediately. This prospect is only slightly more likely.

There are those dog owners, however, who are much more philosophical about the flea, since, like the cockroach, it has been around since the beginning of the world. For instance, that old-time philosopher, David Harum, has been much quoted with his remark, "A reasonable amount of fleas is good for a dog. They keep him from broodin' on bein' a dog." We would rather agree with John Donne who in his *Devotions* reveals that, "The flea, though he kill none, he does all the harm he can." This is especially true if your dog is a show dog! If the scratching doesn't ruin the coat, the inevitable infestation of parasites left by the fleas will!

We readily see that dogs can be afflicted by both internal and external parasites. The external parasites are known as the aforementioned fleas, plus ticks and lice; while all of these are bothersome, they can be treated. However, the internal parasites, or worms of various kinds, are usually well-entrenched before discovery and more substantial means of ridding the dog of them completely are required.

INTERNAL PARASITES

The most common worms are the round worms. These, like many other worms, are carried and spread by the flea and go through a cycle within the dog host. They are excreted in egg or larval form and passed on to other dogs. this manner.

Worm medicine should be prescribed by a veterinarian, and dogs should be checked for worms at least twice a year—or every three months if there is a known epidemic in your area— and during the summer months when fleas are plentiful.

Major types of worms are hookworms, whipworms, tapeworms (the only non-round worms in this list), ascarids (the "typical" round worms), heartworms, kidney and lung worms. Each can be peculiar to a part of the country or may be carried by a dog from one area to another. Kidney and lung worms are fortunately quite rare; the others are not. Some symptoms for worms are vomiting intermittently, eating grass, lack of pep, bloated stomach, rubbing the tail along the ground, loss of weight, dull coat, anemia and pale gums, eye discharge, or unexplained nervousness and irritability. A dog with worms will usually eat twice as much as he normally would.

Never worm a sick dog or a pregnant bitch after the first two weeks she has been bred, and never worm a constipated dog . . . it will retain the strong medicine within the body for too long a time.

HOW TO TEST FOR WORMS

Worms can kill your dog if the infestation is severe enough. Even light infestations of worms can debilitate a dog to the point where he is more susceptible to other serious diseases that can kill.

Today's medication for worming is relatively safe and mild, and worming is no longer the traumatic experience for either the dog or owner that it used to be. Great care must be given, however, to the proper administration of the drugs. Correct dosage is a "must" and clean quarters are essential to rid your kennel of these parasites. It is almost impossible to find an animal that is completely free of parasites, so we must consider worming as a necessary evil.

However mild today's medicines may be, it is inadvisable to worm a dog unnecessarily. There are simple tests to determine the presence of worms and this chapter is designed to help you learn how to administer these tests yourself. Veterinarians charge a nominal fee for this service, if it is not part of their regular office visit examination. It is a simple matter to prepare fecal slides that you can read yourself on a periodic basis.

All that is needed by way of equipment is a microscope with 100X power. These can be purchased in the toy department of a department or regular toy store for a few dollars. The basic, least expensive sets come with the necessary glass slides and attachments.

After the dog has defecated, take an applicator stick, a toothpick with a flat end, or even an old-fashioned wooden matchstick and gouge off a piece of the stool about the size of a small pea. Have one of the glass slides ready with a large drop of water on it. Mix the two together until you have a cloudy film over a large area of the slide. This smear should be covered with another slide or a cover slip—though it is possible to obtain readings with just the one open slide. Place your slide under the microscope and prepare to focus in on it. To read the slide you will find that your eye should follow a certain pattern. Start at the top and read from left to right, then right back to the left and then left over to the right side once again until you have looked at every portion of the slide from the top left to the bottom right side.

Make sure that your smear is not too thick or watery or the reading will be too dark and confused to make proper identification. If you decide you would rather not make your own fecal examinations, but would prefer to have the veterinarian do it, the proper way to present a segment of the stool is as follows:

After the dog has defecated, a portion of the stool, say a square inch from different sections of it, should be placed in a glass jar or plastic container and labeled with the dog's name and address of the owner. If the sample cannot be examined within three or four hours after passage, it should be refrigerated. Your opinion as to what variety of worms you suspect is sometimes helpful to the veterinarian and may be noted on the label of the jar you submit to him for the examination.

Checking for worms on a regular basis is advisable not only for the welfare of the dog but for the protection of your family, since most worms are transmissible, under certain circumstances, to humans.

Ch. Wagtime David, owned by Barb White, Columbiana, Ohio, was sired by Ch. Travel On Jackson ex Simpson's Give Me The Nod.

CHAPTER SEVENTEEN

Your Dog, Your Veterinarian and You

Ch. Frandee's Dark N' Handsome is pictured winning Best of Variety from the Classes when on his way to his championship. Handsome, bred and shown by Dee Dee Wood, Norco, California, was later exported to Japan.

The purpose of this chapter is to explain why you should never attempt to be your own veterinarian. Quite the contrary, we urge emphatically that you establish good liaison with a reputable veterinarian who will help you maintain happy, healthy dogs. Our purpose is to bring you up-to-date on the discoveries made in modern canine medicine and to help you work with your veterinarian by applying these new developments to your own animals.

We have provided here "thumbnail" histories of many of the most common types of diseases your dog is apt to come in contact with during his lifetime. We feel that if you know a little something about the diseases and how to recognize their symptoms, your chances of catching them in the preliminary stages will help you and your veterinarian effect a cure before a serious condition develops.

Today's dog owner is a realistic, intelligent person who learns more and more about his dog —inside and out—so that he can care for and enjoy the animal to the fullest. He uses technical terms for parts of the anatomy, has a fleeting knowledge of the miracles of surgery, and is fully prepared to administer clinical care for his animals at home. This chapter is designed for study and/or reference and we hope you will use it to full advantage.

We repeat, we do *not* advocate your playing "doctor." This includes administering medication without veterinary supervision, or even doing your own inoculations. General knowledge of diseases, their symptoms, and side effects will assist you in diagnosing diseases for your veterinarian. He does not expect you to be an expert, but will appreciate your efforts in getting a sick dog to him before it is too late and he cannot save its life.

ASPIRIN: A DANGER

There is a common joke about doctors telling their patients, when they telephone with a complaint, to take an aspirin, go to bed and let him know how things are in the morning. Unfortunately, that is exactly the way it turns out with a lot of dog owners who think aspirins are cure-alls and give them to their dogs indiscriminately. They finally call the veterinarian when the dog has an unfavorable reaction.

Aspirin is not a panacea for everything—certainly not for every dog. In an experiment, fatalities in cats treated with aspirin in one laboratory alone numbered 10 out of 13 within a two-week period. Dogs' tolerance was somewhat better, as to actual fatalities, but there was considerable evidence of ulceration on the stomach linings in varying degrees when necropsy was performed.

Aspirin has been held in the past to be almost as effective for dogs as for people when given for many of the everyday aches and pains. The fact remains, however, that medication of any kind should be administered only after veterinary consultation and a specific dosage suitable to the condition is recommended.

While aspirin is chiefly effective in reducing fever, relieving minor pains, and cutting down on inflammation, the acid has been proven harmful to the stomach when given in strong doses. Only your veterinarian is qualified to determine what the dosage is or whether it should be administered to your particular dog at all.

WHAT THE THERMOMETER CAN TELL YOU

You will notice in reading this chapter dealing with the diseases of dogs that practically everything a dog might contract in the way of sickness has basically the same set of symptoms: loss of appetite, diarrhea, dull eyes, dull coat, warm and/or runny nose and FEVER!

Therefore, it is most advisable to have a thermometer on hand for checking temperature. There are several inexpensive metal rectal-type thermometers that are accurate and safer than the glass variety that can be broken. This may happen either by dropping it or perhaps by its breaking off in the dog because of improper insertion or an aggravated condition with the dog that makes him violently resist the injection of the thermometer.

Whatever type you use, it should first be sterilized with alcohol and then lubricated with Vaseline to make the insertion as easy as possible.

The normal temperature for a dog is 101.5 degrees Fahrenheit, as compared to the human 98.6 degrees. Excitement as well as illness can cause this to vary a degree or two, but any sudden or extensive rise in body temperature must be considered as cause for alarm. Your first indication will be that your dog feels unduly "warm" and this is the time to take the temperature, *not* when the dog becomes very ill or manifests additional serious symptoms. With a thermometer on hand, you can check temperature quickly and perhaps prevent some illnesses from becoming serious.

COPROPHAGY

Perhaps the most unpleasant of all phases of dog breeding is to come up with a dog that takes to eating stool. This practice, which is referred to politely as coprophagy, is one of the unsolved mysteries in the dog world. There simply is no confirmed explanation as to why some dogs do it.

However, there are several logical theories, all or any of which may be the cause. Some people cite nutritional deficiencies; others say that dogs that are inclined to gulp their food (which passes through them not entirely digested) find it still partially palatable. There is another theory that the preservatives used in some meat are responsible for an appealing odor that remains through the digestive process. Then again, poor quality meat can be so tough and unchewable that dogs swallow it whole and it passes through them in large undigested chunks.

There are others who believe the habit is strictly psychological, the result of a nervous condition or insecurity. Others believe the dog cleans up after itself because it is afraid of being punished as it was when it made a mistake on the carpet as a puppy. Some people claim boredom is the reason, or even spite. Others will tell you a dog does not want its personal odor on the premises for fear of attracting other hostile animals to itself or its home.

The most logical of all explanations and the one veterinarians are inclined to accept is that it is a deficiency of dietary enzymes. Too much dry food can be bad and many veterinarians suggest trying meat tenderizers, monosodium glutamate, or garlic powder all of which give the stool a bad odor and discourage the dog. Yeast or certain vitamins or a complete change of diet are even more often suggested. By the time you try each of the above you will probably discover that the dog has outgrown the habit anyway. However, the condition cannot be ignored if you are to enjoy your dog to the fullest.

There is no set length of time that the problem persists, and the only real cure is to walk the dog on leash, morning and night and after every meal. In other words, set up a definite eating and exercising schedule before coprophagy is an established pattern.

MASTURBATION

A source of embarrassment to many dog owners, masturbation can be eliminated with a minimum of training.

The dog that is constantly breeding anything and everything, including the leg of the piano or perhaps the leg of your favorite guest, can be broken of the habit by stopping its cause.

The over-sexed dog—if truly that is what he is —which will never be used for breeding can be castrated. The kennel stud dog can be broken of the habit by removing any furniture from his quarters or keeping him on leash and on verbal command when he is around people or in the house where he might be tempted to breed pillows, people, etc.

Hormone imbalance may be another cause and your veterinarian may advise injections. Exercise can be of tremendous help. Keeping the dog's mind occupied by physical play when he is around people will also help relieve the situation.

Females might indulge in sexual abnormalities like masturbation during their heat cycle, or again, because of a hormone imbalance. But if they behave this way because of a more serious problem, a hysterectomy may be indicated.

A sharp "no!" command when you can anticipate the act, or a sharp "no!" when caught in the act will deter most dogs if you are consistent in your correction. Hitting or other physical abuse will only confuse a dog.

RABIES

The greatest fear in the dog fancy today is still the great fear it has always been—rabies.

What has always held true about this dreadful disease still holds true today. The only way rabies can be contracted is through the saliva of a rabid dog entering the bloodstream of another animal or person. There is, of course, the Pasteur treatment for rabies which is very effective.

It should be administered immediately if there is any question of exposure. There was of late the incident of a little boy, who survived being bitten by a rabid bat. Even more than dogs being found to be rabid, we now know that the biggest carriers are bats, skunks, foxes, rabbits, and other warmblooded animals that pass it from one to another since they do not have the benefit of inoculation. Dogs that run free should be inoculated for protection against these animals. For city or house dogs that never leave their owner's side, it may not be as necessary.

For many years, Great Britain (because it is an island and because of the country's strictly enforced six-month quarantine) was entirely free of rabies. But in 1969 a British officer brought back his dog from foreign duty and the dog was found to have the disease soon after being released from quarantine. There was a great uproar about it, with Britain killing off wild and domestic animals in a great scare campaign, but the quarantine is once again down to six months and things seem to have returned to a normal, sensible attitude.

Health departments in rural towns usually provide rabies inoculations free of charge. If your dog is outdoors a great deal, or exposed to other animals that are, you might wish to call the town hall and get information on the program in your area. One cannot be too cautious about this dread disease. While the number of cases diminishes each year, there are still thousands being reported and there is still the constant threat of an outbreak where animals roam free. Never forget, there is no cure.

Rabies is caused by a neurotropic virus which can be found in the saliva, brain, and sometimes the blood of the afflicted warmblooded animal. The incubation period is usually two weeks or as long as six months, which means you can be exposed to it without any visible symptoms. As we have said, while there is still no known cure, it can be controlled.

You can help effect this control by reporting animal bites, educating the public to the dangers and symptoms, and prevention of it, so that we may reduce the fatalities.

There are two kinds of rabies; one form is called "furious" and the other is referred to as "dumb." The mad dog goes through several stages of the disease. His disposition and behavior change radically and suddenly; he becomes irritable and vicious. The eating habits alter, and he rejects food for things like stones and sticks; he becomes exhausted and drools saliva out of his mouth constantly. He may hide in corners, look glassy eyed and suspicious, bite at the air as he races around snarling and attacking with his tongue hanging out. At this point paralysis sets in, starting at the throat so that he can no longer drink water though he desires it desperately; hence, the term hydrophobia is given. He begins to stagger and eventually convulse, and death is imminent.

In "dumb" rabies paralysis is swift; the dog seeks dark, sheltered places and is abnormally quiet. Paralysis starts with the jaws, spreads down the body, and death is quick. Contact by humans or other animals with the drool from either of these types of rabies on open skin can produce the fatal disease, so extreme haste and proper diagnosis is essential. In other words, you do not have to be bitten by a rabid dog to have the virus enter your system. An open wound or cut that comes in touch with the saliva is all that is needed.

The incubation and degree of infection can vary. You usually contract the disease faster if the wound is near the head, since the virus travels to the brain through the spinal cord. The deeper the wound, the more saliva is injected into the body, and the more serious the infection. So, if bitten by a dog under any circumstances—or any warmblooded animal for that matter—immediately wash out the wound with soap and water, bleed it profusely, and see your doctor as soon as possible.

Also, be sure to keep track of the animal that bit, if at all possible. When rabies is suspected, the public health officer will need to send the animal's head away to be analyzed. If it is found to be rabies free, you will not need to undergo treatment. Otherwise, your doctor may advise that you have the Pasteur treatment, which is extremely painful. It is rather simple, however, to have the veterinarian examine a dog for rabies without having the dog sent away for positive diagnosis of the disease. A ten-day quarantine is usually all that is necessary for everyone's peace of mind.

Rabies is no respecter of age, sex, or geographical location. It is found all over the world from North Pole to South Pole, and has nothing to do with the old wives' tale of dogs going mad in the hot summer months. True, there is an increase in reported cases during summer, but only because that is the time of the year for animals to roam free in good weather and during the mating season when the battle of the sexes is taking place. Inoculation and a keen eye for symptoms and bites on our dogs and other pets will help control the disease until the cure is found.

VACCINATIONS

If you are to raise a puppy, or a litter of puppies, successfully, you must adhere to a realistic and strict schedule of vaccinations. Many puppyhood diseases can be fatal—all of them are debilitating. According to the latest statistics, 98 per cent of all puppies are being inoculated after 12 weeks of age against the dread distemper, hepatitis, and leptospirosis and manage to escape these horrible infections. Orphaned puppies should be vaccinated every two weeks until the age of 12 weeks. Distemper and hepatitis live-virus vaccines should be used, since the puppies are not protected with the colostrum normally supplied to them through the mother's milk. Puppies weaned at six to seven weeks should also be inoculated repeatedly because they will

no longer be receiving mother's milk. While not all will receive protection from the serum at this early age, it should be given and they should be vaccinated once again at both nine and 12 weeks of age.

Leptospirosis vaccination should be given at four months of age with thought given to booster shots if the disease is known in the area, or in the case of show dogs which are exposed on a regular basis to many dogs from far and wide. While animal boosters are in order for distemper and hepatitis, every two or three years is sufficient for leptospirosis, unless there is an outbreak in your immediate area. The one exception should be the pregnant bitch since there is reason to believe that inoculation might cause damage to the fetus.

Strict observance of such a vaccination schedule will not only keep your dog free of these debilitating diseases, but will prevent an epidemic in your kennel, or in your locality, or to the dogs that are competing at the shows.

SNAKEBITE

As field trials and hunts and the like become more and more popular with dog enthusiasts, the incident of snakebite becomes more of a likelihood. Dogs that are kept outdoors in runs or dogs that work the fields and roam on large estates are also likely victims.

Most veterinarians carry snakebit serum, and snakebite kits are sold to dog owners for just such a purpose. To catch a snakebite in time might mean the difference between life and death, and whether your area is populated with snakes or not, it behooves you to know what to do in case it happens to you or your dog.

Your primary concern should be to get to a doctor or veterinarian immediately. The victim should be kept as quiet as possible (excitement or activity spreads the venom through the body more quickly) and if possible the wound should be bled enough to clean it out before applying a tourniquet, if the bite is severe.

First of all, it must be determined if the bite is from a poisonous or non-poisonous snake. If the bite carries two horseshoe-shaped pinpoints of a double row of teeth, the bite can be assumed to be non-poisonous. If the bite leaves two punctures or holes—the result of the two fangs carrying venom—the bite is very definitely poisonous and time is of the essence.

Recently, physicians have come up with an added help in the case of snakebite. A first aid treatment referred to as "hypothermia," which is the application of ice to the wound to lower body temperature to a point where the venom spreads less quickly, minimizes swelling, helps prevent infection, and has some influence on numbing the pain. If ice is not readily available, the bite may be soaked in ice-cold water. But even more urgent is the need to get the victim to a hospital or a veterinarian for additional treatment.

EMERGENCIES

No matter how well you run your kennel or keep an eye on an individual dog, there will almost invariably be some emergency at some time that will require quick treatment until you get the animal to the veterinarian. The first and most important thing to remember is to keep calm! You will think more clearly and your animal will need to know he can depend on you to take care of him. However, he will be frightened and you must beware of fear-biting. Therefore, do not shower him with kisses and endearments at this time, no matter how sympathetic you feel. Comfort him reassuringly, but keep your wits about you. Before getting him to the veterinarian try to alleviate the pain and the shock.

If you can take even a minor step in this direction it will be a help toward the final cure. Listed here are a few of the emergencies that might occur and what you can do AFTER you have called the vet and told him you are coming.

BURNS

If you have been so foolish as to not turn your pot handles toward the back of the stove—for your children's sake as well as your dog's—and the dog is burned, apply ice or ice-cold water and treat for shock. Electrical or chemical burns are treated the same, but with an acid or alkali burn, use, respectively, a bicarbonate of soda and a vinegar solution. Check the advisability of covering the burn when you call the veterinarian.

DROWNING

Most animals love the water but sometimes get in "over their heads." Should your dog take in too much water, hold him upside down and open his mouth so that water can empty from the lungs, then apply artificial respiration or mouth-to-mouth resuscitation. With a large dog, hang the head over a step or off the end of a table while you hoist the rear end in the air by the back feet. Then treat for shock by covering him with a blanket, administering a stimulant such as coffee with sugar, and soothing him with your voice and hands.

FITS AND CONVULSIONS

Prevent the dog from thrashing about and injuring himself, cover with a blanket, and hold down until you can get him to the veterinarian.

FROSTBITE

There is no excuse for an animal getting frostbite if you are "on your toes" and care for the animal; however, should frostbite set in, thaw out the affected area slowly by massaging with a circular motion and stimulation. Use Vaseline to help keep the skin from peeling off and/or drying out.

HEART ATTACK

Be sure the animal keeps breathing by applying artificial respiration. A mild stimulant may be used, and give him plenty of air. Treat for shock as well, and get him to the veterinarian quickly.

SHOCK

Shock is a state of circulatory collapse that can be induced by a severe accident, loss of blood, heart failure, or any injury to the nervous system. Until you can get the dog to the veterinarian, keep him warm by covering him with a blanket and administer a mild stimulant such as coffee or tea with sugar. Try to keep the dog quiet until the appropriate medication can be prescribed. Relapse is not uncommon, so the dog must be observed carefully for several days after initial shock.

SUFFOCATION

Administer artificial respiration and treat for shock with plenty of air.

SUN STROKE

Cooling the dog off immediately is essential. Ice packs, submersion in ice water, and plenty of cool air are needed.

Ch. Schiely's Fudge Ripple is owned and shown by Beverly Schiely of North Olmsted, Ohio. Klein photo.

Ch. Prime-Time Superfly placed third in the Sporting Group at the 1980 Pasadena Kennel Club show. Bob Covey handled for owners Charles and Jackie Rowe, Rowingdale Cockers, La Mesa, California.

WOUNDS

Open wounds or cuts that produce bleeding must be treated with hydrogen peroxide, and tourniquets should be used if bleeding is excessive. Also, shock treatment must be given, and the animal must be kept warm.

THE FIRST AID KIT

It would be sheer folly to try to operate a kennel or to keep a dog without providing for certain emergencies that are bound to crop up when there are active dogs around. Just as you would provide a first aid kit for people, you should also provide a first aid kit for the animals on the premises.

The first aid kit should contain the following items:

BFI or other medicated powder
jar of Vaseline
Q-tip cotton swabs
bandage—1" gauze
adhesive tape
Band-Aids
cotton gauze or cotton balls
boric acid powder

A trip to your veterinarian is always safest, but there are certain preliminaries for cuts and bruises of a minor nature that you can take care of yourself.

Cuts, for instance, should be washed out and medicated powder should be applied with a bandage. The lighter the bandage the better so that the most air possible can reach the wound. Q-tips can be used for removing debris from the eyes, after which a mild solution of boric acid wash can be applied. As for sores, use dry powder on wet sores, and Vaseline on dry sores. Use cotton for washing out wounds and drying them.

A particular caution must be given here on bandaging. Make sure that the bandage is not too tight to hamper the dog's circulation. Also, make sure the bandage is applied correctly so that the dog does not bite at it trying to remove it. A great deal of damage can be done to a wound by a dog tearing at a bandage to get it off. If you notice the dog is starting to bite at it, do it over or put something on the bandage that smells and tastes bad to him. Make sure, however, that the solution does not soak through the bandage and enter the wound. Sometimes, if it is a leg wound, a sock or stocking slipped on the dog's leg will cover the bandage edges and will also keep it clean.

HOW NOT TO POISON YOUR DOG

Ever since the appearance of Rachel Carson's book *Silent Spring*, people have been asking, "Just how dangerous are chemicals?" In the animal fancy where disinfectants, room deodorants, parasitic sprays, solutions, and aerosols are so widely used, the question has taken on even more meaning. Veterinarians are beginning to ask, "What kind of disinfectant do you use?" "Have you any fruit trees that have been sprayed recently?" When animals are brought in to their offices in a toxic condition, or for unexplained death, or when entire litters of puppies die mysteriously, there is good reason to ask such questions.

The popular practice of protecting animals against parasites has given way to their being exposed to an alarming number of commercial products, some of which are dangerous to their very lives. Even flea collars can be dangerous, especially if they get wet or somehow touch the genital regions or eyes. While some products are much more poisonous than others, great care must be taken that they be applied in proportion to the size of the dog and the area to be covered. Many a dog has been taken to the vet with an unusual skin problem that was a direct result of having been bathed with a detergent rather than a proper shampoo. Certain products that are safe for dogs can be fatal for cats. Extreme care must be taken to read all ingredients and instructions carefully before using the products on any animal.

The same caution must be given to outdoor chemicals. Dog owners must question the use of fertilizers on their lawns. Lime, for instance, can be harmful to a dog's feet. The unleashed dog that covers the neighborhood on his daily rounds is open to all sorts of tree and lawn sprays and insecticides that may prove harmful to him, if not as a poison, then as a producer of an allergy.

There are numerous products found around the house that can be lethal, such as rat poison, boric acid, hand soap, detergents, car anti-freeze, and insecticides. These are all available in the house or garage and can be tipped over easily and consumed. Many puppy fatalities are reported as a result of puppies eating mothballs. All poisons should be placed on high shelves out of the reach of *both* children and animals.

Perhaps the most readily available of all household poisons are plants. Household plants are almost all poisonous, even if taken in small quantities. Some of the most dangerous are the elephant ear, the narcissus bulb, any kind of ivy leaves, burning bush leaves, the jimson weed, the dumb cane weed, mock orange fruit, castor beans, Scottish broom seeds, the root or seed of the plant called "four o'clock," cyclamen, pimpernel, lily of the valley, the stem of the sweet pea, rhododendrons of any kind, spider lily bulbs, bayonet root, foxglove leaves, tulip bulbs, monkshood roots, azalea, wisteria, poinsettia leaves, mistletoe, hemlock, locoweed, and arrowglove. In all, there are over 500 poisonous plants in the United States. Peach, elderberry, and cherry trees can cause cyanide poisoning if the bark is consumed. Rhubarb leaves, either raw or cooked, can cause death or violent convulsions. Check out your closets, fields, and grounds around your home, and especially the dog runs, to see what should be eliminated to remove the danger to your dogs.

Am., Can. Ch. Calypso's L'il Peoples Chico pictured winning under judge Ted Eldridge. Chico is handled by Michael Lannie for owners Terri Frazier and Tom and Laurie Acklin. The sire was Ch. Windy Hill's Makes-Its-Point ex Calypso's Tanfastic Action.

SYMPTOMS OF POISONING

Be on the lookout for vomiting, hard or labored breathing, whimpering, stomach cramps, and trembling as a prelude to convulsions. Any delay in a visit to your veterinarian can mean death. Take along the bottle or package or a sample of the plant you suspect to be the cause to help the veterinarian determine the correct antidote.

The most common type of poisoning, which accounts for nearly one-fourth of all animal victims, is staphylococcic—infected food. Salmonella ranks third. These can be avoided by serving fresh food and not letting it lie around in hot weather.

There are also many insect poisonings caused by animals eating cockroaches, spiders, flies, butterflies, etc. Toads and some frogs give off a fluid that can make a dog foam at the mouth—and even kill him—if he bites just a little too hard!

Some misguided dog owners think it is "cute" to let their dogs enjoy a cocktail with them before dinner. There can be serious effects resulting from encouraging a dog to drink—sneezing fits, injuries as a result of intoxication, and heart stoppage are just a few. Whiskey for medicinal purposes, or beer for brood bitches should be administered only on the advice of your veterinarian.

There have been cases of severe damage and death when dogs have emptied ash trays and eaten cigarettes, resulting in nicotine poisoning. Leaving a dog alone all day in a house where there are cigarettes available on a coffee table is asking for trouble. Needless to say, the same applies to marijuana. The narcotic addict who takes his dog along with him on "a trip" does not deserve to have a dog. All the ghastly side effects are as possible for the dog as for the addict, and for a person to submit an animal to this indignity is indeed despicable. Don't think it doesn't happen. Unfortunately, in all our major cities the practice is becoming more and more a problem for the veterinarian.

Be on the alert and remember that in the case of any type of poisoning, the best treatment is prevention.

THE CURSE OF ALLERGY

The heartbreak of a child being forced to give up a beloved pet because he is suddenly found to be allergic to it is a sad but true story. Many families claim to be unable to have dogs at all; others seem to be able only to enjoy them on a restricted basis. Many children know animals only through occasional visits to a friend's house or the zoo.

While modern veterinary science has produced some brilliant allergists, the field is still working on a solution for those who suffer from exposure to their pets. There is no permanent cure as yet.

Over the last quarter of a century there have been many attempts at a permanent cure, but none has proven successful because the treatment was needed too frequently, or was too expensive to maintain over extended periods.

However, we find that most people who are allergic to their animals are also allergic to a variety of other things as well. By eliminating the other irritants, and by taking medication given for the control of allergies in general, many are able to keep pets on a restricted basis. This may necessitate the dog's living outside the house, being groomed at a professional grooming parlor instead of by the owner, or merely being kept out of the bedroom at night. A discussion of this "balance" factor with your medical and veterinary doctors may give new hope to those willing to try.

A paper presented by Mathilde M. Gould, M.D., a New York allergist, before the American Academy of Allergists in the 1960's and reported in the September-October 1964 issue of the *National Humane Review* magazine, offered new hope to those who are allergic by a method referred to as hyposensitization. You may wish to write to the magazine and request the article for discussion of your individual problem with your medical and veterinary.

Surely, since the sixties there have been additional advances in the field of allergy since so many people—and animals—are affected in so many ways.

ALLERGIES IN DOGS

It used to be that you recognized an allergy in your dog when he scratched out his coat and developed a large patch of raw skin or sneezed himself almost to death on certain occasions. A trip to the veterinarian involved endless discussion as to why it might be and an almost equally endless "hit and miss" cure of various salves and lotions with the hope that one of them would work. Many times the condition would correct itself before a definite cure was affected.

However, during the 1970's through preliminary findings at the University of Pennsylvania Veterinary School there evolved a diagnosis for allergies that eliminated the need for skin sensitivity tests. It is called RAST, and is a radioallergosobant test performed with a blood serum sample. It is not even necessary in all cases for the veterinarian to see the dog.

A cellulose disc laced with a suspected allergen is placed in the serum, and if the dog is allergic to that particular allergen the serum will contain a specific antibody that adheres to the allergen on the disc. The disc is placed in a radioactively "labeled" antiserum that is attracted to that particular antibody. The antiserum binds with the antibody and can be detected with a radiation counter.

Furthermore, the scientists at the University of Pennsylvania also found that the RAST test has shown to be a more accurate diagnostic tool than skin testing because it measures the degree, and not merely the presence, of allergic reactions.

DO ALL DOGS CHEW?

Chewing is the best possible method of cutting teeth and exercising gums. Every puppy goes through this teething process, and it can be destructive if the puppy uses shoes or table corners or rugs instead of the proper item for the best possible results. All dogs should have a Nylabone available for chewing, not only to teethe on but also for inducing growth of the permanent teeth, to assure normal jaw development, and to settle the permanent teeth solidly in the jaws. Chewing on a Nylabone also has a cleaning effect and serves as a "massage" for the gums, keeping down the formation of tartar that erodes tooth enamel.

When you see a puppy pick up an object to chew, immediately remove it from his mouth with a sharp "No!" and replace the object with a Nylabone. Puppies take anything and everything into their mouths so they should be provided with several Nylabones to prevent damage to the household. This same Nylabone elimi-

Nylabone® is the perfect chewing pacifier for young dogs in their teething stage and even for older dogs to help satisfy that occasional urge to chew. Unlike many other dog bones on the market today, Nylabone® does not splinter or fall apart; it will last indefinitely and as it is used it frills, becoming a doggie toothbrush that cleans teeth and massages gums.

nates the need for the kind of "bone" which may chip your dog's mouth or stomach or intestinal walls. Cooked bones, soft enough to be powdered and added to the food, are also permissible if you have the patience to prepare them, but Nylabone serves all the purposes of bones for chewing that your dog may require, so why take a chance on meat bones?

Electrical cords and wires of any kind present a special danger that must be eliminated during puppyhood, and glass dishes that can be broken and played with are also hazardous.

The answer to the question about whether all dogs chew is an emphatic *yes*, and the answer if even more emphatic in the case of puppies.

SOME REASONS FOR CHEWING

Chewing can also be a form of frustration or nervousness. Dogs sometimes chew for spite, if owners leave them alone too long or too often. Bitches will sometimes chew if their puppies are taken away from them too soon; insecure puppies often chew thinking they're nursing. Puppies that chew wool, blankets, carpet corners, or certain other types of materials may have a nutritional deficiency or something lacking in their diet, such as the starch that might be left in material after washing. Perhaps the articles have been near something that tastes good and they have retained the odor of food.

The act of chewing has no connection with particular breeds or ages, any more than there is a logical reason for dogs to dig holes outdoors or dig on wooden floors indoors.

So we repeat, it is up to you to be on guard at all times until the need—or habit—passes.

HIP DYSPLASIA

Hip dysplasia, or HD, is one of the most widely discussed of all animal afflictions, since it has appeared in varying degrees in just about every breed of dog. True, the larger breeds seem most susceptible, but it has hit the small breeds and is beginning to be recognized in cats as well.

While HD in man has been recorded as far back as 370 B.C., HD in dogs was more than likely referred to as rheumatism until veterinary research came into the picture. In 1935 Dr. Otto Schales, at Angell Memorial Hospital in Boston, wrote a paper on hip dysplasia and classified the four degrees of dysplasia of the hip joints as follows:

Grade 1—slight (poor fit between ball socket)
Grade 2—moderate (moderate but obvious shallowness of the socket)
Grade 3—severe (socket quite flat)
Grade 4—very severe (complete displacement of head of femur at early age)

HD is an incurable, hereditary, though not congenital disease of the hip sockets. It is transmitted as a dominant trait with irregular manifestations. Puppies appear normal at birth but the constant wearing away of the socket means the animal moves more and more on muscle, thereby presenting a lameness, a difficulty in getting up, and severe pain in advanced cases.

The degree of severity can be determined around six months of age, but its presence can be noticed from two months of age. The problem is determined by X-ray, and if pain is present it can be relieved temporarily by medication. Exercise should be avoided since motion encourages the wearing away of the bone surfaces.

Dogs with HD should not be shown or bred, if quality in the breed is to be maintained. It is essential to check a pedigree for dogs known to be dysplastic before breeding, since this disease can be dormant for many generations.

ELBOW DYSPLASIA

The same condition can also affect the elbow joints and is known as elbow dysplasia. This also causes lameness, and dogs so affected should not be used for breeding.

PATELLAR DYSPLASIA

Some of the smaller breeds of dogs suffer from patella dysplasia, or dislocation of the knee. This can be treated surgically, but the surgery by no means abolishes the hereditary factor; therefore, these dogs should not be used for breeding.

All dogs—in any breed—should be X-rayed before being used for breeding. The X-ray should be read by a competent veterinarian, and the dog declared free and clear.

THE UNITED STATES REGISTRY

In the United States we have a central Hip Dysplasia Foundation, known as the OFA (Orthopedic Foundation for Animals). This HD control registry was formed in 1966. X-rays are sent for expert evaluation by qualified radiologists.

All you need do for complete information on getting an X-ray for your dog is to write to the Orthopedic Foundation for Animals at 817 Virginia Ave., Columbia, MO. 65201, and request their dysplasia packet. There is no charge for this kit. It contains an envelope large enough to hold your X-ray film (which you will have taken by your own veterinarian), and a drawing showing how to position the dog properly for X-rays. There is also an application card for proper identification of the dog. Then, hopefully, your dog will be certified "normal." You will be given a registry number which you can put on his pedigree, use in your advertising, and rest assured that your breeding program is in good order.

All X-rays should be sent to the address above. Any other information you might wish to have may be requested from Mrs. Robert Bower, OFA, Route 1, Constantine, Mo. 49042.

We cannot urge strongly enough the importance of doing this. While it involves time and effort, the reward in the long run will more than pay for your trouble. To see the heartbreak of parents and children when their beloved dog has to be put to sleep because of severe hip dysplasia as the result of bad breeding is a sad experience. Don't let this happen to you or to those who will purchase your puppies!

Additionally, we should mention that there is a method of palpation to determine the extent of affliction. This can be painful if the animal is not properly prepared for the examination. There have also been attempts to replace the animal's femur and socket. This is not only expensive, but the percentage of success is small.

For those who refuse to put their dog down, there is a new surgical technique that can relieve pain but in no way constitutes a cure. This technique involves the severing of the pectinius muscle which for some unknown reason brings relief from pain over a period of many months— even up to two years. Two veterinary colleges in the United States are performing this operation at the present time. However, the owner must also give permission to "de-sex" the dogs at the time of the muscle severance. This is a safety measure to help stamp out hip dysplasia, since obviously the condition itself remains and can be passed on through generations.

HD PROGRAM IN GREAT BRITAIN

The British Veterinary Association (BVA) has made an attempt to control the spread of HD by appointing a panel of members of their profession who have made a special study of the disease to read X-rays. Dogs over one year of age may be X-rayed and certified as free. Forms are completed in triplicate to verify the tests. One copy remains with the panel, one copy is for the owner's veterinarian, and one for the owner. A record is also sent to the British Kennel Club for those wishing to check on a particular dog for breeding purposes.

GERIATRICS

If you originally purchased good healthy stock and cared for your dog throughout his life, there is no reason why you cannot expect your dog to live to a ripe old age. With research and the remarkable foods produced for dogs, especially in this past decade or so, his chances of longevity have increased considerably. If you have cared for him well, your dog will be a sheer delight in his old age, just as he was while in his prime.

We can assume you have fed him properly if he is not too fat. Have you ever noticed how fat people usually have fat dogs because they indulge their dog's appetite as they do their own? If there has been no great illness, then you will find that very little additional care and attention are needed to keep him well. Exercise is still essential, as is proper food, booster shots, and tender loving care.

Even if a heart condition develops, there is still no reason to believe your dog cannot live to an old age. A diet may be necessary, along with medication and limited exercise, to keep the condition under control. In the case of deafness, or partial blindness, additional care must be taken to protect the dog, but neither infirmity will in any way shorten his life. Prolonged exposure to temperature variances; overeating; excessive exercise; lack of sleep; or being housed with younger, more active dogs may take an unnecessary toll on the dog's energies and induce serious trouble. Good judgment, periodic veterinary checkups, and individual attention will keep your dog with you for many added years.

When discussing geriatrics, the question of when a dog becomes old or aged usually is asked. We have all heard the old saying that one year of a dog's life is equal to seven years in a human. This theory is strictly a matter of opinion, and must remain so, since so many outside factors enter into how quickly each individual dog "ages." Recently, a new chart was devised that is more realistically equivalent:

DOG	HUMAN
6 months	10 years
1 year	15 years
2 years	24 years
3 years	28 years
4 years	32 years
5 years	36 years
6 years	40 years
7 years	44 years
8 years	48 years
9 years	52 years
10 years	56 years
15 years	76 years
21 years	100 years

It must be remembered that such things as serious illnesses, poor food and housing, general neglect, and poor beginnings as puppies will take their toll of a dog's general health and age him more quickly than a dog that has led a normal, healthy life. Let your veterinarian help you determine an age bracket for your dog in his later years.

While good care should prolong your dog's life, there are several "old age" disorders to watch for no matter how well he may be doing. The tendency toward obesity is the most common, but constipation is another. Aging teeth and a slowing down of the digestive processes may hinder digestion and cause constipation, just as any major change in diet can bring on diarrhea. There is also the possibility of loss or impairment of hearing or eyesight which will also tend to make the dog wary and distrustful. Other behavioral changes may result as well, such as crankiness, loss of patience, and lack of interest; these are the most obvious changes. Other ailments may manifest themselves in the form of rheumatism, arthritis, tumors and warts, heart disease, kidney infections, male prostatism, and female disorders. Of course, all these require a veterinarian's checking the degree of seriousness and proper treatment.

Ch. Memoir's Devil May Care wins Best of Opposite Sex over Specials from the Classes, and Best of Winners under judge Dick Duding, at the Cocker Spaniel Club of Rhode Island Specialty. Owner and breeder was Anita Roberts.

DOG INSURANCE

Much has been said for and against canine insurance, and much more will be said before this kind of protection for a dog becomes universal and/or practical. There has been talk of establishing a Blue Cross-type plan similar to the one now existing for humans. However, the best insurance for your dog is YOU! Nothing compensates for tender, loving care. Like the insurance policies for humans, there will be a lot of fine print in the contracts revealing that the dog is not covered after all. These limited conditions usually make the acquisition of dog insurance expensive and virtually worthless.

Blanket coverage policies for kennels or establishments that board or groom dogs can be an advantage, especially in transporting dogs to and from their premises. For the one-dog owner, however, whose dog is a constant companion, the cost for limited coverage is not necessary.

THE HIGH COST OF BURIAL

Pet cemeteries are mushrooming across the nation. Here, as with humans, the sky can be the limit for those who wish to bury their pets ceremoniously. The costs of plots and satin-lined caskets, grave stones, flowers, etc., run the gamut of prices to match the emotions and means of the owner.

IN THE EVENT OF YOUR DEATH

This is a morbid thought perhaps, but ask yourself the question, "If death were to strike at this moment, what would become of my dogs?"

Perhaps you are fortunate enough to have a relative, child, spouse, or friend who would take over immediately, if only on a temporary basis. Perhaps you have already left instructions in your last will and testament for your pet's housing, as well as a stipend for its care.

Provide definite instructions before a disaster occurs or your dogs are carted off to the pound to be destroyed, or stolen by commercially inclined neighbors with "resale" in mind. It is a simple thing to instruct your lawyer about your wishes in the event of sickness or death. Leave instructions as to feeding, etc., posted on your kennel room or kitchen bulletin board, or wherever your kennel records are kept. Also, tell several people what you are doing and why. If you prefer to keep such instructions private,

merely place them in sealed envelopes in a known place with directions that they are to be opened only in the event of your death. Eliminate the danger of your animals suffering in the event of an emergency that prevents your personal care of them.

KEEPING RECORDS

Whether you have one dog or a kennel full of them, it is wise to keep written records. It takes only a few moments to record dates of inoculations, trips to the vet, tests for worms, etc. It can avoid confusion or mistakes or having your dog not covered with immunization if too much time elapses between shots because you have to guess at the date of the last shot.

Make the effort to keep all dates in writing rather than trying to commit them to memory. A rabies injection date can be a problem if you have to recall that "Fido had the shot the day Aunt Mary got back from her trip abroad, and, let's see, I guess that was around the end of June."

In an emergency, these records may prove their value if your veterinarian cannot be reached and you have to call on another, or if you move and have no case history on your dog for the new veterinarian. In emergencies, one does not always think clearly or accurately, and if dates, types of serums used, and other information are a matter of record, the veterinarian can act more quickly and with more confidence.

Ch. Pett's Rhythm Step is pictured winning at a Cocker Spaniel Specialty show. Breeder-owners are Mr. and Mrs. Roland Pett of Dennis Port, Massachusetts.

From the Classic Kennels of Linda Hay are the bitch Classic's Coming Attraction and the dog Classic's Repeat Performance. The sire of these year-old black and whites was Ch. Baliwick Bricklayer out of Ch. Painted Acre Pucker Power. "Erin," the bitch, is owned by Linda Hay; the dog, "Adolf," is co-owned by her and Ted and Lynnette Jacobson.

CHAPTER EIGHTEEN

Pursuing a Career in Dogs

Ch. Pett's Handsome Harry, pictured at 16 months of age, is owned by the Roland Petts of Dennis Port, Massachusetts.

One of the biggest joys for those of us who love dogs is to see someone we know or someone in our family grow up in the fancy and go on to enjoy the sport of dogs in later life. Many dog lovers, in addition to leaving codicils in their wills, are providing in other ways for veterinary scholarships for deserving youngsters who wish to make their association with dogs their profession.

Unfortunately, many children who have this earnest desire are not always able to afford the expense of an education that will take them through veterinary school, and they are not eligible for scholarships. In the 1960's during my tenure as editor of *Popular Dogs* magazine, I am happy to say I had something to do with the publicizing of college courses whereby those who could not go all the way to a veterinary degree could earn an Animal Science degree and thus still serve the fancy in a significant way. The Animal Science courses cost less than half of what it would take to become a veterinarian, and those achieving these titles have become a tremendous assistance to the veterinarian.

We all have experienced the more and more crowded waiting rooms at the veterinary offices, and are aware of the demands on the doctor's time, not just for office hours but for his research, consultation, surgery, etc. The tremendous increase in the number of dogs and cats and other domestic animals, both in cities and the suburbs, has resulted in an almost overwhelming consumption of veterinarians' time.

Until recently most veterinary assistance was made up of kennel men or women who were restricted to services more properly classified as office maintenance rather than actual veterinary aid. Needless to say, their part in the operation of a veterinary office is both essential and appreciated, as are the endless details and volumes of paperwork capably handled by office secretaries and receptionists. However, still more of a veterinarian's duties could be handled by properly trained semi-professionals.

With exactly this additional service in mind, many colleges are now conducting two-year courses in animal science for the training of such para-professionals, thereby opening a new field for animal technologists. The time saved by the assistance of these trained technicians, who now relieve the veterinarians of the more mechanical chores and allow them additional time for diagnosing and general servicing of their clients, will be beneficial to all involved.

"Delhi Tech," the State University Agricultural and Technical College at Delhi, New York, was one of the first to offer the required courses for this degree. Now, many other institutions of learning are offering comparable courses at the college level. Entry requirements are usually that each applicant must be a graduate of an ap-

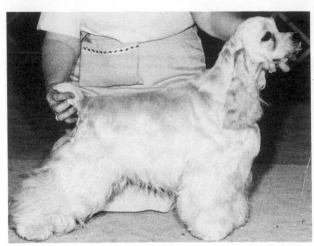

Ch. Pett's Calendar Girl is the dam of six champions, including the well-known Ch. Pett's Gentleman Jim. Calendar Girl was a show winner in the 1960's and an outstanding brood bitch at the kennels of Dorothy and Roland Pett of Dennis Port, Massachusetts.

proved high school or have taken the State University admissions examination. In addition, each applicant for the Animal Science Technology program must have some previous credits in mathematics and science, with chemistry an important part of the science background.

The program at Delhi was a new educational venture dedicated to the training of competent technicians for employment in the biochemical field and has been generously supported by a five-year grant, designated as a "Pilot Development Program in Animal Science." This grant provided both personal and scientific equipment with obvious good results when it was done originally pursuant to a contract with the United States Department of Health, Education, and Welfare. Delhi is a unit of the State University of New York and is accredited by the Middle States Association of Colleges and Secondary Schools. The campus provides offices, laboratories, and animal quarters and is equipped with modern instruments to train technicians in laboratory animal care, physiology, pathology, microbiology, anesthesia, X-ray, and germ-free techniques. Sizable animal colonies are maintained in air-conditioned quarters: animals housed include mice, rats, hamsters, guinea pigs, gerbils and rabbits, as well as dogs and cats.

First-year students are given such courses as livestock production, dairy food science, general, organic and biological chemistry, mammalian anatomy, histology and physiology, pathogenic microbiology, and quantitative and instrumental analysis, to name a few. Second year students matriculate in general pathology, animal para-

sitology, animal care and anesthesia, introductory psychology, animal breeding, animal nutrition, hematology and urinalysis, radiology, genetics, food sanitation and meat inspection, histological techniques, animal laboratory practices, and axenic techniques. These, of course, may be supplemented by electives that prepare the student for contact with the public in the administration of these duties. Such recommended electives include public speaking, botany, animal reproduction, and other related subjects.

In addition to Delhi, one of the first to offer this program was the State University of Maine. Part of their program offered some practical training for the students at the Animal Medical Center in New York City. Often after this initial "in the field" experience, the students could perform professionally immediately upon entering a veterinarian's employ as personnel to do laboratory tests, X-rays, blood work, fecal examinations, and general animal care. After the courses at college, they were equipped to perform all of the following procedures as para-professionals:

* Recording of vital information relative to a case. This would include such information as the client's name, address, telephone number, and other facts pertinent to the visit. The case history would include the breed, age of animal, its sex, temperature, etc.
* Preparation of the animal for surgery.
* Preparation of equipment and medicaments to be used in surgery.
* Preparation of medicaments for dispensing to clients on prescription of the attending veterinarian.
* Administration and application of certain medicines.
* Administration of colonic irrigations.
* Application or changing of wound dressings.
* Cleaning of kennels, exercise runs, and kitchen utensils.
* Preparation of food and the feeding of patients.
* Explanation to clients on the handling and restraint of their pets, including needs for exercise, house training, and elementary obedience training.
* First-aid treatment for hemorrhage, including the proper use of tourniquets.
* Preservation of blood, urine, and pathologic material for the purpose of laboratory examination.
* General care and supervision of the hospital or clinic patients to insure their comfort. Nail trimming and grooming of patients.

Credits are necessary, of course, to qualify for this program. Many courses of study include biology, zoology, anatomy, genetics, and animal diseases, and along with the abovementioned courses the fields of client and public relations are touched upon as well as a general study of the veterinary medical profession.

By the mid-seventies there were a reported 30,000 veterinarians practicing in the United States. It is estimated that within the following decade more than twice that number will be needed to take proper care of the domestic animal population in this country. While veterinarians are graduated from 22 accredited veterinary colleges in this country and Canada, recent figures released by the Veterinary Medical Society inform us that only one out of every seven applicants is admitted to these colleges. It becomes more and more obvious that the para-professional person will be needed to back up the doctor.

Students having the desire and qualifications to become veterinarians, however, may suffer financial restrictions that preclude their education and licensing as full-fledged veterinarians. The Animal Science Technologist with an Associate degree in Applied Science may very well become the answer as a profession in an area close to their actual desire.

Their assistance in the pharmaceutical field, where drug concerns deal with laboratory animals, covers another wide area for trained assistants. The career opportunities are varied and reach into job opportunities in medical centers, research institutions, and government health agencies; at present, the demand for graduates far exceeds the current supply of trained personnel.

As to financial remuneration, beginning yearly salaries are relatively low and estimated costs of basic college expenses relatively high but the latter include tuition, room and board, college fees, essential textbooks, and limited personal expenses. These personal expenses, of course, will vary with individual students, as well as their other expenses, though the costs are about half of those involved in becoming a full-fledged veterinarian.

High school graduates with a sincere affection and regard for animals and a desire to work with veterinarians and perform such clinical duties as mentioned above will find they fit in especially well.

Those interested in pursuing a career of this nature might obtain the most current list of accredited colleges and universities offering these programs by consulting the American Veterinary Medical College, 600 S. Michigan Avenue, Chicago, Illinois 60605.

As the popularity of this profession increased, additional attention was given to the list of services, and the degrees to which one could aspire was expanded. There are para-professionals with Associate of Science degrees, and some colleges and universities have extended the courses to four years' duration which lead to Bachelor of Science degrees.

At the University of Minnesota Technical College, a two year course offers a degree of Associate in Applied Science after the successful completion of 108 credit hours. This Animal Health Technology course prepares the students for future careers in the following fields:

* Laboratory Animal Technician (Junior)
* Experimental Animal Technician
* Clinical Laboratory Animal Assistant
* Laboratory Animal Assistant in Radiology
* Laboratory Animal Research Assistant
* Small Animal Technician (General)
* Small Animal Veterinarian's Assistant
* Small Animal Veterinarian's Receptionist
* Animal Hospital Technician
* Zoo Technician
* Large Animal Technician (General)
* Large Animal Veterinarian's Receptionist
* Large Animal Clinic Assistant
* Meat Animal Inspection Technician

An 11-week-old puppy named Rubin at the home of his breeder-owner, Pam Burrows of Gainesville, Florida. Rubin was sired by Ch. Trojan's Tocayo ex Ch. Karavan's Cartoon Character.

PART-TIME KENNEL WORK

Youngsters who do not wish to go on to become veterinarians or animal technicians can get valuable experience and extra money by working part-time after school and on weekends, or full-time during summer vacations, in a veterinarian's office. The exposure to animals and office procedure will be time well spent.

Kennel help is also an area that is wide open for retired men and women. They are able to help out in many areas where they can learn and stay active, and most of the work allows them to set their own pace. The understanding and patience that age and experience brings is also beneficial to the animals they will deal with; for their part, these people find great reward in their contribution to animals and will be keeping active in the business world as well.

Ch. Pett's Daddy's Mink is pictured winning the Sweepstakes competition at the Southern Wisconsin Cocker Spaniel Specialty show. This beautiful tri-color bitch was handled by Ron Fabis for breeder-owners Mr. and Mrs. Roland Pett.

Ch. Scioto Bluffs High Hope is the first champion for the kennels of Mrs. Robert Fellows of Clarks Summit, Pennsylvania. "Thistle" was sired by Ch. Scioto Bluffs Sinbad out of Scioto Bluffs Carlene. She is pictured with handler David J. Lowe.

PROFESSIONAL HANDLING

For those who wish to participate in the sport of dogs and whose interests or abilities do not center around the clinical aspects of the fancy, there is yet another avenue of involvement.

For those who excel in the show ring, who enjoy being in the limelight and putting their dogs through their paces, a career in professional handling may be the answer. Handling may include a weekend of showing a few dogs for special clients, or it may be a full-time career that can also include boarding, training, conditioning, breeding, and showing dogs for several clients.

Depending on how deep is your interest, the issue can be solved by a lot of preliminary consideration before it becomes necessary to make a decision. The first move would be to have a long, serious talk with a successful professional handler to learn the pros and cons of such a profession. Watching handlers in action from ringside as they perform their duties can be revealing. A visit to their kennels for an on-the-spot revelation of the behind-the-scenes responsibilities is essential. Working for them full or part time would be the best way of all to resolve any doubt you might have.

Professional handling is not all glamour in the show ring. There is plenty of "dirty work" behind the scenes 24 hours of every day. You must have the necessary ability and patience for this work, as well as the ability and patience to deal with the CLIENTS—the dog owners who value their animals above almost anything else and would expect a great deal from you in the way of care and handling. The big question you must ask yourself first of all is: do you *really* love dogs enough to handle it . . .

DOG TRAINING

Like the professional handler, the professional dog trainer has a most responsible job. You need not only to be thoroughly familiar with the correct and successful methods of training a dog but must also have the ability to communicate with dogs. True, it is very rewarding work, but training for the show ring, obedience, or guard dog work must be performed exactly right for successful results to maintain a good business reputation.

An American Kennel Club judge pauses to give one final (and studious) look at a winner before awarding the ribbons. It is apparent that he appreciates the breed.

Training schools are quite the vogue nowadays, with all of them claiming success. Careful investigation should be made before enrolling a dog, and even more careful investigation should be made of their methods and of their actual successes before becoming associated with them.

GROOMING PARLORS

If you do not wish the 24-hour a day job that is required by a professional handler or professional trainer, but still love working with and caring for dogs, there is always the very profitable grooming business. Poodles started the ball rolling for the swanky, plush grooming establishments that sprang up all over the major cities, many of which seem to be doing very well. Here again, handling dogs and the public well is necessary for a successful operation, in addition to skill in the actual grooming of dogs of all breeds.

While shops flourish in the cities, some of the suburban areas are now featuring mobile units which by appointment will visit your home with a completely equipped shop on wheels and will groom your dog right in your own driveway.

THE PET SHOP

Part-time or full-time work in a pet shop can help you make up your mind rather quickly as to whether you would like to have a shop of your own. For those who love animals and are concerned with their care and feeding, the pet shop can be a profitable and satisfying association. Supplies that are available for sale in these shops are almost limitless, and a nice living can be garnered from pet supplies if the location and population of the city you choose warrant it.

DOG JUDGING

There are also those whose professions, age, or health prevent them from owning, breeding, or showing dogs, and who turn to judging at dog shows after their active years in the show ring are no longer possible. Breeder-judges make a valuable contribution to the fancy by judging in accordance with their years of experience in the fancy, and the assignments are enjoyable. Judging requires experience, a good eye for dogs, and an appreciation of a good animal.

Ch. Trojan's New Dawn, red and white bitch whelped in 1965, is shown going Best of Opposite Sex to Best of Variety. Owned and handled by Alice Kaplan, Magnolia, Texas.

CHAPTER NINETEEN

A Glossary of Cocker Spaniel Terms

Lady Beverly Boots retrieving, owned by the Cal-Ore Kennels of Mr. and Mrs. Fredrick N. Ray, Brooks, Oregon. Boots was whelped in June 1969 and enjoyed a full ten years of field work with the Ray family.

A

Abortion	premature Explusion of fetus
Afterbirth	placenta or embryonic tissues to which puppies are attached by umbilical cords and from which they receive nourishment during gestation
Albino	pigment deficiency, usually a congenital fault, that renders skin, hair, and eyes pink; a dog with lack of coloring due to recessive genes
Allele (noun)	a gene, factor, or trait, that differs from its sister gene. *See* Allelomorphs
Allelomorphs	(noun; adj., allelomorphic) genes, factors, traits, or types that segregate as alternatives; contrasting gene pattern
Allergy	hypersensitivity to one of any number of things such as insect bites, foods, carpet lint, detergents, etc
Alter	to neuter or spay
American Kennel Club	registering body for canine world in the United States; headquarters for the stud book, dog registrations, and federation of kennel clubs. They also create and enforce the rules and regulations governing dog shows in the U.S.A
Amnion	the fetal sac enclosing the fetus
Amniotic fluid	protective fluid within the amnion
Angulation	the angles formed by the meeting of the bones
Anus	anterior opening found under the tail for purposes of alimentary canal elimination
Apple-head	an irregular roundness of topskull; a domed skull
Apron	on long-coated dogs, the longer hair that frills outward from the neck and chest
Autosomes	(noun; adj., autosomal) paired, ordinary chromosomes, similar in both sexes as differentiated from the sex chromosomes

B

Babbler   hunting dog that barks or howls while out on scent

Balanced   a symmetrical, correctly proportioned animal; one with correct balance with one part in regard to another

Barrel   rounded rib section, thorax; chest

Bay   the howl or bark of the hunting dog

Beauty spot   usually roundish colored hair on a blaze of another color. Found mostly between the ears

Beefy   overdevelopment or overweight in a dog, particularly in the hindquarters

Bevy   a flock of birds

Birdy   a dog with strong bird-hunting instinct

Bitch   a female dog

Blaze   a type of marking; white stripe running up the center of the face between the eyes

Blind   the place, manmade or natural, that the hunter uses as cover when hunting

Blocky   square head

Bloom   dogs in top condition are said to be "in full bloom"

Bossy   overdevelopment of the shoulder muscles

Bowlegged   front legs curving outward when viewed from the front

Brace   two dogs (a matched pair) that move as a pair in unison

Break   failure to stop at flush, shot, or command

Breeching   tan-colored hair on inside of the thighs

Brisket   the forepart of the body below the chest

Broken color   a color broken by white or another color or patches of another color

Broken-haired   a wiry coat

Brood bitch   a female used for breeding

Burr   inside part of the ear that is visible to the eye

Butterfly nose   parti-colored nose or entirely flesh color

Bye   in a field trial the odd dog left after braces are drawn

C

Canine   animals of the Canidae family which includes not only dogs, but foxcs, wolves, and jackals

Canines   the four large teeth in the front of the mouth often referred to as fangs

Castrate   the surgical removal of the testicles on the male dog

Cat-foot   round, tight, high-arched feet said to resemble those of a cat

Character   the general appearance or expression said to be typical of the breed

Cheeky   fat cheeks or protruding cheeks.

Chest   forepart of the body between the shoulder blades and above the brisket

China eye   a clear blue wall-eye

Chiseled   a clean cut head, especially when chiseled out below the eye

Chromosomes   small microscopic bodies within the cells of all living things. When division of cells begins, the chromosomes appear as short strings of beads or rods

Clip   method of trimming coats according to individual breed standards

Cloddy   thick set or plodding dog

Close-coupled   a dog short in loins; comparatively short from withers to hipbones

Cobby   short-bodied; compact

Collar   usually a white marking, resembling a collar, around the neck

Condition   general appearance of a dog showing good health, grooming, and good care

Conformation   the form and structure of the bone or framework of the dog in comparison with requirements of the Standard for the breed

Corky   an active and alert dog

Couple   two dogs

Coupling   leash or collar-ring for a brace of dogs

Couplings   body between withers and the hipbones

Cowhocked	when the hocks turn toward each other and sometimes touch
Crest	arched portion of the back of the neck
Crossbred	a dog whose sire and dam are of two different breeds
Crossing-over	(noun) an exchange of inheritance factors or genes between related chromosomes
Croup	the back part of the back above the hind legs; area from hips to tail
Crown	the highest part of the head; the topskull
Cryptorchid	male dog with neither testicle visible
Culotte	the long hair on the back of the thighs
Cushion	fullness of upper lips

D

Dappled	mottled marking of different colors with none predominating
Decoy	fake bird or waterfowl used to lure birds of like species to gun
Dentition	arrangement of teeth
Dewclaws	extra claws, or functionless digits on the inside of the front and/or rear legs
Dewlap	loose, pendulous skin under the throat
Delivery	the act of surrendering retrieved game (or object) to handler
Derby	field trial competition for young, novice sporting dogs
Dish-faced	when nasal bone is so formed that nose is higher at the end than in the middle or at the stop
Disqualification	a dog that has a fault marking it ineligible to compete in dog show competition
Distemper teeth	discolored or pitted teeth as a result of having had distemper.
Dock	to shorten the tail by cutting
Dog	a male dog, though used freely to indicate either sex
Domed	evenly rounded in topskull; not flat but curved upward
Dominant	(adj.) a trait or character that is seen; indicates that a trait contributed by one parent conceals that from the other parent. For example, dark eyes are dominant over light eyes
Down-faced	when nasal bone inclines toward tip of nose
Down in pastern	weak or faulty pastern joints; a let-down foot
Drawing	selection of lots of dogs to be run in pairs in field trial stake
Drop ear	the leather pendant which is longer than the leather of the button ear
Dry neck	taut skin
Dudley nose	flesh-colored or light brown pigmentation in the nose
Dummy	object used to teach dog to retrieve

E

Elbow	the joint between the upper arm and the forearm
Elbows out	turning out or off the body and not held close to the sides
Epistasis	(noun; adj., epistatic) similar to hypostasis; like dominance but epistasis occurs between factors not alternative or allelomorphic. Breeding term
Ewe neck	curvature of the top of the neck
Expression	color, size, and placement of the eyes which give the dog the typical expression associated with the breed

F

Factor	(noun) a simple Mendelian trait; may be considered synonymous with gene. Breeding term
Faking	changing the appearance of a dog by artificial means to make it more closely resemble the Standard, i.e., white chalk to white white fur
Feathering	longer hair fringe on ears, legs, tail, or body
Feet East and West	toes turned out
Femur	the large heavy bone of the thigh
Fetch	to retrieve and return downed game (or object) to handler
Fiddle Front	forelegs out at elbows, pasterns close, and feet turned out

299

Field Trial	competition for sporting dogs which is judged for the breed's specific ability
Flag	a long-haired tail
Flank	the side of the body between the last rib and the hip
Flare	a blaze that widens as it approaches the topskull
Flat bone	when girth of the leg bones is correctly eliptical rather than round
Flat sided	ribs insufficiently rounded as they meet the breastbone
Flews	upper lips, particularly at inner corners
Flush	to drive birds or game from cover
Forearm	bone of the foreleg between the elbow and the pastern
Foreface	front part of the head; before the eyes; muzzle
Frogface	usually overshot jaw where nose is extended by the receding jaw
Fringes	*See* feathering
Front	forepart of the body as viewed head-on
Furrow	slight indentation or median line down center of the skull to the top
Futurity Stakes	a class at field trials (or dog shows) for young dogs that have been nominated before birth

G

Game	prey or hunted quarry
Gay tail	tail carried above the topline
Gene	(noun; adj., genotypic) a single unit of inheritance (Mendel's "determiners") a microscopic part of a chromosome
Genotype	(noun; adj., genotypic) the hereditary composition of an individual. The sum total of every animal's dominant and recessive traits
Gestation	the period during which bitch carries her young; 63 days in the dog
Get	puppies or offspring
Goose rump	too steep or too sloping a croup
Gun dog	a dog that is trained to work to the gun

Guns	the men or women who shoot the flushed game at the field trials
Gun-shy	when a dog fears gun shots or the sight of the gun
Guard hairs	the longer, stiffer hairs that protrude through the undercoat

H

Hard-mouthed	the dog that bites or leaves tooth marks on the game in retrieve
Hare foot	a narrow foot
Haw	a third eyelid or membrane at the inside corner of the eye
Heel	the same as the hock; also an obedience command
Height	vertical measurement from the withers to the ground or shoulder to the ground
Heterozygous	(adj.) possessing contrasting genes (or allelomorphs). Where dominant and recessive genes are both present for any trait or traits
Hie on	a hunting command to urge the dog on while hunting or at field trials
Hock	the tarsus bones of the hind leg that form the joint between the second thigh and the metatarsals
Hocks well let down	when distance from hock to the ground is close to the ground
Homozygous	(adj.) pure for a given trait, or possessing matched genes for that trait. The opposite of heterozygous. (Thus, inbred strains are said to be homozygous, and out-crossed animals to be heterozygous. Degree must be substantiated.)
Hound	dogs commonly used for hunting by scent
Hound marked	three color dogs, white, tan, and black; pre-dominating color mentioned first
Hucklebones	the top of the hipbones
Humerus	the bone of the upper arm
Hup	command given to gun dogs to sit (at flush or at shot)

Hypostasis (noun; adj., epistatic). The masking of the effect of another factor, not an allelomorph, i.e., the masking of the ticking factor in dogs by solid color

I

Inbreeding the mating of closely related dogs of the same breed, usually brother to sister

Incisors the cutting teeth found between the fangs in the front of the mouth

K

Knuckling over an insecurely knit pastern joint often causes irregular motion while dog is standing still

L

Layback well placed shoulders

Layback receding nose accompanied by an undershot jaw

Leather the flap of the ear

Level bite the front or incisor teeth of the upper and lower jaws meet exactly

Line breeding the mating of related dogs of the same breed to a common ancestor. Controlled inbreeding. Usually grandmother to grandson, or grandfather to granddaughter

Lippy lips that do not meet perfectly

Loaded shoulders when shoulder blades are out of alignment due to overweight or overdevelopment on this particular part of the body

Loin the region of the body on either side of the vertebral column between the last ribs and the hindquarters

Lower thigh same as the second thigh

Lumber excess fat on a dog

Lumbering awkward gait on a dog

M

Mane profuse hair on the upper portion of the neck

Mantle dark-shaded portion of the coat or shoulders, back, and sides

Mark pinpointing the spot where game fell so direct retrieve can be made

Mask shading on the foreface

Median line See furrow

Molar rear teeth used for actual chewing

Molera abnormal ossification of the skull

Mongrel puppy or dog whose parents are of two different breeds

Monorchid a male dog with only one testicle apparent

Mute to trail game without baying or barking

Muzzle the head in front of the eyes; this includes nose, nostrils, and jaws, as well as the foreface

Muzzle-band white markings on the muzzle

N

Nose scenting ability

Noslip retriever the dog at heel and retrieves game on command

Nictitating eyelid the thin membrane at the inside corner of the eye which is drawn across the eyeball. Sometimes referred to as the third eyelid

O

Occiput the upper crest or point at the top of the skull

Occipital protuberance the raised occiput itself

Occlusion the meeting or bringing together of the upper and lower teeth

Olfactory pertaining to the sense of smell

Out at shoulder the shoulder blades are set in such a manner that the joints are too wide, hence jut out from the body

Outcrossing the mating of unrelated individuals of the same breed

Overhang a very pronounced eyebrow

Overshot the front incisor teeth on top overlap the front teeth of the lower jaw. Also called pig jaw

P

Pack several dogs kept together in one kennel. A term usually applied to hounds

Paddling	moving with the forefeet wide, to encourage a body roll motion
Pads	the underside, or soles, of the feet
Parti-color	variegated in patches of two or more colors. More detailed explanation can be found in text
Pastern	the collection of bones forming the joint between the radius and ulna, and the metacarpals
Peak	same as occiput
Phenotype	(noun; adj., phenotypic) the external appearance of an individual. The outward manifestation of all dominant genetic material (or double recessive. *See* Recessive.)
Pied	comparatively large patches of two or more colors. Also called parti-colored or piebald
Pigeon-breast	a protruding breastbone
Pig jaw	jaw with overshot bite
Pile	the soft hair in the undercoat
Pincer bite	a bite where the incisor teeth meet exactly
Plain	old expression used to indicate lack in stop
Potterer	a dog that is slow or sometimes unsure on scent
Puppy	a dog under one year of age

Q

Quality	refinement, fineness
Quarter	the process by which the dog works in the field ahead of the gun
Quarters	hind legs as a pair

R

Racy	of comparatively slight build, said to be fast
Recessive	(adj.) a trait or character that is concealed by a like dominant character. Exception: when no dominant is present and recessive genes pair for a certain trait. Paired recessive = Visibility
Retrieve	the act of finding and returning shot game to handler
Ringer	a substitute for close resemblance
Roach back	convex or upward curvature of back; poor topline
Roan	a mixture of colored hairs with white hairs
Rounding	cutting or trimming the ends of the ear leather
Ruff	the longer hair growth around the neck
Runner	a shot bird that runs through cover to escape

S

Saddle	a marking over the back, like a saddle
Scapula	the shoulder blade
Scent	the odor left by an animal in passing, on ground, or in the air
Scissors bite	a bite in which the upper teeth just barely overlap the lower teeth
Self color	one color with lighter shadings
Septum	the line extending vertically between the nostrils
Shelly	a narrow body that lacks the necessary size required by the breed Standard
Slab sides	insufficient spring of ribs
Sloping shoulder	the shoulder blade which is set obliquely or "laid back"
Snowshoe foot	slightly webbed between the toes
Soft-mouthed	a dog (usually a puppy) who constantly drops its birds
Soundness	the general good health and appearance of a dog in its entirety
Spayed	a female whose ovaries have been surgically removed
Specialty Club	an organization to sponsor and promote an individual breed
Specialty Show	a dog show devoted to the promotion of a single breed
Spectacles	shading or dark markings around the eyes or from eyes to ears
Splashed	irregularly patched; color on white or vice versa
Splay foot	a flat or open-toed foot
Spread	the width between the front legs

Spring	*See* Flush
Spring of ribs	the degree of rib roundness
Stake	in field trial competition, the designation of a class
Stance	manner of standing
Staring Coat	dry harsh hair, sometimes curling at the tips
Station	comparative height of a dog from the ground, either high or low
Stern	tail (or rudder) of a sporting dog or hound
Sternum	breastbone
Stifle	joint or hind leg between thigh and second thigh.
Stilted	choppy, up-and-down gait of straight-hocked dog
Stop	the step-up from nose to skull between the eyes
Straight-hocked	without angulation; straight behind
Substance	good bone. Or in good weight, or well-muscled dog
Superciliary arches	the prominence of the frontal bone of the skull over the eye
Swayback	Concave or downward curvature of the back between the withers and the hipbones. Poor topline

T

Team	three or more (usually four) dogs working together in unison
Tender-mouthed	a dog who handles game correctly without damage to it
The Fall	where a shot bird came down
Thigh	the hindquarter from hip joint to stifle
Throatiness	excessive loose skin under the throat
Ticked	small isolated areas of black or colored hairs on another color background
Timber	bone, especially of the legs
Topknot	tufts of hair on the top of the head
Trail	to hunt by following scent left on ground by game or quarry

Triangular eye	the eye set in surrounding tissue or triangular shape; a three-cornered eye
Tri-color	three colors on a dog; tan, black, and white
Trumpet	depression or hollow on either side of the skull just behind the eye socket; comparable to the temple area in man
Tuck-up	body depth at the loin
Turn up	uptilted jaw
Type	the distinguishing characteristics of a dog to measure its worth against the Standard for the breed

U

Undershot	the front teeth of the lower jaw overlapping or projecting beyond the front teeth of the upper jaw when the mouth is closed
Upper-arm	the humerus bone of the foreleg between the shoulder blade and forearm

V

Vent	area under the tail

W

Walleye	a blue eye also referred to as a fish or pearl eye
Weaving	when the dog is in motion, the forefeet or hind feet cross
Weedy	a dog too light of bone
Wheaten	pale yellow or fawn color
Wheel back	backline arched over the loin; roach back
Whelps	unweaned puppies
Wing-clipped	a bird not wounded but unable to fly due to shot through wing feathers
Wire-haired	a hard wiry coat
Withers	the peak of the first dorsal vertebra; highest part of the body just behind the neck
Wrinkle	loose, folding skin on forehead and/or foreface

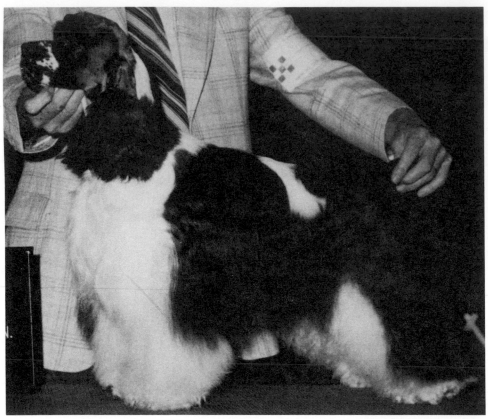

Schiely's Fudge Fever is pictured winning on the
way to championship. Fudge is owned by Annette
and Al Davies.

Ch. Bondale's Marylou, with handler Ray McGinnis, winning points toward championship. Owner,
Marjorie E. Bond.

Bondale's Bullet is pictured winning Best of Winners on the way to championship at the Channel City Kennel Club show in 1980. Owner Marjorie Bond, Bondale Kennels. Jerry Moon, handler; Barbara McCormick, judge.

Milru's Cheery Cherub, U.D., pictured winning under Dorothy Grover at the 1959 Cocker Spaniel Club of Long Island show. Walter Tuddenham, president of the club, presented the trophy to Ruth Muller, who handled her own dog to this win.

Cocker Spaniel Statistics

THE TOP THIRTY WINNING COCKER SPANIELS IN BREED HISTORY
(Based on winnings through December 31, 1980 shows)

NAME	GROUP POINTS	BIS	BB	1	2	3	4	BV
* 1. Ch. Sagamore Toccoa (buff)	73595	39	5	74	24	14	15	196
2. Ch. Kamp's Kaptain Kool (R&W)	53037	20**	15	68	35	17	9	200
* 3. Ch. Shardeloe's Selena (black)	51557	19**	18	86	37	23	23	247
* 4. Ch. Tabaka's Tidbit o'Wynden C.D.X. (black)	43185	16**	18	50	34	10	19	173
5. Ch. Liz Bar Magic of Music (black)	34393	8	25	42	17	18	9	163
6. Ch. Kapewood Prince Matchebelli (buff)	31203	16	2	49	29	5	7	122
7. Ch. Pinetop's Fancy Parade (B&T)	24525	35**	20	86	19	15	8	169
8. Ch. Rexpointe Kojak (B&W)	21458	3	—	23	21	26	12	139
9. Ch. Gail's Ebony Don D (black)	21368	25	8	70	23	3	3	117
10. Ch. Rinky Dink's Socko (black)	19174	12	6	39	12	11	14	110
11. Ch. Butch's Kountry Boy (black)	19003	4	6	16	16	6	11	84
12. Ch. Clarkdale Capital Stock (black)	18545	17**	25	53	31	12	6	144
13. Ch. Burson's Blarney (B&W)	18375	5	12	31	38	15	16	180
14. Ch. Westphal's Limelight (buff)	18340	1	—	13	21	14	26	118
15. Ch. Forjay's Winterwood (red)	17840	5	4	14	17	18	9	97
16. Ch. Forjay's Sundown (B&T)	17394	12	10	43	18	11	9	128
17. Ch. Hugomar Headliner (Tri)	15770	3	2	26	18	18	13	168
18. Ch. Treasure Hill Masterpiece (black)	15708	2	—	30	29	28	29	210
*19. Ch. Liz Bar Chances Are (black)	15402	4	13	14	13	6	6	70
20. Ch. Bigg's Snow Prince (buff)	14825	15	5	32	9	7	3	74
21. Ch. Pinefair Password (black)	14756	4	3	18	21	12	6	71
22. Ch. Artru Patent Leather (black)	14457	1	4	23	17	13	9	138
*23. Ch. Russ' Winter Beauty (red)	13974	3**	14	12	15	8	4	85
24. Ch. Kaplar's Royal Kavalier (B&T)	13631	1**	13	15	17	10	13	142
25. Ch. Ardee's Trademark (black)	13421	2	15	13	36	9	23	183
26. Ch. Artru Hot Rod (buff)	13344	13**	26	33	22	10	7	120
27. Ch. Carmor's Rise and Shine (buff)	12763	10	17	16	5	4	1	46
28. Ch. Stonewalk Squareshooter (R&W)	11081	1	2	20	33	34	28	177
29. Ch. Dream Echo Magic Trouch (black)	10677	3**	8	19	31	17	15	137
30. Ch. Orient's Pleasing You (B&W)	10545	3	2	18	23	25	24	154

* Indicates bitch

** Indicates at least one BIS won at the American Spaniel Club January show, a limited breed show

TOP TEN WINNING COCKER SPANIELS — 1959

NAME	GROUP POINTS	BIS	BB	1	2	3	4	BV
1. Ch. Clarkdale Capital Stock (black)	7933	7	11	21	15	5	2	56
2. Ch. Pinetop's Fancy Parade (B&T)	6443	5	10	22	14	9	5	75
3. Ch. Holly Tree High Knight (black)	3474	2	2	4	2	5	1	21
4. Ch. Windjammer's Passkey (black)	3088	2	—	6	3	1	2	16
5. Ch. Mel Lar's Prince Fredrick (R&W)	2450	1	2	7	9	3	6	52
6. Ch. Hickory Hill High Catch (black)	1816	2	3	15	4	1	2	30
7. Ch. Dau Han's Dan Morgan (R&W)	1761	2	—	3	1	2	3	26
8. Ch. Merryhaven Strutaway (black)	1531	—	2	2	8	2	1	29
9. Ch. Gayhurst Whiz On (black)	1489	—	—	4	3	1	4	18
10. Ch. Nor Mar's Nujac (buff)	1250	—	2	4	1	4	2	22

TOP TEN WINNING COCKER SPANIELS — 1960

NAME	GROUP POINTS	BIS	BB	1	2	3	4	BV
1. Ch. Pinetop's Fancy Parade (B&T)	16319	28	9	63	5	3	3	91
2. Ch. Clarkdale Capital Stock (black)	5559	5	8	19	9	3	2	44
3. Ch. Holly Tree High Knight (black)	4082	4	8	14	5	5	5	45
4. Ch. Try Cob's Spectacular (B&T)	2141	1	3	3	2	1	4	22
5. Ch. Nor Mar's Nujac (buff)	1534	—	1	3	2	4	1	18
6. Ch. Mel Lar's Prince Fredrick (R&W)	1487	—	2	3	6	4	5	42
7. Ch. Hickory Hill High Catch (black)	1374	1	1	3	2	—	2	12
8. Ch. Dau Han's Dan Morgan (R&W)	1195	1	—	1	5	4	2	18
9. Ch. Shunga's Capital Heir (black)	927	—	—	3	2	4	1	22
10. Ch. Rexpointe Frostee Dutchman (B&W)	794	—	—	—	1	5	3	23

TOP TEN WINNING COCKER SPANIELS — 1961

NAME	GROUP POINTS	BIS	BB	1	2	3	4	BV
1. Ch. Whitfield Why Certainly (black)	4307	4	—	9	4	4	—	22
2. Ch. Har-Dee's Hell Bender II (black)	2949	3	2	7	8	4	4	33
3. Ch. Silver Maple Jimmy Stardust (buff)	2947	1	2	16	8	7	6	51
4. Ch. My Idaho Promise to Marysville (R&W)	2514	1	1	10	15	4	3	35
5. Ch. Shady Hill Bit o'Copper (B&T)	2134	1	2	8	3	3	—	29
6. Ch. Van Valzah's Vintage (buff)	1792	—	1	4	5	3	6	38
7. Ch. Pinetop's Fancy Parade (B&T)	1763	2**	—	1	—	1	—	3
* 8. Ch. Camby's Susan (B&W)	1576	1	—	3	—	—	1	10
9. Ch. Shunga's Capital Heir (black)	1566	—	2	7	4	8	1	26
10. Ch. Clarkdale Capital Stock (black)	1125	1	1	2	—	—	1	5

*Indicates bitch

**Indicates BIS at the American Spaniel Club January show, a limited breed show

TOP TEN WINNING COCKER SPANIELS — 1962

NAME	GROUP POINTS	BIS	BB	1	2	3	4	BV
1. Ch. My Idaho Promise to Marysville (R&W)	3973	3	1	18	9	3	1	35
2. Ch. Silver Maple Jimmy Stardust (buff)	3445	3	1	14	10	5	4	44
3. Ch. Fraclin Colonel Caridas (B&W)	3236	1	2	7	3	4	4	34
4. Ch. Whitfield Why Certainly (black)	2359	1	—	8	3	4	1	19
5. Ch. Lurola's Leading Issue (black)	2257	1	—	3	10	7	7	37
6. Ch. Artru Johnny Be Good (buff)	2131	—	3	5	6	6	7	39
7. Ch. Shady Hill Bit o'Copper (B&T)	2031	1**	3	—	5	4	4	21
8. Ch. Rozal's Restock (black)	1616	2	2	4	6	7	1	23
9. Ch. Scioto Bluff's Sinbad (R&W)	1378	—	5	2	2	4	4	28
10. Ch. Van Valzah's Vintage (buff)	1059	—	—	2	4	3	2	28

**Indicates BIS at the American Spaniel Club January show, a limited breed show

TOP TEN WINNING COCKER SPANIELS — 1963

NAME	GROUP POINTS	BIS	BB	1	2	3	4	BV
1. Ch. Bigg's Snow Prince (buff)	3357	3	6	8	4	1	3	30
2. Ch. Lurola's Leading Issue (black)	2891	1	1	10	6	6	4	42
3. Ch. Merikay's Dynamite (B&W)	1492	—	—	2	3	4	3	21
4. Ch. Flo Bob's Noble Knight (black)	1478	—	2	4	6	6	1	24
* 5. Ch. Nosowea's Spring Nosegay (R&W)	1351	—	5	1	4	1	2	30
6. Ch. Artru Johnny Be Good (buff)	1326	—	2	2	7	2	3	24
7. Ch. Scioto Bluff's Sinbad (R&W)	1250	1**	—	2	4	4	1	18
8. Ch. Har Ken's Tee Vee Tony (B&T)	1248	—	—	—	2	1	3	25
9. Ch. Maindale's Golden Touch (buff)	1034	1	—	4	1	1	2	20
10. Ch. Baliwick Baghdad (R&W)	1006	1	1	1	1	1	—	11

* Indicates bitch
** Indicates BIS at the American Spaniel Club January show, a limited breed show

TOP TEN WINNING COCKER SPANIELS — 1964

NAME	GROUP POINTS	BIS	BB	1	2	3	4	BV
1. Ch. Bigg's Snow Prince (buff)	9065	8	2	23	5	5	—	40
2. Ch. Forjay's Sundown (B&T)	4791	4	3	9	6	3	5	42
3. Ch. Hi Boot's Such Brass (B&T)	3730	—	2	2	8	9	6	44
4. Ch. Orient's Pleasing You (B&W)	3082	1	—	5	8	4	7	49
5. Ch. Nelson's Royal Ripper (black)	2244	3	—	4	1	2	—	13
6. Ch. Artru Available (R&W)	2119	1	2	2	5	6	5	49
7. Ch. Pacemaker Photograph (B&T)	1745	—	1	4	9	5	5	34
8. Ch. Stonewalk Squareshooter (R&W)	1719	1	1	2	3	3	3	22
9. Ch. Mijo's Momentum (black)	1595	—	2	3	4	3	4	27
10. Ch. Heatherway Hillbilly (R&W)	1397	—	2	2	7	2	—	33

TOP TEN WINNING COCKER SPANIELS — 1965

NAME	GROUP POINTS	BIS	BB	1	2	3	4	BV
1. Ch. Forjay's Sundown (B&T)	10388	8	6	30	9	2	1	53
2. Ch. Hi Boot's Such Brass (B&T)	4539	1	1	9	10	8	6	44
3. Ch. Orient's Pleasing You (B&W)	4139	—	2	7	10	17	8	59
4. Ch. Mijo's Momentum (black)	3790	1	—	12	5	2	4	29
5. Ch. Pinefair Password (black)	2646	1	—	3	2	1	—	7
6. Ch. Bigg's Snow Prince (buff)	2403	1	1	1	—	1	—	4
7. Ch. Scioto Bluff's Sin Bahr (R&W)	2111	—	—	5	4	4	5	41
8. Ch. Treasure Hill Masterpiece (black)	1835	—	—	7	2	3	6	29
9. Ch. Maribeau's Master Sargent (B&W)	1699	1**	—	1	2	2	—	27
10. Ch. Dream Echo Magic Touch (black)	1652	—	—	1	6	6	4	29

** Indicates BIS at American Spaniel Club January show, a limited breed show

TOP TEN WINNING COCKER SPANIELS — 1966

NAME	GROUP POINTS	BIS	BB	1	2	3	4	BV
1. Ch. Pinefair Password	8999	3	2	12	16	6	5	46
2. Ch. Hopewood Headstrong	4711	4	5	7	6	1	2	29
3. Ch. Treasure Hill Masterpiece	3648	—	—	7	8	5	9	47
4. Ch. Orient's Pleasing You	3171	2	—	6	5	4	8	43
5. Ch. Camby's Contribution	2952	—	1	6	3	3	2	25
6. Ch. Stonewalk Squareshooter	2598	—	—	4	9	14	8	44
7. Ch. Shiloh Dell's Sho Kan	2060	—	—	2	4	6	5	28
8. Ch. Dream Echo Magic Touch	1713	—	2	2	4	4	6	39
9. Ch. Forjay's Sundown	1538	—	1	4	—	1	2	13
10. Ch. Smytholme's Beach Boy	1519	2	1	3	1	—	—	19

TOP TEN WINNING COCKER SPANIELS — 1967

NAME	GROUP POINTS	BIS	BB	1	2	3	4	BV
1. Ch. Dream Echo Magic Touch (black)	5743	2	4	13	17	6	4	56
2. Ch. Treasure Hill Masterpiece (black)	4244	1	—	9	7	9	5	50
3. Ch. Hugomar Headliner (tri)	3717	—	—	3	6	9	4	57
4. Ch. Whirlybird's Top Hit (B&T)	3208	1	5	4	8	4	4	37
5. Ch. Pinefair Password (black)	2825	—	1	3	3	4	1	16
6. Ch. Camby's Contribution (R&W)	2587	—	4	1	4	5	6	36
7. Ch. Essanar Eden Roc, C.D. (black)	2570	1	1	1	2	1	2	15
8. Ch. Bar C Kar's Mr. Chips (buff)	2030	—	2	2	4	4	2	31
* 9. Ch. Dreamridge Dinner Date (B&W)	1965	—	7	3	3	1	4	34
10. Ch. Hi Fi's Show Time (black)	1963	1	—	3	6	4	8	34

* Indicates bitch

TOP TEN WINNING COCKER SPANIELS — 1968

NAME	GROUP POINTS	BIS	BB	1	2	3	4	BV
1. Ch. Hugomar Headliner (tri)	8271	2	2	15	8	6	8	63
2. Ch. Burson's Blarney (B&W)	5349	2	4	8	11	3	8	56
3. Ch. Heyday Hobbit (B&T)	4577	1	9	4	5	11	6	72
4. Ch. Treasure Hill Masterpiece (black)	4130	1	—	5	8	8	7	45
5. Ch. Stonewalk Squareshooter (R&W)	2162	—	1	—	4	3	12	39
6. Ch. Smytholme's Beach Boy (B&T)	1896	—	1	—	3	3	3	20
7. Ch. Three Crown's Tomahawk (B&T)	1675	—	2	1	3	4	4	27
8. Ch. Dreamridge Magic Touch (black)	1569	1**	2	3	2	1	3	14
* 9. Ch. La Mar's Ivory Summer (buff)	1479	—	—	1	4	5	—	18
10. Ch. Hi Fi's Show Stopper (black)	1453	—	—	3	5	7	3	43

* Indicates bitch

** Indicates BIS at American Spaniel Club January show, a limited breed show

TOP TEN WINNING COCKER SPANIELS — 1969

NAME	GROUP POINTS	BIS	BB	1	2	3	4	BV
1. Ch. Burson's Blarney (B&W)	6227	1	4	15	13	5	2	56
2. Ch. Silver Maple Star Performer (buff)	4009	4	—	6	15	2	7	40
* 3. Ch. La Mar's Ivory Summer (buff)	3562	3	—	6	2	4	2	24
4. Ch. Hugomar Headliner (tri)	2711	1	—	6	2	1	—	16
5. Ch. Hi Fi's Show Stopper (black)	2461	1	—	4	4	5	5	29
6. Ch. Shoestring Shootin' Match (black)	2298	—	1	5	2	6	5	43
7. Ch. Newton's Speedy Gonzales (black)	2247	1	—	3	1	2	6	20
8. Ch. Burson's Bonanza (R&W)	1968	1	1	4	—	1	4	13
9. Ch. Be Gay's Tan Man (tri)	1906	—	1	3	3	3	3	37
10. Ch. Alco's Arnie (B&W)	1571	—	1	—	2	2	2	31

*Indicates bitch

TOP TEN WINNING COCKER SPANIELS — 1970

NAME	GROUP POINTS	BIS	BB	1	2	3	4	BV
1. Ch. Burson's Blarney (B&W)	5894	2	3	8	11	6	1	40
* 2. Ch. Sagamore Toccoa (buff)	4073	1	1	3	3	1	9	57
3. Ch. Be Gay's Tan Man (tri)	3681	1**	7	3	4	5	1	36
4. Ch. Newton's Speedy Gonzales (black)	3308	—	—	6	5	6	6	46
5. Ch. Seenar's Ali Baba (black)	1900	1	1	3	1	—	1	14
6. Ch. Shoestring Shootin' Match (black)	1889	—	—	2	4	3	6	44
7. Ch. Rob Mar's Jack Frost (buff)	1755	1	1	1	1	3	—	21
* 8. Ch. Lurola's Skip To M'Lou (black)	1725	—	7	3	—	2	4	33
9. Ch. Ramrod Sherman (tri)	1588	—	1	2	2	1	5	24
10. Ch. Rexpointe Flying Dutchman (B&W)	1046	—	1	1	2	1	2	16

* Indicates bitch

** Indicates BIS at the American Spaniel Club January show, a limited breed show

TOP TEN WINNING COCKER SPANIELS — 1971

NAME	GROUP POINTS	BIS	BB	1	2	3	4	BV
* 1. Ch. Sagamore Toccoa (buff)	16753	8	3	14	14	5	6	59
2. Ch. Ramrod Sherman (tri)	4151	1	1	8	8	2	3	37
3. Ch. Seenar's Ali Baba (black)	3772	—	—	2	7	4	2	30
* 4. Ch. Shardeloe's Selena (black)	2630	—	2	6	—	1	8	30
5. Ch. Regalia's Snowdrifter (B&W)	2582	1	2	4	3	1	2	23
6. Ch. Lurola's Royal Lancer (B&T)	2419	—	15	2	1	2	—	27
7. Ch. Van Matre's Charger (black)	2048	—	—	—	3	8	6	40
8. Ch. Silver Maple Shannon (R&W)	1874	—	—	2	2	7	3	41
9. Ch. Alco's Arnie (B&W)	1863	—	—	1	2	4	2	40
10. Ch. Laynewood Lancer (black)	1411	—	2	1	2	3	1	30

* Indicates bitch

TOP TEN WINNING COCKER SPANIELS — 1972

NAME	GROUP POINTS	BIS	BB	1	2	3	4	BV
* 1. Ch. Sagamore Toccoa (buff)	51998	30	—	56	7	8	—	74
* 2. Ch. Shardeloe's Selena (black)	5720	1	5	9	7	5	5	47
3. Ch. Regalia's Snowdrifter (B&W)	4459	2	1	6	2	2	6	26
4. Ch. Ardee's Trademark (black)	3532	1	5	2	2	2	5	54
5. Ch. Nor Mar's Nautilus (B&T)	3148	—	2	1	1	3	7	31
6. Ch. Van Matre's Charger (black)	2560	—	—	2	3	4	7	40
7. Ch. Briarhaven Bourbon Baron (B&T)	2386	—	2	5	3	5	1	34
8. Ch. Silver Maple Shannon (R&W)	1815	1	—	2	2	—	2	26
9. Ch. Talisman's Magic Trumpeteer (black)	1787	—	—	—	1	4	6	21
*10. Ch. Sagamore Sprite (buff)	1690	—	—	3	3	—	5	21

* Indicates bitch

TOP TEN WINNING COCKER SPANIELS — 1973

NAME	GROUP POINTS	BIS	BB	1	2	3	4	BV
* 1. Ch. Shardeloe's Selena (black)	19449	8**	7	34	11	7	2	79
2. Ch. Soundview Sir Nutley (buff)	4221	—	—	6	5	7	1	30
3. Ch. Ardee's Trademark (black)	3483	1	3	5	7	1	5	37
4. Ch. Deep River Decision (R&W)	2816	—	—	—	4	5	9	48
5. Ch. Nor Mar's Nautilus (B&T)	2514	—	—	—	1	3	6	27
6. Ch. Vista G Altair (B&W)	2380	—	1	2	—	4	3	30
7. Ch. Seenar's Con Man (black)	2325	—	1	1	2	2	3	27
8. Ch. Dream Echo Golden Touch (buff)	1992	—	2	5	5	1	2	28
9. Ch. Van Matre's Charger (black)	1773	—	—	—	3	2	5	22
10. Ch. Star Trek Midnight Sun (black)	1552	1	—	3	1	1	2	23

* Indicates bitch
** One BIS at the American Spaniel Club January show, a limited breed show

TOP TEN WINNING COCKER SPANIELS — 1974

NAME	GROUP POINTS	BIS	BB	1	2	3	4	BV
* 1. Ch. Shardeloe's Selena (black)	23664	10**	4	37	19	10	7	90
2. Ch. Westphal's Limelight (buff)	9170	—	—	6	14	6	14	56
3. Ch. Bobwin's Boy Eagle (buff)	4578	1	3	3	1	2	4	22
4. Ch. Ardee's Trademark (black)	3394	—	3	5	6	2	7	38
5. Ch. Vista G Altair (B&W)	3232	—	1	—	2	2	7	26
6. Ch. Pryority's Patriot (black)	2977	—	7	1	3	4	3	31
7. Ch. Forjay's Winterwood (red)	2929	—	—	1	3	6	4	38
8. Ch. Van Matre's Charger (black)	2065	—	—	1	1	5	4	27
9. Ch. Cuidado's Pecas (R&W)	1727	—	—	2	3	3	2	22
9. Ch. Seenar's Back Talk (black)	1727	—	—	—	—	3	3	24
10. Ch. Travel On Jackson (black)	1668	—	—	1	2	2	6	27

* Indicates bitch
** Indicates one BIS at the ASC Flushing specialty, a limited breed show

TOP TEN WINNING COCKER SPANIELS — 1975

NAME	GROUP POINTS	BIS	BB	1	2	3	4	BV
1. Ch. Forjay's Winterwood (red)	14911	5	4	13	14	12	5	59
2. Ch. Westphal's Limelight (buff)	9170	1	—	7	7	8	12	62
3. Ch. Artru Patent Leather (black)	7158	—	1	14	12	3	6	80
4. Ch. Travel On Jackson (black)	4605	—	—	6	7	8	7	49
5. Ch. Sagamore Strutter (buff)	4111	1	1	6	5	4	5	36
* 6. Ch. Tabaka's Tidbit of Wynden, C.D.	3428	1	1	4	—	2	8	22
7. Ch. Dreamridge Dandiman (R&W)	3186	1**	1	4	1	3	3	24
8. Ch. Ardee's Trademark (black)	2703	—	4	1	7	3	6	43
9. Ch. Pryority's Patriot (black)	2592	1	1	1	1	3	3	14
10. Ch. Shelbyshire's Citation (black)	2443	1	—	3	2	2	1	20

* Indicates bitch
** Indicates BIS at the American Spaniel Club January show, a limited breed show

TOP TEN WINNING COCKER SPANIELS — 1976

NAME	GROUP POINTS	BIS	BB	1	2	3	4	BV
1. Ch. Liz Bar Magic of Music (black)	12163	2	13	18	5	9	5	64
2. Ch. Rexpointe Kojak (B&W)	10750	2	—	10	9	14	6	66
* 3. Ch. Tabaka's Tidbit o'Wynden, C.D.X.	8972	4	5	13	5	2	3	38
4. Ch. Artru Patent Leather (black)	7299	1	1	9	5	10	3	58
5. Ch. Bondalc's Willic Thompson (R&W)	4544	1	1	4	3	1	7	39
6. Ch. Kaplar's Royal Kavalier (B&T)	3870	—	4	5	4	5	4	43
7. Ch. Travel On Jackson (black)	3766	—	—	3	5	9	3	43
8. Ch. Gemini's Sales Talk (black)	3379	1	—	1	1	—	1	11
9. Ch. Willwyn With Style o'Nosowea	2831	1	—	4	6	5	—	20
10. Ch. Dreamridge Don Juan (R&W)	2795	—	—	1	2	4	3	38

* Indicates bitch

TOP TEN WINNING COCKER SPANIELS — 1977

NAME	GROUP POINTS	BIS	BB	1	2	3	4	BV
1. Ch. Liz Bar Magic of Music (black)	20071	6	4	23	9	7	2	63
2. Ch. Rexpointe Kojak (B&W)	9133	1	—	12	11	9	5	58
3. Ch. Heyday Henchman (black)	6371	1	2	5	14	7	3	77
4. Ch. Kaplar's Royal Kavalier (R&T)	5473	1**	4	7	7	1	4	42
5. Ch. Artru Jan Myr's Camelot (buff)	4325	—	1	10	7	7	4	44
6. Ch. Bondale's Willie Thompson (R&W)	3784	—	1	2	5	4	3	44
* 7. Ch. Russ' Winter Beauty (red)	3153	—	5	1	5	4	2	35
* 8. Ch. Tabaka's Tidbit o'Wynden, C.D.X. (black)	2722	—	6	5	1	1	1	23
9. Ch. Wagtime David (black)	2539	—	—	1	4	4	6	32
10. Ch. Buckingham's Action Packed (red)	1777	—	—	2	1	3	4	23

* Indicates bitch

** Indicates BIS at American Spaniel Club show (January), a limited breed show

TOP TEN WINNING COCKER SPANIELS — 1978

NAME	GROUP POINTS	BIS	BB	1	2	3	4	BV
* 1. Ch. Tabaka's Tidbit o'Wynden, C.D.X. (black)	27488	11**	6	28	27	5	7	88
* 2. Ch. Russ' Winter Beauty (red)	10014	2	8	11	10	4	2	47
3. Ch. Kapewood's Prince Matchebelli (buff)	9627	6	1	14	12	3	3	55
4. Ch. Chess King's Board Boss (B&T)	4045	—	3	2	2	4	7	33
5. Ch. Kaplar's Royal Kavalier (B&T)	3987	—	4	3	6	4	5	50
6. Ch. Heyday Henchman (black)	3895	1	—	3	4	3	3	22
7. Ch. Butch's Kountry Boy (black)	3478	—	1	6	2	4	4	32
* 8. Ch. Butch's Liisa (red)	3361	—	2	6	6	3	3	45
9. Ch. Butch's King Coal (black)	2731	—	—	—	5	5	2	33
10. Ch. Artru Jan Myr's Camelot (buff)	2198	1	1	5	1	5	2	27

* Indicates bitch

** One BIS won at the American Spaniel Club January show, a limited breed show

TOP TEN WINNING COCKER SPANIELS — 1979

NAME	GROUP POINTS	BIS	BB	1	2	3	4	BV
1. Ch. Kapewood Prince Matchebelli (buff)	21576	10	1	35	17	2	4	67
2. Ch. Kamps' Kaptain Kool (R&W)	20198	6	5	26	14	9	5	82
3. Ch. Rinky Dink's Socko (black)	8267	5	3	21	4	4	6	52
* 4. Ch. Liz Bar Chances Are (black)	8029	2	6	6	10	3	4	43
5. Ch. Butch's Kountry Boy (black)	5232	2	—	5	3	3	2	27
6. Ch. Karga's Krackerjax Kandyman (buff)	4087	1	1	6	—	2	2	26
7. Ch. Wynden Bellevue Blarney (R&W)	4076	1	—	7	4	1	—	34
8. Ch. Feinlyne By George (B&W)	3639	—	1	4	7	2	3	44
9. Ch. Do It Tovarich (black)	3638	1	—	2	5	2	1	34
10. Ch. Checkerboard Ric Rac (B&W)	3179	—	1	3	5	1	2	30

* Indicates bitch

TOP TEN WINNING COCKER SPANIELS — 1980

(based on shows held from Jan. 1, 1980 thru Dec. 31, 1980)

NAME	*GROUP POINTS*	*BIS*	*BB*	*1*	*2*	*3*	*4*	*BV*
1. Ch. Kamps' Kaptain Kool	32032	14**	8	42	21	8	4	96
2. Ch. Butch's Kountry Boy	13771	2	3	11	13	3	9	57
3. Ch. Rinky Dink's Socko	10907	7	3	18	8	7	8	58
* 4. Ch. Liz Bar Chances Are	7373	2	7	8	3	3	2	27
* 5. Ch. Eli Fran's Diane	6854	1	4	17	5	3	4	48
6. Ch. Do It Tovarich	5906	1	1	12	8	3	5	47
7. Ch. Denzil's Super Daddy	5176	—	2	2	6	3	4	52
8. Ch. Homestead's Ragtime Cowboy	4627	—	—	12	8	2	6	50
9. Ch. Karga's Krackerjax Kandyman	4314	—	3	6	5	2	2	28
10. Ch. Kanchant's Diffrent Strokes	3162	1	—	4	2	1	—	34

* Indicates bitch

** Indicates one BIS won at the American Spaniel Club Flushing Show, a limited breed show

Ch. Kapewoods Rowesbeau won Best of Variety at the 1980 Eugene Kennel Club show with handler Bob Covey. Owner, Rowingdale Kennels; judge, Hayward Hock.

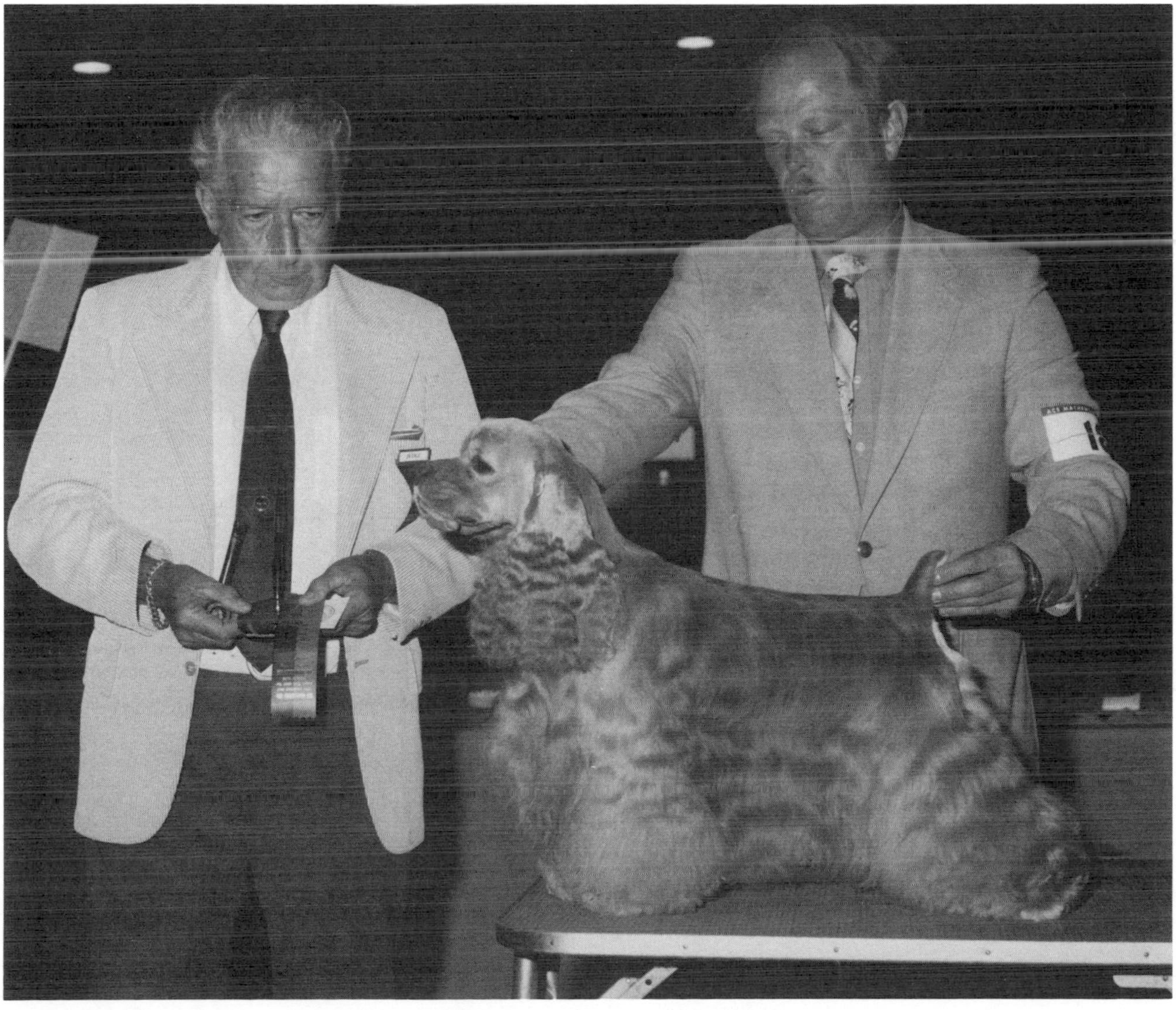

TOP TEN PRODUCING SIRES IN COCKER HISTORY

NAME	COLOR	TOTAL
1. Ch. Scioto Buff's Sinbad	R&W	118
2. Orient's Its a Pleasure	R&W	103
3. Ch. Dreamridge Dominoe	B&W	100
4. Ch. Rinky Dink's Sir Lancelot	B&T	83
5. Ch. Stockdale Town Talk	black	80
6. Ch. Clarkdale Capital Stock	black	76
7. Ch. Crackerbox Certainly	B&T	72
8. Ch. Artru Sandpiper	buff	68
9. Ch. Maddies Vagabond Return	buff	60
10. Ch. Artru Skyjack	buff	56

TOP PRODUCING BITCHES IN BREED HISTORY

NAME	COLOR	TOTAL
1. Ch. Seenar's Seductress	black	15
2. Artru Delightful II	buff	14
2. Ch. Honey Creek Vivacious	R&W	14
3. Ch. Fran Dee's Susan	B&W	13
4. Ch. Fi Fo's Fiesta	tri	11
4. Ch. Hallway Fancy Free	B&W	11
4. Ch. Hickory Hill High Night	black	11
4. Lanebrook's Dash o'Flash	black	11
4. Ch. Laurim's Star Performance	R&W	11
5. Ch. Bar C Kar's Peau Rouge	buff	10
5. Ch. Essanar Evening Song	black	10
5. Ch. Fancy Free Carmen	R&W	10
5. Ch. Hickory Hill High Barbaree	black	10
5. Ch. Honey Creek Cricket	R&W	10
5. Ch. Misty Mornin' Motif	black	10
5. Ch. Nor Mar's Nice N' Neat	B&W	10
5. Pounette Perrette	R&W	10
5. Ch. Tallylyn's My Liza Love	black	10
6. Ch. Candylane Coquette	R&W	9
6. Ch. Dreamridge Dinner Date	B&W	9
6. Ch. Dur Bet's Leading Lady	buff	9
6. Hickory Hill High Pitch	black	9
6. Lurola's Leilanni	buff	9
6. Ch. Magicour's Amy Lou	buff	9
6. Ch. Nonquitt Notable Pride	black	9
6. Ch. Nonquitt Nowanda	B&T	9
6. Ch. Shardeloe's Selena	black	9
6. Ch. Shiloh Dell's Sadie	black	9
6. Ch. Shiloh Dell's Sashay	black	9
6. Willhall Tranquility	B&W	9

TOP TEN LIVING SIRES AS OF 1980

NAME	COLOR	TOTAL
1. Ch. Dreamridge Dominoe	B&W	100
2. Ch. Rinky Dink's Sir Lancelot	B&T	83
3. Ch. Artru Skyjack	buff	56
4. Ch. Artru Action	red	54
5. Ch. La Mar's London	buff	53
6. Ch. Lurola's Royal Lancer	B&T	51
7. Ch. Windy Hill Tis Demi's Demon	B&T	44
8. Ch. Shiloh Dell's Salute	black	39
9. Ch. Dur Bet's Knight to Remember	black	32
10. Ch. Forjay's Winterwood	red	31

TOP LIVING PRODUCING BITCHES

NAME	COLOR	TOTAL
1. Ch. Fran Dec's Susan	B&W	13
2. Ch. Fi Fo's Fiesta	tri	11
2. Ch. Laurim's Star Performance	R&W	11
3. Ch. Essanar Evening Star	black	10
3. Ch. Tallylyn My Liza Love	black	10
4. Ch. Shardeloe's Selena	black	9
5. Ch. Artru Cricket	black	8
5. Ch. Dur Bet's Tantalizer	B&T	8
5. Ch. Essanar Eastwind	black	8
5. Forjay's Bridget	black	8
5. Ch. Kaplar's Cameo Caper	buff	8
5. Liz Bar Summer Magic	black	8
5. Norrisim's No Choice	R&W	8
6. Ch. Artru I'm a Rinky Dink	black	7
6. Ch. Bobwin's Thumbellina	buff	7
6. Byrge's Princess Pat	R&W	7
6. Ch. Dorobin Dance with Me	red	7
6. Ch. Jan Myr Artru Melody of Love	red	7
6. Juniper's Janina	buff	7
6. Ch. Kaembourne Short N' Sweet	R&W	7
6. Ch. Kaplar's Kolleen	red	7
6. Ch. Lea Lad's April Love	black	7
6. Sandrex Sangarita	red	7
6. Ch. Seven Acre's Sunshine	R&W	7
6. Ch. Smarti Parti Sugar Pie Tri, C.D.X.	tri	7

TOP PRODUCING SIRES — 1980

NAME	COLOR	TOTAL
1. Ch. Feinlyne By George	B&W	17
2. Ch. Artru Skyjack	buff	14
3. Ch. Rinky Dink's Sire Lancelot	B&T	13
4. Ch. Bobwin's Sir Ashley	black	10
4. Ch. Fran Dee's Declaration	B&W	10
5. Ch. Dreamridge Dominoe	B&W	9
5. Ch. Rexpointe Shazam	B&W	9
6. Ch. Forjay's Winterwood	red	8
7. Ch. Kamps' Kaptain Kool	R&W	7
7. Ch. Windy Hill Eagle Scout	buff	7
7. Ch. Windy Hill Makes Its Point	B&T	7
8. Ch. Dur Bet's Tartan	B&T	6
8. Ch. Fran Dee's Bill of Rights	R&W	6
9. Ch. Artru Getaway, C.D.	buff	5
9. Ch. Champagne's Dynamic	black	5
9. Ch. Merryhaven Minute Man	black	5
9. Ch. Pett's Yachtsman	R&W	5
10. Ch. Alorah En Garde	B&T	4
10. Ch. Aquitaine's Anubis	black	4
10. Ch. Chess King's Board Boss	B&T	4
10. Ch. Jus Us Buster Brown	brown	4
10. Ch. Kapewood Coty	buff	4
10. Ch. Liz Bar Magic of Music	black	4
10. Ch. M Bar's Hi Roller of Tru Valu	tri	4
10. Ch. Memoir's Billy Hilder	buff	4
10. Ch. Piner's Point of View	black	4
10. Ch. Pineshadow's Persuader	B&T	4
10. Ch. Rexpointe Reprint	B&W	4
10. Ch. Rexpointe Top Banana	B&W	4
10. Ch. Rinky Dink's Socko	black	4
10. Ch. Woodlane Dan Patch	tri	4

Special thanks go to Margaret Saari, D.V.M., for her painstaking efforts in compiling and tabulating the important statistics found on the pages of this section.

TOP PRODUCING BITCHES — 1980

NAME	COLOR	TOTAL
1. Ch. Eli Fran's Tri Dee of Illomar	tri	5
1. Liz Bar Summer Magic	black	5
1. Norrisim's No Choice	R&W	5
2. Enos Acres Devine Miss M	buff	4
2. Ch. Kamps' Kountry Kiss	R&W	4
2. Ch. Laurim's Star Performance	R&W	4
2. Ch. Pett's Silver Dream	buff	4
3. Ch. Airen's Agena	R&W	3
3. Bellburn's But I'm Speshul	black	3
3. Ch. Charmin Miss Carolyn	R&W	3
3. Ch. Cobb's Pale Moon	buff	3
3. Ch. Da Dar's Daydream of Altamira	B&W	3
3. Ch. Fran Dee's Celebration	R&W	3
3. Ch. Libertyville Belinda	black	3
3. Ch. M-Bar's Sno Body Like Me	R&W	3
3. Ch. My Cyn Luxury Item	B&W	3
3. Ch. Rexpointe Dutch Kiss	B&W	3
3. Ch. Sher Ron's Ebony Elegance	black	3
3. Tamburlaine's Cinnamon Kiss	buff	3
3. Ch. Windy Hill Tis Sum-Thin Else	buff	3

PERPETUAL WHELPING CHART

Bred—Jan.	1	2	3	4	5	6	7	8	9	10	11	12	13	14	15	16	17	18	19	20	21	22	23	24	25	26	27			28	29	30	31				
Due—March	5	6	7	8	9	10	11	12	13	14	15	16	17	18	19	20	21	22	23	24	25	26	27	28	29	30	31		April	1	2	3	4				
Bred—Feb.	1	2	3	4	5	6	7	8	9	10	11	12	13	14	15	16	17	18	19	20	21	22	23	24	25	26				27	28						
Due—April	5	6	7	8	9	10	11	12	13	14	15	16	17	18	19	20	21	22	23	24	25	26	27	28	29	30			May	1	2						
Bred—Mar.	1	2	3	4	5	6	7	8	9	10	11	12	13	14	15	16	17	18	19	20	21	22	23	24	25	26	27	28	29		30	31					
Due—May	3	4	5	6	7	8	9	10	11	12	13	14	15	16	17	18	19	20	21	22	23	24	25	26	27	28	29	30	31	June	1	2					
Bred—Apr.	1	2	3	4	5	6	7	8	9	10	11	12	13	14	15	16	17	18	19	20	21	22	23	24	25	26	27	28			29	30					
Due—June	3	4	5	6	7	8	9	10	11	12	13	14	15	16	17	18	19	20	21	22	23	24	25	26	27	28	29	30		July	1	2					
Bred—May	1	2	3	4	5	6	7	8	9	10	11	12	13	14	15	16	17	18	19	20	21	22	23	24	25	26	27	28	29		30	31					
Due—July	3	4	5	6	7	8	9	10	11	12	13	14	15	16	17	18	19	20	21	22	23	24	25	26	27	28	29	30	31	August	1	2					
Bred—June	1	2	3	4	5	6	7	8	9	10	11	12	13	14	15	16	17	18	19	20	21	22	23	24	25	26	27	28	29			30					
Due—August	3	4	5	6	7	8	9	10	11	12	13	14	15	16	17	18	19	20	21	22	23	24	25	26	27	28	29	30	31	Sept.		1					
Bred—July	1	2	3	4	5	6	7	8	9	10	11	12	13	14	15	16	17	18	19	20	21	22	23	24	25	26	27	28	29		30	31					
Due—September	2	3	4	5	6	7	8	9	10	11	12	13	14	15	16	17	18	19	20	21	22	23	24	25	26	27	28	29	30	Oct.	1	2					
Bred—Aug.	1	2	3	4	5	6	7	8	9	10	11	12	13	14	15	16	17	18	19	20	21	22	23	24	25	26	27	28	29		30	31					
Due—October	3	4	5	6	7	8	9	10	11	12	13	14	15	16	17	18	19	20	21	22	23	24	25	26	27	28	29	30	31	Nov.	1	2					
Bred—Sept.	1	2	3	4	5	6	7	8	9	10	11	12	13	14	15	16	17	18	19	20	21	22	23	24	25	26	27	28			29	30					
Due—November	3	4	5	6	7	8	9	10	11	12	13	14	15	16	17	18	19	20	21	22	23	24	25	26	27	28	29	30		Dec.	1	2					
Bred—Oct.	1	2	3	4	5	6	7	8	9	10	11	12	13	14	15	16	17	18	19	20	21	22	23	24	25	26	27	28	29		30	31					
Due—December	3	4	5	6	7	8	9	10	11	12	13	14	15	16	17	18	19	20	21	22	23	24	25	26	27	28	29	30	31	Jan.	1	2					
Bred—Nov.	1	2	3	4	5	6	7	8	9	10	11	12	13	14	15	16	17	18	19	20	21	22	23	24	25	26	27	28	29			30					
Due—January	3	4	5	6	7	8	9	10	11	12	13	14	15	16	17	18	19	20	21	22	23	24	25	26	27	28	29	30	31	Feb.		1					
Bred—Dec.	1	2	3	4	5	6	7	8	9	10	11	12	13	14	15	16	17	18	19	20	21	22	23	24	25	26	27			28	29	30	31				
Due—February	2	3	4	5	6	7	8	9	10	11	12	13	14	15	16	17	18	19	20	21	22	23	24	25	26	27	28		March	1	2	3	4				

Ch. Fellows Highland Fling, bred and owned by Mrs. Robert Fellows of Clarks Summit, Pennsylvania, was sired by Ch. Blue Bays Ring Leader ex Ch. Scioto Bluffs High Hope. Art Benhoff handling.

A Prayer for Animals

Hear our humble prayer, O God, for our friends the animals, especially for animals who are suffering; for any that are hunted or lost or deserted or frightened or hungry; for all that must be put to death. We entreat for them all Thy mercy and pity, and for those who deal with them we ask a heart of compassion and gentle hands and kindly words. Make us, ourselves, to be true friends to animals and so to share the blessings of the merciful.

Albert Schweitzer

Ch. Blue Gates Sky King goes all the way to Best in Show at the 1951 Long Island Kennel Club show under judge Anna Katherine Nicholas. Dorothy Callahan handled for owner George Sperakis. The late Mrs. William Long presented the trophy. Shafer photo.

Cocker Spaniel Conformation

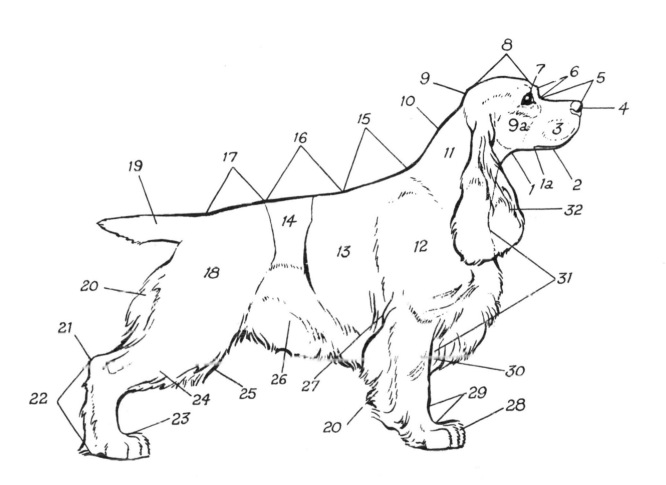

PARTS OF THE COCKER SPANIEL

1 Throat. **1A** Lip corner (flew). **2** Under jaw. **3** Muzzle. **4** Nose. **5** Foreface. **6** Stop. **7** Eye. **8** Skull. **9** Occiput. **9A** Cheek. **10** Crest (of neck). **11** Neck. **12** Shoulders. **13** Ribbing. **14** Loin. **15** Withers. **16** Back. **17** Croup. **18** Thigh (quarter, haunch). **19** Tail. **20** Feathering. **21** Point of hock. **22** Hock (metatarsus). **23** Foot. **24** Lower thigh. **25** Stifle. **26** Abdomen. **27** Elbow. **28** Foot. **29** Pastern. **30** Forearm. **31** Forechest. **32** Ear (leather).

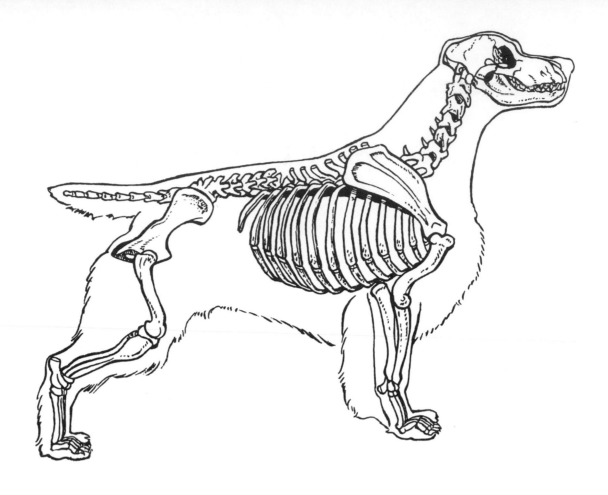

Above: Skeletal Structure of the Cocker Spaniel. **Below:** Musculature of the Cocker Spaniel. Both drawings by E.H. Hart.

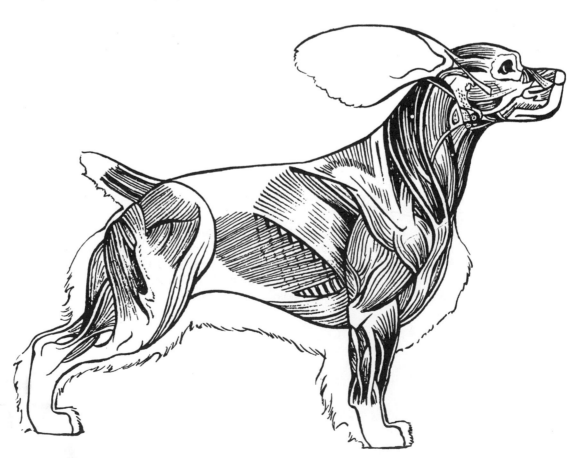

Structural Faults of the Cocker Spaniel. **Above:** Hind legs lack angulation; wet throat; short neck; tail too long and set too low; not enough angulation in shoulder; soft in pastern; croup too rounded; sway back; too leggy. **Below:** Roach back; mutton withers (too flat); tail too short, legs too short; loin too long; hare foot; angulation too extreme in hindquarters. Both drawings by E.H. Hart.

Faulty Heads. **Left:** Too short in muzzle; dish faced; domed skull; eye haw. **Right:** Occiput not strongly defined; stop not sharp enough; roman nose; heavy flews; muzzle not square or deep enough; ears too short, set too high, too thick at attachment to skull.

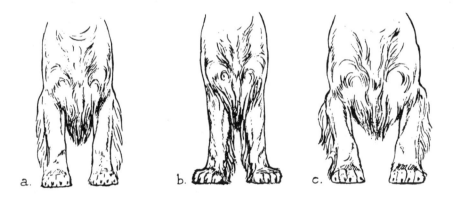

Cocker Fronts. **Left:** Excellent. **Center:** Too narrow; feet east and west. **Right:** Loaded shoulder; out at elbow.

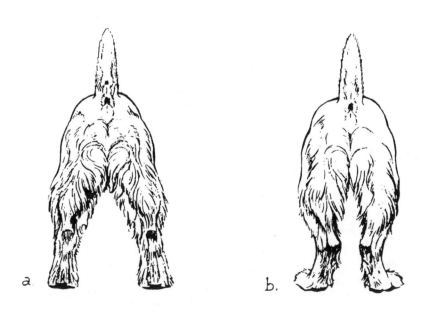

Cocker Rears. **Left:** Excellent. **Right:** Cowhocked and dewclaws.

Ch. Bo-Mar's Ballyhoo, C.D., pictured finishing for her championship. Ballyhoo finished with a Group 4 from the Puppy Classes and is the dam of several champions campaigned during the early 1960's. She was Michael Allen's first brood bitch and did much to help establish the kennel name.

Ch. Corwin Calico, owned by Helen A. Rice, winning under judge Helen Walsh in 1966. Calico had an influence on the breed during the decade of the sixties.

327

INDEX

This index is composed of three separate parts: a general index, an index of kennels, and an index of names of persons mentioned in the text.

General Index

A
Adult stock (cost), 140
Advertising, 25
All About the Cocker Spaniel, 13
Allergies, 284
All-meat diet, 253
American Cocker Review, 51, 59, 98, 198, 199
American Field Trophy, 81
American Kennel & Sporting Field, 232
American Kennel Club (A.K.C.), 20, 83, 91, 129, 137, 232, 234
American Kennel Gazette, 98, 185, 186, 201, 203
American Spaniel Club (A.S.C.), 81, 82, 83, 84, 233
American Stock-Keeper, 25, 98
Artificial insemination, 242
A.S.C. Centennial Celebration, 88
A.S.C. yearbooks, 84, 85
Aspirin (danger), 277

B
Baiting, 182
Bathing, 144-145
Benched dog show, 156
Best-in-Show Winners, 28, 31, 35, 44, 54
Booke of Faulconorie, 15
"Breaking", 231
Breech births, 244
Breed development, 12
Breed survey, 97
Breeder of the century, 89
Breeders, 101
Breeders, top ten, 101
Breeding, 239
British Dogs, 17
Burial, 289
Burns, 281
Buying (first Cocker Spaniel), 129, 130, 131
Buying (older field dog), 245
Buying (show puppy), 138

C
Caesarian section, 245
Call of the Wild, 225
Career in Dogs, 291
Castrating, 248
Catalogs, 89
Centennial Books, 86
Century of Spaniels, 86, 89, 98
Check points (obedience competitions), 227
Chewing, 285
Children in the show ring, 182
Clipping. 145
Cocker Spaniel
  in America, 23-64
  in art, 106
  in England, 17-20
  in foreign lands, 110
  in literature, 108
  in politics, 109
  in publications, 98
  in tales, 103
Cocker Spaniel Pictured, 85
Cocker Spaniel Sportsman, 98
Cocker Spaniel Visitor, 98
Color jurisdictions, 84
Colors, 95
Combing, 147
Conditions of sale, 137-138
Convulsions, 281
Coprophagy, 278
Crufts Competition, 20
Cryptorchids, 134

D
Dam and Get Trophy, 53
Death, 289
Delaney System, 203
Dingo, 12
Disqualifications, 94
Dog Breaking, 231
Dog insurance, 289
Dog judging, 295
Dog show photographers, 155
Dog show world, 151-159
Dog shows, 18
Dog training, 295
Dog World, 98

Double-handling, 182
Drowning, 281
Dry births, 245
Dysplasia, 286

E
Early records, 15
Elbow dysplasia, 286
Emergency, 281
Entering the ring, 178
Episiotomy, 246
Espaigneul, 13

F
False pregnancy, 245
Feeding (adult), 252
Feeding (puppies), 251, 255
The Field, 15, 229, 230
Field dog (buying), 234
Field dog (choosing), 234
Field Dog Stud Book, 232
Field Trial Club, 234
Field trials
  in America, 232
  eligibility, 235
  in England, 19
  entering, 235
  guns, 237
  kinds of, 234
  special awards, 235
  stakes, 236
  today, 233
  turn of the century, 231
First aid kit, 282
Fits, 281
Flush, 13
Foreign Cocker Spaniels, 110-111
Formal school training, 227
Front and Finish, 202, 203, 204, 205
Frostbite, 281
Futurity, 88

G
Gaines Dog Research Center, 105, 207, 208
Gastric torsion, 255
Geriatics, 287
Gestation period, 242

Glossary, 297
Grooming, 143-149
  equipment, 144
  parlors, 295
  shops, 149

H
Handlers, 102, 158-159
Handling (professional), 294
Health (breeding stock), 240
Heart attack, 281
HD program in Great Britain, 287
History, 11

I
Individual gaiting, 180, 181
Internal parasites, 275
Irish Red Spaniels, 95
It's a Dog's Life, 225

J
Jaguar Cave Dogs, 11
Judges, 234
Junior showmanship, 88
Junior showmanship competition, 155

K
Kennel club (England), 19-20
"Kennel Gazette", 19
Kennel Review, 32
Kennel work, 294

L
Labor, 243
Laws of Hornel, 15
Litter (evaluating), 247-248
London Gazette, 229

M
Male or female, 134, 135
Masturbation, 279
Mating, 240, 241
Miacis, 11
Modern Dogs, 18
Monorchids, 134

N
National Championship Stakes, 236
Newsworthy Cocker Spaniels, 104
Nylabone, 285

O
Obedience, 201
  activities, 225
  degrees, 227
  and movies, 225
  rating system, 202-203
  rules and regulations, 225
  trials, 155
Obedience trial championship titles, 227
Obesity, 254
Obo strain, 17
Official Obedience Regulations, 155
Old timers group, 62
On the Dog, 237
Our Prize Dogs, 24
Owners, 102

P
Palegawra, 11

Parasites, 273
Pedigrees, 239
Pet shops, 295
Phillips System, 35, 185-186
Planned parenthood, 135
Point show classes, 153-154
Poisoning, 284
Popular Dogs, 9, 34, 98, 188, 189, 195, 197, 198
Prize ribbons, 157
Probing (puppies), 243
Professional handlers, 158, 159
Publications, 98
Puppies (orphaned), 254
Puppies and worms, 136
Puppy (socializing), 246
Puppy (what to look for), 131
Purchase price (adult stock), 140

Q
Qualifying (championship), 158

R
Rabies, 279-280
Record-keeping, 289
Registry, 286
Reward method, 226
Ribbons and prizes, 235

S
Second Hundred Years, 89
Self service, 105
Sensory perceptions, 13
Shock, 281
Showdogs, 195, 198
Show puppy (buying), 138
Showing and judging, 177-183
Shuman System, 203
Sins (when showing dogs), 183
Snakebite, 280
Spaniel (name origin), 13
Spanish dog, 13
Spaying, 248
"Spinners", 131
Sportsman's Newspaper of America, 232
Standard, 84, 89, 91-94
  Cocker Spaniel, 91
  revision, 84
Standards (what are), 91
Sterilizing, 249
Story of Pedigreed Dogs, 15
Stud fee, 241
Suffocation, 28
Sun stroke, 281

T
Temperature, 278
Tomacartus, 11
Top sires and dams, 197
Training, 225, 226, 231
Training equipment, 226
Tranquilizing dogs, 149
Trimming, 145
Trophies, 89

U
Unbenched dog shows, 156

V
Vaccination, 280
Veterinarian (attendance), 243
Veterinary inspections, 136-137

W
Weaning, 252
When to breed, 240
Working titles, 233
Worms, 136
Worms (test), 136
Wounds, 282
Wyf of Bathes Prologue, 15

Z
Zoological chart, 97

Index of Kennels

A
Abbi, 38, 40, 139, 251
Alderbrook, 32
Argyll, 37
Astrawin, 20

B
Bar-Nan, 31
Bartonblount, 20
B-Gae, 29
Be Gay, 90, 113, 136
Belle Isles, 25
Bellemore, 25
Benbow, 31
Beswell, 31
Biggs, 31
Black Crest, 28, 29
Bobb's, 31
Bobsday, 52
Bobwin, 15, 46, 47, 48, 75, 111, 154, 170, 246
Bondale, 10, 255
Bramlyn, 20
Brookside, 25, 26, 29
Broomleaf, 20

C
Cal-Ore, 59, 60, 61, 123
Cambys, 46
Cap Mar, 31
Cassilis, 26, 29
Charmarel, 29
Classic, 290
Claythorne, 31
Cogges Hall, 29
Colinwood, 20
Corwin, 40, 41
Cottespur, 31
Courtdale, 20
Crackerbox, 197
Curtwin, 29

D
Dalecarlia, 31
Darlingdale, 31
Denniston, 25
Dennydene, 20
De Tourney, 52
Ditan, 31
Doggone, 59
Dorswick, 20
Downsbragh, 31
Dreamridge, 44, 101, 107, 110, 155, 268

Duckwin, 52
Dungarvan, 31
Durban, 20
Dur Bet, 60, 101
Dutchtown, 31

E
Eastlands, 20
Eby, 52
Eldwythe, 20
Essanar, 41

F
Florister, 31
Forjay, 56
Frandee, 49, 86, 93, 133, 260

G
Gatehampton, 20
Gildran, 31
Ging, 45, 72
Giralda, 28
Glencora, 20
Glendorgal, 20
Goldenfields, 20
Golden Gate, 25

H
Hallway, 49
Hardee, 56
Harlanhaven, 101
Havoc, 25
Heyday, 101
Hi Jack Ramrod, 56
High Hampton, 29
Honey Creek, 101
Hornell, 26

I
Idahurst, 24
Ide, 20
Ivy Hill, 31
Ivy Lanes, 29

J
Joywyns, 20

K
Kay Emms, 29
Kekko, 63
Kenavond, 20
Klyru, 31
Knebworth, 25, 31, 36, 61, 62
Kressingham, 52

L
Lachine, 81
Larrabee, 31
Lawlock, 29
Lindaire, 31
Lochranza, 20
Lucklena, 20
Lucknow, 26

M
Mahaska, 31
Marbo, 52
Marianna, 31
Maribeau, 101
Mariquita, 37
Marjolear, 29
Marymack, 52

Memoir, 46, 116, 132, 134
Mepal, 25, 26, 29, 83
Merribark, 50, 51, 127, 150
Merry Hill, 31
Merry Lee, 103
Merry-Way, 52
Merryworth, 20
Me Tu, 59
Midkiff, 26
Milru, 59, 208
Misbourne, 20
Mission, 25
Molinero, 31
Monterey, 33
Mount Vernon, 25
Moyhill, 20
My Own, 28, 37
My Rhythm, 29
Myroy, 32, 37

N
Newcastle, 25
Nonquitt, 31, 32, 37
Nor-Mar, 56
Nostrebor, 20

O
Oak Manor, 31
Ossies, 52
Overcross, 26
Oxshott, 20

P
Petts, 33, 87
Philsworth, 29, 52
Pinefair, 31, 37
Pryority, 51

Q
Quettadene, 20

R
Ramblelot, 29
Rees, 26, 28
Robinhurst, 26
Roblen, 46, 47, 153, 256
Rocky Point, 28
Ronfil, 20
Rosajo, 31
Rosamaude, 25
Rowcliff, 26
Rowingdale, 80, 119, 171, 315
Rural, 31

S
Sahadi Kennels and Cattery, 9
San-D-Glyn, 77
Sand Spring, 26
Scioto, 26
Sea Swing, 188
Seenar, 56
Shadowridge, 49, 248
Shardeloe, 56
Shootingbox, 29
Sills, 31
Silver Maple Farms, 31, 52, 101 194
Sixshot, 20
Sogo, 31
Southfair, 31
Spirit, 59
Sporting Dog, 52

Springback, 20
Stockdale, 28, 31, 33, 35, 37, 101
Stonehenge, 56
Strathmore, 31
Sugartown, 28
Sundust, 15
Sunshine, 93, 158
Swiss Mountain, 25, 83

T
Tabaka, 48
Tedwin, 197
Thurlyn Acre, 31
Tideway, 20
Tip Coe, 29
Topbrands, 20
Topflite, 32
Torchlight, 98
Torohill, 28, 37
Traquair, 20
Travel On, 51, 96
Treetops, 28
Trojan, 38, 39, 108, 130, 250, 268
Try-Cob, 31, 32

U
Ulwood, 20

V
Vickery Gaming Acres, 32
V-Jon, 52

W
Ware, 20
Waterloo, 52
Weirdene, 20
White Deer, 60
Willwyn, 259
Wilmarray, 52
Windridge, 29, 59
Windsweep, 31
Windy Hill, 59
Woodlane, 31
Wynehaven, 31

Index of People

A
Ablett, Miss Martha Jane, 222
Acklin, Tom and Laurie, 109, 219, 283
Allen, Michael, 8, 13, 53, 54, 55, 56, 64, 89, 96, 106, 107, 109, 112, 114, 118, 128, 135, 159, 161, 163, 224, 256, 258
Alton, Lloyd, 44, 45, 71, 72, 91, 117, 122, 141, 175, 272, 247
Ambler, Mary, 52
Anderson, Carl, 223
Anderson, Edward, 202
Andrews, John, 31
Anselmi, Edna, 59, 109
Arkwright, Mr., 230
Arnsten, Adelaide, 89
Austin, Norman, 34, 35, 40, 44, 49, 89, 91, 95, 98, 102, 186, 187, 188

B
Bacall, Lauren, 103
Backman, Irwin, 52

Baker, Mrs. B, 205
Ballantine, Billie and Chuck, 12, 97
Bang, Peggy, 108, 268
Barclay, W., 25
Barney, Jean, 137
Beale, Raymond, 41
Beam, N. and R., 204
Bebeau, Marion, 101
Benhoff, Art, 87, 320
Benhoff, Mrs. Arthur, Jr., 27, 89,
    101, 107
Bergen, S. and S., 205
Bewick, 17
Biggs, Mr. & Mrs. Robert W., 52
Bishop, Mrs. Clinton, 199
Blacke, Tom, 104
Blair, Mr. & Mrs. Leon, 103
Blake, Dennis, 82
Blakiston, Elliott, 202
Blick, Samuel, 202
Bloch, W. N., 194
Bloodgood, Hildreth, K., 25, 101
Bloom, P. and R., 203
Boehmer, Leonie, 52
Bond, Marjorie, 10, 255, 304, 305
Bouley, Bill and Mary, 115, 166
Boyd, J. H., 93
Boyer, R., 204
Brady, Judge, 88
Bridson, Elmer and Laverne, 105
Brodhagen, Jean, 108
Brown, Paul, 105
Browning, Elizabeth Barrett, 108
Bryson, P. H., 232
Buck, Mrs. Leonard J., 28
Buding, B., 189
Burgess, Lucille, 31
Burgess, T., Esq., 18
Burns, Mrs. Chalmers, 32
Burrows, Pam, 50, 134, 143, 201,
    214, 293
Bush, Barbara, 215
Bush, Vice President George, 105, 109

C
Callahan, Clint, 32, 102
Calussen, Howard P., 202
Campbell, Hugh, 57
Cane, Col., 17
Cansino, Margarita (Rita Hayworth),
    103
Cantrell, Mona, 59
Carpenter, Mrs. Mary A., 264
Cattanack, Dr. J. S., 81
Cecil, Sir Robert, 14
Chalong, Henry Barrent, 81
Chapin, Mr. & Mrs. Howard, 105
Charles, John Bailey, 102
Chaucer, 15
Clark, Leslie E. and Elizabeth C., 35,
    187
Cleary, Kevin, 105
Cobb, Bain and Ken, 102
Cobb, William, 86
Cole, Norman, 50
Colton, Ben and Kathryn, 52
Conner, Mary Lester, 26
Covey, Bob, 46, 80, 270, 282,
    315
Covey, Byron, 51
Covey, Mrs. Byron A., 5, 28, 47,
    49, 199, 209

Covey, Mrs. Cameron, 88, 153
Covey, Judy, 46
Cowan, Roy, 32
Craig, Pat Vincent, 42
Craig, Ralph, 32
Cross, Howard E., 202
Cumbers, Anne, 21
Cummings, C. B., 81

D
D'Ambrisi, Richard H., 202
Davies, Al, 57, 304
Davies, Annette, 57, 263, 304
Davis, Mark, 155
Davis, L. Wilson, 202
Dda, Howel, 15
Dean, Everett, 116, 187
Dearinger, James E., 202
Deffenbaugh, Barbara, 158
Delaney, Kent, 203
Dennehy, Cindy and Steve, 93, 158
Dimon, C. E., 186
Dodge, Mrs. Geraldine, 28
Dodsworth, Miss Alice A., 199
Douglas, George, 25, 101
Douglas, John, 229
Downey, Larry, 57
Draper, Dr. Samuel, 37, 62
Drew, Lynn, 109
Duding, Dick, 215, 288
Duncan, Tad and Barbara, 49
Dupree, M., 204
Durland, Elizabeth, 57, 60, 101, 263

E
Earl, George, 18
Eash, Dr. John, 33
Eastman, Mrs. E. Albert, 52
Elder, Steward, 42
Elridge, Ted, 283
Erdahls, 40
Ernst, Bill, 102
Ernst, Gay, 58, 90, 113, 125, 136
Ernst, Wendy, 136
Essenbager, Jay, 52
Evans, Dr. J. S., 52

F
Fabis, Ron, 34, 51, 86, 101, 102,
    157, 158, 164
Falkner, James, 202
Farley, Mrs. Radcliff, 201
Farrow, James, 17, 25
Fellows, J. Otis, 81
Fellows, Mrs. Robert, 87, 259, 261,
    267, 294, 320
Ferrero, J. and M., 194
Field, Dr. William, 85
Fink, Doris, 60, 257, 263
Fiore, Frank, 45
Flugel, Martin, 219
Flynn, Jean, 122
Foley, George, 201
Fordyce, Donald, 201
Frailey, Howard, 216
Francis, Arlene, 103, 104
Franzen, Oscar, 202
Fraser, Mr. & Mrs. R. O., 199
Frazier, Mr. & Mrs. Jack, 41
Frazier, Terri, 283
Friend, Venetia, 69
Fritsch, Ida E., 62
Frosch, Lynn, 203

G
Galassi, Shirley, 114
Gamble, Ellsworth, 164
Garrigan, Mike, 158
Gaynor, Eugene, 101
Gilbert, E. C., 26, 203
Gillies, Bill, 48
Gillis, Jean, 48
Gilman, O. B., 24, 101
Gleason, Jack, 102
Goddefroy, A. E., 81
Godsell, Mrs. Bryand, 201
Goldstein, Alan 187
Goldstein, Natalie, 35, 187
Gonce, Noreen, 264
Goodman, Leo, 31
Gordon, John and Gail, 50
Gorodner, Bill, 8, 45, 71, 72, 91,
    98, 117, 122, 141, 175, 247, 272
Graham, Betty, 197
Graham, Robert, 197, 198, 217
Grant, Frank, 202
Gray, Fred and Margaret, 57
Green, James M., 88
Greer, Frances, 86, 88, 89, 98
Greer, George, 84, 88, 101
Grossman, Dr. Alvin, 88, 152
Guyer, Kathleen, 92

H
Hall, Mr. & Mrs. James, 49
Halsey, Mr. A. E., 19
Hammond, F. and S., 204
Hark, W. G., 101
Harrington, L., 204
Hay, Lindy, 13, 14, 92, 118, 135,
    221, 256, 269, 290
Hayes, J., 203
Hayworth, Rita, 103
Heckmann, Winifred, 41
Henderson, Clyde, 202
Henderson, Dr. & Mrs. L. C., 32
Henry II, 14
Henry VII, 15
Henson, Harold and Kap, 124
Henson, Laura, 88
Hering, Louise, 15, 25, 101
Heseltone, Col., 19
Hester, Mrs., 25
Hickey, Bob, 105
Higgs, Mrs. Sara, 31
Hipsley, Paul C. Sr., 156
Hock, Hayward, 315
Hockman, Gail, 35
Hoel, Harlan, 70, 101, 176, 203
Hopkins, Lydia, 25
Hoversen, A. B., 204
Hughes, Gertrude and Oscar, 52
Hunt, Fred, 88
Hutchinson, Gen. W. N., 231

I
Imrie, Mildred Vogel, 102
Iremonger, Miss P.A., 20
Iremonger, Mrs. W. J., 20
Irick, Mackey, 95

J
Jacobson, J., 203, 290
Jacobson, Lynnette, 290
Jewell, Stephan, 88
Johnson, Joyce and Steve, 168, 212
Johnson, Violet, 52

Johnston, Helen L. and Robert A., 46, 47, 153, 256
Jones, Nancy, 50, 70
Jones, Oren O., 194
Jones, Pat, 49
Judy, Mrs. Will, 49
Juelich, Mr. & Mrs. J. L., 194

K
Kane, Diane, 169
Kaplan, Alice, 38, 39, 42, 108, 121, 141, 167, 191, 268
Kapnek, Theodore, 202
Kay, Nicholas, 99
Keith, M., 205
Kelley, Susan, 59, 74, 200
Kennedy, J., 25
Kessler, Lorine and Melvin, 187
Khatoonian, Irene Phillips, 35
Kinnane, Mrs. Virginia, 157
Kinney, Mrs. Robert J., 52
Kinschular, Michael, 88, 102
Kirk, J. F., 81
Kirkland, Joy, 214
Kittredge, David, 57
Klaiss, Lillian and Theodore J., 55
Knapper, Mrs. Yvonne, 15, 16, 17, 20, 21, 89
Knauss, C., 205
Knott, Thomas, 202
Knox, Dr., 26
Kodis, Samuel W., 202
Koehler, William, 225
Kornhaber, S., 204
Koskey, George, 154
Kraeuchi, Lee, 101
Kraeuchi, Mr. & Mrs. Lee C., 52
Kraeuchi, Ruth, 34, 101, 187
Krandell, Dr., 26
Kress, Mr. & Mrs. Herman, 52

L
Lacy, H. W., 25
Laffon, William J., Jr., 44
Lake, Robert, 88
Landry, Sharon, 210
Lang, E. R., 203
Lannie, Michael, 283
Larrabee, Parley, 102
Larsen, Niels, 104
Laubecker, C., 195
Lauerbach, Muriel, 52
Lee, Rawdon B., 18
Lee, Tami, 182
L'Hommedieu, S. Y., 84
L'Homedius, Dorothy L, 26
Lilley, Diane, 48, 216
Little, James L., 25
Lloyd, Freeman, 15
Lloyd, H. S., 15
Loustalot, Julie, 14
Lowe, David J., 180, 294

M
Mack, Pamela, 52
Marquez, Gabriel, 48
Marquez, Karen, 253
Marshall, Carol Moorland, 32
Marston, Joel, 37, 62
Martin, Carol Ann and Robert L., 187
Mason, Mr., 24

Mathis, Col. Lamar, 218
Mauchel, Mrs. Robert, 187
McCannon, Mrs. W. L., 201
McCollom, A., 81
McCoon, Mr. M. P., 81
McCormick, Barbara, 305
McCue, T. and J., 204
McDonald, Lillian and Stephen, 8
McDougall, George D., 81, 94
McEnany, Betty and Janet, 42
McGauvran, F. J., 101
McGinnis, Ray, 10, 41, 165, 192, 304
McGivern, Dr. Bernard, 57
McGowan, B., 203
McInnes, Dr. B. Kater, 52
McNeil, Dr. Cheryl, 49, 50, 69, 70, 141, 215, 248
Mellen, Peggy, 225
Mellenthin, Herman E., 25, 31, 101, 102, 199
Merkel, Rudolph, 88
Merson, Ron, 88
Miller, Bette, 42
Miller, D. and D., 205
Miller, George, 52
Miller, Ken, 42, 157
Mills, Carol Ann, 88
Mitchell, Ferne, 31
Moffit, Mrs. Ella B., 26
Monteverde, Mr. & Mrs. Richard, 59
Moon, Jerry, 85, 151, 172, 176, 218, 305
Moore, A. H., 81
Morgan, Mrs. Carl E., 28, 199
Morril, Dr. J.,L., 81
Moseley, R. A., 52
Moulton, C. C., 25
Muller, Milton, 43, 208
Muller, Ruth, 43, 105, 131, 208, 246
Muller, Virginia, 32

N
Nakayama, Mr. Shuiti, 48
Neeb, Lucy, 202
Neff, John C., 202
Neilson, C. F., 199
Nelson, C., 14
Nelson, Roy, 37, 62
Nilsson, Robin, Enos and Rune, 58
Nishi, Kathy and Gary, 141
Niven, Dr. J. S., 81
Nixon, President Richard M., 109
Norman, Aaron, 8

O
Obriecht, Leo and Carole, 248
O'Brien, Mary Anne, 221
O'Conner, Laura Watt, 58, 98, 217
O'Connor, Thomas, 202
Oldham, Ed, 83
O'Neal, Thomas F., 44, 101, 110, 155, 268
Otto, Mrs. George, 30

P
Page, Mrs. Wheeler H., 201
Paine, Joyce Scott, 56
Pancoast, Mr. A. W., 25
Parker, Wilma, 88
Payne, William T., 25, 28, 101, 199

Pennix, R., 203
Perry, Vincent, 62
Petersen, Jean and William, 88
Peterson, Marie, 28
Pett, Dorothy, 22, 33, 34, 35, 66, 85, 86, 87, 93, 100, 101, 126, 164, 244, 266, 289, 291, 292, 294, 306
Pett, Roland, 12, 22, 33, 34, 35, 66, 85, 86, 87, 93, 100, 101, 126, 164, 244, 266, 273, 289, 291, 292, 294, 306
Petty, Glyn, 77, 225
Petty, Mrs. S., 203
Pfaffenberger, Clarence, 202
Phillips, Helen F., 202
Phillips, Irene (now Mrs. Harold Schlintz), 185, 198
Phillips, Sara, 52
Phillips, William, 202
Phillips, Dr., 26
Pitcher, F. F., 17
Ploke, Don, 210, 237
Poole, Elane, 50, 51, 59, 120, 127, 150
Poquette, Neil, 122
Post, Louise, 61, 88
Price, R. T. L., 18
Pryor, Bill, 51
Pryor, Marilyn, 51
Pugh, George S., 202
Pulitzer, David and Joanne, 88
Pusey, Ruth, 34

R
Rainey, Tom, 121
Ralston, Mrs. William, 25
Randall, Mr. & Mrs. William L., 188
Rathbone, Basil, 103
Ray, Frederick, 59, 60
Ray, Lisa, 60, 123, 264
Ray, Love, 60
Ray, Monique, 60
Ray, Nancy L., 51, 59, 60, 61, 77, 123, 138, 206, 225, 264
Rayne, Derek, 42
Regan, J & A, 205
Reichar, Agnes, 32
Reno, Mrs. Harry, 38, 40, 41, 89, 129, 139, 140, 144, 188
Reno, Howard, 102
Reusch, M., 204, 205
Reusch, W. H., 203, 204
Rice, Helen A., 27, 40, 41, 49, 160
Rice, Joe, 25
Richardson, Mrs. Arthur F., 33
Richardson, Marguerite, 30
Richter, Chris, 125
Rickenbacker, Capt. Eddie, 103
Riggs, J., 25
Rivero, Pedro, 102
Robbins, Mrs. Rose, 144, 186, 188
Roberts, Anita B., 46, 78, 79, 116, 132, 134, 141, 173, 252, 288
Roberts, Charles R., 46
Roberts, Randy, 46
Roberts, Scott, 225
Robinson, H., 205
Roland, Arthur, 15
Roling, Judge, 88
Romanski, Kate, 98
Rothman, Marty and Bobby, 195
Rowe, Charles, 80, 119

Rowe, Jacquelyn, 80, 282
Rowe, Dr. N., 81
Ruffer, Madam, 51

S

Saari, Margaret M., D.V.M., 8, 98, 106, 171, 198, 199
St. John, P. and R., 194
Sangster, George, 187
Sangster, Harry, 32
Saunders, Blanche, 201, 202
Savage, Phil, 105
Scudder, Townshend, 102
Schiely, Beverly, 220, 282
Schlintz, Mrs. Harold, 185, 198
Schnabel, Debbie, 163
Schooley, Eileen and Robert, 214
Seager, Dr. Stephen W. J., 242
Sedgwick, D. and J., 194
Seger, Pat, 96
Self, Charles, 69, 88
Sharpe, Mr. Isaac, 19
Sherrick, John and Laura, 215
Shomer, Robert, 8
Shuman, Nancy, 36, 203
Shute, Helen, 25, 26, 27, 35, 61
Shute, Richard, 25, 26, 35, 61
Sidewater, Mrs. Evelyn P., 188
Sickierski, Al, 194
Skarda, Langdon, 123, 270
Smith, Ann, 141, 156
Smith, Clarence A., 101
Smith, Dr. C. A., 195
Smith, Julian, 156
Smith, Myrtle, 31, 101
Smith, Mrs. Pat, 51
Smith, Sandy, 213
Smith, T., 204
Smithwick, L., 203
Smythe, Mrs. H. E., 25, 83
Spitz, Carl, 225
Steele, K. and R., 203
Stifel, William F., 86
Stimpfig, A. T., 101
Stonehenge, 14
Strang, Ellen, 115
Strom, C., 205

Strong, C., 205
Swalwell, Arline, 26
Swiderski, Alice, 49, 150
Symmonds, Lee Ann, 88

T

Tabaka, Ruth, 48, 58, 216, 217
Tashimo, Masao, 48
Telfer, Dorothy W., 32
Terry, Thomas H., 83
Thelander, Henry, 107
Thompson, Becky and Ron, 49
Thompson, Clark, 180
Tinsley, E., 81
Topham, F. H., 25
Tramp, S., 204
Treen, Mrs. Esmee, 202
Tremain, Mrs. Aurelia, 201
Tumerville, George, 15
Turner, W. E., 106
Twelvetrees, Mrs. Myrtle, 37, 52

U

Ulltugit-Moe, A. and H., 48

V

Van Horn, Gladys, 58
Van Ingen, Mrs. Terrell H., 191
Van Meter, C. B., 31, 35, 101, 199
Van Paten, Jean, 59
Von Horn, Debbie, 168, 196, 212
Von Horn, Gladys, 76, 85, 141, 151, 176, 210, 218, 253, 270
Vick, Mr. & Mrs. Robert, 138
Vick, Mrs. Winnie, 15, 47, 48, 75, 154, 222, 247, 260
Vickery, Mrs. Milo G., 32

W

Walker, Mrs. Helen Whitehouse, 201, 202
Walsh, J. H. (Stonehenge), 229
Walsh, Rev. William, 30
Ward, Jack, 202
Washington, Porter, 188
Waterman, Joe, 195
Watson, Frances, 141

Watson, James, 24, 81, 83, 84
Weber, Josef, 201, 202
Westland, Georgia, 153
Westphal, Peggy, 57, 194, 195, 199
White, Barbara, 51, 96, 164, 245, 276
White, Lynn, 51
Whitebread, Samuel, 229
Whiting, Mary Lee, 202, 203, 204, 205, 207, 211, 226
Whitman, J. H., 81
Wilcox, Ramona, 52
Wilhelm, M., 205
Willet, Steve, 207
Willey, Mr. J. P., 117
Williams, Mrs. Katheryn, 105
Wills, Robert, 52, 181
Wilmerding, A. Clinton, 81, 82, 83, 84
Wilmot, V., 204
Wilson, C. and K., 204
Wilson, D. J., 204
Wilson, Mai, 28, 58, 88, 199, 205, 209
Winsop, Myrtle, 69
Wolfe, John, 49, 59, 174
Wolfe, Julie, 49, 59, 65, 124, 174
Wood, Dee Dee, 41, 49, 58, 64, 86, 93, 99, 102, 151, 156, 162, 166, 167, 169, 172, 175, 213, 248, 260, 262, 271, 277
Wood, Frank, 49, 58, 64, 86, 99, 102, 156, 162, 166, 167, 169, 175, 233, 248, 260, 266
Wood, Mr. & Mrs. Frank, 42, 49
Wooley, Mary, 96
Woolf, Virginia, 13, 108

Y

Young, Owen L., Ph.D., 98
Young, Ted Jr., 28, 43, 56, 57, 93, 102, 175, 186, 187, 188, 190, 191, 194, 195, 197, 208, 217
Young, Ted Sr., 102

Z

Zimmerman, D., 204
Zimmerman, Irene Gaddy, 8, 30, 35, 37, 60, 88, 102, 223

The author with a puppy from Ging's Kennels, now located in Leesburg, Virginia. Photo by Aaron Norman.